Twenty-third Edition

Rugg's

Recommendations

on the

Colleges

*Compiled and Edited by the College Staff of
Rugg's Recommendations*

by Frederick E. Rugg

Rugg's Recommendations • Fallbrook, California

To
Barbara, Betsie, and Sue

TABLE OF CONTENTS

Some Notes from the Author vii
Some Notes on the Twenty-second Edition xi
Acknowledgments xi

SECTION ONE - Recommended Undergraduate Programs 1
Agriculture 2
American Studies.................................... 3
Anthropology 4
Architecture 6
Art (Studio) 7
Art History 11
Astronomy 12
Biochemistry (Molecular Biology) 13
Biology 14
Botany / Plant Science 19
Business Administration 20
Chemistry 27
Classics 31
Computer Science 32
Dance/Drama/Theater 35
Economics 38
Education 41
Engineering 47
English 50
Foreign Languages................................ 55
Forestry 58
Geography 59
Geology 60
History 62
Home Economics / Family Studies 66
Journalism/Communications 67
Mathematics 70
Music 73
Nursing 78
Pharmacy 82
Philosophy 83
Physics 86
Political Science 89
Pre-Law 92
Pre-Med/Pre-Dental.............................. 96
Psychology 100
Religious Studies 105
Sociology 108
Zoology 111

SECTION TWO - Miscellaneous Majors 113
Africana Studies 114
Alternative Colleges 114
Animal Science 114
Applied Mathematics 115
Archaeology 116
Art Therapy 116
Atmospheric Sciences 117
Audiology/Speech/Language Therapy 117
Aviation Management 118
Aviation Science 118
Biomedical Engineering 119
Biophysics 119
Ceramics 119
Cinematography/Film Studies/Video Production ... 120
Computer Engineering 121
Computer Graphics 122
Creative Writing 122
Criminal Justice 123
Design/Commercial Art 125
East Asian Studies............................... 126

E-Commerce 126
Entomology 127
Entrepreneur Studies 127
Environmental Studies 128
Equestrian Studies 129
Exercise Science/Wellness/Movement 130
Fashion Design/Merchandising............... 131
Forensic Science/Technology.................. 131
Genetics 132
Gerontology/Geriatric Services 132
Health Services Administration 133
Hispanic Studies/Latin American Studies 133
Horticulture.. 134
Hotel and Restaurant Management 135
Human Resources Management 136
Industrial Arts 136
Industrial Design 137
Interior Design 137
International Relations/Studies 138
Japanese Studies 140
Jazz 140
Linguistics 141
Marine Science 142
Medical Technology.............................. 143
Middle Eastern Studies 143
Mortuary Science 144
Music Therapy 144
Musical Theater 145
Naval Architecture 145
Neuroscience 145
Nutritional Science 146
Occupational Therapy 147
Orthotics / Prosthetics 147
Parks and Recreation Services 148
Peace and Conflict Studies 149
Photojournalism 149
Physical Education 150
Physical Therapy 151
Physician Assistant 152
Pre-Veterinary 152
Public Health 153
Range Management 153
Social and Rehabilitation Services 154
Social Work... 154
Special Education 156
Sports Medicine / Athletic Training......... 157
Sports Sciences / Sports Management 158
Urban Studies 159
Voice.. 160
Wildlife/Wildlands Mangement 160
Women's Studies 161

SECTION THREE - Avg. SAT-1, New SAT-1 & ACT Totals / Recommended Majors 163
SECTION FOUR - Appendices 221
A. The 1050 Colleges Used in This Study 222
B. The Miscellaneous Majors Colleges Used in This Study 243
C. Single Sex Colleges Used in This Study 245
D. Wellness Residence Hall and Wellness Course Information.............................. 245
E. A Simplified Timetable and Checklist for Seniors Planning on College 246
F. The Get-Going Form 247
About the Author...................................... 249
From Rugg's Recs—Other Resources 250

SOME NOTES FROM THE AUTHOR

WHY THIS BOOK?

As a secondary school college counselor, I heard the following question from a student or parent almost daily: "Can you please give us a list of quality colleges where one can major in psychology (or engineering or business or whatever)?"

For many years I pulled out the college handbooks and came up with a list of hundreds of colleges for each category and spent too much time with the student sifting through the multitude of schools, trying to narrow down the huge list.

I thought about a way out of this dilemma for a long time. People from Harvard would find an easy solution. They might tell the parents and student not to worry about a college major—just go to a fine liberal arts college (like Harvard) and everything will fall into place. After all, it's not the major and professors that count, it's the wonderful student body that makes a great college great. Right?

Well...over the years, I had trouble convincing parents of the merits of that argument. I guess they realize that all good universities are not good in every field.

Today, there's just so much pressure on young people to line up their careers and pick their occupations in life early. Career education seems to start in kindergarten these days. I've noticed that many parents pick right up on it and give Johnny the business if he hasn't chosen his career by the sophomore year of high school or earlier. No matter what I told Johnny and his parents, they still wanted a list of "the quality colleges with a good psychology (or whatever) department."

This book lists the quality departments at quality colleges and it will make the school counselor's job easier. For example, a public school counselor can use it constantly in January when juniors (and sometimes sophomores) line up outside his/her office, asking for a list of colleges to "go with" their PSAT scores. Probably a prep school counselor, a junior and community college transfer counselor, or a librarian might even find more use of this guide for college majors. Since this book is for the aid of the counselor, it is, then, also a guide for students and their parents in the college admissions process.

WHY THESE 1050 COLLEGES?

From our experience in the college admissions process, we have chosen 1000 quality four-year colleges (out of over 2000 that offer bachelor degrees) to study. We began with the 275 colleges that have survived the careful screening process involved in the granting of a Phi Beta Kappa chapter. The Phi Beta Kappa schools are listed in Appendix A. These colleges received chapters for superior undergraduate performance in the liberal arts and sciences.

To this list were added 775 colleges—schools that our staff felt are as good (or better) as several of the Phi Beta Kappa colleges or have excellent specialized programs. We should also note that, in general, the more well-respected the college, the more departments and majors were included. Berkeley is listed under 33 departments while some others only under one. The typical school in the study was noted with 8.5 departments. A departmental page averages 155 recommended colleges.

HOW IT'S DONE

Over the years, college students have been surveyed - the number well into five figures. If you want a straight answer, the young folks seldom waver. We also receive monthly evaluations from secondary school counselors around the country. Some colleges submit to us departments at their schools that they consider "hidden gems". They also send us departments they consider their "strongholds". Weekly, a variety of college personnel lobby for a certain program at their university. Also, almost every week we get "tipped off" on a great department at a college at workshops I present around the U.S.A. on the college admissions process. Almost every year since 1977 I've added 300 departments to my list. This year the number is over 700.

What can eliminate a department or stop its consideration? No balance. For example, too many professors from the same alma mater in a department, or too many professors in a department graduating from that very college. If the average college in America gives out 10% of it's degrees in, say, the field of Psychology, and the department in question is at a 5% level, this sets up a "red flag", too.

HOW DO YOU USE THIS BOOK?

If you know what you want to major in at college—great!—just look it up. In most cases, you will find each departmental section organized into three groups of colleges:

Group I—Most Selective Colleges

Colleges here are among the 100 most selective colleges in America. They accept very few students with high school averages below 80 (top prep schools can, of course, lower this figure significantly) and College Board scores below 1800 (New SAT-1) and 27 (on the American College Test).

Group II—Very Selective Colleges

Many of the students at these colleges have "B" averages (80-90), and College Board scores between 1650 and 1800 (New SAT-1) and ACTs between 24 and 26.

Group III—Selective Colleges

Although these colleges are, in general, easier to get into than Group I and II colleges, please keep in mind that they are, in our opinion at least, among the top 1000 colleges in the country. Many students at these colleges have College Board scores just under 1650 (New SAT-1), or just under 24 on the ACTs.

Now that we have an idea of the group breakdown, a student may need help deciding from which group(s) to select his/her colleges. The guidance counselor can help here—having knowledge of colleges and a student's grade point average, class rank, board scores, etc. Most students will want to start with a group of 8 to 10 colleges from the departmental major page. This "major page" is a starting point. Schools can be added to the student's list by his/her counselor—from the counselor's own knowledge of the student, and knowledge of other colleges that might "fit" the student. Schools can be eliminated from a student's list after reviewing the college catalogs (see Appendix F—The Get Going Form), checking out undesirable features (city vs. rural setting, etc.), visiting the colleges, and other personal preferences. If the student does not have a major in mind, he or she should go to a typical liberal arts (e.g., English or Math) page to get started. I've also included a letter code system for the college's enrollment figure. The enrollment letter appears beside each college name with the following code:

XL = Extra Large Enrollment (over 20,000 students)
L = Large Enrollment (from 8,000 to 20,000 students)
M = Medium Enrollment (from 3,000 to 8,000 students)
R = Moderate Enrollment (from 1,000 to 3,000 students)
S = Small Enrollment (under 1,000 students)

SOME PARTING SHOTS

I don't care to go into the argument of "Picking a college because it has a great Mathematics Department" vs. "Picking a school because the school overall is great (Yeah Harvard!) and you'll probably change your major anyway." The fact of the matter is that parents, career educators, and other educators are telling 16-year-olds (and younger) to have a career and a major all mapped out and I bet will continue to do so. I'm sure high school counselors will continue to be asked to help Suzy find a list of quality schools with "excellent majors in mathematics." Personally, I see nothing wrong with a high school senior, who loves mathematics, trying to pick a quality school where the math department at that institution is ranked by its students as one of the top majors at that school and is generally recognized as being top notch by college counselors. If Suzy changes her mind after a year or two, she's at least given it a good shot with a premier math department. And chances are excellent that if she changes her major, it was because another outstanding department at that school helped her grow and reassess her career goals. She'll probably stay with that department for her new major. No harm done.

A few other comments on this book and some random thoughts...

1. Some state universities, like Penn State, are very competitive for out-of-staters. A university such as this may be in Group II for in-staters, but, in reality, is a Group I school for "outsiders."

2. In general, a college that is competitive is that way for all majors—but there are some departments that are exceptions. For example, engineering is a tough major and must be considered "Group II" at a "Group III" school.

3. A knowledgeable observer of the college scene will note that some competitive "alternative" colleges do not appear in this work, e.g., Hampshire College (MA), St. John's (MD). The jury is not unanimous on these progressive schools, and they are not included in this book except under "Miscellaneous Majors Pages."

4. A few majors in this book, such as engineering, have not been broken down into subdivisions (Civil, Electrical, Mechanical, etc.). Students will have to research these majors more fully. Well, what's wrong with that? Good to have the youngsters doing some hard work and research on the college admissions process. Foreign Languages, however, is broken down.

5. Every year a few more colleges close their doors. Today, colleges are under pressure to compete and "Be Hot." We need a college guide to weed things out a bit, a consumer-oriented handbook. We hope this helps.

6. Don't overlook the good small liberal arts college. Too many large universities are too impersonal. But some kids love a big school. Some thrive in the anonymity of a huge lecture hall.

7. Keep in mind that weak departments at Harvard, Yale, Stanford, Princeton, etc. might be equal to or better than the strongest departments at many colleges and universities.

8. This book is an aid for counselors, parents, and kids—nothing more. It is not a guide for the colleges to compare themselves one with the other.

9. Do not be surprised if you discover that the best of the more expensive schools are actually least expensive—because they have financial aid, the part-time jobs, etc. They're able to meet a student's financial need in many cases.

10. Students should discuss with their counselors the socioeconomic factors of the colleges they are considering. Will the college of your choice have several students enrolled with your socioeconomic background? And, please get in your college visits.

11. When you visit a college, seek out the students who attend and ask them the following question: "When you sign up for classes, do you get 100% of your choices, or only 4 out of 10 courses, or...?" Also, does the faculty seem to be there, to like to talk to you, to meet and greet you? Or are they not to be found?

12. Most states have a "flagship" university, the leader of the system (e.g., The University of North Carolina at Chapel Hill). In this book it is listed as just "No. Carolina." The other members of the University system are listed as follows: No. Carolina (Asheville), No. Carolina (Charlotte), No. Carolina (Greensboro), No. Carolina (Pembroke), No. Carolina (Wilmington).

13. Some colleges do a great job with private school youngsters, others do a fantastic job with public school youngsters. Some colleges are outstanding with both groups. A very fine college with an outstanding record with public school youngsters is Virginia's Roanoke College.

14. A tip for the high school senior: Don't ease up in your senior year. Take a tough course load with courses such as Physics. College admissions people aren't stupid. The first thing they look at when they review your high school record is the quality of your high school courses.

15. To parents and counselors: Hang tough. The pieces will finally fit.

16. Keep in mind that a starter list of colleges to consider for your daughter #1 may be a terrible list for your daughter #2.

17. I received a phone call from a community college instructor in the Mid-West. He also consults with companies recruiting college graduates, and has found my lists to be the best. He said to me on the phone, "The true test of any college guidebook or college list is, 'Does the information work?' So if the best information comes from college janitors, you go after college janitors."

18. I give an apology now to many of the top secondary prep schools in the country. Many of you may not be happy with my recent emphasis on adding departments to the Cal States, the Mass States, Connecticut States, Pennsylvania States, Michigan and Illinois States, etc. But the public school counselors and parents need these recommendations and they are over 90% of my customer base.

19. This book is not perfect. It has never claimed to be perfect. Our study is not scientific. It has never claimed to be. But it is a good place to start and represents tens of thousands of contacts. I'll repeat that. We have never claimed to be perfect. There is no expert in the field. There never will be. The field is too big. We've even moved to many parts of the country to try to put together "the big picture." We do our best.

Frederick E. Rugg

San Diego County, California
January, 2006 (23rd Edition)

SOME NOTES ON THE TWENTY-THIRD EDITION

The twenty-third edition contains over 1000 entry changes since the twenty-second edition. All 100 plus majors have been revised and changed. Interior Design and Voice - these two majors have been added.

The "Average SAT-1/Average New SAT/ACT Total/Recommended majors" pages are included mainly because of counselors' requests. School counselors wanted average score comparisons and an index of colleges showing recommended majors. In all cases, SAT Total Scores are noted and the equivalent ACT score is provided. These scores are the best estimate by our staff for the entering fall class of 2006. Especially young counselors tell us this section is a quick ready reference—a marker for them. And if you're looking for schools that do not require SAT's, please see "www.fairtest.org" for the latest list.

As in the past, when a state university is noted like Wisconsin, we mean the flagship at Madison, if no other city follows in parenthesis.

Finally, in the middle of the book, you will find every college's website. You know to add the "www." up front.

Frederick E. Rugg

San Diego County, California
January, 2006 (23rd Edition)

ACKNOWLEDGMENTS

I would like to thank the following for their help in the preparation of this guidebook: Phi Beta Kappa Office, Bureau of Educational Statistics, our Research Aides, Officers of Institutional Research who returned our requests, and especially the great number of secondary counselors who've filled out questionnaires and tip me off on quality departments to look at. I am independent of the colleges and these people are, too.

A "Thank You" also goes to the counselors and students I've worked with who have contributed each in their own way. At last count, I've worked 25,000 hours in five secondary school guidance cubicles with 30 counselors, and conducted over 600 workshops with over 8000 counselors. Of course I've learned from them. Together we've probably done the college admissions process a million times. Also I thank the counselors and students and university officials in the United States and abroad for their help, suggestions, and, yes, their complaints. I appreciate, too, those departments who have sent us vitae on their professors. College PR officers who write always get a reading. And the same goes for anyone who e-mails me. Eighty percent of college personnel who write me and tip me off on a great major at their school find it in the next year's book!

I am also grateful to George Gibbs, Ed Wall, Reg Alexander, Arvin R. Anderson, Howard Ahlskog, Hy Kleinman, Michele M. Charles, Gary Metras, Edward Field, Betty Rossie, Horacio Rodriquez, A.P. Stevens, Madeline Field, Cyrus Benson, John Barker, Fred Ames, Matthew Jagielski, Gilbert Field, Jeff Sheehan, Charles Doebler, Joan Girard, Mrs. Fran Fisher, Ralph Strycharz, Dennis Gurn, John DeBonville, Sammy Edwards, Eric Goodhart, Kevin L. Miller, Gloria Broecker, Hoover Sutton, Francona, J.R., Rebecca Lou, Cousin Leonard, professional photographer Lynn C. Henkel of Bradenton, Florida, Dave Congalton, Steve Stassen, Dwayne Copeland, Dianne Pelletier, Art Northrop, Roger Dexter, Peter Frederick Stassen, and to all the secretaries I've worked with over the years.

And finally, a special thanks to my wife, Barbara, for her patience and industry, and daughters, Betsie and Susan.

Inquiries and comments about this guide should be addressed to:

Rugg's Recommendations
P.O. Box 417
Fallbrook, CA 92088

SECTION ONE
RECOMMENDED UNDERGRADUATE PROGRAMS

AGRICULTURE

Author's Note: *Students in the schools of Agriculture, in general, tend to have median college test scores below the University's overall median.*

━━ GROUP I ━━
Most Selective

Cornell (NY)	L	Iowa State	XL
Florida, U. of	XL	Pennsylvania State	XL
Illinois, U. of (Urbana-Champaign)	XL	Rutgers (NJ)	L

━━ GROUP II ━━
Very Selective

Auburn (AL)	L	Michigan State	XL
California, U. of (Davis)	L	Minnesota, U. of	XL
California, U. of (Riverside)	L	Missouri, U. of	XL
Cal. Poly. State U. (San Luis Obispo)	L	New Hampshire, U. of	L
Clemson (SC)	L	North Carolina State	L
Connecticut, U. of	XL	Purdue (IN)	XL
Drury (MO)	R	Texas A&M	XL
Hawaii, U. of	L	Vermont, U. of	M
Kansas State	L	Virginia Tech.	L
Maine, U. of	L	Wisconsin, U. of	XL
Maryland, U. of	XL		

━━ GROUP III ━━
Selective

Arizona, U. of	XL	New Mexico State U.	L
Arkansas, U. of	L	North Dakota State	L
Berea (KY)	R	Ohio State	XL
Cal. Poly. State U. (Pomona)	L	Oklahoma State	L
California State U. (Chico)	L	Oregon State	L
California State U. (Fresno)	L	Ozarks, College of the (MO)	R
Colorado State	L	Southwest Texas State	L
Delaware Valley (PA)	R	Tarleton State (TX)	M
Dordt (IA)	R	Tennessee, U. of	XL
Georgia, U. of	XL	Texas Tech U.	L
Idaho, U. of	L	Tuskegee University (AL)	M
Kentucky, U. of	L	Utah State	L
Louisiana State	XL	Washington State	L
Mississippi State	L	Western Illinois	L
Montana State	L	Western Kentucky	L
Murray State (KY)	M	Wilmington (OH)	S
Nebraska, U. of	L	Wisconsin, U. of (Platteville)	M
Nevada, U. of (Reno)	L	Wyoming, U. of	L

Enrollment Code
■ *Men Only* ▲ *Women Only* | S = Small (less than 1000 students)   R = Moderate (1000-3000 students)   M = Medium (3000-8000 students)
L = Large (8000-20,000 students)   XL = Extra Large (over 20,000 students)

AMERICAN STUDIES

GROUP I
Most Selective

American U. (DC) .... M	North Carolina, U. of L
Amherst (MA)..................................... R	Northwestern (IL) .... M
Brandeis (MA) .... M	Pennsylvania, U. of........................... L
Brown (RI) .... M	Pomona (CA) .... R
Buffalo (SUNY) (NY) L	Sarah Lawrence (NY) .... R
California, U. of (San Diego) L	▲ Smith (MA) .... R
Carleton (MN).................................... R	St. Olaf (MN) .... R
Case Western Reserve (OH).............. M	South, U. of the (TN) .... R
Chicago, U. of (IL) .... M	Stanford (CA) .... M
Emory (GA) .... M	Trinity (CT).. R
Franklin & Marshall (PA) .... R	Tulane (LA) .... M
George Washington (DC) .... M	Virginia, U. of L
Georgetown (DC) .... M	Wake Forest (NC) .... M
Harvard (MA)..................................... M	Wesleyan (CT) .... R
Johns Hopkins (MD) .... M	William & Mary (VA) .... R
Kalamazoo (MI) .... R	Williams (MA) .... R
Maryland, U. of (Baltimore County) ...... M	Yale (CT) .... M
Michigan, U. of XL	

GROUP II
Very Selective

Alabama, U. of L	Massachusetts, U. of (Boston) .... M
Arizona, U. of...................................... XL	Minnesota, U. of XL
Bowling Green (OH)............................ L	New Mexico, U. of L
California State U. (Fresno) L	▲ Pine Manor (MA) .... S
California State U. (Fullerton)................ L	Rider (NJ) .... R
California, U. of (Santa Cruz) .... M	Skidmore (NY) .... R
DePaul (IL)... L	South Florida, U. of L
Eastern Connecticut .... M	Texas, U. of XL
Florida State.. L	Wagner (NY)...................................... R
Fredonia (SUNY)(NY)......................... M	Washington College (MD) .... S
George Mason (VA) L	Washington State XL
Hawaii, U. of L	Wells (NY) .... S
Hillsdale (MI) .... R	▲ Wesleyan College (GA) .... S
Hobart & Wm. Smith (NY) .... R	Western Connecticut .... M
Iowa, U. of XL	Wyoming, U. of L
Mary Washington (VA) .... M	

Enrollment Code

■ *Men Only* S = Small (less than 1000 students) R = Moderate (1000-3000 students) M = Medium (3000-8000 students)
▲ *Women Only* L = Large (8000-20,000 students) XL = Extra Large (over 20,000 students)

ANTHROPOLOGY

GROUP I
Most Selective

American (DC) .... M	Johns Hopkins (MD) .... M
Albany (SUNY) (NY) L	Kenyon (OH) .... R
▲Barnard (NY) .... R	Lafayette (PA) .... R
Binghamton (SUNY)(NY) L	Macalester (MN).................. R
Boston U. (MA) L	Michigan, U. of XL
Bowdoin (ME) .... R	New College (FL) .... S
Brandeis (MA) .... R	North Carolina, U. of L
▲Bryn Mawr (PA) .... S	Northwestern (IL) .... M
Buffalo (SUNY) (NY) L	Notre Dame (IN) .... M
California, U. of (Berkeley)...... XL	Pennsylvania, U. of L
California, U. of (Los Angeles) XL	Pitzer (CA) .... S
Case Western Reserve (OH)...... M	Pomona (CA) .... R
Chicago, U. of (IL) .... M	Rice (TX) .... R
Colorado College .... R	Rutgers (NJ) L
Columbia (NY).................... M	Skidmore (NY) .... R
Connecticut College .... R	▲Smith (MA) .... R
Dartmouth (NH) .... M	Southern Methodist (TX)...... M
Duke (NC) .... M	South, U. of the (TN) .... R
Emory (GA) .... M	Stanford (CA) .... M
Florida, U. of XL	Tulane (LA) .... M
Georgetown (DC) .... M	Vanderbilt (TN) .... M
Grinnell (IA)........................ R	Washington U. (MO) .... M
Harvard (MA) .... M	Yale (CT) .... M
Illinois, U. of (Urbana-Champaign) XL	

GROUP II
Very Selective

Alabama, U. of L	Maryland, U. of XL
Arizona, U. of.................... XL	Nevada, U. of (Las Vegas)...... L
Arizona State XL	Oklahoma, U. of XL
Beloit (WI) .... R	Oregon, U. of L
Brown (RI) .... M	Pittsburgh, U. of (PA).......... L
California State U. (Chico)...... L	Principia (IL) .... S
California, U. of (Santa Cruz) ...... M	Rhode Island, U. of L
California, U. of (Davis) L	St. Mary's College of Maryland .... R
City College (CUNY)(NY) L	Sonoma State (CA) .... M
Colorado State L	South Florida, U. of L
Colorado, U. of L	Stony Brook (SUNY)(NY) L
Earlham (IN)........................ R	▲Sweet Briar (VA) .... S
George Mason (VA) L	Syracuse (NY) L
George Washington (DC) ...... M	Texas A&M XL
Grand Valley (MI) L	Towson (MD) L
Hamline (MN)...................... R	Tulsa, U. of (OK) .... M
Hofstra (NY)........................ M	Washington State L
Hunter (CUNY)(NY) L	Washington, U. of................ XL
Indiana (PA) L	Western Washington U. .... R
Iowa, U. of........................ XL	William Paterson (NJ) .... M
Kansas, U. of L	Wisconsin, U. of XL
Knox (IL)............................ R	Wisconsin, U. of (Milwaukee) L
Luther (IA) .... R	

ANTHROPOLOGY, continued

GROUP III
Selective

Alaska, U. of (Fairbanks) .... M	Louisiana State Xl
Arkansas, U. of L	Mercyhurst (PA) .... R
Ball State (IN) L	New Mexico State U. L
California State U. (Fullerton) L	New Mexico, U. of L
California State U. (Long Beach) L	Pittsburgh, U. of (Greensburg) .... R
California State U. (Sacramento) ...... M	Queens (CUNY) (NY) L
Central Washington L	Southwest Texas State L
Colorado, U. of (Colorado Springs) . M	Tennessee, U. of XL
Fort Lewis (CO) .... M	Western Connecticut .... M
Hawaii, U. of L	Wyoming, U. of L

ARCHITECTURE

GROUP I
Most Selective

▲ Barnard (NY)	R	Miami U. (OH)	L
Buffalo (SUNY) (NY)	L	Michigan, U. of	XL
California, U. of (Berkeley)	XL	MIT (MA)	M
Carnegie Mellon (PA)	M	New Jersey Inst. of Tech	M
Columbia (NY)	M	Notre Dame (IN)	M
Cooper Union (NY)	S	Princeton (NJ)	M
Cornell (NY)	L	Rensselaer (NY)	M
Florida, U. of	XL	Rice (TX)	R
Georgia Inst. of Tech.	L	Temple (PA)	XL
Illinois Inst. of Tech.	R	Tulane (LA)	M
Illinois, U. of (Urbana-Champaign)	XL	Virginia, U. of	L
Lehigh (PA)	M	Washington U. (MO)	M
Maryland, U. of	XL	Yale (CT)	M

GROUP II
Very Selective

Arizona State	XL	Miami, U. of (FL)	L
Arizona, U. of	XL	Milwaukee Sch. of Engineering (WI)	R
Auburn (AL)	L	Montana State	L
Boston Arch. Center (MA)	S	Nebraska, U. of	L
California College of Art & Crafts	S	North Carolina State	L
Cal. Poly. State U. (San Luis Obispo)	L	Northeastern (MA)	L
Catholic U. (DC)	M	Oklahoma, U. of	XL
Cincinnati, U. of (OH)	L	Oregon, U. of	L
Clemson (SC)	L	Pennsylvania State	XL
Detroit Mercy, U. of (MI)	M	Rhode Island School of Design (RI)	R
Drexel (PA)	M	Southern California, U. of	L
Drury (MO)	R	Syracuse (NY)	L
Florida International	L	Tennessee, U. of	XL
Kentucky, U. of	L	Texas A&M	XL
Houston, U. of (TX)	L	Texas Tech U.	L
Illinois, U. of (Chicago)	L	Texas, U. of (Austin)	XL
Iowa State	XL	Utah, U. of	L
Kansas State	L	Virginia Tech.	L
Kansas, U. of	L	Washington State	L
Kentucky, U. of	L	Washington, U. of	XL

GROUP III
Selective

Andrews (MI)	R	North Carolina (Charlotte)	L
Arkansas, U. of	L	North Dakota State	L
Cal. Poly. State U. (Pomona)	L	Norwich (VT)	R
City College (CUNY) (NY)	L	Ohio State	XL
Florida A&M	M	Pratt Inst. (NY)	R
Howard (DC)	M	Roger Williams (RI)	M
Idaho, U. of	L	Southern Polytechnic (GA)	R
Kent State (OH)	L	Texas, U. of (Arlington)	L
Louisiana State	XL	Texas, U. of (San Antonio)	L
Mississippi State	L	Tuskegee University (AL)	M
Morgan State (MD)	M	Wisconsin, U. of (Milwaukee)	L
Nevada, U. of (Las Vegas)	L	Woodbury (CA)	S
New York Institute of Tech	M		

ART (STUDIO)

GROUP I
Most Selective

Albany (SUNY)(NY)	L	Lawrence (WI)	R
American U. (DC)	M	Macalester (MN)	R
Bard (NY)	R	Michigan, U. of	XL
Bates (ME)	R	Middlebury (VT)	R
Binghamton (SUNY)(NY)	L	New Jersey, College of	M
Boston College (MA)	L	New York U.	L
Boston U. (MA)	L	Pennsylvania, U. of	L
Brown (RI)	M	R.I. School of Design	R
▲Bryn Mawr (PA)	S	Rhodes (TN)	R
Buffalo (SUNY)(NY)	L	Rochester, U. of (NY)	M
Carnegie Mellon (PA)	M	Sarah Lawrence (NY)	R
Centre (KY)	R	▲Scripps (CA)	S
Chicago, U. of (IL)	M	Skidmore (NY)	R
Colby (ME)	R	▲Smith (MA)	R
Colgate (NY)	R	Southwestern (TX)	R
Colorado College	R	Stanford (CA)	M
Connecticut College	R	St. Olaf (MN)	R
Cooper Union (NY)	S	Trinity (TX)	R
Cornell (NY)	L	Tulane (LA)	M
Cornish (WA)	S	Vassar (NY)	R
Dallas, U. of (TX)	R	Virginia, U. of	L
Dartmouth (NH)	M	Washington & Lee (VA)	R
DePauw (IN)	R	Washington U. (MO)	M
Drew (NJ)	R	▲Wellesley (MA)	R
Florida, U. of	XL	Wesleyan (CT)	R
Furman (SC)	R	Wheaton (IL)	R
Harvard (MA)	M	Whitman (WA)	R
Haverford (PA)	S	Williams (MA)	R
Kenyon (OH)	R	Wisconsin, U. of (Madison)	XL
Lafayette (PA)	R	Yale (CT)	M

GROUP II
Very Selective

▲Agnes Scott (GA)	S	Augustana (IL)	R
Alabama, U. of	L	Belmont (TN)	R
Alaska, U. of (Anchorage)	M	Birmingham-Southern (AL)	R
Albright (PA)	R	Bowling Green (OH)	L
Alfred (NY)	R	Bradley (IL)	M
Alma (MI)	R	Brigham Young (UT)	XL
Arizona, U. of	XL	Butler (IN)	R
Art Center College of Design (CA)	R	California College of Arts & Crafts	S
Art Institute of Chicago (IL)	R	California Institute of the Arts	S
Asbury (KY)	R	California, U. of (Davis)	L
Auburn (AL)	L		

GROUP II continues next page

Enrollment Code

■ *Men Only*　　S = Small (less than 1000 students)　　R = Moderate (1000-3000 students)　　M = Medium (3000-8000 students)
▲ *Women Only*　　　　L = Large (8000-20,000 students)　　XL = Extra Large (over 20,000 students)

ART (STUDIO), continued

•• ━━━━━━━━━━━ GROUP II, continued ━━━━━━━━━━━ ••

California, U. of (Irvine)	L
California, U. of (Merced)	R
California, U. of (Santa Barbara)	L
Carroll (WI)	R
Centenary (LA)	S
Cincinnati, U. of (OH)	L
Clarke (IA)	S
Cleveland Institute of Art (OH)	S
Coastal Carolina (SC)	M
Coe (IA)	R
Colorado State	L
Connecticut, U. of	XL
▲ Converse (SC)	S
Cornell (IA)	R
Creighton (NE)	M
Dana (NE)	S
Delaware, U. of	L
Denison (OH)	R
Denver, U. of (CO)	M
Drake (IA)	M
East Carolina (NC)	L
Florida International	L
Florida State	L
Gordon (MA)	R
Guilford (NC)	R
Hamline (MN)	R
Hofstra (NY)	M
▲ Hollins (VA)	S
Houghton (NY)	S
Houston, U. of (TX)	L
Hunter (CUNY) (NY)	L
Illinois, U. of (Chicago)	L
Indiana (PA)	L
Iowa State	XL
Iowa, U. of	XL
James Madison (VA)	R
Juniata (PA)	R
Kansas, U. of	L
Kansas State	L
Knox (IL)	R
Lake Forest (IL)	R
Lebanon Valley (PA)	R
Lindenwood (MO)	R
Loras (IA)	R
Loyola Marymount (CA)	M
Manhattanville (NY)	S
Marietta (OH)	R
Maryland Institute–College of Art	S
Maryland, U. of (Baltimore County)	M
Mass. College of Art	R
Messiah (PA)	R
▲ Mills (CA)	S
Missouri, U. of (Kansas City)	M
Montana State	L
Moore College of Art (PA)	S
Moravian (PA)	R
Morningside (IA)	S
Muhlenberg (PA)	R
North Dakota, U. of	M
Ohio State	XL
Ohio U.	L
Oregon, U. of	L
Otis Art Institute (CA)	S
Pacific, U. of the (CA)	M
Parsons School of Design (NY)	R
Portland State (OR)	M
Principia (IL)	S
Purchase (SUNY)(NY)	R
▲ Randolph-Macon Woman's Col. (VA)	S
Redlands, U. of (CA)	R
▲ Rosemont (PA)	R
Rowan (NJ)	M
▲ St. Mary's College (IN)	R
St. Rose (NY)	R
Salisbury State (MD)	M
San Diego State (CA)	XL
San Francisco Art Institute (CA)	S
Sch. of the Art Institute of Chicago	S
Shepherd (WV)	M
Southern Methodist (TX)	M
Syracuse (NY)	L
Temple (PA)	L
Tennessee, U. of	XL
Tulsa, U. of (OK)	R
Utah, U. of	L
Washington & Jefferson (PA)	R
Washington, U. of	XL
▲ Wesleyan Col. (GA)	S
Western Washington U.	L
Westminster (UT)	R
West Virginia, U. of	L
Wheaton (MA)	R
Whitworth (WA)	R
Wisconsin Lutheran	S
Wisconsin, U. of (Steven's Point)	L
Wittenberg (OH)	R

ART (STUDIO), continued

GROUP III
Selective

Abilene Christian (TX)	M	Fontbonne (MO)	R
Adrian (MI)	R	Fort Hays (KS)	M
Anna Maria (MA)	S	Fort Lewis (CO)	M
Aquinas (MI)	R	Frostburg (MD)	M
Arcadia (PA)	R	George Fox (OR)	R
Arizona State	XL	Georgia Southern	L
Arts, U. of the (PA)	R	Goucher (MD)	R
Ball State (IN)	L	Grand Valley (MI)	L
Belhaven (MS)	R	Hawaii, U. of	L
Berea (WV)	R	Humboldt State (CA)	M
Bloomsburg (PA)	M	Indiana State	L
Boise State (ID)	L	Jacksonville (FL)	R
Brescia (KY)	S	Judson (AL)	S
Briar Cliff (IA)	R	Kansas City Art institute (MO)	S
California College of Arts & Crafts	S	Keene State (NH)	R
California State U. (Channel Islands)	R	Kent State (OH)	L
California State U. (East Bay)	M	Kutztown (PA)	M
California State U. (Fresno)	L	Lambuth (TN)	S
California State U. (Long Beach)	L	Lewis-Clark State (ID)	R
California State U. (Los Angeles)	L	Lock Haven (PA)	M
California State U. (Monterey Bay)	R	Long Island U. (C.W.Post)(NY)	M
California State U. (Northridge)	L	Louisiana-Lafayette	L
California State U. (San Bernardino)	M	Louisiana State	XL
California State U. (San Jose)	L	Lycoming (PA)	R
Case Western Reserve (OH)	M	▲Mary Baldwin (VA)	S
Castleton State (VT)	R	Marymount Manhattan (NY)	R
▲Cedar Crest (PA)	S	Maryville (St. Louis) (MO)	R
▲Chatham (PA)	S	Marywood (PA)	R
Chowan (NC)	S	Massachusetts, U. of (Dartmouth)	M
Coker (SC)	S	McPherson (KS)	S
Colorado, U. of (Denver)	M	Memphis College of Art (TN)	S
Columbia (MO)	R	Memphis, U. of (TN)	L
Culver-Stockton (MO)	S	Mercyhurst (PA)	R
Dordt (IA)	R	Millersville (PA)	M
East Tennessee	L	Millikin (IL)	R
Eastern Illinois	L	Minnesota, U. of (Duluth)	M
Edgewood (WI)	S	Minnesota State U. (Moorhead)	M
Edinboro (PA)	M	Monmouth (NJ)	R
Emmanuel (MA)	S	Montana State (Billings)	R
Emporia State (KS)	M	Montclair State (NJ)	M
Endicott (MA)	R	Montevallo (AL)	R
Fairleigh Dickinson (NJ)	M		

GROUP III continues next page

ART (STUDIO), continued

● ● ● ━━━━━━━━━ **GROUP III, continued** ━━━━━━━━━ ● ● ●

Montserrat (MA)	S
Mount St. Joseph (OH)	R
Murray State (KY)	M
Museum of Fine Arts, School of (MA)	R
Nevada, U. of (Las Vegas)	L
New Mexico, U. of	L
North Carolina (Asheville)	R
North Carolina (Greensboro)	M
Northern Illinois U.	L
Northern Iowa	L
Northern Michigan	M
Old Dominion (VA)	L
Otterbein (OH)	R
Ozarks, College of the (MO)	R
Pennsylvania Acad. of the Fine Arts	S
Potsdam (SUNY)(NY)	R
Roanoke (VA)	R
Rockford (IL)	S
Rocky Mountain (MT)	S
St. Edward's (TX)	M
▲ Salem College (NC)	S
Salem State (MA)	M
Santa Fe, College of (NM)	S
▲ Seton Hill (PA)	S
Shawnee State (OH)	R
Siena Heights (MI)	S
South Dakota, U. of	M
Southern Maine	M
Southern Oregon State U.	M
Texas A&M (Corpus Christi)	M
Texas Tech. U.	L
Texas, U. of (San Antonio)	L
Towson (MD)	L
Union University (TN)	R
Virginia Commonwealth U.	L
Visual Arts, School of (NY)	R
Weber State (UT)	L
West Chester (PA)	M
West Virginia Wesleyan	R
Western Connecticut	M
Western Michigan	L
Wingate (NC)	R
Winthrop (SC)	M
Wisconsin, U. of (Green Bay)	M
Youngstown State (OH)	L

ART HISTORY

GROUP I
Most Selective

Albany (SUNY)(NY) L	Oberlin (OH) .... R
▲Barnard (NY)............ R	Pennsylvania, U. of............ L
Binghamton (SUNY)(NY) L	Pittsburgh, U. of (PA) L
Boston U. (MA)............ L	Pomona (CA) .... R
Bowdoin (ME) .... R	Princeton (NJ) .... M
Brown (RI) .... M	Reed (OR) .... R
▲Bryn Mawr (PA) .... S	Rochester, U. of (NY) .... M
California, U. of (Los Angeles) XL	Rutgers (NJ)............ L
Case Western Reserve U. (OH) .... M	Sarah Lawrence (NY) .... R
Chicago, U. of (IL) .... M	▲Scripps (CA) .... S
Colgate (NY) .... R	Skidmore (NY) .... R
Colorado College .... R	▲Smith (MA) .... R
Columbia (NY)............ M	Stanford (CA) .... M
Connecticut College .... R	Swarthmore (PA) .... R
Cornell (NY)............ L	Syracuse (NY) L
Emory (GA) .... M	Trinity (CT)............ R
Georgetown (DC) .... M	Trinity (TX) .... R
George Washington (DC) .... M	Vanderbilt (TN) .... M
Harvard (MA)............ M	Vassar (NY) .... R
Johns Hopkins (MD) .... M	Washington U. (MO) .... M
Michigan, U. of XL	▲Wellesley (MA)............ R
▲Mount Holyoke (MA) .... R	Willamette (OR) .... R
New York U............ L	Williams (MA) .... R
North Carolina, U. of L	Wisconsin, U. of XL
Northwestern (IL) .... M	Yale (CT) .... M

GROUP II
Very Selective

California State U. (Northridge) L	Kansas, U. of L
California, U. of (Riverside) L	Lake Forest (IL) .... R
California, U. of (Santa Barbara) L	Manhattanville (NY)............ S
California, U. of (Santa Cruz) .... M	Massachusetts, U. of (Lowell) .... M
City College (CUNY)(NY) L	Minnesota, U. of XL
Clarke (IA) .... S	Missouri, U. of XL
College of Charleston (SC) L	Missouri, U. of (Kansas City) .... M
Colorado State L	Oregon, U. of L
Columbia College (IL)............ M	▲Pine Manor (MA) .... S
Delaware, U. of L	Queens (CUNY)(NY) L
Denison (OH) .... R	▲Rosemont (PA) .... S
Denver, U. of (CO) .... M	▲Salem College (NC) .... S
East Carolina L	San Diego State U. (CA) XL
Eastern Connecticut .... M	Sonoma State (CA) .... M
Edinboro (PA) .... M	Southern Methodist (TX)............ M
Florida State............ L	Stony Brook (SUNY)(NY) L
George Mason (VA) L	▲Sweet Briar (VA) .... S
Georgia, U. of XL	Utah, U. of............ L
▲Hollins (VA) .... S	Washington, U. of............ XL
Hunter (CUNY) (NY) L	Wheaton (MA) .... R
Illinois, U. of (Chicago)............ L	Wooster (OH) .... R
Indiana (PA) L	

ASTRONOMY

GROUP I
Most Selective

Amherst (MA)..................................... R
Boston U. L
Brigham Young (UT) XL
▲ Bryn Mawr (PA) .... S
California Inst. of Tech. .... S
Case Western Reserve U. (OH) .... M
Cornell (NY)....................................... L
Harvard (MA)..................................... M
Haverford (PA) .... S
Illinois, U. of (Urbana-Champaign) XL
Michigan, U. of XL
MIT (MA).. M

▲ Mount Holyoke (MA) .... R
Northwestern (IL) .... M
Pennsylvania, U. of........................... L
Pennsylvania State XL
Vassar (NY) .... R
Villanova (PA) .... M
Virginia, U. of L
▲ Wellesley (MA) .... R
Wesleyan (CT) .... R
Whitman (WA).................................... R
Williams (MA) .... R
Wisconsin, U. of XL

GROUP II
Very Selective

Arizona, U. of.................................... XL
Colorado, U. of L
Drake (IA) .... M
Earlham (IN)...................................... R
Florida Inst. of Tech. .... R
Florida, U. of XL
Georgia, U. of XL
Hawaii, U. of L
Indiana U.. XL
Iowa, U. of... XL
Kansas, U. of L
Maryland, U. of................................. XL
Massachusetts, U. of........................ L

Minnesota, U. of XL
Minnesota State U. (Mankato) L
North Carolina State L
Ohio State U...................................... XL
Oklahoma, U. of XL
Pittsburgh, U. of (PA)....................... L
San Diego State XL
San Francisco State U....................... L
Southern California........................... L
Stony Brook (SUNY) (NY)................. L
Texas, U. of (Austin) XL
Washington, U. of............................. XL
Wheaton (MA) .... R

GROUP III
Selective

Benedictine (KS) .... R
Georgia State L
Louisiana State XL
Lycoming (PA) .... R
Montana, U. of .... M

Nebraska, U. of L
Northern Arizona XL
Western Connecticut .... M
Wisconsin, U. of (La Crosse) L
Wyoming, U. of................................. L

Enrollment Code

■ *Men Only*   S = Small (less than 1000 students)   R = Moderate (1000-3000 students)   M = Medium (3000-8000 students)
▲ *Women Only*   L = Large (8000-20,000 students)   XL = Extra Large (over 20,000 students)

BIOCHEMISTRY (Molecular Biology)

GROUP I
Most Selective

▲Barnard (NY) .... R
Binghamton (SUNY) (NY) L
Bowdoin (ME) .... R
Brandeis (MA) .... R
Brown (RI) .... M
California, U. of (Berkeley) XL
California, U. of (Los Angeles) XL
California, U. of (San Diego) L
Case Western Reserve (OH) .... M
Chicago, U. of (IL) .... M
Clarkson (NY) .... M
Columbia (NY) .... M
Connecticut College .... R
Cornell (NY) L
Dallas, U. of (TX) .... R
DePauw (IL) .... R
Geneseo (SUNY) (NY) .... M
Georgetown (DC) .... M

Georgia, U. of XL
Harvard (MA) .... M
Iowa, U. of XL
Lehigh (PA) .... M
Miami, U. of (FL) L
MIT (MA) .... M
▲Mount Holyoke (MA) .... R
Pennsylvania, U. of............................ L
Princeton (NJ) .... M
Rice (TX) .... R
Rutgers (NJ) L
Rochester, U. of (NY) .... M
Swarthmore (PA) .... R
Tulane (LA) .... M
Virginia, U. of L
Worcester Poly Inst. (MA) .... R
Yale (CT) .... M

GROUP II
Very Selective

Albright (PA) .... R
Arizona State XL
Austin (TX) .... R
Beloit (WI) .... R
Bethel (MN) .... M
California Poly State U. (San Luis Obispo).. L
California, U. of (Davis) L
California, U. of (Riverside) L
Centre (KY) .... R
Clark (MA) .... R
Colorado, U. of L
Connecticut, U. of XL
Denison (OH) .... R
Florida Inst. of Tech. .... R
Ithaca (NY) .... M
Kansas State L
Knox (IL) .... R
Lewis & Clark (OR) .... R
Louisiana State XL
Maine, U. of L
McDaniel (MD) .... R
Michigan State.................................... XL

Minnesota, U. of XL
Mississippi State L
Missouri, U. of XL
Moravian (PA)...................................... R
Muhlenberg (PA) .... R
Ohio State XL
Pennsylvania State XL
Pittsburgh, U. of (PA)......................... L
Purdue (IN) XL
Regis (CO) .... R
Ripon (WI) .... R
Sciences, U. of the (PA) .... S
Siena (NY) .... R
Skidmore (NY) .... R
St. Andrews Presbyterian (NC) .... S
Stony Brook (SUNY) (NY) L
Susquehanna (PA) .... R
Virginia Tech. L
Washington State L
Washington, U. of.............................. XL
Wisconsin, U. of XL

GROUP III
Selective

California State U. (Fullerton) L
Framingham (MA) .... M
Indiana (PA) L
Misericordia, College (PA) .... S
Nevada, U. of (Reno) L

Northern Illinois U. L
Ohio Northern..................................... R
Oregon State....................................... L
Sacred Heart (CT)............................... R
Temple (PA) L

BIOLOGY

—————— **GROUP I** ——————
Most Selective

Albany (SUNY) (NY)	L	Iowa State	XL
Amherst (MA)	R	Johns Hopkins (MD)	M
Austin (TX)	R	Kalamazoo (MI)	R
▲Barnard (NY)	R	Kenyon (OH)	R
Bates (ME)	R	Lafayette (PA)	R
Binghampton (SUNY)(NY)	L	Lawrence (WI)	R
Boston College (MA)	L	Lehigh (PA)	M
Boston University (MA)	L	Macalester (MN)	R
Bowdoin (ME)	R	Miami, U. of (FL)	L
Brandeis (MA)	R	Middlebury (VT)	R
Brown (RI)	M	Minnesota, U. of (Morris)	R
▲Bryn Mawr (PA)	S	Missouri, U. of (Rolla)	M
Bucknell (PA)	R	MIT (MA)	M
California Inst. of Tech.	S	▲Mount Holyoke (MA)	R
California, U. of (Berkeley)	XL	New College (FL)	S
California, U. of (Los Angeles)	XL	North Carolina, U. of	L
California, U. of (San Diego)	L	Oberlin (OH)	R
Carleton (MN)	R	Occidental (CA)	R
Case Western Reserve (OH)	M	Pepperdine (CA)	R
Centre (KY)	R	Pitzer (CA)	S
Chicago, U. of (IL)	M	Pomona (CA)	R
Claremont McKenna (CA)	R	Princeton (NJ)	M
Clarkson (NY)	M	Providence (RI)	M
Colby (ME)	R	Reed (OR)	R
Colgate (NY)	R	Rennselaer (NY)	M
Colorado Col.	R	Rhodes (TN)	R
Columbia (NY)	M	Rice (TX)	R
Connecticut College	R	Richmond, U. of (VA)	R
Cornell (NY)	L	Rochester, U. of (NY)	M
Dallas, U. of (TX)	R	Rutgers (NJ)	L
Dartmouth (NH)	M	Skidmore (NY)	R
Davidson (NC)	R	▲Smith (MA)	R
DePauw (IN)	R	South, U. of the (TN)	R
Dickinson (PA)	R	Southwestern (TX)	R
Duke (NC)	M	Stanford (CA)	M
Emory (GA)	M	St. Mary's Col. of Maryland	R
Franklin & Marshall (PA)	R	St. Olaf (MN)	R
Furman (SC)	R	Swarthmore (PA)	R
Geneseo (SUNY) (NY)	M	Trinity (CT)	R
Georgetown (DC)	M	Tufts (MA)	M
Gettysburg (PA)	R	Tulane (LA)	M
Grinnell (IA)	R	Union (NY)	R
Hamilton (NY)	R	Ursinus (PA)	R
Harvard (MA)	M	Vanderbilt (TN)	M
Harvey Mudd (CA)	S	Vassar (NY)	R
Haverford (PA)	S	Vermont, U. of	L
Holy Cross (MA)	R		
Illinois Wesleyan	R		

GROUP I continues next page

BIOLOGY, continued

GROUP I, continued

Villanova (PA)	M	Wheaton (IL)	R
Virginia, U. of	L	Whitman (WA)	R
■ Wabash (IN)	S	Willamette (OR)	R
Wake Forest (NC)	M	William & Mary (VA)	M
Washington & Lee (VA)	M	Williams (MA)	R
Washington U. (MO)	M	Worcester Poly Inst. (MA)	R
▲ Wellesley (MA)	R	Yale (CT)	M
Wesleyan (CT)	R	Yeshiva (NY)	R

GROUP II
Very Selective

▲ Agnes Scott (GA)	S	Connecticut, U. of	XL
Albertson (ID)	S	Cornell Col. (IA)	R
Albright (PA)	R	Creighton (NE)	M
Allegheny (PA)	R	Delaware, U. of	L
Alfred (NY)	R	Denison (OH)	R
Alma (MI)	R	Denver, U. of (CO)	M
Arizona State	XL	Drake (IA)	M
Arizona, U. of	XL	Drury (MO)	R
Augustana (IL)	R	Duquesne (PA)	M
Augustana (SD)	R	Earlham (IN)	R
Belmont (TN)	R	Eckerd (FL)	R
Beloit (WI)	R	Elizabethtown (PA)	R
Benedictine (IL)	R	Elon (NC)	R
Berry (GA)	R	Erskine (SC)	S
Bethel (MN)	M	Fairfield (CT)	M
Birmingham-Southern (AL)	R	Florida Inst. of Tech	R
Cal. Poly. State U. (San Luis Obispo)	L	Florida International	L
California State U. (Chico)	L	Florida Southern	R
California, U. of (Davis)	L	Georgetown (KY)	R
California, U. of (Irvine)	L	Georgia State	L
California, U. of (Merced)	R	Georgia, U. of	XL
California, U. of (Riverside)	L	Gonzaga (WA)	R
California, U. of (Santa Barbara)	L	Gordon (MA)	R
California, U. of (Santa Cruz)	M	Grove City (PA)	R
Canisius (NY)	M	Guilford (NC)	R
Centenary (LA)	S	Gustavus Adolphus (MN)	R
Central (IA)	R	Hamline (MN)	R
Clark (MA)	R	■ Hampden-Sydney (VA)	S
Clarke (IA)	S	Hendrix (AR)	R
Clemson (SC)	L	Hiram (OH)	R
Coe (IA)	R	Hobart & William Smith (NY)	R
Colorado, U. of	L	Hood (MD)	S
Columbia College (SC)	R	Hope (MI)	R
Concordia (MN)	R		

GROUP II continues next page

Enrollment Code

■ *Men Only* S = Small (less than 1000 students)   R = Moderate (1000-3000 students)   M = Medium (3000-8000 students)
▲ *Women Only*   L = Large (8000-20,000 students)   XL = Extra Large (over 20,000 students)

BIOLOGY, continued

•• ══════════ GROUP II, continued ══════════ ••

Houghton (NY)	S
Hunter (CUNY)(NY)	L
Illinois College	S
Illinois, U. of (Chicago)	L
Indiana (PA)	L
Indiana U.	XL
Juniata (PA)	R
Kansas State	L
Kansas, U. of	L
Kentucky, U.of	L
King's (PA)	R
Knox (IL)	R
Lake Forest (IL)	S
LeMoyne (NY)	R
Lewis & Clark (OR)	R
Lipscomb (TN)	R
Linfield (OR)	R
Loras (IA)	R
Loyola (IL)	M
Loyola (LA)	R
Loyola (MD)	R
Luther (IA)	R
Marist (NY)	M
Marquette (WI)	M
Mary Washington (VA)	M
McDaniel (MD)	R
McKendree (IL)	R
Michigan State	XL
Millersville (PA)	M
Millsaps (MS)	S
Minnesota, U. of (Duluth)	M
Minnesota State U. (Moorhead)	M
Mobile, U. of (AL)	R
Monmouth (IL)	S
Morningside (IA)	S
Mount Mercy (IA)	S
Muhlenberg (PA)	R
Murray State (KY)	M
Nazareth (NY)	R
Nebraska Wesleyan	R
New Hampshire, U. of	L
New Mexico State	L
New Mexico, U. of	L
North Carolina, U. of (Wilmington)	L
North Central (IL)	R
North Dakota, U. of	M
Oglethorpe (GA)	R
Ohio Northern	R
Ohio Wesleyan	R
Oklahoma Christian	R
Oklahoma City U.	R
Oklahoma, U. of	L
Oswego (SUNY)(NY)	M
Pacific Lutheran (WA)	R
Pacific University (OR)	R
Presbyterian (SC)	R
Puget Sound (WA)	R
Randolph-Macon (VA)	R
▲ Randolph-Macon Woman's Col. (VA)	S
Rhode Island, U. of	L
Ripon (WI)	R
Roanoke (VA)	R
Rochester Inst. of Tech. (NY)	L
Salisbury State (MD)	M
Sciences in Philadelphia (PA)	R
Scranton, U. of (PA)	M
▲ Scripps (CA)	S
Seattle Pacific (WA)	R
Siena (NY)	R
Spring Hill (AL)	R
St. John's (MN)	R
St. Louis (MO)	M
St. Michael's (VT)	R
St. Norbert (WI)	R
St. Scholastica (MN)	R
Stonehill (MA)	R
Stony Brook (SUNY) (NY)	L
Susquehanna (PA)	R
Texas, U. of (Austin)	XL
Texas Christian	M
Transylvania (KY)	S
Truman State (MO)	M
Tulsa, U. of (OK)	R
Utah, U. of	L
Valparaiso U. (TN)	M
Virginia Tech.	L

GROUP II continues next page

BIOLOGY, continued

•• GROUP II, continued ••

Washington & Jefferson (PA)	R	William Jewell (MO)	R
Washington College (MD)	S	Winona State U. (MN)	M
Wells (NY)	S	Winthrop (SC)	M
West Chester (PA)	M	Wisconsin, U. of (Milwaukee)	L
Westminster (MO)	S	Wisconsin, U. of (Stevens Point)	M
Westminster (PA)	R	Wittenberg (OH)	R
Westminster (UT)	R	Wofford (SC)	R
Westmont (CA)	R	Wooster (OH)	R
Wheaton (MA)	R	Xavier (OH)	R

••• GROUP III •••
Selective

Alaska, U. of (Fairbanks)	M	Framingham (MA)	M
▲ Alverno (WI)	R	George Fox (OR)	R
Arcadia (PA)	R	Gwynedd-Mercy (PA)	S
Aquinas (MI)	R	Hardin-Simmons (TX)	R
Azusa Pacific (CA)	R	Heidelberg (OH)	S
Baker (KS)	R	Holy Names (CA)	S
Ball State (IN)	L	Houston Baptist (TX)	R
Barry (FL)	R	Jacksonville (FL)	R
Berea (KY)	R	Kentucky Wesleyan	S
Bethany (WV)	S	Lambuth (TN)	S
Blackburn (IL)	S	Lewis-Clark State (ID)	R
Briar Cliff (IA)	R	Lock Haven (PA)	M
Brooklyn (CUNY)(NY)	L	Long Island U. (C.W. Post)(NY)	R
California Poly State U. (Pomona)	L	Louisiana - Lafayette	L
California State U. (Channel Islands)	R	Lycoming (PA)	R
California State U. (Monterey Bay)	R	Lynchburg (VA)	R
Carroll (MT)	R	Lyndon State (VT)	R
▲ Cedar Crest (PA)	S	Maryville (TN)	S
Central Michigan	L	▲ Meredith (NC)	R
College of Charleston (SC)	L	Millersville (PA)	M
Colorado, U. of (Denver)	M	Milligan (TN)	S
Daemen (NY)	R	Misericordia, College (PA)	S
Delaware Valley (PA)	R	Missouri Southern State	M
DeSales (PA)	S	Morgan State (MD)	M
Dillard (LA)	R	Mount St. Mary's (CA)	R
Doane (NE)	S	Nichols State (LA)	M
D'Youville (NY)	R	North Carolina (Pembroke)	R
East Stroudsburg (PA)	M	Northern Illinois U.	L
East Tennessee	L	Northern Michigan	M
Eastern Connecticut	M	Northland (WI)	S
Eastern Oregon	R	Northwestern (IA)	R
Elmhurst (IL)	R	▲ Pine Manor (MA)	S
Emmanuel (MA)	S	Pittsburgh, U. of (Bradford)	S
Fitchburg (MA)	R	Point Park (PA)	R
Fort Lewis (CO)	M		

GROUP III continues next page

BIOLOGY, continued

••• ━━━━━━━━━━━━━━ **GROUP III, continued** ━━━━━━━━━━ •••

Puerto Rico (Cayey), U. of	M	Texas, U. of (San Antonio)	L
Reinhardt (GA)	S	Thomas More (KY)	R
Rhode Island College	M	Tougaloo (MS)	S
Rider (NJ)	R	Utah State	L
Rockford (IL)	S	Virginia Wesleyan	R
Shippensburg (PA)	M	Wartburg (IA)	R
South Alabama	M	Western Colorado	R
South Dakota, U. of	M	Western Kentucky	L
Southern Oregon State U.	M	West Chester (PA)	M
Southwest Texas State	L	West Virginia Wesleyan	R
▲Spelman (GA)	R	Wheeling Jesuit (WV)	R
Saint Scholastica (MN)	R	Wilkes (PA)	R
St. Vincent (PA)	R	Wisconsin, U. of (Eau Claire)	L
Temple (PA)	L	Wisconsin, U. of (Platteville)	M
Texas A&M (Corpus Christi)	M	Wyoming, U. of	L
Texas Lutheran	R	Xavier University of Louisiana	R
Texas, U. of (Arlington)	L		

Enrollment Code

■ *Men Only*   S = Small (less than 1000 students)   R = Moderate (1000-3000 students)   M = Medium (3000-8000 students)
▲ *Women Only*   L = Large (8000-20,000 students)   XL = Extra Large (over 20,000 students)

BOTANY / PLANT SCIENCE

GROUP I
Most Selective

California, U. of (Berkeley) XL
Connecticut College .... R
Cornell (NY) L
Duke (NC) .... M

Florida, U. of XL
Miami U. (OH) L
Michigan, U. of XL
North Carolina, U. of L

GROUP II
Very Selective

California, U. of (Davis) L
California, U. of (Riverside) L
Connecticut, U. of XL
Delaware, U. of L
Maine, U. of L
Maryland, U. of L
Michigan State XL
Montana, U. of .... M
North Carolina State L
Ohio U. L

Ohio Wesleyan .... R
Oklahoma State L
Pennsylvania State XL
Purdue (IN) XL
Tennessee, U. of L
Texas, U. of (Austin) XL
Vermont, U. of L
Washington, U. of XL
Wisconsin, U. of XL

GROUP III
Selective

Alabama, U. of L
Ball State (IN) L
Colorado State L
Eastern Connecticut .... M
Eastern Illinois L
Hawaii, U. of L
Humboldt State (CA) .... M

Louisiana State XL
Northern Arizona XL
Oregon State L
Southeastern Oklahoma State .... M
Southern Illinois U. (Carbondale) L
Wyoming, U. of L

Enrollment Code		
■ *Men Only*	S = Small (less than 1000 students) R = Moderate (1000-3000 students)	M = Medium (3000-8000 students)
▲ *Women Only*	L = Large (8000-20,000 students) XL = Extra Large (over 20,000 students)	

BUSINESS ADMINISTRATION

GROUP I
Most Selective

Albany (SUNY) (NY)	L	Lehigh (PA)	M
American (DC)	M	Miami U. (OH)	L
Babson (MA)	R	Michigan, U. of	XL
Binghamton (SUNY) (NY)	L	Missouri, U. of	XL
Boston College (MA)	L	MIT (MA)	M
Boston U. (MA)	L	Muhlenberg (PA)	R
Bucknell (PA)	R	New York U.	L
Buffalo (SUNY) (NY)	L	North Carolina, U. of	L
California, U. of (Berkeley)	XL	Notre Dame (IN)	M
California, U. of (Los Angeles)	XL	Pennsylvania, U. of	L
Carnegie Mellon (PA)	M	Rensselaer (NY)	M
Case Western Reserve U. (OH)	M	Rhodes (TN)	R
Claremont McKenna (CA)	R	Richmond, U. of (VA)	R
Clarkson (NY)	M	Rutgers (NJ)	L
➤ Colby (ME)	R	Southern California, U. of	L
DePauw (IN)	R	Southwestern (TX)	R
Emory (GA)	M	Syracuse (NY)	L
Fairfield (CT)	R	Trinity (TX)	R
Florida, U. of	XL	Tulane (LA)	M
Florida State	L	U.S. Air Force Academy (CO)	M
Franklin & Marshall (PA)	R	Vermont, U. of	L
Furman (SC)	R	Villanova (PA)	M
Geneseo (SUNY) (NY)	M	Virginia Poly. Institute	L
Georgetown (DC)	M	Virginia, U. of	L
George Washington (DC)	M	Wake Forest (NC)	M
Georgia Inst. of Tech	L	Washington U. (MO)	M
Gettysburg (PA)	R	Washington & Lee (VA)	M
Gustavus Adolphus (MN)	R	William & Mary (VA)	M
Illinois, U. of (Urbana-Champaign)	XL	Wisconsin, U. of	XL
Indiana U.	XL	Worcester Poly Inst. (MA)	R
Lafayette (PA)	R	Yeshiva (NY)	R

➤ *Administrative Science*

GROUP II
Very Selective

Adrian (MI)	R	Belmont (TN)	R
▲ Agnes Scott (GA)	S	Bentley (MA)	M
Alabama, U. of	L	Berry (GA)	R
Alabama, U. of (Huntsville)	M	Birmingham Southern (AL)	R
Alaska Pacific	S	Bowling Green (OH)	L
Albertson (ID)	S	Bradley (IL)	M
Albright (PA)	R	Brigham Young (UT)	XL
Alfred (NY)	R	Bryant (RI)	R
Alma (MI)	R	Buena Vista (IA)	R
Arizona, U. of	XL	Butler (IN)	R
Arizona State	XL	Cal. Poly. State U. (San Luis Obispo)	L
Asbury (KY)	R	California State (Fullerton)	L
Auburn (AL)	L	California, U. of (Riverside)	L
Augsburg (MN)	R	California, U. of (Santa Barbara)	L
Augustana (IL)	R	Capital U. (OH)	R
Austin (TX)	R	Centenary (LA)	S
Baylor (TX)	M		

GROUP II continues next page

BUSINESS ADMINISTRATION, continued

GROUP II, continued

Central Florida, U. of	L
Charleston, College of (SC)	L
Christian Brothers (TN)	R
Cincinnati, U. of (OH)	L
Clark (MA)	R
Clemson (SC)	L
Coe (IA)	R
Colorado, U. of	L
Colorado, U. of (Col. Springs)	M
Columbia College (SC)	R
Concordia (MN)	R
Connecticut, U. of	XL
Creighton (NE)	M
Dayton, U. of (OH)	M
Delaware, U. of	L
Denver, U. of (CO)	M
DePaul (IL)	L
Dominican (IL)	S
Drake (IA)	M
Dubuque, U. of (IA)	S
Duquesne (PA)	M
Eastern Michigan	L
Eckerd (FL)	R
Elizabethtown (PA)	R
Elon (NC)	R
Erskine (SC)	S
Flagler (FL)	R
Florida Atlantic	L
Florida Gulf Coast U.	M
Florida Inst. of Tech.	R
Florida International	M
Fredonia (SUNY) (NY)	M
George Mason (VA)	L
Georgetown College (KY)	R
Gonzaga (WA)	R
Goucher (MD)	S
Grove City (PA)	R
Guilford (NC)	R
Hampton (VA)	M
Hanover (IN)	R
Harding (AR)	M
Hendrix (AR)	R
Hillsdale (MI)	R
Hofstra (NY)	M
Hood (MD)	S
Houston, U. of (TX)	L
Idaho, U. of	L

Illinois College	S
Illinois, U. of (Chicago)	L
Indiana U. of Pennsylvania	L
Iowa State	XL
Iowa, U. of	XL
Ithaca (NY)	M
James Madison (VA)	M
John Carroll (OH)	M
▲ Judson (AL)	S
Juniata (PA)	R
Kansas State	L
Kentucky, U. of	L
LaSalle (PA)	M
Lebanon Valley (PA)	R
LeMoyne (NY)	R
LeTourneau (TX)	R
Lewis & Clark (OR)	R
Lindenwood (MO)	R
Lipscomb (TN)	R
Longwood (VA)	R
Loras (IA)	R
Lowell, U. of (MA)	L
Loyola (MD)	R
Loyola (LA)	R
Loyola Marymount (CA)	M
Luther (IA)	R
Manhattan (NY)	M
Manhattanville (NY)	R
Marietta (OH)	R
Marist (NY)	M
Marquette (WI)	M
Maryland, U. of	XL
Mary Washington (VA)	M
Massachusetts, U. of	L
Master's (CA)	R
McDaniel (MD)	R
Messiah (PA)	R
Michigan, U. of (Dearborn)	M
Michigan State	XL
Michigan Tech	M
Millersville (PA)	M
Millsaps (MS)	S
Minnesota, U. of	XL
Mississippi College	R
Mississippi, U. of	L

GROUP II continues next page

Enrollment Code

■ *Men Only*
▲ *Women Only*

S = Small (less than 1000 students)   R = Moderate (1000-3000 students)   M = Medium (3000-8000 students)
L = Large (8000-20,000 students)   XL = Extra Large (over 20,000 students)

BUSINESS ADMINISTRATION, continued

======================== **GROUP II, continued** ========================

Mississippi U. for Women .... R	Ripon (WI) .... R
Missouri, U. of (Kansas City) .... M	Roanoke (VA) .... R
Missouri, U. of (St. Louis) .... M	Rochester Inst. of Tech (NY) L
Mobile, U. of (AL) .... R	Rockhurst (MO) .... R
Monmouth (IL) .... S	Rowan (NJ) .... M
Moravian (PA) .... R	Salem College (NC) .... S
Nazareth (NY) .... R	Samford (AL) .... R
New Hampshire, U. of L	San Diego State U. (CA) XL
Newman University (KS) .... S	San Diego, U. of (CA) .... M
New Mexico, U. of L	San Francisco, U. of (CA) .... M
New Mexico State L	Santa Clara U. (CA) .... M
New Paltz (SUNY) (NY) .... M	Sciences, U. of the (PA) .... S
North Carolina, U. of (Greensboro) ...... M	Scranton, U. of (PA) .... M
North Carolina, U. of (Wilmington L	Seton Hall (NJ) .... M
North Dakota, U. of .... M	Shaw (NC) .... R
Northeastern (MA) L	Shepherd (WV) .... M
Northwestern (MN) .... R	Siena (NY) .... R
Northern Arizona XL	▲Simmons (MA) .... R
North Florida .... M	Skidmore (NY) .... R
Oglethorpe (GA) .... R	Southern Methodist (TX) .... M
Ohio U. L	Spring Hill (AL) .... R
Oklahoma City U. (OK) .... R	St. Bonaventure (NY) .... R
Oklahoma State L	▲St. Catherine (MN) .... R
Oklahoma, U. of XL	St. John's (MN) .... R
Old Dominion (VA) L	St. Joseph's U. (PA) .... R
Oregon, U. of L	St. Louis U. (MO) .... M
Oswego (SUNY) (NY) .... M	St. Mary's Col. of CA .... R
Pacific Lutheran (WA) .... R	▲St. Mary's Col. (IN) .... R
Pacific, U. of the (CA) .... M	St. Mary's Col. (MN) .... R
Pacific University (OR) .... R	St. Michael's Col. (VT) .... R
Palm Beach Atlantic (FL) .... R	St. Norbert (WI) .... R
Pennsylvania State XL	# St. Scholastica (MN) .... R
Pepperdine (CA) .... R	Southern Oregon State U. .... M
Pittsburgh, U. of (PA) L	Stetson (FL) .... R
Plattsburgh (SUNY) (NY) .... M	Stonehill (MA) .... R
Portland State (OR) L	Susquehanna U. (PA) .... R
Portland, U. of (OR) .... R	Temple (PA) L
Presbyterian (SC) .... R	Texas A&M XL
Principia (IL) .... S	Texas A&M at Galveston .... S
Providence (RI) .... M	Texas Christian .... M
Puerto Rico, U. of L	Texas Tech U. L
Puget Sound (WA) .... R	Texas, U. of (Austin) XL
Purdue (IN) XL	Texas, U. of (Dallas) .... M
Queens (NC) .... S	Transylvania (KY) .... S
Randolph-Macon (VA) .... R	▲Trinity (DC) .... S
Redlands, U. of (CA) .... R	
Richard Stockton (NJ) .... M	

 # Also, Organizational Behavior and Marketing

GROUP II continues next page

Enrollment Code

■ Men Only | S = Small (less than 1000 students) | R = Moderate (1000-3000 students) | M = Medium (3000-8000 students)
▲ Women Only | L = Large (8000-20,000 students) | XL = Extra Large (over 20,000 students)

BUSINESS ADMINISTRATION, continued

GROUP II, continued

Truman State (MO)	M
Tulsa, U. of (OK)	R
Ursinus (PA)	R
Utah, U. of	L
Valparaiso (IN)	M
Virginia Tech.	R
Wartburg (IA)	R
Washington College (MD)	S
Washington State	L
Washington, U. of	XL
Wells (NY)	S
▲Wesleyan College (GA)	S
Western Michigan	L
Westminster (MO)	S
Westminster (UT)	R
West Virginia U.	L
Whitworth (WA)	R
Wilberforce (OH)	S
William Jewell Col. (MO)	R
Winona State U. (MN)	M
Wisconsin, U. of (Milwaukee)	L
Wisconsin, U. of (Stevens Point)	M
Wittenberg (OH)	R
Wofford (SC)	R
Wyoming, U. of	L
Xavier (OH)	R

GROUP III
Selective

Abilene Christian (TX)	M
Akron, U. of (OH)	L
Alabama, U. of (Birmingham)	M
Alaska, U. of (Anchorage)	M
Alaska, U. of (Fairbanks)	M
Alderson-Broaddus (WV)	S
▲Alverno (WI)	R
American International (MA)	R
Anna Maria (MA)	S
Appalachian State (NC)	L
Arkansas, U. of	L
Ashland (OH)	R
Assumption (MA)	R
Averett (VA)	S
Avila (MO)	S
Azusa Pacific (CA)	R
Baker (KS)	R
Baldwin-Wallace (OH)	R
Barry (FL)	R
▲Bay Path (MA)	R
Baruch (CUNY) (NY)	L
Belhaven (MS)	R
Bellarmine (KY)	R
Belmont Abbey (NC)	S
Benedictine (KS)	R
Benedictine (IL)	R
▲Bennett (NC)	S
Berea (KY)	R
Bethel (MN)	R
Blackburn (IL)	S
Bloomsburg (PA)	M
Bluffton (OH)	S
Boise State (ID)	L
Brescia (KY)	S
Briar Cliff (IA)	R
Bridgewater (VA)	R
Brockport (SUNY) (NY)	M
Caldwell (NJ)	S
California Lutheran	R
California Maritime Academy	S
Cal. Poly. State U. (Pomona)	L
California State U. (Bakersfield)	M
California State U. (Channel Islands)	R
California State U. (Dominguez Hills)	M
California State U. (East Bay)	M
California State U. (Fresno)	L
California State U. (Fullerton)	L
California State U. (Los Angeles)	L
California State U. (Northridge)	L
California State U. (Sacramento)	M
California State U. (San Bernardino)	M
California State U. (San Marcos)	M
California State U. (Stanislaus)	M
Campbell (NC)	R
Canisius (NY)	M
Carthage (WI)	R
Castleton (VT)	R
Catawba (NC)	S
Cedarville (OH)	R
Central Arkansas	M
Central Connecticut	M
Central Oklahoma	L
Central Washington	L
Chaminade (HI)	R
π Champlain (VT)	R

π *Also, Electronic Games & Interactive Development*

GROUP III continues next page

BUSINESS ADMINISTRATION, continued

••• ────────────── **GROUP III, continued** ────────────── •••

Chapman (CA)	R	Grambling (LA)	M
▲Chatham (PA)	S	Green Mountain (VT)	S
Chowan (NC)	S	Hartford, U. of (CT)	M
Christopher Newport (VA)	M	Hartwick (NY)	R
Cincinnati, U. of (OH)	L	Hastings (NE)	R
Citadel, The (SC)	R	Hawaii Pacific	M
Clark Atlanta (GA)	M	Heidelberg (OH)	S
Coastal Carolina (SC)	M	Henderson State (AR)	M
Coker (SC)	S	Hillsdale (MI)	R
Colorado State	L	Howard (DC)	M
Colorado, U. of (Denver)	M	Husson (ME)	S
Columbia College (MO)	R	Immaculata (PA)	S
Concordia (CA)	R	Indiana Institute of Tech.	S
Concordia (NE)	R	Indiana State U.	L
Culver-Stockton (MO)	S	Iona (NY)	M
Daemen (NY)	R	Jacksonville (FL)	R
Delaware Valley (PA)	R	Kennesaw State (GA)	R
Dillard (LA)	R	Kentucky Wesleyan (KY)	S
Doane (NE)	S	King's (PA)	R
East Tennessee	L	LaSell (MA)	S
Eastern (PA)	R	LaVerne, U. of (CA)	R
Eastern Connecticut	M	Lenoir-Rhyne (NC)	R
Eastern Illinois	L	Lesley (MA)	S
Eastern Nazarene (MA)	R	Linfield (OR)	R
Eastern Oregon	R	Long Island U. (C.W. Post) (NY)	R
Edgewood (WI)	S	Louisiana-Lafayette	L
Elmhurst (IL)	R	Louisville (KY)	L
Elmira (NY)	R	Maine (Farmington)	R
Emory & Henry (VA)	S	Maine, U. of	L
Endicott (MA)	R	Malone (OH)	R
Eureka (IL)	S	Manchester (IN)	R
Fairleigh Dickinson (NJ)	M	Marshall (WV)	L
Fairmont State (WV)	M	▲Mary Baldwin (VA)	S
Faulkner (AL)	R	Marygrove (MI)	R
Ferris State (MI)	L	Mass. Col. of Lib. Arts (N. Adams)	R
Fisk (TN)	S	Massachusettes, U. of (Boston)	M
Florida A&M	M	McMurray (TX)	R
Framingham (MA)	M	Mercer (GA)	R
Freed-Hardeman (TN)	R	Mercyhurst (PA)	R
Frostburg (MD)	M	▲Meredith (NC)	R
Gannon (PA)	M	Merrimack (MA)	R
Gardner-Webb (NC)	S	Middle Tennessee	L
George Fox (OR)	R	Milligan (TN)	S
Georgia Southern	L	Mississippi State	L
Georgia State	L	Missouri Southern State	M
Graceland (IA)	R		

GROUP III continues next page

Enrollment Code

■ *Men Only*	S = Small (less than 1000 students) R = Moderate (1000-3000 students) M = Medium (3000-8000 students)
▲ *Women Only*	L = Large (8000-20,000 students) XL = Extra Large (over 20,000 students)

BUSINESS ADMINISTRATION, continued

GROUP III, continued

Monmouth (NJ)	R
Montana, U. of	M
Montclair State (NJ)	M
Montreat (NC)	S
■ Morehouse (GA)	R
Mount Mercy (IA)	S
Mount St. Joseph (OH)	R
Mount St. Mary's (CA)	R
Mount St. Mary's (MD)	R
Mount Union (OH)	S
Muskingum (OH)	R
Nebraska, U. of	L
Nebraska, U. of (Kearney)	M
Nebraska, U. of (Omaha)	L
Nevada, U. of (Las Vegas)	L
Nevada, U. of (Reno)	L
New Orleans, U. of	L
Niagara (NY)	R
North Carolina, U. of (Charlotte)	L
North Carolina, U. of (Pembroke)	R
North Georgia	R
Northern Arizona	L
Northern Colorado	L
Northern Illinois	L
Northern Iowa, U. of	L
Northern Kentucky	L
Northwestern U. of Louisiana	L
Northwood University (MI)	R
Nova Southeastern (FL)	R
Nyack (NY)	R
Oakland U. (MI)	M
Oakland City U. (IN)	R
Ohio Northern	R
Ohio State	XL
Oral Roberts (OK)	M
Oregon Inst. of Tech.	R
Ozarks, College of the (MO)	R
Pace (NY)	R
Penn State (Erie)(PA)	M
Peru State (NE)	R
Philadelphia U. (PA)	R
▲ Pine Manor (MA)	S
Pittsburg State (KS)	M
Pittsburgh, U. of (Greensburg)	R
Pittsburgh, U. of (Johnstown)	R
Point Loma (CA)	R
Potsdam (SUNY) (NY)	M
Presentation (SD)	S
Puerto Rico (CAYEY), U. of	M
Quincy (IL)	R
Quinnipiac (CT)	R
Phillips (OK)	R
Radford (VA)	M
Ramapo (NJ)	M
Regis (CO)	R
Reinhardt (GA)	S
Rider (NJ)	M
Robert Morris (PA)	M
Rockford (IL)	S
Roger Williams (RI)	M
Roosevelt (IL)	R
Sacred Heart (CT)	R
San Jose State (CA)	L
Schreiner (TX)	S
Seattle U. (WA)	R
Shippensburg (PA)	M
Silver Lake (WI)	S
Simpson (IA)	R
Sonoma State (CA)	M
South Alabama	M
South Carolina, U. of	L
South Dakota, U. of	M
Southeastern Missouri State	L
Southeastern Oklahoma State	M
Southern Illinois	L
Southern Maine	M
Southern Mississippi	L
Southern Oregon State U.	M
South Florida, U. of	XL
Southwestern Oklahoma	M
Southwest Texas State	L
▲ Stephens (MO)	S
St. Ambrose (IA)	R
St. Andrews Presbyterian (NC)	S
St. Edward's (TX)	M
St. Francis (NY)	R
St. John Fisher (NY)	L
St. John's (NY)	L
St. Joseph's (IN)	S
St. Joseph's (NY)	R
St. Martin's (WA)	S
St. Mary's (TX)	R
St. Rose (NY)	R
St. Thomas (MN)	M
St. Vincent's (PA)	R
Suffolk (MA)	R
Tampa, U. of (FL)	R
Taylor (IN)	R

GROUP III continues next page

BUSINESS ADMINISTRATION, continued

GROUP III, continued

Tennessee, U. of	L	West Florida, U. of	M
Texas A&M (Corpus Christi)	M	Western Carolina (NC)	M
Texas Lutheran	R	Western Connecticut State	M
Texas State U. (San Marcos)	L	Western New England (MA)	R
Texas Wesleyan	R	Western State (CO)	R
Texas, U. of (San Antonio)	L	Whittier (CA)	R
Texas, U. of (Tyler)	R	Wichita State (KS)	M
Thomas More (KY)	R	Widener (PA)	R
Toledo, U. of	L	Winthrop (SC)	M
Towson (MD)	L	Wisconsin, U. of (Eau Claire)	L
Troy State (AL)	M	Wisconsin, U. of (Green Bay)	M
Utica College (NY)	R	Wisconsin, U. of (LaCrosse)	L
Virginia Commonwealth	L	Wisconsin, U. of (Stout)	M
Virginia Wesleyan	R	Woodbury (CA)	S
Visual Arts, School of (NY)	R	Worcester State (MA)	M
Wagner (NY)	R	Xavier U. of Louisiana	R
Washington & Jefferson (PA)	R	York (PA)	M
Weber State (UT)	L	Youngstown State (OH)	L
West Chester (PA)	M		

CHEMISTRY

GROUP I
Most Selective

Albany (SUNY)(NY)	L	Kalamazoo (MI)	R
Allegheny (PA)	R	Kenyon (OH)	R
Amherst (MA)	R	Lafayette (PA)	R
▲Barnard (NY)	R	Lawrence (WI)	R
Bates (ME)	R	Macalester (MN)	R
Binghamton (SUNY)(NY)	L	MIT (MA)	M
Boston College (MA)	L	Michigan, U. of	XL
Boston U. (MA)	L	Missouri, U. of (Rolla)	M
Bowdoin (ME)	R	▲Mount Holyoke (MA)	R
Brandeis (MA)	M	New College (FL)	S
Brown (RI)	M	New Mexico Inst. of Tech.	R
▲Bryn Mawr (PA)	S	North Carolina, U. of	L
Bucknell (PA)	M	Northwestern (IL)	M
Buffalo (SUNY)(NY)	L	Notre Dame (IN)	M
California Inst. of Tech.	S	Oberlin (OH)	R
California, U. of (Berkeley)	XL	Occidental (CA)	R
California, U. of (Los Angeles)	XL	Pennsylvania State	XL
California, U. of (San Diego)	L	Pomona (CA)	R
Carleton (MN)	R	Princeton (NJ)	M
Carnegie Mellon (PA)	M	Puget Sound (WA)	R
Case Western Reserve U. (OH)	M	Reed (OR)	R
Centre (KY)	R	Rennselaer (NY)	M
Chicago, U. of (IL)	M	Rhodes (TN)	R
Claremont McKenna (CA)	R	Rice (TX)	R
Clarkson (NY)	M	Richmond (VA)	R
Colby (ME)	R	Rochester, U. of (NY)	M
Colgate (NY)	R	Rose-Hulman (IN)	R
Colorado College	R	Rutgers (NJ)	L
Columbia (NY)	M	Siena (NY)	R
Connecticut College	R	Skidmore (NY)	R
Cornell (NY)	L	South, U. of the (TN)	R
Dartmouth (NH)	M	Southwestern (TX)	R
Davidson (NC)	R	St. Olaf (MN)	R
DePauw (IN)	R	Stanford (CA)	M
Drew (NJ)	R	Trinity (CT)	R
Duke (NC)	M	Trinity (TX)	R
Emory (GA)	M	Tufts (MA)	M
Franklin & Marshall (PA)	R	Union (NY)	R
Furman (SC)	R	United States Naval Academy (MD)	M
Georgetown (DC)	M	Virginia, U. of	L
Georgia Inst. of Tech	L	■Wabash (IN)	S
Gonzaga (WA)	M	Wake Forest (NC)	M
Grinnell (IA)	R	Washington U. (MO)	M
Gustavus Adolphus (MN)	R	▲Wellesley (MA)	R
Hamilton (NY)	R	Wesleyan (CT)	R
Harvard (MA)	M	Wheaton (IL)	R
Harvey Mudd (CA)	S	Whitman (WA)	R
Haverford (PA)	S	Willamette (OR)	R
Holy Cross (MA)	R	Williams (MA)	R
Illinois Wesleyan	R	Wisconsin, U. of	XL
Illinois, U. of (Urbana-Champaign)	XL	Worcester Poly Inst.(MA)	R
Iowa State	XL		
Johns Hopkins (MD)	M		

CHEMISTRY continues next page

CHEMISTRY, continued

GROUP II
Very Selective

Albertson (ID)	S	Goucher (MD)	S
Alfred (NY)	R	Hamline (MN)	R
Alma (MI)	R	Hanover (IN)	R
Arcadia (PA)	R	Hendrix (AR)	R
Arizona, U. of	XL	Hiram (OH)	R
Augustana (SD)	R	Hobart & William Smith (NY)	R
Austin (TX)	R	▲ Hollins (VA)	S
Baylor (TX)	M	Hope (MI)	R
Bemidji State (MN)	M	Houghton (NY)	S
Berea (KY)	R	Hunter (CUNY)(NY)	L
Berry (GA)	R	Huntingdon (AL)	S
Bethany (WV)	S	Indiana U.	XL
Birmingham-Southern (AL)	R	Ithaca Col.	M
Bradley (IL)	M	Juniata (PA)	R
Brigham Young (UT)	L	Kansas, U. of	L
Brooklyn College (CUNY)(NY)	L	Knox (IL)	R
Butler (IN)	R	Lake Forest (IL)	R
California, U. of (Davis)	L	LaSalle (PA)	R
California, U. of (Irvine)	L	Lehigh (PA)	M
California, U. of (Santa Barbara)	L	Linfield (OR)	R
California, U. of (Santa Cruz)	M	Lipscomb (TN)	R
Capital (OH)	R	Loras (IA)	R
Carroll (WI)	R	Louisiana State	XL
Centenary (LA)	S	Louisiana-Lafayette	L
Central (IA)	R	Louisville (KY)	L
Citadel, The (SC)	R	Loyola (LA)	R
City College (CUNY)(NY)	L	Lycoming (PA)	R
Clark (MA)	R	Maine, U. of	L
Clarke (IA)	S	Mansfield (PA)	R
Clemson (SC)	L	Marquette (WI)	M
Coe (IA)	R	Maryland, U. of (Baltimore County)	M
Colorado, U. of	L	Mary Washington (VA)	M
Concordia (MN)	R	Massachusetts, U. of	L
Converse (SC)	S	McKendree (IL)	R
Creighton (NE)	R	Michigan State	XL
Delaware, U. of	L	Michigan, U. of (Dearborn)	M
Denver, U. of (CO)	M	Millsaps (MS)	S
DePaul (IL)	L	Minnesota, U. of (Morris)	R
Drake (IA)	M	Missouri, U. of (Kansas City)	M
Duquesne (PA)	M	Monmouth (IL)	S
Earlham (IN)	R	Murray State (KY)	M
Eastern Michigan	L	Nebraska Wesleyan	R
Elmhurst (IL)	R	New Hampshire, U. of	L
Florida Inst. of Tech	R	New Mexico State	L
Florida Southern	R	North Carolina, U. of (Charlotte)	L
Florida State	L	North Carolina, U. of (Wilmington)	L
Georgetown (KY)	R	North Carolina State	L
George Washington (DC)	M	North Central (IL)	R
Georgia, U. of	XL		

GROUP II continues next page

CHEMISTRY, continued

GROUP II, continued

North Dakota, U. of	M
Ohio Northern	R
Ohio State	XL
Ohio University	L
Ohio Wesleyan	R
Oklahoma, U. of	XL
Oregon, U. of	L
Otterbein (OH)	R
Pittsburgh, U. of (PA)	L
Portland, U. of (OR)	R
Providence (RI)	M
Puerto Rico, U of (Mayaguez)	L
Puget Sound (WA)	R
Purdue (IN)	XL
Richard Stockton (NJ)	M
Ripon (WI)	S
Roanoke (VA)	R
Rochester, U. of (NY)	M
Rochester Institute of Tech. (NY)	L
Rockhurst (MO)	R
Rollins (FL)	R
St. John's (MN)	R
St. Louis (MO)	M
St. Michael's (VT)	R
St. Thomas (MN)	R
St. Thomas (TX)	R
St. Vincent (PA)	R
San Diego State U. (CA)	XL
Sciences in Philadelphia (PA)	R
Seattle Pacific (WA)	R
Seattle U. (WA)	R
Shepherd (WV)	M
South Florida, U. of	L
▲ Spelman (GA)	R
Spring Hill (AL)	R
Stetson (FL)	R
Stonehill (MA)	R
Stony Brook (SUNY) (NY)	L
Susquehanna (PA)	R
▲ Sweet Briar (VA)	S
Syracuse (NY)	L
Temple (PA)	L
Texas A&M	XL
Transylvania (KY)	S
Truman State (MO)	M
Ursinus (PA)	R
Utah State	L
Utah, U. of	L
Vermont, U. of	L
Virginia Military Inst.	R
Virginia Tech.	L
Viterbo (WI)	R
Washington & Jefferson (PA)	R
Washington, U. of	XL
Wells (NY)	S
West Florida, U. of	M
Westminster (UT)	R
Westmont (CA)	R
Whitworth (WA)	R
Wiliam Jewell (MO)	R
Winthrop (SC)	M
Wisconsin Lutheran	S
Wisconsin, U. of (Milwaukee)	L
Wittenberg (OH)	R
Wofford (SC)	R
Wooster (OH)	R

CHEMISTRY continues next page

Enrollment Code

■ *Men Only*
▲ *Women Only*

S = Small (less than 1000 students)   R = Moderate (1000-3000 students)   M = Medium (3000-8000 students)
L = Large (8000-20,000 students)   XL = Extra Large (over 20,000 students)

CHEMISTRY, continued

GROUP III
Selective

Abilene Christian (TX)	M	Mount St. Joseph (OH)	R
Akron, U. of (OH)	L	Muskingum (OH)	R
Alabama, U. of (Birmingham)	M	Nichols State (LA)	M
Alabama, U. of (Huntsville)	M	Northern Illinois U.	L
Andrews (MI)	R	Northern Michigan	M
Aquinas (MI)	R	Northwestern (IA)	R
Ashland (OH)	R	Oakland U. (MI)	M
Baldwin-Wallace (OH)	R	Puerto Rico, U. of (Cayey)	L
Benedictine (KS)	R	Rider (NJ)	R
Bethany (KS)	S	St. John's (NY)	L
Bluffton (OH)	S	St. Mary's (MN)	R
California (PA)	M	St. Scholastica (MN)	R
California State U. (Chico)	L	Salem State (MA)	M
California State U. (Dominguez Hills)	M	Shippensburg (PA)	M
California State U. (Fresno)	L	Shorter (GA)	R
California State U. (Fullerton)	L	Sonoma State (CA)	M
California State U. (Long Beach)	L	Southern Connecticut	M
California State U. (San Jose)	L	Southern Illinois U. (Carbondale)	L
California State U. (San Marcos)	M	Southern Maine	M
Carroll (MT)	R	Southern Oregon State U.	M
Carson-Newman (TN)	R	Southwestern Oklahoma	M
Central Washington	L	▲ Sweet Briar (VA)	S
College of Charleston (SC)	L	Tennessee, U. of	XL
Cumberland (KY)	R	Texas A&M (Corpus Christi)	M
Delaware Valley (PA)	R	Texas Lutheran	R
DeSales (PA)	S	Thomas More (KY)	R
Eastern Washington	L	Towson (MD)	L
Emporia State (KS)	M	Union (TN)	R
Framingham (MA)	M	Washington & Lee (VA)	R
Gannon (PA)	M	Wayne State (NE)	R
Georgia State	L	West Chester (PA)	M
Houston Baptist (TX)	R	Western Carolina (NC)	M
Kennesaw State (GA)	R	Western Illinois	L
Kentucky Wesleyan	R	Wheeling Jesuit (WV)	R
King's (PA)	R	Whittier (CA)	R
Lewis-Clark State (ID)	R	Winona State (MN)	M
Lock Haven (PA)	M	Wisconsin, U. of (Eau Claire)	L
Long Island U. (Brooklyn)(NY)	M	Wisconsin, U. of (LaCrosse)	L
Long Island U. (C.W. Post)(NY)	R	Wisconsin, U. of (Platteville)	M
Marshall (WV)	L	Wisconsin, U. of (Stevens Point)	M
▲ Mary Baldwin (VA)	S	Worcester State (MA)	M
Maryville (TN)	R	Wyoming, U. of	L
Massachusetts, U. of (Dartmouth)	M	Xavier (OH)	R
Millersville (PA)	M	Xavier U. of Louisiana	R
Milligan (TN)	S		

Enrollment Code

■ *Men Only*   S = Small (less than 1000 students)   R = Moderate (1000-3000 students)   M = Medium (3000-8000 students)
▲ *Women Only*   L = Large (8000-20,000 students)   XL = Extra Large (over 20,000 students)

CLASSICS

━━━━━━━━━━━━━━━ **GROUP I** ━━━━━━━━━━━━━━━
Most Selective

Agnes Scott (GA)	S	Maryland, U. of (Baltimore County)	M
Amherst (MA)	R	Michigan, U. of	XL
▲ Barnard (NY)	R	Middlebury (VT)	R
Bowdoin (ME)	R	New York U.	M
Brown (RI)	M	North Carolina, U. of	L
▲ Bryn Mawr (PA)	S	Northwestern (IL)	M
Buffalo (SUNY)(NY)	L	Oberlin (OH)	R
California, U. of (Berkeley)	XL	Pennsylvania, U. of	L
Carleton (MN)	R	Pittsburgh, U. of (PA)	L
Case Western Reserve (OH)	M	Princeton (NJ)	M
Centre (KY)	R	Rhodes (TN)	R
Chicago, U. of (IL)	M	St. Olaf (MN)	R
Colgate (NY)	R	▲ Scripps (CA)	S
Columbia (NY)	M	Skidmore (NY)	R
Connecticut College	R	Stanford (CA)	M
Dallas, U. of (TX)	R	Swarthmore (PA)	R
Dartmouth (NH)	M	Texas, U. of (Austin)	XL
Drew (NJ)	R	Trinity (TX)	R
Duke (NC)	M	Tufts (MA)	M
Emory (GA)	M	Vanderbilt (TN)	M
Georgetown (DC)	M	Virginia, U. of	L
Grinnell (IA)	R	■ Wabash (IN)	S
Gustavus Adolphus (MN)	R	Whitman (WA)	R
Harvard (MA)	M	Willamette (OR)	R
Holy Cross (MA)	R	William & Mary (VA)	R
Johns Hopkins (MD)	M	Williams (MA)	R
Kalamazoo (MI)	R	Wisconsin, U. of	XL
Kenyon (OH)	R	Yale (CT)	M
Macalester (MN)	R		

━━━━━━━━━━━━━━━ **GROUP II** ━━━━━━━━━━━━━━━
Very Selective

Baylor (TX)	M	Millsaps (MS)	S
Beloit (WI)	R	Misericordia, College (PA)	S
Brooklyn College (CUNY)(NY)	L	Montana, U. of	L
California State U. (Long Beach)	L	Montclair State (NJ)	M
California, U. of (Santa Barbara)	L	North Carolina (Asheville)	R
Catholic U. (DC)	M	North Carolina (Greensboro)	M
Cincinnati, U. of	L	Ohio State	XL
Creighton (NE)	M	Oklahoma, U. of	XL
Duquesne (PA)	M	▲ Randolph-Macon Woman's Col. (VA)	S
Florida State	L	Rollins (FL)	R
Florida, U. of	XL	St. Anselm (NH)	R
Fordham (NY)	L	St. John's/St. Benedict (MN)	R
Georgia, U. of	L	Southwest Missouri	L
■ Hampden-Sydney (VA)	S	Tennessee, U. of	XL
Hunter (CUNY)(NY)	L	Virginia Tech.	L
Illinois, U. of (Chicago)	L	Washington, U. of	XL
Kentucky, U. of	L	Wooster, College of the (OH)	R
π Mary Washington (VA)	M	Xavier (OH)	R
Massachusetts, U. of (Boston)	M		

π *Also, Classical Archeology*

COMPUTER SCIENCE

GROUP I
Most Selective

Albany, (SUNY)(NY)	L	Iowa State	XL
Binghamton (SUNY)(NY)	L	Johns Hopkins (MD)	M
Boston College (MA)	L	Lafayette (PA)	R
Brandeis (MA)	R	Lehigh (PA)	M
Brown (RI)	M	Maryland, U. of (Baltimore County)	M
Bucknell (PA)	R	Maryland, U. of	XL
California, U. of (Berkeley)	XL	Michigan, U. of	XL
California, U. of (Los Angeles)	XL	MIT (MA)	M
Carleton (MN)	R	Missouri, U. of (Rolla)	M
Carnegie Mellon (PA)	M	New Mexico Inst. of Tech.	R
Case Western Reserve U. (OH)	M	Pennsylvania State	XL
Chicago, U. of (IL)	M	Pittsburgh, U. of (PA)	L
Clarkson (NY)	M	Princeton (NJ)	M
Colgate (NY)	R	Rensselaer (NY)	M
Colorado School of Mines	R	Rice (TX)	R
Cornell (NY)	L	Rochester, U. of (NY)	M
Dallas, U. of (TX)	R	Rose-Hulman (IN)	R
Dartmouth (NH)	M	Stanford (CA)	M
Denison (OH)	R	Stevens Inst. of Tech. (NJ)	R
DePauw (IN)	R	United States Air Force Academy (CO)	M
Dickinson (PA)	R	Vassar (NY)	R
Furman (SC)	R	Washington, U. of	XL
George Washington (DC)	M	Washington U. (MO)	M
Georgia Institute of Tech.	M	William & Mary (VA)	M
Grinnell (IA)	R	Williams (MA)	R
Hamilton (NY)	R	Wisconsin, U. of	XL
Harvard (MA)	M	Worcester Poly. Tech. (MA)	R
Harvey Mudd (CA)	S	Yeshiva (NY)	R
Illinois, U. of	XL		

GROUP II
Very Selective

Alabama, U. of (Huntsville)	M	Cal. Poly. State U. (San Luis Obispo)	L
Alfred (NY)	R	California, U. of (Irvine)	L
Allegheny (PA)	R	California, U. of (Merced)	R
Alma (MI)	R	California, U. of (San Diego)	L
Arcadia (PA)	R	California, U. of (Santa Barbara)	L
Auburn (AL)	L	California, U. of (Santa Cruz)	M
Augsburg (MN)	R	Capital (OH)	R
Bemidji State (MN)	M	Carroll (MT)	R
Benedictine (IL)	R	Carroll (WI)	R
▲ Bennett (NC)	S	Central (IA)	R
Bradley (IL)	M	Central Florida, U. of	L
Brooklyn College (CUNY)(NY)	L	Clarke (IA)	S
Bryant (RI)	R	Clemson (SC)	L
Buena Vista (IA)	R		
Butler (IN)	R		

GROUP II continues next page

COMPUTER SCIENCE, continued

GROUP II, continued

Cogswell (CA)	S	Oklahoma City U.	R
Colorado State	L	Oregon, U. of	L
Denver, U. of (CO)	M	Pace (NY)	M
DePaul (IL)	L	Pacific Lutheran (WA)	R
Drexel (PA)	M	Pacific University (OR)	R
Eckerd (FL)	R	Pepperdine (CA)	R
Embry-Riddle (FL)	M	Pittsburgh, U. of (Johnstown)	R
Florida Inst. of Tech	M	Portland State (OR)	L
Florida State	L	Potsdam (SUNY) (NY)	M
George Mason (VA)	L	Queens (CUNY)(NY)	L
Goucher (MD)	R	Regis (CO)	R
Hendrix (AR)	R	Rhode Island, U. of	L
Hiram (OH)	R	Rochester Inst. of Tech (NY)	L
Hunter (CUNY) (NY)	L	Rowan (NJ)	M
Idaho, U. of	L	Rutgers (Camden) (NJ)	M
Illinois College	S	Santa Clara U. (CA)	M
Iowa, U. of	XL	St. Ambrose (IA)	R
James Madison (VA)	M	St. Cloud (MN)	L
Kansas State	L	St. Edward's (TX)	M
Kent State (OH)	L	St. John's (MN)	R
LaSalle (PA)	M	St. Norbert (WI)	R
Maine, U. of	M	St. Scholastica (MN)	R
Marist (NY)	M	Sciences, U. of the (PA)	S
Marquette (WI)	M	Shippensburg (PA)	M
Mary Washington (VA)	M	South Carolina, U. of	L
Massachusetts, U. of	L	Stetson (FL)	R
Massachusetts, U. of (Lowell)	M	Stonehill (MA)	R
McKendree (IL)	R	Stony Brook (SUNY) (NY)	L
Michigan, U. of (Dearborn)	M	Syracuse (NY)	L
Millsaps (MS)	S	Taylor (IN)	R
Minnesota, U. of (Morris)	R	Texas, U. of	XL
Missouri, U. of (Kansas City)	M	Texas, U. of (Dallas)	M
Mobile, U. of (AL)	R	Transylvania (KY)	S
Montana State	L	Tulsa, U of (OK)	R
Montana Tech.	R	Utah, U. of	L
Montana, U. of	M	Virginia Tech.	L
Moravian (PA)	R	Webster (MO)	R
Murray State (KY)	M	Westminster (PA)	R
New Jersey Inst. of Tech	M	Westminster (UT)	R
New Mexico State	L	William Jewell (MO)	R
North Central (IL)	R	Winona State U. (MN)	M
Northeastern (MA)	L	Wofford (SC)	R

COMPUTER SCIENCE continues next page

Enrollment Code		
■ *Men Only*	S = Small (less than 1000 students)	R = Moderate (1000-3000 students) M = Medium (3000-8000 students)
▲ *Women Only*	L = Large (8000-20,000 students)	XL = Extra Large (over 20,000 students)

COMPUTER SCIENCE, continued

---- **GROUP III** ----
Selective

Adrian (MI) .... R	Millersville (PA) .... M
Alabama, U. of (Birmingham) .... M	Minnesota State U. (Mankato) L
Arkansas, U. of L	Minnesota, U. of (Duluth) L
Arizona State XL	Mississippi State L
Baker (KS) .... R	Monmouth (NJ) .... M
Baldwin-Wallace (OH) .... R	■ Morehouse (GA) .... R
Ball State (IN) L	Mount St. Joseph (OH) .... R
Baruch (CUNY)(NY) L	Mount Union (OH) .... S
Belhaven (MS) .... R	Muskingum (OH) .... R
Benedictine (KS) .... R	Nebraska, U. of (Omaha) L
Bloomsburg (PA) .... M	Nevada, U. of (Reno) L
Brockport (SUNY) (NY) .... M	Northeastern Illinois .... M
Cal. Poly. State U. (Pomona) L	Northern Michigan .... M
California State U. (Chico) L	Northwestern Louisiana L
California State U. (East Bay) .... M	North Carolina (Greensboro) .... M
California State U. (Monterey Bay) ...... R	North Florida .... M
California State U. (Northridge) L	Oakland U. (MI) .... M
California State U. (Sacramento) .... M	Oswego (SUNY)(NY) .... M
California State U. (San Bernardino) ...... M	Ozarks, College of the (MO) .... R
California State U. (San Jose) L	Pittsburgh, U. of (Bradford) .... R
California State U. (San Marcos) .... M	Quinnipiac (CT) .... R
California State U. (Stanislaus) .... M	Ramapo (NJ) .... M
Canisius (NY) .... M	Rider (NJ) .... M
Catawba (NC) .... S	Robert Morris (PA) .... R
π Champlain (VT) .... R	Roosevelt (IL) .... R
Charleston Southern (SC) .... R	St. Joseph's (NY) .... R
Christopher Newport (VA) .... M	St. Mary (KS) .... S
Chowan (NC) .... S	▲ St. Mary (NE) .... S
Clark Atlanta (GA) .... M	St. Mary's (MN) .... R
Coastal Carolina (SC) .... M	Salem State (MA) .... M
Colorado, U. of (Col. Springs) .... M	San Jose State U. (CA) L
Colorado, U. of (Denver) .... M	Southeastern Louisiana L
East Stroudsburg (PA) .... M	Southern Connecticut .... M
Eastern Connecticut .... M	Southern Maine .... M
Eastern Michigan L	Southern Polytechnic (GA) .... R
Eureka (IL) .... S	Southwest Texas State L
Evansville (IN) .... R	▲ Spelman (GA) .... R
Ferris State (MI) L	Temple (PA) L
Florida Gulf Coast U. .... M	Texas, U. of (Arlington) L
Frostburg (MD) .... M	Texas, U. of (Tyler) .... R
Gardner-Webb (NC) .... R	Thomas More (KY) .... R
Georgia State L	Weber State (UT) L
Great Falls (MT) .... S	West Chester (PA) .... M
Hawaii Pacific .... M	West Florida, U. of .... M
High Point (NC) .... R	West Virginia Wesleyan .... R
Husson (ME) .... S	Western Carolina (NC) .... M
Jacksonville State (AL) .... M	Western Kentucky L
Jamestown (ND) .... R	Western Michigan L
Kansas Wesleyan .... S	Western New England (MA) .... R
Liberty (VA) .... R	Wilkes (PA) .... R
Louisiana-Lafayette L	William Paterson (NJ) .... M
Loyola U. (LA) .... M	Wisconsin (LaCrosse) L
Marygrove (MI) .... R	

π *Electronic Games &*
Interactive Development

DANCE/DRAMA/THEATER

GROUP I
Most Selective

Allegheny (PA)...................................... R	Juilliard (NY).. S
American Acad. of Dramatic Arts (NY) ... S	Kenyon (OH) .... R
Amherst (MA)....................................... R	Knox (IL)... R
▲Barnard (NY)..................................... R	Lawrence (WI) .... R
Binghamton (SUNY)(NY) L	Macalester (MN)................................. R
Boston College (MA)........................... L	Maryland, U. of (Baltimore County)...... M
Boston U. (MA)................................... L	Miami, U. of (FL) L
Brandeis (MA) .... R	Middlebury (VT) .... R
Bucknell (PA) .... M	Milliken (IL) .... R
California, U. of (Los Angeles) XL	▲Mount Holyoke (MA) .... R
California, U. of (San Diego) L	New School U. (Eugene Lang)(NY) .... S
Carleton (MN)...................................... R	New York U. L
Carnegie Mellon (PA) .... M	North Carolina, U. of L
Case Western Reserve (OH).............. M	Northwestern (IL) .... M
Colgate (NY) .... R	Oberlin (OH) .... R
Colorado College .... R	Princeton (NJ) .... M
Columbia (NY)..................................... M	Rutgers (NJ).. L
Connecticut College .... R	St. Olaf (MN) .... R
Cornell (NY).. L	Sarah Lawrence (NY) .... R
Dallas, U. of (TX) .... R	Skidmore (NY) .... R
Dartmouth (NH) .... M	South, U. of the (TN) .... R
Davidson (NC)..................................... R	Southwestern (TX) .... R
Denison (OH) .... R	Tufts (MA) .... M
Drew (NJ) .... R	Tulane (LA) .... M
George Washington (DC) .... M	Vassar (NY) .... R
Gettysburg (PA) .... R	Wesleyan (CT) .... R
Hamilton (NY) .... R	Whitman (WA)..................................... R
Illinois, U. of XL	William & Mary (VA) .... R
Illinois Wesleyan .... R	Yale (CT) .... M

DANCE / DRAMA / THEATER continues next page

DANCE/DRAMA/THEATER, continued

GROUP II
Very Selective

Alabama, U. of L	Loyola (IL) .... M
Arizona, U. of XL	Lyon (AR) .... S
Arizona State XL	Maine, U. of L
Bard (NY) .... R	Manhattanville (NY) .... R
Baylor (TX) .... M	McDaniel (MD) .... R
Beloit (WI) .... R	Millsaps (MS) .... S
Bennington (VT) .... S	Minnesota State U. (Mankato) L
Birmingham-Southern (AL)................ R	Minnesota, U. of XL
Brooklyn College (CUNY)(NY) L	Muhlenberg (PA) .... R
Butler (IN) .... R	Nevada, U. of (Las Vegas) .... M
California Institute of the Arts .... S	New Hampshire, U. of .... R
California, U. of (Irvine).................... L	New Mexico, U. of L
California, U. of (Riverside) L	No. Carolina School of the Arts .... S
Catholic U. (DC) .... M	Occidental (CA) .... R
Central Florida, U. of L	Ohio U. L
Charleston, College of (SC).............. L	Oklahoma City U. .... R
Clarke (IA) .... S	Oklahoma, U. of XL
Coe (IA) .... R	Oklahoma State L
Columbia College (IL) .... M	Purchase (SUNY) (NY) .... R
Columbia College (SC) .... R	Rollins (FL) .... R
Cornish (WA) .... S	▲Scripps (CA) .... S
Creighton (NE) .... M	Seattle Pacific (WA) .... R
DePaul (IL) L	Shepherd (WV) .... R
Drake (IA) .... M	South Carolina, U. of........................ L
π Elon (NC) .... R	Southern California L
Florida, U. of XL	Southern Methodist (TX).................. M
Florida State.................................... L	Stanford (CA) .... M
Florida Southern.............................. R	Susquehanna (PA) .... R
Fordham (NY) L	▲Sweet Briar (VA) .... S
George Mason (VA) L	Syracuse (NY) L
Georgia, U. of L	Texas Christian .... M
Goucher (MD) .... S	Texas, U. of XL
Grand Valley (MI) L	Utah State L
Hanover (IN) .... R	Utah, U. of L
Hawaii, U. of L	Virginia Commonwealth U. L
Hofstra (NY).................................... M	Viterbo (WI) .... R
▲Hollins (VA) .... S	Washington, U. of XL
Hunter (CUNY)(NY) L	Wells (NY) .... S
Indiana U. XL	Western Maryland............................ R
Iowa, U. of...................................... XL	West Virginia U. L
James Madison (VA)........................ M	Wheaton (MA) .... R
Kansas, U. of L	Wisconsin, U. of XL
Kansas State L	Wisconsin, U. of (Milwaukee) L
LeMoyne (NY).................................. R	Wisconsin, U. of (Stevens Point)...... M
Lindenwood (MO) .... R	Wooster (OH) .... R
Linfield (OR) .... R	
Long Island U.(C.W. Post)(NY) .... R	

π *Music Theatre*

DANCE / DRAMA / THEATER continues next page

DANCE/DRAMA/THEATER, continued

GROUP III
Selective

+ + Akron, U. of (OH) L	McPherson (KS) .... S
Alabama, U. of (Birmingham) .... M	Montana, U. of .... M
Alaska, U. of (Fairbanks) .... M	Niagara (NY) .... R
Arcadia (PA)..................................... R	Northwestern College (IA) .... R
Arts, U. of the (PA)........................... R	Ohio State XL
Barry (FL) .... R	Otterbein (OH) .... R
Bethany (WV) .... S	# Point Park (PA) .... R
Belhaven (MS) .... R	Rockford (IL) .... S
✳✳ Benedictine (KS)............................. R	Rocky Mountain (MT) .... S
Boise State (ID)................................ L	Salem State (MA) .... M
Brenau (GA) .... R	San Francisco State (CA) L
Brockport (SUNY)(NY) .... M	Santa Fe, College of (NM) .... S
California State U. (Long Beach) L	Seattle U. (WA) .... R
California State U. (Northridge) L	▲Seton Hill (PA) .... S
California State U. (Sacramento) .... M	++ Slippery Rock (PA) .... M
Catawba (NC) .... S	Southern Maine .... M
Central Michigan L	Southern Missippi L
Coker (SC) .... S	Southern Utah .... M
Converse College (SC) .... S	South Florida, U. of L
Dana (NE) .... S	Southwest Missouri L
DeSales (PA) .... S	Southwest Texas State L
Emerson (MA) .... R	St. Edward's (TX) .... M
Evansville (IN) .... R	St. Mary's (MN) .... R
Fontbonne (MO) .... R	Sterling (KS) .... S
Franklin (IN) .... S	Stephens (MO) .... S
Greensboro College (NC) .... S	Tarleton State (TX) .... M
Hartford, U. of (CT) .... M	Temple (PA) L
Illinois State L	Towson (MD) L
Indiana State L	Wagner (NY) .... R
Jacksonville (FL) .... R	Weber State (UT) L
Johnson State (VT) .... R	Webster (MO) .... R
Keene State (NH).............................. R	Western Michigan L
Longwood (VA).................................. R	✳ Western St. Coll. of Colorado........... R
Marymount Manhattan (NY) .... R	π West Virginia Wesleyan .... R
▲Mary Baldwin (VA) .... S	++Winthrop(SC) .... M

π *Music Theater*
++ *Especially Dance*
# *Musical Theater and Dance*
✳✳ *Also, Theater Management*
✳ *Communication and Theater - One Major*

Enrollment Code		
■ **Men Only**	S = Small (less than 1000 students)	R = Moderate (1000-3000 students)	M = Medium (3000-8000 students)
▲ **Women Only**	L = Large (8000-20,000 students)	XL = Extra Large (over 20,000 students)

ECONOMICS

GROUP I
Most Selective

Albany (SUNY)(NY)	L	Lafayette (PA)	R
American U. (DC)	M	Lehigh (PA)	M
Amherst (MA)	R	Macalester (MN)	R
Babson (MA)	R	Miami, U. of (OH)	L
▲Barnard (NY)	R	Michigan, U. of	XL
Bates (ME)	R	MIT (MA)	M
Boston College (MA)	L	Middlebury (VT)	R
Boston University (MA)	L	▲Mount Holyoke (MA)	R
Bowdoin (ME)	R	New York U.	L
Brandeis (MA)	R	Northwestern (IL)	M
Brown (RI)	M	Occidental (CA)	R
▲Bryn Mawr (PA)	S	Pennsylvania, U. of	L
Bucknell (PA)	M	Pomona (CA)	R
California, U. of (Los Angeles)	XL	Princeton (NJ)	M
California, U. of (San Diego)	L	Reed (OR)	R
Carleton (MN)	R	Rhodes (TN)	R
Carnegie Mellon (PA)	M	Richmond (VA)	R
Case Western Reserve (OH)	M	Rochester, U. of (NY)	M
Chicago, U. of (IL)	M	Rose-Hulman (IN)	R
Claremont McKenna (CA)	R	Rutgers (NJ)	L
Colby (ME)	R	▲Smith (MA)	R
Colgate (NY)	R	St. Mary's Col. of Maryland	R
Colorado College	R	St. Olaf (MN)	R
Colorado School of Mines	R	South, U. of the (TN)	R
Columbia (NY)	M	Southwestern (TX)	R
Connecticut College	R	Stanford (CA)	M
Cornell (NY)	L	Swarthmore (PA)	R
Dallas, U. of (TX)	R	Trinity (CT)	R
Dartmouth (NH)	M	Trinity (TX)	R
Davidson (NC)	R	Tufts (MA)	M
DePauw (IN)	R	U.S. Military Academy (NY)	M
Drew (NJ)	R	Vanderbilt (TN)	M
Duke (NC)	M	Vassar (NY)	R
Emory (GA)	M	Villanova (PA)	M
Franklin & Marshall (PA)	R	Virginia, U. of	L
Furman (SC)	R	■Wabash (IN)	S
George Washington (DC)	M	Wake Forest (NC)	M
Georgetown (DC)	M	Washington & Lee (VA)	R
Georgia Inst. of Tech.	M	▲Wellesley (MA)	R
Gettysburg (PA)	R	Wesleyan (CT)	R
Grinnell (IA)	R	Whitman (WA)	R
Hamilton (NY)	R	Willamette (OR)	R
Harvard (MA)	M	William & Mary (VA)	R
Haverford (PA)	S	Williams (MA)	R
Holy Cross (MA)	R	Worcester Poly. Inst. (MA)	R
Kalamazoo (MI)	R	Yale (CT)	M
Kenyon (OH)	R		

ECONOMICS continues next page

Enrollment Code

■ *Men Only*　**S** = Small (less than 1000 students)　**R** = Moderate (1000-3000 students)　**M** = Medium (3000-8000 students)
▲ *Women Only*　**L** = Large (8000-20,000 students)　**XL** = Extra Large (over 20,000 students)

ECONOMICS, continued

GROUP II
Very Selective

▲ Agnes Scott (GA) .... S
Alaska, U. of (Anchorage) .... M
\# Albion (MI) .... R
Allegheny (PA) .... R
Assumption (MA) .... R
Auburn (AL) .... M
Baruch (CUNY)(NY) L
Beloit (WI) .... R
Bentley (MA) .... M
Bethany (WV) .... S
Bradley (IL) .... M
Brigham Young (UT) L
California, U. of (Davis) L
California, U. of (Merced) .... R
California, U. of (Santa Cruz) .... M
California State U. (Bakersfield) .... M
California State U. (Long Beach) L
California State U. (Santa Barbara) L
Centre (KY) .... R
City College (CUNY)(NY) L
Clark (MA) .... R
Clemson (SC) L
Colorado, U. of L
Connecticut, U. of XL
Cornell College (IA) .... R
Delaware, U. of L
Denison (OH) .... R
Drake (IA) .... M
Florida State L
George Mason (VA) L
Georgia State L
Georgia, U. of XL
Grove City (PA) .... R
Guilford (NC) .... R
■ Hampden-Sydney (VA) .... S
Hendrix (AR) .... R
Hobart & William Smith (NY) .... R
Illinois Col. .... S
Illinois, U. of (Chicago) L
Iowa State XL
Kansas, U. of L
Lake Forest (IL) .... R
Linfield (OR) .... R
Loras (IA) .... R
Loyola (LA) .... R
Maine, U. of L

Manhattanville (NY) .... R
Maryland, U. of XL
Maryland, U. of (Baltimore County) .... M
Mary Washington (VA) .... M
Massachusetts, U. of L
Michigan State XL
Michigan, U. of (Dearborn) .... M
Minnesota, U. of XL
Missouri, U. of (Kansas City) .... M
Nebraska, U. of L
New Mexico, U. of L
North Carolina State L
Oglethorpe (GA) .... R
Ohio State XL
Ohio Wesleyan (OH) .... R
Oklahoma, U. of XL
Oregon State L
Puget Sound (WA) .... R
Oneonta (SUNY) (NY) .... M
Randolph-Macon (VA) .... R
Richard Stockton (NJ) .... M
Ripon (WI) .... S
▲ Salem Col. (NC) .... S
San Francisco, U. of .... M
St. John's (MN) .... R
St. Lawrence (NY) .... R
St. Thomas (MN) .... R
Seattle U. (WA) .... R
Southern Methodist (TX) L
▲ Spelman (GA) .... R
Susquehanna (PA) .... R
Texas A&M XL
Texas, U. of (Dallas) .... M
Truman State (MO) .... M
Ursinus (PA) .... R
Vermont, U. of L
Virginia Military Inst. .... R
Washington & Jefferson (PA) .... R
Washington, U. of XL
Westminster Col. (MO) .... S
Westmont Col. (CA) .... R
Wheaton (MA) .... R
Wofford (SC) .... R
Wooster (OH) .... R
Xavier (OH) .... R

\# *Also, Economics & Business*

ECONOMICS, continued

••• ———————————————— **GROUP III** ———————————————— •••
Selective

Arkansas, U. of	L	Monmouth (IL)	S
Baldwin-Wallace (OH)	R	Montana State	L
Bellarmine (KY)	R	Nebraska, U. of (Kearney)	M
Berea (WV)	R	Northern Iowa	L
California State U. (Bakersfield)	M	Oakland U. (MI)	M
California State U. (Channel Islands)	R	Old Dominion (VA)	L
California State U. (Chico)	L	Northern Colorado	L
California State U. (East Bay)	M	Queens (CUNY)(NY)	L
California State U. (Northridge)	L	Rhode Island College	M
Central Missouri	L	St. Anselm (NH)	R
Central Oklahoma	L	Shippensberg (PA)	M
East Carolina	L	South Dakota State U.	M
East Tennessee	L	Southern Connecticut	M
Eastern Connecticut	M	Southern Utah	M
Eastern Washington	L	Toledo, U. of (OH)	L
Framingham (MA)	M	Washington State	L
Hardin-Simmons (TX)	R	Weber State (UT)	L
Hawaii Pacific	M	Whittier (CA)	R
Heidelberg (OH)	S	Wilson (PA)	S
Indiana U.-Purdue U.-Indianapolis (IN)	L	Wisconsin, U. of (Milwaukee)	L
Louisiana State	XL	Wright State (OH)	L
Marshall (WV)	L	Wyoming, U. of	L
Millersville (PA)	M		

Enrollment Code

■ *Men Only*   S = Small (less than 1000 students)   R = Moderate (1000-3000 students)   M = Medium (3000-8000 students)
▲ *Women Only*   L = Large (8000-20,000 students)   XL = Extra Large (over 20,000 students)

EDUCATION

GROUP I
Most Selective

Albany (SUNY)(NY) L	North Carolina, U. of L
Boston U. (MA)................................. L	Pittsburgh, U. of (PA)........................ L
Bucknell (PA) .... R	Occidental (CA) .... R
Buffalo (SUNY) (NY) L	Rutgers (NJ) L
Connecticut Col. .... R	Skidmore (NY) .... R
Dallas, U. of (TX) .... R	Southern California L
Dickinson (PA) .... R	Stanford (CA) .... M
Earlham (IN)................................... R	Swarthmore (PA) .... S
Geneseo (SUNY) (NY)...................... M	Trinity (TX) .... R
Illinois, U. of XL	➤ Tufts (MA) .... M
Iowa, U. of...................................... XL	Vanderbilt (TN) .... M
Miami, U. of (FL)............................. M	▲Wellesley (MA)................................ R
Miami U. (OH) L	Wheaton (IL) .... R
Michigan, U. of XL	William & Mary (VA) .... M
New Jersey, College of .... M	
New School U. (Lang)(NY)................ S	➤ *Child Study*

GROUP II
Very Selective

Adelphi (NY)................................... M	Central (IA) .... R
Adrian (MI) .... R	Centre (KY) .... R
Alaska Pacific .... S	Chestnut Hill (PA) .... S
Albertson (ID) .... S	Christian Brothers (TN)...................... R
Alfred (NY) .... R	Cincinnati, U. of (OH) L
Alma (MI) .... R	Clarke (IA) .... S
Arizona, U. of.................................. XL	Clemson (SC) L
Asbury (KY) .... R	Coe (IA) .... R
Auburn (AL) L	Columbia College (SC) .... R
Augustana (IL)................................. R	Concordia (MN) .... R
Augustana (SD) .... R	Connecticut, U. of XL
Austin (TX) .... R	Cornell College (IA) .... R
Baylor (TX) L	Creighton (NE) .... M
Berry (GA) .... R	Dayton, U. of (OH) .... M
π Bethel (IN)..................................... R	Delaware, U. of................................ L
Biola (CA) .... R	DePaul (IL) L
Birmingham Southern (AL) .... R	Drake (IA) .... M
Bradley (IL) .... M	Drury (MO) .... R
Bridgewater (MA) .... M	Duquesne (PA)................................. M
Brigham Young (UT) XL	Eastern Michigan.............................. L
Bryan (TN) .... S	Elizabethtown (PA) .... R
Buena Vista (IA) .... R	Elon (NC) .... R
Butler (IN) .... R	Erskine (SC)..................................... S
California, U. of (Riverside).............. L	π Flagler (FL) .... R
California, U. of (Santa Barbara) L	Florida International L
Calvin (MI) .... M	Florida Southern............................... R
Capital U. (OH) .... R	
Carroll (WI) .... R	π *Also American Sign Language / Deaf Interpretation*
Centenary (LA)................................ S	

GROUP II continues next page

EDUCATION, continued

GROUP II, continued

Florida State	L
Fredonia (SUNY) (NY)	M
Georgetown College (KY)	R
Georgia, U. of	XL
Gonzaga (WA)	R
Goucher (MD)	R
Grove City (PA)	R
Guilford (NC)	R
Gustavus Adolphus (MN)	R
Hamline (MN)	R
Hanover (IN)	R
Harding (AR)	M
Hillsdale (MI)	R
Hiram (OH)	R
Hood (MD)	S
Houghton (NY)	S
Hunter (CUNY) (NY)	L
Illinois College	S
Indiana, U.	XL
Indiana, U. of (PA)	L
Iowa State	XL
James Madison (VA)	M
Juniata (PA)	R
Kansas State	L
Kentucky, U. of	L
Lake Forest (IL)	R
Lindenwood (MO)	R
Lipscomb (TN)	R
Loras (IA)	R
Luther (IA)	R
Lyon (AR)	S
Manhattan (NY)	M
Manhattanville (NY)	R
Maryland, U. of	XL
McDaniel (MD)	R
Mercer (GA)	R
Messiah (PA)	R
Michigan State	XL
Millersville (PA)	M
▲ Mills (CA)	S
Minnesota State U. (Moorhead)	M
Minnesota, U. of	XL
Minnesota, U. of (Duluth)	M
Minnesota, U. of (Morris)	R
Mississippi, U. of	L
Mississippi U. for Women	R
Missouri, U. of (St. Louis)	M
Moravian (PA)	R

Morningside (IA)	S
Mount St. Mary's (MD)	R
Nazareth (NY)	R
Nebraska, U. of	L
New Hampshire, U. of	L
New Mexico State	L
New Orleans (LA)	L
New Paltz (SUNY) (NY)	M
North Carolina, U. of (Asheville)	R
North Carolina, U. of (Greensboro)	M
North Dakota, U. of	M
North Florida	M
Ohio U.	L
Oklahoma, U. of	XL
Oklahoma State	L
Oneonta (SUNY)(NY)	M
Oregon, U. of	L
Oswego (SUNY)(NY)	M
Pacific Lutheran (WA)	R
● * Pacific Oaks (CA)	S
Pacific, U. of the (CA)	M
Palm Beach Atlantic (FL)	R
Pennsylvania State	XL
Portland, U. of (OR)	R
Potsdam (SUNY) (NY)	R
Principia (IL)	S
Providence (RI)	M
Puerto Rico, U. of	L
Queens (CUNY) (NY)	L
Redlands, U. of (CA)	R
Regis (CO)	R
Rockhurst (MO)	R
Rowan (NJ)	M
St. Bonaventure (NY)	R
St. Catherine (MN)	R
St. John's/ St. Benedict (MN)	R
St. Louis (MO)	M
St. Martin's (WA)	S
St. Mary's Col. (CA)	R
▲ St. Mary's Col. (IN)	R
St. Mary's Col. (MN)	R
St. Michael's (VT)	R
St. Norbert (WI)	R
St. Thomas (MN)	R
Salisbury State (MD)	M

● *Junior Year Standing*

* *Especially Child Development*

GROUP II continues next page

EDUCATION, continued

San Diego State U. (CA) XL
Seattle Pacific (WA) .... R
Shepherd (WV) .... M
Shippensburg (PA) .... M
South Florida, U. of L
Southwest Missouri L
Stetson (FL) .... R
Susquehanna (PA) .... R
Tennessee, U. of XL
Tennessee Tech .... M
Texas A&M XL
Texas Christian .... M
Texas, U. of (Austin) XL
Towson (MD) L
Transylvania (KY) .... R
Truman State (MO) .... M
Ursinus (PA) .... R
Valparaiso (IN) .... R

Washington & Jefferson (PA)............. R
Washington State L
Washington, U. of XL
Wells (NY) .... S
Western Michigan L
Western Washington U. L
Westminster (UT) .... R
Whitworth (WA) .... R
William Jewell Col. (MO) .... R
Winona State U. (MN) .... M
Wisconsin Lutheran .... S
Wisconsin, U. of XL
Wisconsin, U. of (Milwaukee) L
Wisconsin, U. of (Stevens Point) ...... M
Wittenberg (OH) .... R
Wofford (SC) .... R
York (PA) .... M

GROUP III
Selective

Akron, U. of (OH) L
Alaska, U. of (Anchorage) .... M
Alderson-Broaddus (WV) .... S
▲ Alverno (WI) .... R
Anderson (IN) .... R
Appalachian State (NC) L
Arcadia (PA) .... R
Arkansas, U. of L
Arizona State XL
Ashland (OH) .... R
Assumption (MA) .... R
Augsburg (MN) .... R
Averett (VA) .... S
Avila (MO) .... S
Baker (KS) .... R
Baldwin-Wallace (OH) .... R
Ball State (IN) L
Barry (FL) .... R
Belhaven (MS) .... R
Bellarmine (KY) .... R
Belmont (TN) .... R
Bemidji State (MN) .... M
▲ Bennett (NC) .... S
Berea (KY) .... R

Bethany (KS) .... S
Bethany (WV) .... S
Bethel (KS) .... S
Bethel (MN) .... R
Blackburn (IL) .... S
Bluffton (OH) .... S
Boise State (ID) L
Bowling Green (OH) L
Bloomsburg (PA) .... M
Brescia (KY) .... S
Brockport (SUNY) (NY) .... M
Brooklyn College (CUNY)(NY) L
Caldwell (NJ) .... S
California Lutheran .... R
California State U. (Bakersfield) .... M
California State U. (Channel Islands) .... R
California State U. (Fresno) L
California State U. (Monterey Bay) .... R
California State U. (Los Angeles)........... L
California State U. (Sacramento) .... M
California State U. (San Bernardino) ...... M
California State U. (San Marcos) .... M

GROUP III continues next page

Enrollment Code
■ *Men Only* S = Small (less than 1000 students) R = Moderate (1000-3000 students) M = Medium (3000-8000 students)
▲ *Women Only* L = Large (8000-20,000 students) XL = Extra Large (over 20,000 students)

EDUCATION, continued

••• ━━━━━━━━━━━━━ **GROUP III, continued** ━━━━━━━━━━━━━ •••

California State U. (Stanislaus) .... M	Florida Gulf Coast U. .... M
California (PA) .... M	Fontbonne (MO) .... R
Canisius (NY) .... M	Fort Hays (KS) .... M
Carson-Newman (TN) .... R	Framingham State (MA) .... M
Castleton State (VT) .... R	Franklin (IN) .... S
Catawba (NC) .... S	Freed-Hardeman (TN) .... R
Cedarville (OH) .... R	Friends (KS) .... R
Central Connecticut .... M	Frostburg (MD) .... M
Central Michigan U. L	Geneva (PA) .... R
Central Oklahoma L	George Fox (OR) .... R
Chaminade (HI) .... R	Georgia Southern L
Charleston Southern (SC) .... R	Georgia Southwestern .... R
Citadel, The (SC) .... R	Georgia State L
City College (CUNY) (NY) L	Gordon (MA) .... R
Clark Atlanta (GA) .... M	Graceland (IA) .... R
Coastal Carolina (SC) .... M	Grambling (LA) .... M
Coker (SC) .... S	Great Falls (MT) .... S
College of Charleston (SC) .... M	Greensboro College (NC) .... S
Colorado, U. of (Colorado Springs) .... M	Hannibal-La Grange (MO) .... R
Concordia (NE) .... R	Hardin-Simmons (TX) .... R
▲Converse (SC) .... S	Hastings (NE) .... R
Cumberland (KY) .... R	Heidelberg (OH) .... S
Daemen (NY) .... R	Henderson State (AR)...................... M
Dana (NB) .... S	Herbert Lehman (CUNY) (NY) L
Dillard (LA) .... R	Holy Names (CA) .... S
Doane (NE) .... S	Huntingdon (AL) .... S
Dominican (CA) .... S	Huntington (IN) .... S
Dordt (IA) .... R	Husson (ME) .... S
Dubuque, U. of (IA) .... S	Illinois State L
D'Youville (NY) .... R	Indiana State U. L
East Carolina (NC) L	Indiana U.-Purdue U.-Indianapolis (IN) L
East Central State (OK) .... M	Jacksonville State (AL) .... M
Eastern Connecticut .... M	Jamestown (ND) .... R
Eastern Illinois L	Johnson State (VT) .... R
Eastern Kentucky L	▲Judson (AL) .... S
Eastern Mennonite (VA)................... R	Kansas Wesleyan .... S
Eastern Oregon .... R	Kean (NJ) .... M
Edgewood (WI) .... S	Keene State (NH)........................... R
Edinboro (PA) .... M	Kent State (OH) L
Elmhurst (IL)................................ R	Kentucky Wesleyan .... S
Elmira (NY) .... R	King (TN)..................................... S
Elms (MA) .... S	Kutztown (PA) .... M
Emporia State (KS) .... M	Lamar (TX) .... M
Eureka (IL) .... S	Lambuth (TN)............................... S
Fairmont (WV) .... M	Lasell (MA) .... S
Fitchburg State (MA) .... R	Laverne, U. of (CA) .... R
Florida A&M .... M	
Florida Atlantic L	

GROUP III continues next page

EDUCATION, continued

GROUP III, continued

Lesley (MA)	S
Lewis-Clark State (ID)	R
Liberty (VA)	R
Linfield (OR)	R
Lock Haven (PA)	M
Long Island U. (C.W.Post)(NY)	M
Longwood (VA)	R
Louisiana College	R
Louisiana-Lafayette	L
Maine (Farmington)	R
Manchester (IN)	R
Mansfield (PA)	R
Marshall (WV)	L
Maryville (St. Louis) (MO)	R
Marywood (PA)	R
Mass. Coll. of Lib. Arts (N. Adams)	R
Mass. St. Col. System	M
McPherson (KS)	S
Memphis, U. of (TN)	L
Middle Tennessee	L
Millikin (IL)	R
Misericordia, College (PA)	S
Mississippi College	R
Mississippi State	L
Missouri Baptist	M
Missouri Southern State	M
Mobile, U. of (AL)	R
Monmouth (IL)	S
Montana, U. of	M
Montana State (Billings)	R
Montclair State (NJ)	M
Montevallo (AL)	R
Mount St. Joseph (OH)	R
Mount Mercy (IA)	S
Mount Union (OH)	R
Murray State (KY)	M
Muskingum (OH)	R
Nebraska, U. of (Omaha)	L
Nevada, U. of (Las Vegas)	L
Nevada, U. of (Reno)	L
New Mexico, U. of	L
Nichols State (LA)	M
North Dakota State	L
Northeastern Illinois	M
Northeastern State (OK)	L

Northern Arizona	L
Northern Colorado	L
Northern Illinois U.	L
Northern Iowa	L
Northern Kentucky	L
Northern Michigan	M
Northwestern (IA)	R
Northwestern (MN)	R
Northwestern Louisiana	L
Nyack (NY)	R
Oakland City U. (IN)	R
Ohio State	L
Oklahoma Baptist	R
Olivet Nazarene (IL)	R
Oral Roberts (OK)	M
Ouachita Baptist (AR)	R
Ozarks, College of the (MO)	R
Peru State (NE)	R
Philadelphia Biblical (PA)	S
Pittsburg State (KS)	M
Pittsburgh, U. of (Johnstown)	R
Plymouth State (NH)	M
Point Loma (CA)	R
Puerto Rico (Cayey), U. of	L
Radford (VA)	M
Robert Morris (PA)	R
Rhode Island College	M
Rider (NJ)	R
Rocky Mountain (MT)	S
Roger Williams (RI)	R
Saginaw Valley (MI)	M
St. Ambrose (IA)	R
St. Andrews Presbyterian (NC)	S
St. Cloud (MN)	L
St. Edward's (TX)	M
Saint Rose (NY)	R
St. Joseph's (IN)	S
St. Joseph's (ME)	S
St. Joseph's (NY)	R
▲ St. Joseph Col. (CT)	S
St. Mary (KS)	S
St. Mary (NE)	S
St. Scholastica (MN)	R

GROUP III continues next page

Enrollment Code

■ *Men Only*   S = Small (less than 1000 students)   R = Moderate (1000-3000 students)   M = Medium (3000-8000 students)
▲ *Women Only*   L = Large (8000-20,000 students)   XL = Extra Large (over 20,000 students)

EDUCATION, continued

•••══════════════════ GROUP III, continued ══════════════════•••

St. Thomas Aquinas (NY)	R	Thomas More (KY)	R
Salem State (MA)	M	Tougaloo (MS)	S
Santa Fe, College of (NM)	S	Troy State (AL)	M
Seton Hall (NJ)	M	Utah State	L
Shawnee State (OH)	R	Wagner (NY)	R
Shorter (GA)	R	Walsh (OH)	R
Silver Lake (WI)	S	Wartburg (IA)	R
Simpson (IA)	S	Washburn (KS)	M
Slippery Rock (PA)	M	Weber State (UT)	L
Southeast Missouri State	L	Western Carolina (NC)	M
Southeastern Louisiana	L	Western Connecticut	M
Southern Connecticut	M	Western Illinois	L
Southern Illinois U. (Edwardsville)	L	Western Kentucky	L
Southern Mississippi	L	Western New England (MA)	R
Southern Nazarene (OK)	R	Westfield State (MA)	M
Southern Oregon State U.	M	West Florida, U. of	M
Southern Utah	M	West Virginia Wesleyan	R
Southwest Baptist (MO)	R	▲ Wheelock (MA)	S
Southwest Texas State	L	Whittier (CA)	R
Southwestern Oklahoma	M	Widener (PA)	R
▲ Stephens (MO)	S	Wilmington (OH)	S
Sterling (KS)	S	Winthrop (SC)	M
Tabor (KS)	S	Wisconsin, U. of (Platteville)	M
Texas A&M (Corpus Christi)	M	Worcester State (MA)	M
Texas Lutheran	R	Wyoming, U. of	L
Texas Tech. U.	L	Xavier U. of Louisiana	R
Texas Wesleyan	R	York (NE)	S

ENGINEERING

GROUP I
Most Selective

Binghamton (SUNY)(NY) L	Missouri, U. of (Rolla) .... M
Boston U. (MA)................................. L	New Mexico Inst. of Mining & Tech. .... R
Brown (RI) .... M	New Jersey, College of .... M
Bucknell (PA).................................. M	Northwestern (IL) .... M
Buffalo (SUNY) (NY) L	Notre Dame (IN) .... M
California Inst. of Tech. .... S	Olin (MA)... S
California, U. of (Berkeley) XL	Pennsylvania State XL
California, U. of (Davis) L	Pennsylvania, U. of........................... L
California, U. of (Los Angeles) XL	Princeton (NJ) .... M
California, U. of (San Diego) L	Rensselaer (NY) .... M
California, U. of (Santa Barbara) L	Rice (TX) .... R
Carnegie Mellon (PA) .... M	Rochester, U. of .... M
Case Western Reserve U. (OH) .... M	Rose-Hulman (IN) .... R
Clarkson (NY) .... M	Rutgers (NJ) L
Colorado School of Mines .... R	▲ Smith (MA) .... R
Columbia (NY)................................. M	Southern California, U. of.................. L
Cooper Union (NY) .... S	Stanford (CA) .... M
Cornell (NY).................................... L	Stevens Inst. of Tech. (NJ) .... R
Dartmouth (NH) .... M	Swarthmore (PA) .... R
Duke (NC) .... M	Texas, U. of (Austin)......................... XL
Florida, U. of XL	Trinity (CT)....................................... R
George Washington (DC) .... M	Tufts (MA) .... M
Georgia Inst. of Tech. .... M	Tulane (LA) .... M
Harvey Mudd (CA) .... S	Union (NY) .... R
Illinois Inst. of Tech........................ R	U.S. Air Force Academy (CO)........... M
Illinois, U. of (Urbana-Champaign) XL	U.S. Coast Guard Academy (CT) .... S
Iowa State XL	U.S. Military Academy (NY) .... M
Iowa, U. of XL	U.S. Naval Academy (MD)................. M
Johns Hopkins (MD) .... M	Vanderbilt (TN) .... M
Kettering (MI).................................. R	Villanova (PA) .... M
Lafayette (PA)................................. R	Virginia, U. of L
Lehigh (PA) .... M	Washington U. (MO) .... M
Maryland, U. of XL	Washington, U. of............................. L
MIT (MA)... M	Worcester Poly. Tech. (MA).............. R
Michigan, U. of XL	

GROUP II
Very Selective

Akron, U. of (OH) L	Auburn (AL) L
Alabama, U. of L	Baylor (TX) .... M
Alabama, U. of (Birmingham)........... M	Boise State (ID)................................. L
Alabama, U. of (Huntsville) .... M	Bradley (IL) .... M
Alaska, U. of (Fairbanks) .... M	Brigham Young (UT) L
Alfred (NY)...................................... R	Butler (IN) .... R
Arizona, U. of.................................. XL	California State U. (Fresno) L
Arizona State XL	
Arkansas, U. of L	*GROUP II continues next page*

ENGINEERING, continued

GROUP II, continued

California State U. (Fullerton)	L
California State U. (Los Angeles)	L
California State U. (Northridge)	L
California State U. (Sacramento)	M
California, U. of (Irvine)	L
California, U. of (Merced)	R
California, U. of (Riverside)	L
California, U. of (Santa Cruz)	M
California Maritime Academy	S
Cal. Poly State U. (Pomona)	L
Cal. Poly. State U. (San Luis Obispo)	L
Calvin (MI)	M
Carroll (MT)	R
Catholic U. (DC)	M
Central Connecticut	M
Central Florida, U. of	L
Christian Brothers (TN)	R
Cincinnati, U. of (OH)	L
Citadel, The (SC)	R
City College (CUNY)(NY)	L
Clemson (SC)	L
Cogswell (CA)	S
Colorado State	L
Colorado, U. of	L
Colorado, U. of (Col. Springs)	R
Connecticut, U. of	XL
Dayton, U. of (OH)	M
Delaware, U. of	L
Denver, U. of (CA)	M
Detroit Mercy (MI)	M
Dordt (IA)	R
Drexel (PA)	M
Embry-Riddle (FL)	M
Florida A&M	M
Florida Atlantic	L
Florida Inst. of Tech.	R
Florida International	L
Gannon (PA)	R
Geneva (PA)	R
Gonzaga (WA)	R
Grand Valley (MI)	L
Grove City (PA)	R
Hartford, U. of (CT)	M
Houston, U. of (TX)	L
Howard (DC)	M
Idaho, U. of	L
Illinois, U. of (Chicago)	L

Indiana U./Purdue U./Indianapolis	L
Kansas, U. of	L
Kansas State	L
Kentucky, U. of	L
Lamar (TX)	M
Letourneau College (TX)	S
Lipscomb (TN)	R
Louisiana-Lafayette	L
Louisiana State	XL
Louisville (KY)	L
Lowell, U. of (MA)	L
Loyola (MD)	R
Loyola Marymount (CA)	M
Maine, U. of	L
Manhattan (NY)	M
π Marietta (OH)	R
Maritime College (SUNY)(NY)	S
Marquette (WI)	M
Massachusetts, U. of	L
# Massachusetts, U. of (Dartmouth)	M
Massachusetts, U. of (Lowell)	M
Mass. Maritime Academy	S
Memphis, U. of (TN)	L
Mercer (GA)	R
Messiah (PA)	R
Michigan State	XL
Michigan Tech.	M
Michigan, U. of	XL
Michigan, U. of (Dearborn)	M
Milwaukee Sch. of Engine (WI)	R
Minnesota State U. (Mankato)	L
Minnesota, U. of	XL
Minnesota, U. of (Duluth)	M
Mississippi State	L
Mississippi, U. of	L
Missouri, U. of	XL
Montana Tech.	R
Montana State	L
Morgan State (MD)	M
Nebraska, U. of	L
Nevada, U. of (Las Vegas)	L
Nevada, U. of (Reno)	L
New Hampshire, U. of	L

π *Petroleum Engineering*
Also, Textile Science / Industry

GROUP II continues next page

ENGINEERING, continued

GROUP II, continued

New Jersey Inst. of Tech.	M
New Mexico, U. of	L
New Mexico State U.	L
New Orleans, U. of	L
New Paltz (SUNY)(NY)	M
New York Institute of Tech	M
North Carolina, U. of (Charlotte)	L
North Carolina State	L
North Dakota State	L
North Dakota, U. of	M
Northeastern (MA)	L
Northern Illinois U.	L
Oakland U. (MI)	M
Ohio Northern	R
Ohio State	XL
Ohio U.	L
Oklahoma, U. of	XL
Old Dominion (VA)	L
Oregon Inst. of Tech.	R
Oregon State	L
Pacific, U. of the (CA)	R
Pittsburgh, U. of	L
Pittsburgh, U. of (Johnstown)	R
Polytechnic Univ. of NY	R
Portland, U. of (OR)	R
Puerto Rico, U. of (Mayaguez)	L
Purdue (IN)	XL
+ Rhode Island, U. of	L
Rochester Inst. of Tech. (NY)	L
Roger Williams (RI)	M
Rowan (NJ)	M
St. Louis U. (MO)	M
St. Martin's (WA)	S
San Diego State (CA)	XL
San Jose State (CA)	L
Santa Clara U. (CA)	M
Seattle Pacific (WA)	R
Seattle U. (WA)	R
South Carolina, U. of	L
So. Dakota School of Mines	R
South Dakota State U.	M
Southern Illinois U. (Carbondale)	L
Southern Illinois U. (Edwardsville)	L
Southern Maine, U. of	M
Southern Methodist (TX)	L
Southern Polytechnic (GA)	R
South Florida, U. of	L
Stony Brook (SUNY) (NY)	L
▲ Sweet Briar (VA)	S
Syracuse (NY)	L
Tennessee Tech	M
Tennessee, U. of	XL
Texas A&M	XL
Texas A&M (Kingsville)	M
Texas Tech U.	L
Texas, U. of (Arlington)	L
Texas, U. of (Dallas)	M
Texas, U. of (San Antonio)	L
Texas, U. of (Tyler)	R
Toledo, U. of (OH)	L
Tri-State (IN)	R
Tulsa, U. of (OK)	R
Tuskegee University (AL)	M
Utah, U. of	L
Utah State	L
Valparaiso (IN)	M
Virginia Commonwealth	L
Virginia Military Inst.	R
Virginia Tech.	L
Walla Walla (WA)	R
Washington State	L
Wayne State (MI)	L
West Virginia U.	L
Western Michigan	L
Western New England (MA)	R
Westminster (UT)	R
Widener (PA)	R
Wilkes (PA)	R
Wisconsin, U. of	XL
Wisconsin, U. of (Platteville)	M
Wright State (OH)	L
Wyoming, U. of	L

+ *And International Engineering*

Enrollment Code
■ *Men Only*   S = Small (less than 1000 students)   R = Moderate (1000-3000 students)   M = Medium (3000-8000 students)
▲ *Women Only*   L = Large (8000-20,000 students)   XL = Extra Large (over 20,000 students)

ENGLISH

GROUP I
Most Selective

Allegheny (PA)	R	Lawrence (WI)	R
Amherst (MA)	R	Lehigh (PA)	m
Bard (NY)	R	Macalester (MN)	R
▲ Barnard (NY)	R	Miami U. (OH)	L
Bates (ME)	R	Michigan, U. of	XL
Binghamton (SUNY)(NY)	L	Middlebury (VT)	R
Boston Col. (MA)	L	▲ Mount Holyoke (MA)	R
Bowdoin (ME)	R	New (FL)	S
Brandeis (MA)	R	North Carolina, U. of	L
Brown (RI)	M	New Jersey, College of	M
▲ Bryn Mawr (PA)	S	New School U. (Lang)(NY)	S
Bucknell (PA)	M	Northwestern (IL)	M
Buffalo (SUNY) (NY)	L	Notre Dame (IN)	M
California, U. of (Berkeley)	XL	Oberlin (OH)	R
California, U. of (Los Angeles)	XL	Pennsylvania, U. of	L
Carleton (MN)	R	Pitzer (CA)	S
Carnegie Mellon (PA)	M	Pomona (CA)	R
Centre (KY)	R	Princeton (NJ)	M
Chicago, U. of (IL)	M	Puget Sound, U. of (WA)	R
Claremont McKenna (CA)	R	Reed (OR)	R
Colby (ME)	R	Rhodes (TN)	R
Colgate (NY)	R	Rice (TX)	R
Colorado College	R	Richmond, U. of (VA)	R
Columbia (NY)	M	Rochester, U. of (NY)	M
Connecticut Col.	R	Rutgers (NJ)	L
Cornell (NY)	L	Sarah Lawrence (NY)	R
Dallas, U. of (TX)	R	Skidmore (NY)	R
Dartmouth (NH)	M	▲ Smith (MA)	R
Davidson (NC)	R	South, U. of the (TN)	R
DePauw (IN)	R	Southwestern (TX)	R
Dickinson (PA)	R	Stanford (CA)	M
Drew (NJ)	R	St. Olaf (MN)	R
Duke (NC)	M	Swarthmore (PA)	R
Emory (GA)	M	Trinity (CT)	R
Florida, U. of	XL	Trinity (TX)	R
Franklin & Marshall (PA)	R	Tufts (MA)	M
Geneseo (SUNY)(NY)	M	Vanderbilt (TN)	M
Georgetown (DC)	M	Vassar (NY)	R
Gettysburg (PA)	R	Virginia, U. of	L
Grinnell (IA)	R	■ Wabash (IN)	S
Gustavus Adolphus (MN)	R	Wake Forest (NC)	M
Hamilton (NY)	R	Washington & Lee (VA)	R
Harvard (MA)	M	Washington U. (MO)	M
Haverford (PA)	S	▲ Wellesley (MA)	R
Holy Cross (MA)	R	Wesleyan (CT)	R
Illinois, U. of	XL	Wheaton (IL)	R
Illinois Wesleyan	R	Whitman (WA)	R
Iowa, U. of	XL	Willamette (OR)	R
Kalamazoo (MI)	R	William & Mary (VA)	R
Kenyon (OH)	R	Williams (MA)	R
Knox (IL)	R	Wisconsin, U. of	XL
Lafayette (PA)	R	Yale (CT)	M

ENGLISH, continued

GROUP II
Very Selective

▲Agnes Scott (GA)	S	Elizabethtown (PA) .... R
Alabama, U. of	L	Emerson (MA) .... R
Albertson (ID)	S	Florida State L
Albion (MI)	R	Franciscan U. of Steubenville (OH) ... R
Alfred (NY)	R	Fredonia (SUNY)(NY) ... M
Alma (MI)	R	Fordham (NY) ... L
Arizona, U. of	XL	George Mason (VA) ... L
Arizona State	XL	Georgetown College (KY) ... R
Auburn (AL)	L	Georgia, U. of ... XL
Augustana (IL)	R	Gonzaga (WA) ... R
Augustana (SD)	R	Gordon (MA) ... R
Baylor (TX)	M	Goucher (MD) ... R
Belmont (TN)	R	Grand Valley (MI) ... L
Beloit (WI)	R	Grove City (PA) ... R
Bennington (VT)	S	Guilford (NC) ... R
Berea (KY)	R	Hamline (MN) ... R
Berry (GA)	R	■ Hampton-Sydney (VA) ... S
Bethany (WV)	S	Hanover (IN) ... R
Birmingham-Southern (AL)	R	Hendrix (AR) ... R
Bradley (IL)	M	Hiram (OH) ... R
Brigham Young (UT)	XL	Hobart & Wm. Smith (NY) ... R
Bryn Athyn (PA)	S	▲Hollins (VA) ... S
California, U. of (Davis)	L	▲Hood (MD) ... S
California, U. of (Irvine)	L	Hunter (CUNY) (NY) ... L
Cal Poly State U. (San Luis Obispo)	L	Illinois, U. of (Chicago) ... L
Calvin (MI)	M	Iowa State ... XL
Canisius (NY)	M	John Carroll (OH) ... M
Catholic (DC)	M	▲Judson (AL) ... S
Centenary (LA)	S	Juniata (PA) ... R
Central (IA)	R	Kansas State ... L
Central Florida	L	Kentucky, U. of ... L
Central Michigan	L	Kentucky Wesleyan ... S
Chapman (CA)	R	Lake Forest (IL) ... R
Cincinnati, U. of (OH)	L	LaSalle (PA) ... M
Clark (MA)	R	LeMoyne (NY) ... R
Clemson (SC)	L	Lewis & Clark (OR) ... R
Coe (IA)	R	Lipscomb (TN) ... R
Colorado, U. of	L	Loras (IA) ... R
Concordia (MN)	R	Loyola (LA) ... R
Cornell Col. (IA)	R	Luther (IA) ... R
Delaware, U. of	L	Lycoming (PA) ... R
Denison (OH)	R	Lyon (AR) ... S
DePaul (IL)	L	Manhattanville (NY) ... R
Denver, U. of (CO)	M	Marietta (OH) ... R
Drake (IA)	M	Marquette (WI) ... M
Drury (MO)	R	Mary Washington (VA) ... M
Earlham (IN)	R	Massachusetts, U. of ... L
Eckerd (FL)	R	

GROUP II continues next page

Enrollment Code
■ *Men Only* S = Small (less than 1000 students)   R = Moderate (1000-3000 students)   M = Medium (3000-8000 students)
▲ *Women Only*   L = Large (8000-20,000 students)   XL = Extra Large (over 20,000 students)

ENGLISH, continued

════════ GROUP II, continued ════════

Master's (CA) .... R	Rollins (FL) .... R
Messiah (PA) .... R	Rutgers (Camden) NJ .... M
Michigan State XL	St. Anselm (NH) .... R
Millsaps (MS) .... S	St. Bonaventure (NY) .... R
Minnesota, U. of (Morris) .... R	▲ St. Catherine (MN) .... R
Mississippi, U. of L	St. Joseph's U. (PA) .... R
Mississippi U. for Women .... R	St. Lawrence (NY) .... R
Missouri, U. of XL	St. Louis U. (MO) .... M
Missouri, U. of (Kansas City) .... M	▲ St. Mary's Col. (IN) .... R
Montana, U. of .... M	St. Mary's College of Maryland .... R
Mount Mercy (IA) .... S	St. Norbert (WI) .... R
Muhlenberg (PA) .... R	St. Scholastica (MN) .... R
Murray State (KY) .... M	San Diego State (CA) XL
Nazareth (NY) .... R	Santa Clara U. (CA) .... M
Nevada, U. of (Las Vegas) L	▲ Scripps (CA) .... S
Nevada, U. of (Reno) L	Seattle Pacific (WA) .... R
New Hampshire, U. of L	Shepherd (WV) .... M
New Mexico State U. L	South Carolina, U. of L
New Orleans (LA) L	Spring Hill (AL) .... R
New Paltz (SUNY)(NY) .... M	Stetson (FL) .... R
North Carolina, U. of (Wilmington) L	Stony Brook (SUNY) (NY) L
North Dakota, U. of .... M	Susquehanna (PA) .... R
Northeastern (MA) L	Texas A&M XL
Oglethorpe (GA) .... R	Truman State (MO) .... M
Ohio State XL	Tulsa, U. of (OK) .... R
Ohio U. L	Utah State L
Oklahoma Baptist .... R	Virginia Poly. Institute L
Oklahoma City U. .... R	Warren Wilson (NC) .... S
Oklahoma, U. of XL	Wartburg (IA) .... R
Oklahoma State L	Washington & Jefferson (PA) .... R
Oneonta (SUNY)(NY) .... M	Washington, U. of XL
Oregon, U. of L	Washington State L
Oswego (SUNY)(NY) .... M	Wells (NY) .... S
Otterbein (OH) .... R	West Chester (PA) .... M
Pacific University (OR) .... R	Western Michigan L
Pittsburgh, U. of (PA) L	Western Washington U. L
Portland State (OR) L	Westminster (MO) .... S
Presbyterian (SC) .... R	Westminster (UT) .... R
Principia (IL) .... S	Wheaton (MA) .... R
Providence (RI) .... M	Whitworth (WA) .... R
Purchase (SUNY) (NY) .... R	William Jewell (MO) .... R
Queens (NC) .... S	Winona State U. (MN) .... M
Queens (CUNY)(NY) L	Winthrop (SC) .... M
Randolph-Macon (VA) .... R	Wittenberg (OH) .... R
▲ Randolph-Macon Woman's Col. (VA) .... S	Wofford (SC) .... S
Redlands, U. of (CA) .... R	Wooster (OH) .... R
Ripon (WI) .... S	Wyoming, U. of L
Roanoke (VA) .... R	

Enrollment Code

■ *Men Only*	S = Small (less than 1000 students) R = Moderate (1000-3000 students) M = Medium (3000-8000 students)
▲ *Women Only*	L = Large (8000-20,000 students) XL = Extra Large (over 20,000 students)

ENGLISH, continued

GROUP III
Selective

Adrian (MI)	R	Eureka (IL)	S
Alabama, U. of (Birmingham)	M	Fairleigh Dickinson (NJ)	M
Alabama, U. of (Huntsville)	M	Florida A&M	M
▲ Alverno (WI)	R	Florida Gulf Coast U.	M
Appalachian State (NC)	L	Fort Hays (KS)	M
Aquinas (MI)	R	Fort Lewis (CO)	M
Arkansas, U. of	L	Friends (KS)	R
Arcadia (PA)	R	Georgia Southwestern	R
Assumption (MA)	R	Goshen (IN)	R
Augsburg (MN)	R	Gwynedd-Mercy (PA)	S
Augusta (GA)	M	Howard (DC)	M
Azusa Pacific (CA)	R	Jamestown (ND)	R
Baldwin-Wallace (OH)	R	Johnson State (VT)	R
Bellarmine (KY)	R	Keene State (NH)	R
Bethel (IN)	R	Kennesaw State (GA)	R
Brescia (KY)	S	King (TN)	S
Briar Cliff (IA)	R	Illinois College	S
California (PA)	M	Lewis-Clark State (ID)	R
California State U. (Bakersfield)	M	Long Island U. (Brooklyn)(NY)	R
California State U. (Channel Islands)	R	Long Island U. (C.W. Post)(NY)	R
California State U. (East Bay)	M	Longwood (VA)	R
California State U. (Fresno)	L	Louisiana College	R
California State U. (Fullerton)	L	Louisiana-Lafayette	L
California State U. (Monterey Bay)	R	Louisiana State	XL
California State U. (Northridge)	L	Lyndon State (VT)	R
California State U. (Sacramento)	M	Mansfield (PA)	R
Campbell (NC)	R	Mass. Coll. of Lib. Arts (N. Adams)	R
Carson-Newman (TN)	R	Massachusetts, U. of (Boston)	M
Central Washington	L	Memphis, U. of (TN)	L
Charleston Southern (SC)	R	Mercyhurst (PA)	R
Chestnut Hill (PA)	S	▲ Meredith (NC)	R
Chowan (NC)	S	Merrimack (MA)	R
Christopher Newport (VA)	M	Middle Tennessee	L
Citadel, The (SC)	R	Millersville (PA)	M
City College (CUNY)(NY)	L	Misericordia (PA)	S
Daemen (NY)	R	Montclair State (NJ)	M
Dana (NB)	S	Montevallo (AL)	R
DeSales (PA)	S	Mount St. Joseph (OH)	R
Doane (NE)	S	Niagara (NY)	R
Dordt (IA)	R	Northeastern Illinois	M
D'Youville (NY)	R	Northeastern State (OK)	L
East Carolina	L	Northern Iowa	L
East Central State (OK)	R	Northern Kentucky	L
East Tennessee	L	Northern Michigan	M
Eastern Illinois	L	Northwestern (IA)	R
Eastern Michigan	L	Oklahoma Christian	R
Eastern Nazarene (MA)	R	Penn State (Erie)(PA)	M
Eastern Oregon	R	Pittsburgh, U. of (Greensburg)	R
Eastern Washington	L	Point Park (PA)	R
Edinboro (PA)	M		

GROUP III continues next page

ENGLISH, continued

●●● ━━━━━━━━━━━━━━━━━ **GROUP III,** continued ━━━━━━━━━━━━━ ●●●

Plymouth State (NH) .... M	Temple (PA) L
▲ Regis (MA) .... S	Tennessee, U. of XL
Rhode Island, U. of........................... L	Texas, U. of (San Antonio) L
Robert Morris (PA) .... R	Texas, U. of (Tyler) .... R
Rockford (IL) .... S	Texas A&M (Corpus Christi) .... M
Rocky Mountain (MT) .... S	Texas Tech. U. L
▲ Rosemont (PA) .... S	Troy State (AL) .... M
St. Edward's (TX) .... M	Utah, U. of.. L
St. Mary (KS) .... S	Walla Walla (WA) .... R
St. Mary's U. of San Antonio (TX) .... R	Walsh (OH).. R
St. Peter's (NJ) .... R	Western Carolina (NC) .... M
▲ Salem Col. (NC) .... S	Western Connecticut .... M
San Francisco State (CA) L	Western Illinois L
Schreiner (TX).................................. S	Western St. Coll. of Colorado............ R
Seattle U. (WA) .... R	Westfield (MA) .... M
Shippensburg (PA)............................ M	West Virginia Wesleyan .... R
Slippery Rock (PA) .... M	Wheeling Jesuit (WV) .... R
South Alabama .... M	Wichita State (KS) .... M
South Dakota, U. of .... M	Whittier (CA) .... R
Southeastern Louisiana...................... L	Wilkes (PA) .... R
Southern Connecticut .... M	William Paterson (NJ) .... M
Southern Nazarene (OK) .... R	Wilmington (OH) .... S
Southern Utah .... M	Wisconsin, U. of (Eau Claire) L
Southwestern (KS) .... S	Wisconsin, U. of (Milwaukee) .... R
▲ Spelman (GA) .... R	Wisconsin, U. of (Platteville)............ M
Tarleton State (TX) .... M	

FOREIGN LANGUAGES

GROUP I
Most Selective

Albany (SUNY)(NY) L	Kalamazoo (MI) .... R
Allegheny (PA)................................... R	Lawrence (WI) .... R
Bard (NY) .... R	Macalester (MN)................................ R
▲ Barnard (NY) .... R	Michigan, U. of XL
Bates (ME) .... R	Middlebury (VT) .... R
Binghamton (SUNY)(NY) L	Minnesota, U. of XL
Boston College (MA) L	▲ Mt. Holyoke (MA) .... R
Boston U. (MA).................................... L	New York U. .... M
Bowdoin (ME)..................................... R	North Carolina, U. of L
Brown (RI) .... M	Notre Dame (IN) .... M
▲ Bryn Mawr (PA) .... S	Pennsylvania, U. of............................ L
California, U. of (Berkeley).............. XL	Pomona (CA) .... R
California, U. of (Los Angeles) XL	Princeton (NJ) .... M
Carleton (MN).................................... R	Reed (OR) .... R
Chicago, U. of (IL) .... M	Rhodes (TN) .... R
Colby (ME) .... R	Rochester, U. of (NY) .... M
Colgate (NY) .... R	Rutgers (NJ).. L
Columbia (NY) .... M	▲ Scripps (CA) .... S
Connecticut College .... R	Skidmore (NY) .... R
Dallas, U. of (TX) .... R	▲ Smith (MA) .... R
Dartmouth (NH) .... M	South, U. of the (TN) .... R
DePauw (IN) .... R	Southwestern (TX) .... R
Dickinson (PA) .... R	Stanford (CA) .... M
Drew (NJ) .... R	Trinity (TX) .... R
Emory (GA) .... M	Tulane (LA) .... M
Florida, U. of XL	Virginia, U. of L
Franklin & Marshall (PA) .... R	Wake Forest (NC) .... M
Georgetown (DC) .... M	Washington & Lee (VA) .... R
Grinnell (IA).. R	Washington U. (MO) .... M
Gustavus Adolphus (MN) .... R	▲ Wellesley (MA) .... R
Harvard (MA)...................................... M	Whitman (WA).................................... R
Haverford (PA)..................................... S	William & Mary (VA) .... M
Holy Cross (MA) .... R	Yale (CT) .... M
Illinois, U. of (Urbana-Champaign) XL	

FOREIGN LANGUAGES continues next page

FOREIGN LANGUAGES, continued

GROUP II
Very Selective

▲ Agnes Scott (GA) .... S
  Alabama, U. of L
  Arizona, U. of XL
  Arizona State XL
  Beloit (WI) .... R
  Brigham Young (UT) XL
  California, U. of (Santa Barbara) L
  Calvin (MI) .... M
  Catholic (DC) .... M
  Central (IA) .... R
  Centre (KY) .... R
  Charleston, College of (SC) L
  Clark (MA) .... R
  Clemson (SC) L
  Concordia (MN) .... R
  Drake (IA) .... M
  Earlham (IN) .... R
  Eckerd (FL) .... R
  Georgia, U. of XL
  Grand Valley (MI) L
  Gustavus Adolphus (MN) .... R
  Hawaii, U. of L
  Herbert Lehman (CUNY)(NY) .... M
▲ Hollins (VA) .... S
  Illinois College .... S
  Illinois, U. of (Chicago) L
  Indiana U. XL
  Iowa, U. of XL
  James Madison (VA) L
  Kansas, U. of L
  Kansas State L
  Lake Forest (IL) .... R
  Lewis & Clark (OR) .... R
  Linfield (OR) .... R

  Lyon (AR) .... S
▲ Mills (CA) .... S
  Minnesota, U. of (Morris) .... R
  Moravian (PA) .... R
  Nazareth (NY) .... R
  Nebraska, U. of L
  New Paltz (SUNY)(NY) .... M
  North Carolina (Charlotte) L
  Ohio State XL
  Oregon, U. of L
  Pacific University (OR) .... R
  Pepperdine (CA) .... R
  Pittsburgh, U. of (PA) L
  Portland State (OR) L
  Puerto Rico, U. of (Mayaguez) L
▲ Rosemont (PA) .... S
  St. Anselm (NH) .... R
  South Carolina, U. of L
  Stony Brook (SUNY)(NY) L
▲ Sweet Briar (VA) .... S
  Temple (PA) L
  Texas, U. of (Austin) XL
▲ Trinity (DC) .... S
  Truman State (MO) .... M
  Utah, U. of L
  Valparaiso U. (IN) .... M
  Vermont, U. of L
  Virginia Commonwealth L
  Wells (NY) .... S
  West Chester (PA) .... M
  Wheaton (MA) .... R
  Wisconsin, U. of XL
  Wofford (SC) .... R

GROUP III
Selective

  Bethany (WV) .... S
  California State U. (Sacramento) ...... M
  Carthage (WI) .... R
  Eastern Washington .... M
  Emory & Henry (VA) .... S
  Mansfield (PA) .... R
  Montana State L
  New Mexico, U. of L
  Northwestern (IA) .... R

  Slippery Rock (PA) .... M
  South Alabama .... M
  South Florida, U. of L
  Southern Oregon State U. .... M
  Wayne State (MI) L
  Western Michigan L
  Wisconsin, U. of (Milwaukee) L

FOREIGN LANGUAGES continues next page

Enrollment Code		
■ *Men Only*	S = Small (less than 1000 students)	R = Moderate (1000-3000 students)	M = Medium (3000-8000 students)
▲ *Women Only*	L = Large (8000-20,000 students)	XL = Extra Large (over 20,000 students)	

FOREIGN LANGUAGES, continued

Some Recommendations by Specific Departments

Compiled initially with the help of Minnesota's Jeff Sheehan, Secondary School Counselor

FRENCH

Arizona, U. of XL
California, U. of (Berkeley) XL
Central (IA) .... R
Colby (ME) .... R
Columbia (NY) .... M
Dartmouth (NH) .... M
Emory (GA) .... R
Georgetown (DC) .... M
Harvard (MA) .... M
Holy Cross (MA) .... M
Indiana U. XL
Indiana (PA) L
▲ Mills (CA) .... S

▲ Mount Holyoke (MA) .... R
North Carolina, U. of L
Northwestern (IL) .... M
Princeton (NJ) .... M
Rhodes (TN) .... R
San Diego State U. (CA) L
▲ Scripps (CA) .... S
Tufts (MA) .... M
Tulane (LA) .... M
Vassar (NY) .... R
Washington U. (MO) .... M
▲ Wellesley (MA) .... R
Wittenberg (OH) .... R

GERMAN

Boston College (MA) L
Brown (RI) .... M
California, U. of (Berkeley) XL
California, U. of (Santa Barbara) L
Colorado, U. of L
Hunter (CUNY)(NY) L
Illinois, U. of (Urbana-Champaign) XL
Indiana U. XL
Indiana (PA) L
Michigan State XL

Penn State XL
Pennsylvania, U. of L
Princeton (NJ) .... M
Rhode Island., U. of L
Stanford (CA) .... M
Texas, U. of (Austin) XL
Williams (MA) .... R
Wisconsin, U. of XL
Wofford (SC) .... R

JAPANESE

Brigham Young (UT) XL
Connecticut College .... R
Harvard (MA) .... M
Hawaii, U. of (Manoa) L
Ohio State L
Oregon, U. of L

Pacific University (OR) .... R
Pennsylvania, U. of L
Pittsburgh, U. of (PA) L
Washington, U. of XL
Wisconsin, U. of XL

SPANISH

Bradley (IL) .... M
Brigham Young (UT) XL
Buffalo (SUNY) (NY) L
California State U. (San Marcos) ...... M
California, U. of (Irvine) .... M
California, U. of (San Diego) L
California, U. of (Santa Barbara) L
Central (IA) .... R
Colby (ME) .... R
George Washington (DC) .... M
Greensboro College (NC) .... S
Indiana U. XL
Kansas, U. of L
Lawrence (WI) .... R
Lyon (AR) .... S

Maryland, U. of XL
Massachusetts, U. of (Dartmouth) .... M
Messiah (PA) .... R
Northwestern (IA) .... R
Pittsburgh, U. of L
Puerto Rico, U. of (Mayaguez) L
Rutgers (NJ) L
San Diego State U. (CA) L
▲ Scripps (CA) .... S
Southern Connecticut .... M
Texas, U. of XL
Utah, U. of L
Vanderbilt (TN) .... M
Wisconsin, U. of XL
Worcester State (MA) .... M

FORESTRY

• ━━━━━━━━━━━━━━ **GROUP I** ━━━━━━━━━━━━━━ •
Most Selective

Florida, U. of XL	South, U. of the (TN) .... R
Illinois, U. of XL	SUNY Coll. of Env. Sci. & Forestry .... R
North Carolina State L	

•• ━━━━━━━━━━━━━ **GROUP II** ━━━━━━━━━━━━━ ••
Very Selective

Arizona, U. of XL	Missouri, U. of XL
Auburn (AL) L	Montana State L
Berry (GA) .... R	Oklahoma State L
Clemson (SC) L	Pennsylvania State XL
Colorado State L	Purdue (IN) XL
Connecticut, U. of XL	Syracuse (NY) L
Georgia, U. of L	Tennessee, U. of XL
Iowa State XL	Texas A&M XL
Maine, U. of L	Virginia Tech. L
Michigan State XL	Washington, U. of XL
Michigan Tech .... M	West Virginia U. L
Minnesota, U. of XL	Wisconsin, U. of XL
Mississippi State L	

••• ━━━━━━━━━━━━ **GROUP III** ━━━━━━━━━━━━ •••
Selective

Humboldt State (CA) .... M	Oregon State L
Idaho, U. of L	Southern Illinois (Carbondale) L
Montana, U. of .... M	Stephen F. Austin (TX) L
Northern Arizona XL	Utah State L

Enrollment Code

■ *Men Only* S = Small (less than 1000 students) R = Moderate (1000-3000 students) M = Medium (3000-8000 students)
▲ *Women Only* L = Large (8000-20,000 students) XL = Extra Large (over 20,000 students)

GEOGRAPHY

GROUP I
Most Selective

Boston U. (MA) L	George Washington (DC) .... M
Buffalo (SUNY)(NY) L	Johns Hopkins (MD) .... M
California, U. of (Berkeley) XL	Macalester (MN) .... R
Chicago, U. of (IL) .... M	Michigan, U. of XL
Clark (MA) .... R	Middlebury (VT) .... R
Colgate (NY) .... R	Minnesota, U. of XL
Dartmouth (NH) .... M	Sarah Lawrence (NY) .... R
Florida, U. of XL	

GROUP II
Very Selective

Arizona State XL	Ohio State XL
Bemidji State (MN) .... M	Oklahoma, U. of XL
California, U. of (Santa Barbara) L	Oklahoma State L
Colorado, U. of L	Oregon, U. of L
Colorado, U. of (Colorado Springs) ...... M	Oneonta (SUNY)(NY) .... M
Denver, U. of (CO) .... M	Pennsylvania State XL
DePaul (IL) L	Radford (VA) .... M
Florida International L	San Diego State U. (CA) L
Georgia, U. of L	South Carolina, U. of L
Hunter (CUNY)(NY) L	Syracuse (NY) L
Indiana U. XL	Texas, U. of (Austin) XL
Kansas State L	Vermont, U. of L
Kansas, U. of L	Virginia Poly. Institute L
Louisiana State XL	Western Washington U. L
Mary Washington (VA) .... M	Wisconsin, U. of (Madison) XL
Michigan State XL	Wittenberg (OH) .... R
New Paltz (SUNY)(NY) .... M	

GROUP III
Selective

Ball State (IN) .... M	Keene State (NH) .... R
Bloomsburg (PA) .... M	Maine (Farmington) .... R
Bridgewater (MA) .... M	Mansfield (PA) .... R
California State U. (Chico) L	Massachusetts, U. of (Boston) .... M
California State U. (Long Beach) L	New Orleans (LA) L
California State U. (Northridge) L	North Carolina (Charlotte) L
California State U. (Stanislaus) .... M	Salem State (MA) .... M
Carthage (WI) .... R	Sonoma State (CA) .... M
Central Connecticut .... M	Southern Connecticut .... M
Central Michigan L	Southern Illinois U. (Carbondale) L
Central Washington L	Southwest Texas State L
Edinboro (PA) .... M	Texas A&M (Corpus Christi) .... M
π Elmhurst (IL) .... R	Western Illinois L
Frostburg (MD) .... M	Wisconsin, U. of (LaCrosse) L
++ Indiana (PA) L	Wyoming, U. of L
Indiana State L	

++ *Especially Regional Planning*
π *Geography and Environmental Planning*

GEOLOGY

━━━━━━━━━━━━━━ **GROUP I** ━━━━━━━━━━━━━━
Most Selective

Amherst (MA)	R	Hamilton (NY)	R
▲Barnard (NY)	R	Harvard (MA)	M
Bates (ME)	R	Lafayette (PA)	R
Binghamton (SUNY)(NY)	L	Lehigh (PA)	M
Bowdoin (ME)	R	MIT (MA)	M
Brown (RI)	M	▲Mount Holyoke (MA)	R
▲Bryn Mawr (PA)	R	Pennsylvania, U. of	L
California Inst. of Tech.	S	Pomona (CA)	R
California, U. of (Berkeley)	XL	Princeton (NJ)	M
Carleton (MN)	R	Rennselaer (NY)	M
Chicago, U. of (IL)	M	Rochester, U. of (NY)	M
Colgate (NY)	R	Skidmore (NY)	R
Colorado Col.	R	▲Smith (MA)	R
Colorado School of Mines	R	South, U. of the (TN)	R
Columbia (NY)	M	Vanderbilt (TN)	M
Dartmouth (NH)	M	Washington & Lee (VA)	R
Franklin & Marshall (PA)	R	Washington U. (MO)	M
Furman (SC)	R	Whitman (WA)	R
Geneseo (SUNY) (NY)	M	William & Mary (VA)	M
Gustavus Adolphus (MN)	R		

━━━━━━━━━━━━━━ **GROUP II** ━━━━━━━━━━━━━━
Very Selective

Alaska, U. of (Fairbanks)	M	Guilford (NC)	R
Albany (SUNY) (NY)	L	Hanover (IN)	R
Alabama, U. of	L	Hope (MI)	R
Allegheny (PA)	R	Idaho, U. of	L
Arizona State	XL	Indiana U.	XL
Arizona, U. of	XL	Juniata (PA)	R
Beloit (WI)	R	Michigan Tech	M
Bowling Green (OH)	L	Millsaps (MS)	S
Brigham Young (UT)	XL	Minnesota, U. of	XL
California, U. of (Davis)	L	Minnesota, U. of (Duluth)	M
California, U. of (Santa Barbara)	L	Minnesota, U. of (Morris)	R
Centenary College (LA)	S	New Hampshire, U. of	L
College of Charleston (SC)	L	New Mexico Inst. of Mining & Tech.	R
Colorado State	L	New Mexico, U. of	L
Colorado, U. of	L	Oklahoma, U. of	XL
Cornell Col. (IA)	R	Oklahoma State	L
Dayton, U. of (OH)	M	Purdue (IN)	XL
Denison (OH)	R	St. Lawrence (NY)	R
Denver, U. of (CO)	M	St. Thomas (MN)	M
Earlham (IN)	R		
Eastern Washington	L		

GROUP II continues next page

GEOLOGY, continued

GROUP II, continued

San Diego State (CA)	L	Tulsa, U. of (OK)	M
π South Carolina, U. of	L	Utah, U. of	L
South Dakota School of Mines	R	Vermont, U. of	M
Stony Brook (SUNY) (NY)	L	Washington, U. of	XL
Texas A&M	XL	Wisconsin, U. of	XL
Texas Christian	M	Wooster, College of (OH)	R
Texas, U. of (Austin)	XL		

π *Also Geophysics*

GROUP III
Selective

Bloomsburg (PA)	M	Louisiana State	XL
Boise State (ID)	L	Muskingum (OH)	R
Brockport (SUNY)(NY)	M	Nevada, U. of (Reno)	L
Brooklyn College (CUNY) (NY)	L	North Carolina (Wilmington)	M
California State U. (Bakersfield)	M	Northland (WI)	S
California State U. (Chico)	L	Northern Illinois U	L
California State U. (East Bay)	M	Oneonta (SUNY)(NY)	M
California State U. (Sacramento)	M	Plattsburgh (SUNY)(NY)	M
Edinboro (PA)	M	Salem State (MA)	M
Emporia State (KS)	M	Texas A&M (Corpus Christi)	M
Fort Lewis (CO)	M	West Chester (PA)	M
Hartwick (NY)	R	Western State Coll. of Colorado	R
Lamar (TX)	M	Wright State (OH)	L
Louisiana-Lafayette	L	Wyoming, U. of	L

Enrollment Code

■ *Men Only*   S = Small (less than 1000 students)   R = Moderate (1000-3000 students)   M = Medium (3000-8000 students)
▲ *Women Only*   L = Large (8000-20,000 students)   XL = Extra Large (over 20,000 students)

HISTORY

GROUP I
Most Selective

Albertson (ID) .... S	Kenyon (OH) .... R
Albion (MI) .... R	Lafayette (PA) .... R
American (DC) .... M	Lawrence (WI) .... R
Amherst (MA) .... R	Lehigh (PA) .... M
▲Barnard (NY) .... R	Macalester (MN) .... R
Bates (ME) .... R	Miami, U. of L
Binghamton (SUNY)(NY) L	Michigan, U. of XL
Boston Col. (MA) L	Middlebury (VT) .... R
Boston U. (MA) L	Missouri, U. of (Rolla) .... M
Bowdoin (ME) .... R	▲Mount Holyoke (MA) .... R
Brandeis (MA) .... R	North Carolina, U. of L
Brown (RI) .... M	Northwestern (IL) .... M
▲Bryn Mawr (PA) .... S	Notre Dame (IN) .... M
Bucknell (PA) .... M	Oberlin (OH) .... R
Buffalo (SUNY)(NY) L	Pennsylvania, U. of L
California, U. of (Berkeley) XL	Pitzer (CA) .... S
California, U. of (Los Angeles) XL	Pomona (CA) .... R
Carleton (MN) .... R	Princeton (NJ) .... M
Carnegie Mellon (PA) .... M	Reed (OR) .... R
Case Western Reserve (OH) .... M	Rhodes (TN) .... R
Centre (KY) .... R	Rice (TX) .... R
Chicago, U. of (IL) .... M	Richmond, U. of (VA) .... R
Claremont McKenna (CA) .... R	Rochester, U. of (NY) .... M
Colgate (NY) .... R	Rutgers (NJ) L
Colorado Col. .... R	St. Olaf (MN) .... R
Columbia (NY) .... M	Sarah Lawrence (NY) .... R
Connecticut Col. .... R	▲Smith (MA) .... R
Cornell (NY) L	South, U. of the (TN) .... R
Dallas, U. of (TX) .... R	Southwestern (TX) .... R
Dartmouth (NH) .... M	Swarthmore (PA) .... R
Davidson (NC) .... R	Texas Christian U. (TX) .... M
DePauw (IN) .... R	Trinity (TX) .... R
Dickinson (PA) .... R	Tufts (MA) .... M
Drew (NJ) .... R	Tulane (LA) .... M
Duke (NC) .... M	Union (NY) .... R
Emory (GA) .... M	U.S. Military Academy (NY) .... M
Florida, U. of XL	Vanderbilt (TN) .... R
Furman (SC) .... R	Vassar (NY) .... R
George Washington (DC) .... M	Virginia, U. of L
Georgetown (DC) .... M	■Wabash (IN) .... S
Georgia Institute of Tech. L	Wake Forest (NC) .... M
Gettysburg (PA) .... R	Washington & Lee (VA) .... R
Grinnell (IA) .... R	▲Wellesley (MA) .... R
Hamilton (NY) .... R	Wesleyan U. (CT) .... R
Harvard (MA) .... M	Wheaton (IL) .... R
Haverford (PA) .... S	Whitman (WA) .... R
Holy Cross (MA) .... R	William & Mary (VA) .... M
Illinois, U. of (Urbana-Champaign) XL	Williams (MA) .... R
Johns Hopkins (MD) .... M	Yale (CT) .... M
Kalamazoo (MI) .... R	Yeshiva (NY) .... R

HISTORY, continued

GROUP II
Very Selective

▲ Agnes Scott (GA)	S	Goucher (MD)	S
Albion (MI)	R	Guilford (NC)	R
Alfred (NY)	R	Gustavus Adolphus (MN)	R
Allegheny (PA)	R	■ Hampden-Sydney (VA)	S
Alma (MI)	R	Hamline (MN)	R
Arizona State	XL	Hanover (IN)	R
Arizona, U. of	XL	Hillsdale (MI)	R
Auburn (AL)	L	Hiram (OH)	R
Austin (TX)	R	Hobart & William Smith (NY)	R
Bard (NY)	R	▲ Hollins (VA)	S
Baylor (TX)	M	Hood (MD)	S
Beloit (WI)	R	Illinois College	S
Birmingham-Southern (AL)	R	Illinois, U. of (Chicago)	L
Bryan (TN)	S	Indiana U.	XL
Bryn Athyn (PA)	S	Iowa, U. of	XL
California, U. of (Davis)	L	Juniata (PA)	R
California, U. of (Merced)	R	Kansas, U. of	L
California, U. of (Riverside)	L	Kansas State	L
California, U. of (Santa Cruz)	M	Kentucky, U. of	L
Calvin (MI)	M	Kentucky Wesleyan	S
Canisius (NY)	M	Knox (IL)	R
Christendom (VA)	S	Lake Forest (IL)	R
Cincinnati, U. of (OH)	L	Linfield (OR)	R
City College (CUNY)(NY)	L	Loras (IA)	R
Coe (IA)	R	Loyola (LA)	R
Colorado U. of	L	Luther (IA)	R
Connecticut U. of	XL	Manhattanville (NY)	R
Cornell College (IA)	R	Marquette (WI)	M
Covenant (GA)	S	Maryland, U. of	XL
Delaware, U. of	L	+ Mary Washington (VA)	M
Denison (OH)	R	Massachusetts, U. of	L
DePaul (IL)	L	Miami, U. of (FL)	M
Denver, U. of (CO)	M	Michigan State	XL
Drake (IA)	M	Millersville (PA)	M
East Carolina	L	Millsaps (MS)	S
Eastern Michigan	L	Minnesota, U. of (Morris)	R
Elmira (NY)	R	Missouri, U. of	XL
Erskine (SC)	S	Missouri, U. of (Kansas City)	M
Florida Atlantic	L	■ Morehouse (GA)	R
Florida State	L	Muhlenberg (PA)	R
Georgetown College (KY)	R	New Mexico State U.	L
Georgia, U. of	L		
Gonzaga (WA)	R		

+ And Historic Preservation Major

GROUP III continues next page

Enrollment Code		
■ *Men Only*	S = Small (less than 1000 students)	R = Moderate (1000-3000 students)	M = Medium (3000-8000 students)
▲ *Women Only*	L = Large (8000-20,000 students)	XL = Extra Large (over 20,000 students)	

HISTORY, continued

GROUP II, continued

New Orleans, U. of (LA)	L	Texas Tech U.	L
North Carolina (Asheville)	R	Texas, U. of (Austin)	XL
Northeastern (MA)	L	Texas, U. of (Dallas)	M
Ohio State	XL	Trinity (CT)	R
Ohio U.	L	Tulsa, U. of (OK)	M
Oklahoma, U. of	XL	Utah, U. of	L
Oregon State	L	Vermont, U. of	L
Pittsburgh, U. of (PA)	L	Virginia Tech.	L
Portland, U. of (OR)	R	Virginia Military Institute	R
Providence (RI)	M	Warren Wilson (NC)	S
Queens (NC)	S	Wartburg (IA)	R
Ripon (WI)	S	Washington College (MD)	S
Roanoke (VA)	R	Washington State	L
▲Rosemont (PA)	S	Washington, U. of	XL
Rowan (NJ)	M	Washington & Jefferson (PA)	R
Rutgers (Camden) (NJ)	M	Webster (MO)	R
St. Joseph's (PA)	R	Wells (NY)	S
St. John's/ St. Benedict (MN)	R	Western Michigan	L
St. Mary's College of Maryland	R	Westminster (MO)	S
St. Norbert (WI)	R	Westminster (UT)	S
San Diego State U. (CA)	XL	Wheaton (MA)	R
Santa Clara U. (CA)	M	Whitworth (WA)	R
Seattle U. (WA)	R	Willamette (OR)	R
Shepherd (WV)	M	William Paterson (NJ)	M
South Carolina, U. of	L	Winona State U. (MN)	M
Southern Methodist (TX)	L	Winthrop (SC)	M
Spring Hill (AL)	R	Wisconsin, U. of	XL
Stetson (FL)	R	Wittenberg (OH)	R
Stony Brook (SUNY)(NY)	L	Wofford (SC)	R
Tennessee, U. of	XL	Wooster (OH)	R
Texas A&M	XL	Xavier (OH)	R

| HISTORY, continued |

GROUP III
Selective

Akron, U. of (OH) L	▲ Mary Baldwin (VA) .... S
Alabama, U. of L	Massachusetts U. of (Boston) .... M
Appalachian State (NC) L	Middle Tennessee L
Arkansas, U. of L	Milligan (TN) .... S
Assumption (MA) .... R	Misericordia (PA) .... S
Baldwin-Wallace (OH) .... R	Murray State (KY) .... M
Bellarmine (KY) .... R	Muskingum (OH) .... R
Boise State (ID) L	Nevada, U. of (Las Vegas) L
Briar Cliff (IA) .... R	New Mexico, U. of L
Bridgewater (MA) .... M	Northern Colorado L
Bridgewater (VA) .... R	Northern Iowa L
Brockport (SUNY)(NY) .... M	Northwestern (IA) .... S
California State U. (Channel Islands) .. R	Northwestern Louisiana L
California State U. (East Bay) .... M	Pittsburgh, U. of (Greenburg) .... R
California State U. (Fullerton) L	Quincy (IL) .... R
California State U. (Long Beach) L	Ramapo (NJ) .... M
California State U. (San Marcos) ...... M	Regis (CO) .... R
Campbell (NC) .... R	Rhode Island College .... M
Capital U. (OH) .... R	St. Ambrose (IA) .... R
Carroll (MT) .... R	St. Joseph's (NY) .... R
Carson-Newman (TN) .... R	St. Mary's (MN) .... R
Central Connecticut .... M	Salem State (MA) .... M
Charleston, U. of (WV) .... S	Shippensburg (PA) .... M
Cumberland (KY) .... R	South Dakota, U. of .... M
Delaware State .... R	Southern Illinois U. (Carbondale) L
East Tennessee L	Southern Mississippi L
Eastern Connecticut .... M	Southwest Texas State L
Fairmont State (WV) .... M	Tarleton State (TX) .... M
Fitchburg (MA) .... R	Texas A&M (Corpus Christi) .... M
Fredonia (SUNY)(NY) .... M	Texas Lutheran .... R
Georgia Southern L	Texas, U. of (San Antonio) L
Graceland (IA) .... R	Toledo, U. of L
Hastings (NE) .... R	Western St. Col. of Colorado .... R
Heidelberg (OH) .... S	West Kentucky L
Indiana (PA) L	West Virginia Wesleyan .... R
Kennesaw State (GA) .... R	Wheeling Jesuit (WV) .... R
Kutztown (PA) .... M	Wilkes (PA) .... R
Lambuth (TN) .... S	Wilmington (OH) .... S
Liberty (VA) .... R	Wingate (NC) .... R
Lock Haven (PA) .... M	Wisconsin, U. of (Green Bay) .... M
Louisiana State XL	Wisconsin, U. of (Milwaukee) L

HOME ECONOMICS/FAMILY STUDIES

GROUP I
Most Selective

Florida State.. L

Iowa state... XL

Wisconsin, U. of................................... XL

GROUP II
Very Selective

\# Bradley (IL) .... M

Brigham Young (UT) XL

Connecticut, U. of XL

Georgia, U. of XL

➤ Kansas State L

Michigan State.................................. XL

Nebraska, U. of L

Northern Illinois U. L

Oneonta (SUNY) (NY)........................ M

●* Pacific Oaks (CA) .... S

π Seattle Pacific (WA) .... M

Utah, U. of... L

Utah State L

Western Michigan L

Wisconsin, U. of (Stout) .... M

● *Junior Year Standing*

\# *Family & Consumer Science*

π *Apparel Design, also Clothing*

➤ *Nutritional & Exercise Sciences*

* *Especially Child Development*

GROUP III
Selective

Akron, U. of (OH) L

Berea (KY) .... R

California State U. (Fresno)............... L

California State U. (Sacramento) ...... M

Central Michigan L

Eastern Illinois.................................. L

Framingham State (MA) .... M

Georgia Southern L

Marywood (PA).................................. R

Montclair State (NJ) .... M

Montevallo (AL)................................. R

Oregon State..................................... L

Point Loma (CA) .... R

Texas Tech. U. L

Washington State L

JOURNALISM/COMMUNICATIONS

GROUP I
Most Selective

American U. (DC) .... M	New York U L
Boston College (MA) L	North Carolina, U. of L
Boston U. (MA) L	Northwestern (IL) .... M
California, U. of (Los Angeles) XL	Ohio U. L
California, U. of (San Diego) L	Southern California L
Creighton (NE) .... M	Southwestern (TX) .... R
DePauw (IN) .... R	Stanford (CA) .... M
Florida, U. of XL	Syracuse (NY) L
Gettysburg (PA) .... R	Trinity (TX) .... R
Illinois, U. of (Urbana-Champaign) XL	Villanova (PA) .... M
Macalester (MN) .... R	Washington & Lee (VA) .... R
Miami, U. of (FL) L	Wheaton (IL) .... R
Michigan, U. of XL	Wisconsin, U. of XL

GROUP II
Very Selective

Alabama, U. of L	Fordham (NY) .... M
Alabama, U. of (Huntsville) .... M	Fredonia (SUNY) (NY) .... M
Alma (MI) .... R	Geneva (PA) .... R
Arizona State XL	George Mason (VA) L
Arizona, U. of XL	Georgetown College (KY) .... R
Asbury (KY) .... R	Georgia State L
Auburn (AL) L	Georgia, U. of XL
Bryan (TN) .... S	Gonzaga (WA) .... R
California Poly. State U. (SLO) L	Hanover (IN) .... R
Canisius (NY) .... M	Hastings (NE) .... R
Capital (OH) .... R	Houston, U. of (TX) L
Central Florida, U. of L	Illinois College .... S
Chapman (CA) .... R	Indiana State L
Charleston, College of (SC) L	Indiana U. XL
Clark (MA) .... R	Indiana U. of Pennsylvania L
Clarke (IA) .... S	Iowa, U. of XL
Colorado, U. of L	Ithaca (NY) .... M
Columbia College (IL) .... M	James Madison (VA) .... M
Connecticut, U. of XL	John Carroll (OH) .... M
Dayton, U. of (OH) .... M	Juniata (PA) .... R
Delaware, U. of L	Kansas, U. of L
Denver, U. of (CO) .... M	Kansas State L
DePaul (IL) L	Kentucky, U. of L
Drake (IA) .... M	LeMoyne (NY) .... R
Dubuque, U. of (IA) .... S	Linfield (OR) .... R
Duquesne (PA) .... M	Loras (IA) .... R
Fairfield (CT) .... M	Louisiana State XL
Flagler (FL) .... R	
Florida Inst. of Tech. .... R	*GROUP II continues next page*

GROUP II continues next page

JOURNALISM/COMMUNICATIONS, continued

•• ■─────────── GROUP II, continued ───────────■ ••

Loyola (MD)	R	St. Ambrose (IA)	R
Loyola Marymount (CA)	M	St. Bonaventure (NY)	R
Maine, U. of	L	St. Cloud (MN)	L
Mansfield (PA)	M	St. Louis (MO)	M
Marist (NY)	M	St. Mary's (IN)	R
π Marquette (WI)	M	St. Michael's (VT)	R
Marshall (WV)	L	St. Norbert (WI)	R
Mary Baldwin (VA)	S	St. Thomas (MN)	M
Maryland, U. of	XL	San Diego State U. (CA)	XL
Massachusetts, U. of	L	Santa Clara U. (CA)	M
Master's (CA)	R	Scranton, U. of (PA)	M
Memphis, U. of (TN)	L	▲ Simmons (MA)	R
Michigan State	L	South Alabama	M
Milligan (TN)	S	South Carolina, U. of	L
▲ Mills College (CA)	S	Southern Illinois U. (Carbondale)	L
Minnesota, U. of	XL	Southern Methodist (TX)	M
Minnesota, U. of (Duluth)	M	Spring Hill (AL)	R
Mississippi, U. of	L	▲ Stephens (MO)	S
Missouri, U. of	XL	Suffolk (MA)	R
Missouri, U. of (Kansas City)	M	Susquehanna U. (PA)	R
Montana, U. of	M	Temple (PA)	L
Moravian (PA)	R	Texas A&M	S
Muhlenberg (PA)	R	Texas Christian U.	M
Nevada, U. of (Reno)	L	Texas, U. of (Arlington)	L
New Hampshire, U. of	L	Texas, U. of (Austin)	XL
North Central (IL)	R	Tulsa, U. of (OK)	R
North Florida	M	Virginia Tech.	L
North Texas	L	Wartburg (IA)	R
Ohio Wesleyan	R	Washington State	L
Oklahoma, U. of	XL	West Virginia U.	L
Oregon, U. of	L	Western Michigan	L
Oswego (SUNY)(NY)	M	Western Washington U.	L
Pennsylvania State	XL	Westminster (UT)	R
Pepperdine (CA)	R	Whitworth (WA)	R
Pittsburgh, U. of (PA)	L	William Paterson (NJ)	M
Plattsburgh (SUNY)(NY)	M	Winona State U. (MN)	L
Purchase (SUNY)(NY)	R	Wisconsin Lutheran	S
Quinnipiac (CT)	R	Wisconsin, U. of (Stevens Point)	M
▲ Randolph-Macon Woman's Col. (VA)	S	Xavier (OH)	R
Rhode Island, U. of	L	York (PA)	R
Rowan (NJ)	M		

π *Especially Broadcasting*

JOURNALISM/COMMUNICATIONS continues next page

Enrollment Code	
■ *Men Only*	S = Small (less than 1000 students) R = Moderate (1000-3000 students) M = Medium (3000-8000 students)
▲ *Women Only*	L = Large (8000-20,000 students) XL = Extra Large (over 20,000 students)

JOURNALISM/COMMUNICATIONS, continued

GROUP III
Selective

▲Alverno (WI)	R
Appalachian State (NC)	L
Arkansas, U. of	L
Augsburg (MN)	R
+ Azusa Pacific (CA)	R
Ball State (IN)	L
Bemidji State (MN)	M
Bethany (WV)	S
Bridgewater State (WA)	M
Brockport (SUNY) (NY)	M
Buena Vista (IA)	R
Butler (IN)	R
California Lutheran	R
California State U. (Fullerton)	L
California State U. (Long Beach)	L
California State U. (Northridge)	L
California State U. (Sacramento)	M
California State U. (San Bernardino)	M
Castleton State (VT)	R
Central Missouri	L
▲Chatham (PA)	S
Dana (NE)	S
East Tennessee	L
Eastern Connecticut	M
Eastern Kentucky	L
Elon (NC)	R
Endicott (MA)	R
Fitchburg (MA)	R
Florida A&M	M
Florida Southern	R
Fontbonne (MO)	R
Franklin (IN)	S
Gwynedd-Mercy (PA)	S
Hardin-Simmons (TX)	R
Hawaii Pacific	M
Hofstra (NY)	M
Howard (DC)	M
Hunter (CUNY) (NY)	L
Idaho, U. of	L
Jacksonville (FL)	R
Johnson C. Smith (NC)	R
▲Judson (AL)	S
Keene State (NH)	R
Kent State (OH)	L
Kentucky Wesleyan	S
Lewis-Clark State (ID)	R
Liberty (VA)	R
Loyola (IL)	M
Loyola U. (LA)	M
Lynchburg (VA)	R
• Lyndon State (VT)	R
Marymount Manhattan (NY)	R
Mass. College of Lib. Arts (N. Adams)	R
Minnesota, U. of (Duluth)	M
Misericordia, College (PA)	S
Missouri Southern State	M
Missouri, U. of (St. Louis)	M
Monmouth (NJ)	R
Montana, U. of	M
Morningside (IA)	S
Montevallo (AL)	R
Muskingum (OH)	R
Murray State (KY)	M
Nebraska, U. of	L
North Carolina, U. of (Greensboro)	M
North Carolina, U. of (Pembroke)	R
North Dakota, U. of	M
Northern Illinois U.	L
Northern Iowa	L
Northern Kentucky	L
Oakland U. (MI)	M
Oklahoma City U.	R
Otterbein (OH)	R
▲Pine Manor (MA)	S
Regis (CO)	R
▲Regis (MA)	S
Reinhardt (GA)	S
Rider (NJ)	R
Robert Morris (PA)	R
Roger Williams (RI)	M
Roosevelt (IL)	R
St. Edward's (TX)	M
St. John Fisher (NY)	R
St. Mary's College (MN)	R
Samford (AL)	R
San Jose State (CA)	L
Seton Hall (NJ)	M
Southeastern Louisiana	L
Southern Connecticut	M
Southern Maine	M
Southern Utah	M
Tampa, U. of (FL)	R
Texas Wesleyan	R
Towson (MD)	L
Virginia Wesleyan	R
Walla Walla (WA)	R
Weber State (UT)	L
West Chester (PA)	M
Western Illinois	L
Wichita State (KS)	M
Wingate (NC)	R
Wisconsin, U. of (LaCrosse)	L
Worcester State (MA)	M

+ *Media Studies*
• *Also Broadcasting, also Television Studies*

MATHEMATICS

GROUP I
Most Selective

▲Agnes Scott (GA) .... M
  Albany (SUNY)(NY) L
  American U. (DC) .... M
▲Barnard (NY) .... R
  Bates (ME) .... R
  Binghamton (SUNY) (NY) L
  Boston U. (MA) L
  Bowdoin (ME) .... R
  Brandeis (MA) .... R
▲Bryn Mawr (PA) .... R
  Bucknell (PA) .... M
  Buffalo (SUNY)(NY) L
  California Inst. of Tech. .... S
  California, U. of (Berkeley) XL
  California, U. of (Los Angeles) XL
  California, U. of (San Diego) L
  Carnegie Mellon (PA) .... M
  Carleton (MN) .... R
  Case Western Reserve U. (OH) .... M
  Chicago, U. of (IL) .... M
  Clarkson (NY) .... M
  Colby (ME) .... R
  Colgate (NY) .... R
  Colorado College .... R
  Colorado School of Mines .... R
  Columbia (NY) .... M
  Connecticut College .... R
  Dartmouth (NH) .... M
  Davidson (NC) .... R
  Dickinson (PA) .... R
  Duke (NC) .... M
  Florida, U. of XL
  Georgia Inst. of Tech. L
  Grinnell (IA) .... R
  Harvard (MA) .... M
  Harvey Mudd (CA) .... S
  Holy Cross (MA) .... R
  Illinois Inst. of Tech. .... R
  Illinois, U. of (Urbana-Champaign) XL
  Kenyon (OH) .... R

  Lehigh (PA) .... M
  Michigan, U. of XL
  MIT (MA) .... M
▲Mount Holyoke (MA) .... R
  New College (FL) .... S
  New Jersey, College of .... M
  New York U. L
  Northwestern (IL) .... M
  Notre Dame (IN) .... M
  Oberlin (OH) .... R
  Occidental (CA) .... R
  Pennsylvania, U. of L
  Pittsburgh, U. of (PA) L
  Pomona (CA) .... R
  Princeton (NJ) .... M
  Reed (OR) .... R
  Rensselaer (NY) .... M
  Rice (TX) .... R
  Rose-Hulman (IN) .... R
  Stanford (CA) .... M
  St. Mary's Col. of Maryland .... R
  St. Olaf (MN) .... R
  Trinity (CT) .... R
  Tulane (LA) .... M
  Union (NY) .... R
  United States Air Force Academy (CO) .... M
  Villanova (PA) .... M
■Wabash (IN) .... S
  Wake Forest (NC) .... M
  Washington & Lee (VA) .... R
  Washington U. (MO) .... M
▲Wellesley (MA) .... R
  Wesleyan (CT) .... R
  Wheaton (IL) .... R
  Whitman (WA) .... R
  Willamette (OR) .... R
  Wisconsin, U. of XL
  Worcester Poly Inst. (MA) .... R
  Yale (CT) .... M

Enrollment Code

■ *Men Only*   S = Small (less than 1000 students)   R = Moderate (1000-3000 students)   M = Medium (3000-8000 students)
▲ *Women Only*   L = Large (8000-20,000 students)   XL = Extra Large (over 20,000 students)

MATHEMATICS, continued

GROUP II
Very Selective

Adrian (MI)	R		Michigan, U. of (Dearborn)	M
Alabama, U. of (Huntsville)	M		Millsaps (MS)	S
Albertson (ID)	S		Montana Tech.	R
Albion (MI)	R		Muhlenberg (PA)	R
Arcadia (PA)	R		New Mexico State	L
Arizona State	XL		Newman U. (KS)	S
Auburn (AL)	L		North Carolina State	L
Baylor (TX)	M		North Florida	M
Bellarmine (KY)	R		Ohio State	XL
Belmont (TN)	R		Ohio U.	L
Birmingham-Southern (AL)	R		Oregon, U. of	L
Bowling Green (OH)	L		Otterbein (OH)	R
Bryant (RI)	R		Potsdam (SUNY) (NY)	R
California Poly. State U. (SLO)	L		Puerto Rico, U. of (Mayaguez)	L
California, U. of (Irvine)	L		Roanoke (VA)	R
California, U. of (Riverside)	L		Rochester Inst. of Tech.	L
California, U. of (Santa Cruz)	M		Rockhurst (MO)	R
Carroll (MT)	R		San Diego, U. of (CA)	M
Cincinnati, U. of (OH)	L		Seattle U. (WA)	R
College of Charleston (SC)	L		▲Simmons (MA)	R
Colorado, U. of	L		South Dakota School of Mines	R
Concordia (MN)	R		Southern California, U. of	L
DePaul (IL)	L		Southwest Missouri	L
Earlham (IN)	R		Stetson (FL)	R
Fairfield (CT)	M		▲Sweet Briar (VA)	S
Florida Atlantic	L		Texas, U. of (Austin)	XL
George Mason (VA)	L		▲Trinity (DC)	S
Hendrix (AR)	R		Truman State (MO)	M
Hiram (OH)	R		Valparaiso (IN)	M
Illinois College	S		Vassar (NY)	R
Illinois, U. of (Chicago)	L		Virginia Poly. Institute	L
Kansas State	L		Washington, U. of	XL
Knox (IL)	R		Wheaton (MA)	R
LaSalle (PA)	M		Winthrop (SC)	M
Lebanon Valley (PA)	R		Wisconsin Lutheran	S
Lyon (AR)	S		Wofford (SC)	R
Massachusetts, U. of (Lowell)	M		Wooster (OH)	R
Michigan State	XL			

MATHEMATICS continues next page

MATHEMATICS, continued

GROUP III
Selective

Averett (VA)	S	Louisiana State	XL
Baldwin-Wallace (OH)	R	Lynchburg (VA)	R
Ball State (IN)	L	Malone (OH)	R
▲ Bennett (NC)	S	Montana State (Billings)	R
Bloomsburg (PA)	M	Mount St. Joseph (OH)	R
Bluffton (OH)	S	Murray State (KY)	M
Boise State (ID)	L	Northeastern State (OK)	L
Briar Cliff (IA)	R	Northern State (OK)	L
California State U. (Channel Islands)	R	Northern Michigan	M
California State U. (Dominguez Hills)	M	Ozarks, College of the (MO)	R
California State U. (Monterey Bay)	R	Penn State (Erie)(PA)	M
California State U. (San Jose)	L	St. Joseph's (NY)	R
Christopher Newport (VA)	M	Simpson (IA)	R
Clark Atlanta (GA)	M	South Dakota State U.	M
Colorado, U. of (Denver)	M	Southern Polytechnic (GA)	R
East Carolina	L	Southwest Texas State	L
East Tennessee	L	Texas A&M (Corpus Christi)	M
Eastern Connecticut	M	Texas Tech. U.	L
Eastern Washington	L	Texas, U. of (Tyler)	R
Fisk (TN)	S	Weber State (UT)	L
Fontbonne (MO)	R	Western Carolina (NC)	M
Georgia State	L	Wheeling Jesuit (WV)	R
Indiana (PA)	L	Wilkes (PA)	R
Lewis-Clark State (ID)	R	Wisconsin, U. of (Eau Claire)	L
Louisiana-Lafayette	L	Wisconsin, U. of (Stevens Point)	M

MUSIC

========================= **GROUP I** =========================
Most Selective

▲ Barnard (NY)	R	Lawrence (WI)	R
Beloit (WI)	R	Mannes School of Music (NY)	S
Binghamton (SUNY)(NY)	L	Miami, U. of (FL)	L
Boston College (MA)	L	Miami U. (OH)	L
Boston U. (MA)	L	Michigan, U. of	XL
Bowdoin (ME)	R	Minnesota, U. of	XL
Brandeis (MA)	R	New York U.	L
Bucknell (PA)	R	Northwestern (IL)	M
Buffalo (SUNY)(NY)	L	Oberlin (OH)	R
California, U. of (Berkeley)	XL	Pomona (CA)	R
California, U. of (Los Angeles)	XL	Princeton (NJ)	M
California, U. of (San Diego)	L	Rhodes (TN)	R
Carleton (MN)	R	Rice (TX)	R
Carnegie-Mellon (PA)	M	Rochester, U. of (NY)	M
Case Western Reserve U. (OH)	M	Rutgers (NJ)	L
Chicago, U. of (IL)	M	Sarah Lawrence (NY)	R
Cleveland Inst. of Music (OH)	S	▲ Scripps (CA)	S
Colby (ME)	R	Skidmore (NY)	R
Columbia (NY)	M	▲ Smith (MA)	R
Connecticut College	R	Southern California, U. of	L
π DePauw (IN)	R	Southwestern (TX)	R
Florida, U. of	XL	Stanford (CA)	M
Furman (SC)	R	St. Mary's College of Maryland	R
Geneseo (SUNY) (NY)	M	St. Olaf (MN)	R
Gustavus Adolphus (MN)	R	Texas, U. of (Austin)	XL
Harvard (MA)	M	Vanderbilt (TN)	M
Illinois, U. of (Urbana-Champaign)	XL	Vassar (NY)	R
Illinois Wesleyan	R	Virginia, U. of	L
Indiana U.	XL	Wheaton (IL)	R
Iowa, U. of	XL	Whitman (WA)	R
Johns Hopkins (MD)	M	Willamette (OR)	R
Juilliard (NY)	S	Wisconsin, U. of	XL
Kenyon (OH)	R	Yale (CT)	M
Knox (IL)	R		

π *Music and Music Business*

MUSIC continues next page

Enrollment Code		
■ *Men Only*	S = Small (less than 1000 students)	R = Moderate (1000-3000 students)	M = Medium (3000-8000 students)
▲ *Women Only*	L = Large (8000-20,000 students)	XL = Extra Large (over 20,000 students)

MUSIC, continued

=================================== GROUP II ===================================
Very Selective

Alabama, U. of L	Florida State L
Alaska Pacific .... S	π Florida Southern .... R
Albertson (ID) .... S	π Fredonia (SUNY) (NY) .... M
Arizona State XL	Georgia State L
Asbury (KY) .... R	Georgia, U. of L
Augustana (IL) .... R	Gordon (MA) .... R
Augustana (SD) .... M	Harding (AR) .... M
Bard (NY) .... R	Hiram (OH) .... R
Baylor (TX) .... M	Hofstra (NY) .... M
Bennington (VT) .... S	Hope (MI) .... R
Berklee College of Music (MA) .... R	Houghton (NY) .... S
Birmingham-Southern (AL) .... R	Houston, U. of (TX) L
Boston Conservatory .... S	Idaho, U. of L
Brigham Young (UT) L	Illinois, U. of (Chicago) L
Bryan (TN) .... S	Ithaca (NY) .... M
Butler (IN) .... R	James Madison (VA) L
Cal. Inst. of the Arts .... S	▲ Judson (AL) .... S
California, U. of (Riverside) L	Kansas State L
California, U. of (Santa Barbara) L	Kentucky, U. of L
California, U. of (Santa Cruz) .... M	Lake Forest (IL) .... R
Capital (OH) .... R	Lebanon Valley (PA) .... R
Catholic U. (DC) .... M	Louisiana State XL
Centenary (LA) .... S	Loyola (IL) .... M
Central (IA) .... R	Luther (IA) .... R
Central Florida L	Maine, U. of .... M
Chapman (CA) .... R	Manhattanville (NY) .... R
Cincinnati, U. of L	Manhattan School of Music (NY) ...... S
Clark (MA) .... R	Maryland, U. of XL
Clarke (IA) .... S	Maryville (TN) .... S
Coe (IA) .... R	McDaniel (MD) .... R
Colorado, U. of L	Mercer (GA) .... R
Concordia (CA) .... R	Michigan State XL
Concordia (MN) .... R	Milliken (IL) .... R
▲ Converse (SC) .... S	▲ Mills (CA) .... S
Cornish (WA) .... S	Millsaps (MS) .... S
Covenant (GA) .... S	Missouri, U. of (Kansas City) .... M
Creighton (NE) .... M	Mobile, U. of (AL) .... R
Curtis Institute of Music (PA) .... S	Moravian (PA) .... R
Dayton, U. of (OH) .... M	Morningside (IA) .... S
Denison (OH) .... R	Murray State (KY) .... M
π Denver, U. of .... R	Nebraska, U. of L
DePaul (IL) L	New England Conservatory (MA) .... S
Drake (IA) .... M	
Drury (MO) .... R	π *Music and Music Business*
Evansville (IN) .... R	*GROUP II continues next page*

MUSIC, continued

GROUP II, continued

New Hampshire, U. of L
North Carolina School of the Arts .... S
North Florida .... M
North Texas L
Northwestern (MN) .... R
Ohio State XL
Ohio U. L
π Oklahoma City U. .... R
Oklahoma State L
π Oneonta (SUNY)(NY) .... M
Oregon, U. of L
Pacific Lutheran (WA) .... R
Pacific, U. of the (CA) .... R
Portland State (OR) L
Potsdam (SUNY) (NY) .... M
Purchase (SUNY) (NY) .... R
π Puget Sound (WA) .... R
Queens (NC) .... R
Queens (CUNY)(NY) L
Redlands, U. of (CA) .... R
Rhode Island, U. of L
Roanoke (VA) .... R
Rowan (NJ) .... M
San Francisco Conservatory (CA) .... S
Santa Clara U. (CA) .... M
Shepherd (WV) .... M
▲ St. Catherine (MN) .... R
Stetson (FL) .... R
Stony Brook (SUNY)(NY) L
Susquehanna (PA) .... R
Syracuse (NY) L
Temple (PA) .... M
Texas Christian .... M
Tulsa, U. of (OK) .... M
Utah State L
Valparaiso (IN) .... R
Wartburg (IA) .... R
Webster (MO) .... R
Wells (NY) .... S
West Chester (PA) .... M
West Virginia, U. of L
Western Michigan L
Whitworth (WA) .... R
William Jewell Col. (MO) .... R
Wisconsin Lutheran .... S
Wittenberg (OH) .... R
Wooster, College of (OH) .... R

π *Music and Music Business*

MUSIC continues next page

Enrollment Code

■ *Men Only*
▲ *Women Only*

S = Small (less than 1000 students) R = Moderate (1000-3000 students) M = Medium (3000-8000 students)
L = Large (8000-20,000 students) XL = Extra Large (over 20,000 students)

MUSIC, continued

GROUP III
Selective

Alderson-Broaddus (WV)	S
Anderson (IN)	R
Andrews (MI)	R
Anna Maria (MA)	S
Arkansas, U. of	L
Arts, U. of the (PA)	R
➤Azusa Pacific (CA)	R
Baker (KS)	R
π Baldwin-Wallace (OH)	R
Belhaven (MS)	S
➤Belmont (TN)	R
Benedictine (KS)	R
Berea (WV)	R
Bethany (KS)	S
Bethany (WV)	R
Bethel (IN)	R
Bethel (KS)	S
Bowling Green (OH)	L
Bluffton (OH)	S
Brenau (GA)	R
Briar Cliff (IA)	R
Bridgewater (VA)	R
California State U. (East Bay)	M
California State U. (Fresno)	L
California State U. (Fullerton)	L
California State U. (Long Beach)	L
California State U. (Northridge)	L
California State U. (Sacramento)	M
California State U. (San Jose)	L
Carson-Newman (TN)	R
Carthage (WI)	R
Cedarville (OH)	R
Central Connecticut	M
Central Michigan	L
Central Oklahoma	L
Central Washington	L
Charleston Southern (SC)	R
Christopher Newport (VA)	M
Coker (SC)	S
Cumberland (KY)	R
Dana (NE)	S
Duquesne (PA)	M
East Carolina	L
Eastern Michigan	L
π Elmhurst (IL)	R

➤Five Towns College (NY)	S
Fort Hays (KS)	M
Friends (KS)	R
Goshen (IN)	R
Hannibal-La Grange (MO)	R
Hardin-Simmons (TX)	R
Hartford, U. of (CT)	M
Hartwick (NY)	R
Hastings (NE)	S
Heidelberg (OH)	R
Holy Names (CA)	S
Huntingdon (AL)	S
Indiana (PA)	L
Indiana State	L
Jacksonville (FL)	R
John Brown (AR)	R
Johnson State (VT)	R
Keene State (NH)	R
Kent State (OH)	L
Lock Haven (PA)	M
Longwood (VA)	R
Louisiana College	R
Louisiana-Lafayette	L
Louisville (KY)	L
π Loyola (LA)	M
Marywood (PA)	R
Massachusetts, U. of (Boston)	M
Massachusetts, U. of (Lowell)	M
Memphis, U. of (TN)	L
▲Meredith (NC)	R
Minnesota State U. (Moorhead)	M
Minnesota, U. of (Duluth)	M
Mississippi College	R
π Monmouth (NJ)	R
Montana, U. of	M
Montevallo (AL)	R
Mount St. Joseph (OH)	R
Mount St. Mary's (CA)	R
Muskingum (OH)	R
Nevada, U. of (Las Vegas)	L
Nevada, U. of (Reno)	L

➤ *Music Business*

π *Music and Music Business*

GROUP III continues next page

MUSIC, continued

••• ———— **GROUP III, continued** ———— •••

Northern Colorado	L
Northwestern College (IA)	R
Northwestern Louisiana	L
Nyack (NY)	R
Oklahoma Baptist	R
Oral Roberts (OK)	M
Otterbein (OH)	R
Ouachita (AR)	R
Peru State (NE)	R
Philadelphia Biblical (PA)	S
Pittsburg State (KS)	M
Rhode Island College	M
Rider (NJ)	M
Rocky Mountain (MT)	S
Roosevelt (IL)	R
Samford (AL)	R
▲ Seton Hill (PA)	S
Shenandoah (VA)	R
Shorter (GA)	R
Simpson (IA)	R
Slippery Rock (PA)	M
Sonoma State (CA)	M
South Dakota, U. of	M
South Florida, U. of	L
π Southern Illinois U. (Carbondale)	L
Southern Maine	M
Southern Mississippi	L
Southwest Baptist (MO)	R
Southwestern (KS)	S
Sterling (KS)	S
Tampa, U. of (FL)	R
Tarleton State (TX)	M
Texas Lutheran	R
Texas, U. of (San Antonio)	L
Towson (MD)	L
Union University (TN)	R
Virginia Commonwealth	L
Viterbo (WI)	R
Weber State (UT)	L
Western Carolina (NC)	M
Western Connecticut	M
π Western Illlinois	L
Western St. Coll. of Colorado	R
Westfield (MA)	M
π William Paterson (NJ)	M
Wingate (NC)	R
π Wisconsin, U. of (Stevens Point)	M
Xavier U. of Louisiana	R

π *Music and Music Business*

NURSING

GROUP I
Most Selective

▲Barnard (NY) .... R
  Binghamton (SUNY) (NY) L
  Boston Col. (MA) L
  Buffalo (SUNY)(NY) L
  Case Western Reserve U. (OH) .... M
  Colorado, U. of L
  Columbia (NY) .... M
  Duke (NC) .... M
  Emory (GA) .... M
  Florida, U. of XL
  Gustavus Adolphus (MN) .... R
  Illinois, U. of XL
  Illinois Wesleyan .... R

  Johns Hopkins (MD) .... M
  Missouri, U. of XL
  New York U. L
  North Carolina, U. of L
  Northern Michigan .... M
  Pennsylvania, U. of L
  Rochester, U. of (NY) .... M
  St. Olaf (MN) .... R
  Vanderbilt (TN) .... M
  Villanova (PA) .... M
  Virginia, U. of L
  Washington, U. of XL
  Wisconsin, U. of L

GROUP II
Very Selective

  Adelphi (NY) .... M
  Alabama, U. of (Huntsville) .... M
  Arizona, U. of XL
  Barry (FL) .... R
  Baylor (TX) .... M
  Belmont (TN) .... R
  Bethel (MN) .... R
  Bradley (IL) .... M
  Calvin (MI) .... R
  Capital (OH) .... R
  Carroll (WI) .... R
  Catholic U. (DC) .... M
  Cincinnati, U. of (OH) L
  Clarke (IA) .... S
  Coe (IA) .... R
  Connecticut, U. of XL
  Creighton (NE) .... M
  Daemen (NY) .... R
  Delaware, U. of L
  Detroit Mercy (MI) .... M
  Duquesne (PA) .... M
  Elmira (NY) .... R
  Evansville (IN) .... R
  Fairfield (CT) .... M
  Florida Gulf Coast U. .... M
  Florida International L
  Franciscan U. of Steubenville (OH) .... R
  George Mason (VA) .... M

  Georgetown (DC) .... M
  Gwynedd-Mercy (PA) .... S
  Harding (AR) .... M
  Hunter (CUNY) (NY) L
  Illinois, U. of (Chicago) L
  Indiana U. XL
  Indiana U. of Pennsylvania L
  Iowa, U. of XL
  Lebanon Valley (PA) .... R
  Lipscomb (TN) .... R
  Loyola (IL) .... M
  Luther (IA) .... R
  Maine, U. of L
  Marquette (WI) .... M
➤Maryland, U. of (Baltimore County) .... M
  Massachusetts, U. of L
  McKendree (IL) .... R
  McMurry (TX) .... R
  Michigan, U. of XL
  Milwaukee Sch. of Engine (WI) .... R
  Minnesota, U. of XL
  Mississippi U. for Women .... R
  Missouri, U. of (St. Louis) .... M
  Mobile, U. of (AL) .... R

➤ *Health Policy, also*

GROUP II continues next page

NURSING, continued

GROUP II, continued

Montana Tech. .... R	▲Simmons (MA) .... R
Moravian (PA).................................... R	South Carolina, U. of.......................... L
Morningside (IA) .... S	South Dakota School of Mines .... R
Mount Mercy (IA) .... S	St. Anselm (NH) .... R
New Jersey, College of .... M	▲St. Catherine (MN) .... R
New Mexico, U. of L	St John's/St. Benedict (MN) .... R
North Dakota, U. of........................... M	St. Louis (MO) .... M
North Florida .... M	▲St. Mary's College (IN) .... R
Northeastern (MA) L	Texas Christian U. .... M
Ohio Northern.................................... R	Texas, U. of (Health Sci. Ctr.-S. Antonio) .... R
Ohio State XL	Truman State (MO) .... M
Pace (NY) .... M	Union University (TN) .... R
Pacific Lutheran (WA) .... R	Valparaiso U. (IN)............................... M
Pennsylvania State XL	Vermont, U. of .... M
Pittsburgh, U. of (PA)......................... L	Viterbo (WI) .... R
Portland, U. of (OR)........................... R	Virginia Commonwealth L
Purdue (IN) XL	Webster (MD) .... R
Rockhurst (MO) .... R	Western Michigan L
Samford (AL) .... R	Westminster (UT) .... R
San Diego, U. of (CA) .... M	William Jewell (MO) .... R
San Francisco, U. of (CA) .... M	Wisconsin, U. of (Milwaukee) XL
Seattle Pacific (WA) .... R	Wyoming, U. of.................................. M
Seton Hall (NJ) .... M	York (PA) .... M

NURSING continues next page

NURSING, continued

GROUP III
Selective

Abilene Christian (TX)	M	Eastern Mennonite (VA)	R
Akron, U. of (OH)	L	Eastern Michigan	L
Alabama, U. of (Birmingham)	M	Eastern Oregon	R
Alabama, U. of (Huntsville)	M	Eastern Washington	L
Alaska, U. of (Fairbanks)	M	Edgewood (WI)	S
Alderson-Broaddus (WV)	S	Elmhurst (IL)	R
▲ Alverno (WI)	R	Elms (MA)	S
Andrews (MI)	R	Emporia State (KS)	M
Arizona State	XL	Fairmont State (WV)	M
Avila (MO)	S	Ferris State (MI)	L
Azusa Pacific (CA)	R	Fitchburg (MA)	R
Baker (KS)	R	Fort Hays (KS)	M
Ball State (IN)	L	Gannon (PA)	M
Bellarmine (KY)	R	Georgia Southern	L
Berea (KY)	R	Georgia Southwestern	R
Bethel (IN)	R	Georgia State	L
Bethel (KS)	S	Goshen (IN)	R
Bloomsburg (PA)	M	Graceland (IA)	R
Boise State (ID)	L	Grambling (LA)	M
Briar Cliff (IA)	R	Hardin-Simmons (TX)	R
Brockport (SUNY)(NY)	M	Hartwick (NY)	R
California (PA)	M	Hawaii Pacific	M
California State U. (Bakersfield)	M	Henderson State (AR)	M
California State U. (Chico)	L	Holy Names (CA)	S
California State U. (Dominguez Hills)	M	Howard (DC)	M
California State U. (Fresno)	L	Husson (ME)	S
California State U. (Fullerton)	L	Idaho State	L
California State U. (Los Angeles)	L	Immaculata (PA)	S
California State U. (San Jose)	L	Ind.U.-Purdue U.-Indianapolis (IN)	L
Carroll (MT)	R	Jacksonville (FL)	R
Carson-Newman (TN)	R	Jacksonville State (AL)	M
▲ Cedar Crest (PA)	S	Jamestown (ND)	R
Cedarville (OH)	R	Kansas Wesleyan	S
Central Arkansas	M	Kennesaw State (GA)	R
Central Missouri	L	Kent State (OH)	L
Charleston, U. of (WV)	S	King (TN)	S
Colby-Sawyer (NH)	S	Lewis-Clark State (ID)	R
Colorado, U. of (Colorado Springs)	M	Liberty (VA)	R
Dillard (LA)	R	Long Island U. (Brooklyn)(NY)	M
Dominican (CA)	S	Louisiana College	R
D'Youville (NY)	R	Louisiana-Lafayette	L
East Carolina (NC)	L	MacMurray (IL)	S
East Tennessee	L	Malone (OH)	R
Eastern (PA)	R		
Eastern Kentucky	L		

GROUP III continues next page

NURSING, continued

GROUP III, continued

Marshall (WV)	L
Marymount (VA)	R
Maryville (St. Louis) (MO)	R
Massachusetts, U. of (Boston)	M
Massachusetts, U. of (Dartmouth)	M
Memphis, U. of (TN)	L
Mercy (NY)	M
Midwestern State U. (TX)	M
Milligan (TN)	R
Misericordia, College (PA)	S
Mississippi College	R
Molloy (NY)	R
Montana State	L
Mount St. Joseph (OH)	R
Mount St. Mary's (CA)	R
Mount St. Mary's (NY)	S
Murray State (KY)	M
Nevada, U. of (Las Vegas)	L
Nevada, U. of (Reno)	L
Nichols State (LA)	M
North Carolina, U. of (Charlotte)	L
North Carolina, U. of (Greensboro)	M
Northern Colorado	L
Northern Illinois U.	L
Northwestern Louisiana	L
Oakland (MI)	M
Oklahoma Baptist	R
Oklahoma City U.	R
Olivet Nazarene (IL)	R
Oral Roberts (OK)	M
▲Pine Manor (MA)	S
Pittsburgh, U. of (Bradford)	R
Plattsburgh (SUNY) (NY)	M
Point Loma (CA)	R
Presentation (SD)	S
Regis (CO)	R
Rhode Island, U. of	L
Rockford (IL)	S
Russell Sage (The Sage Colleges)(NY)	R
Saginaw Valley (MI)	M
St. Ambrose (IA)	R
St. Joseph's (ME)	S

St, Mary, College of (NE)	S
# St. Scholastica (MN)	R
Salem State (MA)	M
San Diego State (CA)	L
Seattle U. (WA)	R
Shenandoah (VA)	R
Sonoma State (CA)	M
South Alabama	M
South Dakota, U. of	M
South Florida, U. of	L
Southern Illinois U. (Edwardsville)	L
Southern Maine, U. of	M
Southern Mississippi	L
Southern Nazarene (OK)	R
Southwestern (KS)	S
Texas A&M (Corpus Christi)	M
Texas, U.of (Arlington)	L
Texas, U.of (Tyler)	R
Thomas More (KY)	R
Towson (MD)	L
Troy State (AL)	M
Tuskegee University (AL)	M
Union (NE)	R
Union University (TN)	R
Villa Julie (MD)	R
Walla Walla (WA)	R
Walsh (OH)	R
Washburn (KS)	M
Wayne State (MI)	L
Weber State (UT)	L
Western Carolina (NC)	M
Western Connecticut State	M
Western Kentucky	L
Wheeling Jesuit (WV)	R
Widener (PA)	R
Wilkes (PA)	R
Wisconsin, U. of (Eau Claire)	L
Worcester State (MA)	M
Wright State (OH)	L

 # Also, Health Informatics and Information Systems

Enrollment Code	
■ *Men Only*	S = Small (less than 1000 students) R = Moderate (1000-3000 students) M = Medium (3000-8000 students)
▲ *Women Only*	L = Large (8000-20,000 students) XL = Extra Large (over 20,000 students)

PHARMACY

GROUP I
Most Selective

Buffalo (SUNY) (NY) L	Michigan, U. of XL
Butler (IN) .... R	North Carolina, U. of L
Creighton (NE) .... M	Purdue (IN) XL
Florida, U. of XL	Rutgers (NJ) L
Illinois, U. of XL	Wisconsin, U. of L
Iowa, U. of XL	

GROUP II
Very Selective

Albany Col. of Pharmacy (NY) .... S	North Dakota State L
Arizona, U. of XL	Ohio Northern U. .... R
Auburn (AL) L	Ohio State XL
Campbell (NC) .... R	Pacific, U. of the (CA) .... R
Cincinnati, U. of (OH) L	Palm Beach Atlantic (FL) .... R
Connecticut, U. of XL	Pittsburgh, U. of L
Drake (IA) .... M	Rhode Island, U. of L
Duquesne (PA) .... M	Samford (AL) .... R
Ferris State (MI) L	+ Sciences in Philadelphia, U. of (PA) .... R
Florida A&M L	South Carolina, U. of L
Georgia, U. of L	South Dakota State U. .... M
Idaho State L	Southern California, U. of L
Illinois, U. of (Chicago) L	Southwestern Oklahoma .... M
Kansas, U. of L	St. John's (NY) L
Kentucky, U. of L	St. Louis Col. of Pharmacy (MO) .... S
Maryland, U. of XL	Temple (PA) L
Mass. College of Pharmacy .... R	Texas, U. of (Austin) XL
Mercer (GA) .... R	Toledo, U. of L
Minnesota, U. of XL	Utah, U. of L
Mississippi, U. of L	Virginia Commonwealth U. L
Missouri, U. of (Kansas City) .... M	Washington State L
Montana, U. of .... M	Wayne State (MI) L
New Mexico, U. of L	West Virginia U. L
Northeastern (MA) L	Wyoming, U. of L
Northwestern Louisiana L	Xavier (LA) .... R

+ *Also Pharmaceutical Marketing*

PHILOSOPHY

GROUP I
Most Selective

Albany (SUNY)(NY)	L	Kenyon (OH)	R
American (DC)	M	Lawrence (WI)	R
Austin (TX)	R	Macalester (MN)	R
▲ Barnard (NY)	R	Michigan, U. of	XL
Bates (ME)	R	New College (FL)	S
Binghamton (SUNY) (NY)	L	New York U.	L
Boston Col. (MA)	L	North Carolina, U. of	L
Boston U. (MA)	L	Notre Dame (IN)	M
Bowdoin (ME)	R	Oberlin (OH)	R
Brown (RI)	M	Ohio State	XL
Bucknell (PA)	M	Pennsylvania, U. of	L
California, U. of (Berkeley)	XL	Pittsburgh, U. of (PA)	L
California, U. of (Los Angeles)	XL	Pomona (CA)	R
Carleton (MN)	R	Princeton (NJ)	M
Carnegie Mellon (PA)	M	Reed (OR)	R
Centre (KY)	R	Rhodes (TN)	R
Chicago, U. of (IL)	M	Rochester, U. of (NY)	M
Claremont McKenna (CA)	R	Rutgers (NJ)	L
Colby (ME)	R	▲ Smith (MA)	R
Colgate (NY)	R	Southwestern (TX)	R
Colorado Col.	R	St. Olaf (MN)	R
Columbia (NY)	M	Swarthmore (PA)	R
Connecticut Col.	R	Texas, U. of (Austin)	XL
Cornell (NY)	L	Trinity (CT)	R
Creighton (NE)	M	Trinity (TX)	R
Dallas, U. of (TX)	R	Tufts (MA)	M
Davidson (NC)	R	Tulane (LA)	M
DePauw (IN)	R	Vanderbilt (TN)	M
Duke (NC)	M	Vassar (NY)	R
Florida State	L	Villanova (PA)	M
Florida, U. of	XL	■ Wabash (IN)	S
Geneseo (SUNY)(NY)	M	Washington U. (MO)	M
George Washington (DC)	M	Washington, U. of	XL
Georgetown (DC)	M	Wheaton (IL)	R
Hamilton (NY)	R	Whitman (WA)	R
Harvard (MA)	M	Willamette (OR)	R
Haverford (PA)	S	Willaim & Mary (VA)	R
Holy Cross (MA)	R	Wisconsin, U. of	XL
Johns Hopkins (MD)	M	Yale (CT)	M

PHILOSOPHY continues next page

PHILOSOPHY continues next page

Enrollment Code	
■ *Men Only*	S = Small (less than 1000 students) R = Moderate (1000-3000 students) M = Medium (3000-8000 students)
▲ *Women Only*	L = Large (8000-20,000 students) XL = Extra Large (over 20,000 students)

PHILOSOPHY, continued

GROUP II
Very Selective

Alabama, U. of	L	Fordham (NY)	L
Alabama, U. of (Birmingham)	M	Fort Hays (KS)	M
Alabama, U. of (Huntsville)	M	Franciscan U. of Steubenville (OH)	R
Allegheny (PA)	R	George Mason (VA)	L
Albion (MI)	R	Georgia State	L
Arizona, U. of	XL	Georgia, U. of	L
Asbury (KY)	R	Gonzaga (WA)	E
Assumption (MA)	R	Hanover (IN)	R
Bellarmine (KY)	R	Herbert Lehman (CUNY)(NY)	L
Belmont (TN)	R	Hood (MD)	S
Benedictine (KS)	R	Illinois, U. of (Chicago)	L
Bethel (IN)	R	Indiana (PA)	L
Bethel (MN)	M	Indiana U.	XL
Biola (CA)	R	Iowa State	XL
Bowling Green (OH)	L	John Carroll (OH)	R
Brooklyn (CUNY)(NY)	L	Kansas State	L
California, U. of (Santa Barbara)	L	Loras (IA)	R
California State U. (Dominguez Hills)	M	Louisiana State	XL
California State U. (Fresno)	L	Loyola (IL)	M
California State U. (Hayward)	M	Loyola (LA)	M
California State U. (Long Beach)	L	Lycoming (PA)	R
California State U. (Northridge)	L	Maine, U. of	L
California State U. (Stanislaus)	M	Mansfield (PA)	R
Calvin (MI)	R	Marquette (WI)	M
Carroll (MT)	R	Maryland, U. of	XL
Catholic (DC)	R	Mass. College of Lib. Arts (N.Adams)	R
Central (IA)	R	Massachusetts, U. of (Boston)	M
Central Florida	L	Messiah (PA)	R
Christendom (VA)	S	Milligan (TN)	S
Christopher Newport (VA)	M	Minnesota, U. of	XL
City College (CUNY)(NY)	L	Minnesota, U. of (Morris)	R
Clarke (IA)	S	Missouri, U. of (St. Louis)	M
Coastal Carolina (SC)	M	Mount Mercy (IA)	S
Cornell Col. (IA)	R	Muhlenberg (PA)	R
Denison (OH)	R	New Hampshire, U. of	L
DePaul (IL)	L	New Paltz (SUNY)(NY)	M
DeSales (PA)	S	North Carolina, U. of (Charlotte)	L
Detroit Mercy (MI)	M	Northeastern (MA)	L
Doane (NB)	S	Northern Illinois	`L
Earlham (IN)	R	Oneonta (SUNY)(NY)	M
East Tennessee	L	Oregon State	L
Edinboro (PA)	M	Ozarks, College of the (MO)	R
Elon (NC)	R	Portland, U. of (OR)	R
Frostburg (MD)	M		

GROUP II continues next page

PHILOSOPHY, continued

GROUP II, continued

Providence (RI)	M	Salisbury State (MD)	M
Queens (CUNY)(NY)	L	Santa Clara U. (CA)	M
Regis (CO)	R	Seattle U. (WA)	R
Rhode Island College	M	Seton Hall (NJ)	M
Richard Stockton (NJ)	M	Skidmore (NY)	R
Rowan (NJ)	M	South Alabama	M
St. Ambrose (IA)	R	South Florida, U. of	L
St. Andrews Presbyterian (NC)	S	Stony Brook (SUNY) (NY)	L
St. Bonaventure (NY)	R	Texas A&M	XL
▲St. Catherine (MN)	R	Transylvania (KY)	R
St. Cloud (MN)	L	Utah, U. of	L
St. John's (NY)	L	Webster (MO)	R
St. John's/St. Benedict (MN)	R	West Chester (PA)	M
St. Louis (MO)	M	Westminster (UT)	R
▲St. Mary's College (IN)	R	Wheeling Jesuit (WV)	R
St. Mary's (MN)	R	Wofford (SC)	R
St. Thomas (MN)	M	Worcester State (MA)	M
St. Thomas, U. of (TX)	R	Xavier (OH)	R

Enrollment Code

■ Men Only
▲ Women Only

S = **Small** (less than 1000 students) R = **Moderate** (1000-3000 students) M = **Medium** (3000-8000 students)
L = **Large** (8000-20,000 students) XL = **Extra Large** (over 20,000 students)

PHYSICS

GROUP I
Most Selective

Albany (SUNY)(NY)	L	Kalamazoo (MI)	R
Allegheny (PA)	R	Lawrence (WI)	R
Amherst (MA)	R	Lehigh (PA)	M
▲Barnard (NY)	R	Macalester (MN)	R
Bates (ME)	R	MIT (MA)	M
Binghamton (SUNY) (NY)	L	Michigan, U. of	XL
Boston U. (MA)	L	Michigan, U. of (Dearborn)	M
Brandeis (MA)	M	Middlebury (VT)	R
Brown (RI)	M	New College (FL)	S
▲Bryn Mawr (PA)	S	New Mexico Inst. of Mining & Tech.	R
California Inst. of Tech.	S	New York U.	L
California, U. of (Berkeley)	XL	Notre Dame (IN)	M
California, U. of (San Diego)	L	Oberlin (OH)	R
Carleton (MN)	R	Occidental (CA)	R
Carnegie Mellon (PA)	M	Pennsylvania, U. of	L
Case Western Reserve U. (OH)	M	Pomona (CA)	R
Centre (KY)	R	Princeton (NJ)	M
Chicago, U. of (IL)	M	Reed (OR)	R
Clarkson (NY)	M	Rensselaer (NY)	M
Colorado School of Mines	R	Rhodes (TN)	R
Columbia (NY)	M	Rice (TX)	R
Cornell (NY)	L	Rochester, U. of (NY)	M
Dartmouth (NH)	M	Rose-Hulman (IN)	R
Denison (OH)	R	Rutgers (NJ)	L
DePauw (IN)	R	St. Olaf (MN)	R
Dickinson (PA)	R	▲Smith (MA)	R
Florida, U. of	XL	South, U. of the (TN)	R
Franklin & Marshall (PA)	R	Stanford (CA)	M
Geneseo (SUNY) (NY)	M	Swarthmore (PA)	R
Georgetown (DC)	M	Texas, U. of (Dallas)	M
Georgia Inst. of Tech.	M	Trinity (TX)	R
Grinnell (IA)	R	United States Air Force Academy (CO)	M
Gustavus Adolphus (MN)	R	Vanderbilt (TN)	M
Hamilton (NY)	R	Wake Forest (NC)	M
Harvard (MA)	M	Washington & Lee (VA)	R
Harvey Mudd (CA)	S	Washington, U. of	XL
Haverford (PA)	S	Washington U. (MO)	M
Holy Cross (MA)	R	▲Wellesley (MA)	R
Illinois, U. of (Urbana-Champaign)	XL	Wheaton (IL)	R
Illinois Wesleyan	R	Whitman (WA)	R
Iowa State	XL	William & Mary (VA)	M
Iowa, U. of	XL	Worcester Poly. Inst. (MA)	R
Johns Hopkins (MD)	M	Yeshiva (NY)	R
Kenyon (OH)	R		

PHYSICS, continued

GROUP II
Very Selective

Adelphi (NY) .... M
▲ Agnes Scott (GA) .... S
Arizona State XL
Auburn (AL) L
Augsburg (MN) .... R
Beloit (WI) .... R
Bethany (WV) .... S
Bradley (IL) .... M
Cal. Poly. State U. (San Luis Obispo) L
California, U. of (Davis) L
California, U. of (Irvine) L
California, U. of (Santa Barbara) L
California, U. of (Santa Cruz) .... M
Calvin (MI) .... R
Catholic (DC) .... R
Central Florida L
Clark (MA) .... R
Clemson (SC) L
Coe (IA) .... R
Colorado, U. of L
Colorado, U. of (Colorado Springs) .... M
Creighton (NE) .... M
Denver, U. of (CO) .... M
Elmhurst (IL) .... R
Evansville, U. of (IN) .... R
Fairfield (CT) .... M
Florida Inst. of Tech .... R
Florida State L
George Mason (VA) L
Guilford (NC) .... R
Hamline (MN) .... R
Hanover (IN) .... R
Hendrix (AR) .... R
Idaho, U. of L
Kansas State L
Kent State (OH) L
Knox (IL) .... R
Lewis & Clark (OR) .... R
Linfield (OR) .... R
Loras (IA) .... R
Loyola (IL) .... M
Mansfield (PA) .... R

Marietta (OH) .... R
Maryland, U. of XL
Maryland, U. of (Baltimore County) ...... M
Massachusetts, U. of (Lowell) .... M
Mississippi, U. of L
Montana State L
Nebraska, U. of L
New Hampshire, U. of L
New Orleans (LA) L
North Carolina State L
Ohio State XL
Ohio U. L
Oklahoma State L
Oregon State L
Pacific University (OR) .... R
Pittsburgh, U. of (PA) L
Presbyterian (SC) .... R
Rochester Inst. of Tech. (NY) L
Rollins (FL) .... R
Rowan (NJ) .... M
St. John's (MN) .... R
Santa Clara U. (CA) .... M
Shippensburg (PA) .... M
Sonoma State (CA) .... M
South Carolina, U. of L
South Dakota School of Mines .... R
Stockton State (NJ) .... M
Stony Brook (SUNY) (NY) L
Syracuse (NY) L
Tennessee, U. of XL
Texas, U. of (Austin) XL
Tulsa, U. of (OK) .... M
Ursinus (PA) .... R
Vermont, U. of .... M
Washington State L
Westminster (UT) .... R
Whitworth (WA) .... R
William Jewell (MO) .... R
Wisconsin, U. of XL
Xavier (OH) .... R

PHYSICS continues next page

Enrollment Code
■ *Men Only* | S = Small (less than 1000 students) | R = Moderate (1000-3000 students) | M = Medium (3000-8000 students)
▲ *Women Only* | L = Large (8000-20,000 students) | XL = Extra Large (over 20,000 students)

PHYSICS, continued

GROUP III
Selective

Arkansas, U. of	L	Louisiana State	XL
Ball State (IN)	L	▲ Mary Baldwin (VA)	S
Brooklyn Col. (CUNY) (NY)	L	Mass. College of Lib. Arts (N. Adams)	R
California Poly. State U. (Pomona)	L	Massachusetts, U. of (Boston)	M
California State U. (Dominguez Hills)	M	Millersville (PA)	M
California State U. (Northridge)	L	Minnesota State U. (Moorhead)	M
California State U. (San Jose)	L	Muskingum (OH)	R
Carthage (WI)	R	Nevada, U. of (Reno)	L
Christopher Newport (VA)	M	Northern Illinois U.	L
City Col. (CUNY) (NY)	L	Northern Michigan	M
Clark Atlanta (GA)	M	Northwestern (IA)	R
Doane (NE)	S	Ozarks, College of the (MO)	R
Eastern Michigan	L	Penn State (Erie)(PA)	M
Edinboro (PA)	M	Southern Connecticut	M
Fisk (TN)	S	Thomas More (KY)	R
Florida A&M	M	Tuskegee (AL)	M
Fort Lewis (CO)	M	Union (TN)	R
Georgia State	L	Washburn (KS)	M
Goshen (IN)	R	Weber State (UT)	L
Hastings (NE)	R	π West Virginia Wesleyan	R
Indiana (PA)	L	Western Kentucky	L
Indiana State	L	Western Michigan	L
Jacksonville (FL)	R	Wisconsin, U. of (Milwaukee)	L
Louisiana-Lafayette	L		

π *Engineering Physics*

POLITICAL SCIENCE

●━━━━━━━━━━━━ **GROUP I** ━━━━━━━━━━━━●
Most Selective

American U. (DC)	M	Michigan, U. of	XL
Amherst (MA)	R	Middlebury (VT)	R
Binghamton (SUNY)(NY)	L	▲Mount Holyoke (MA)	R
▲Barnard (NY)	R	North Carolina, U. of	L
Bates (ME)	R	Northwestern (IL)	M
Boston College (MA)	L	Notre Dame (IN)	M
Boston U. (MA)	L	Oberlin (OH)	R
Bowdoin (ME)	R	Occidental (CA)	R
Brandeis (MA)	R	Pennsylvania, U. of	L
Brown (RI)	M	Pomona (CA)	R
California, U. of (Berkeley)	XL	Princeton (NJ)	M
California, U. of (Los Angeles)	XL	Rhodes (TN)	R
California, U. of (San Diego)	L	Richmond, U. of (VA)	M
Carleton (MN)	R	Rochester, U. of (NY)	M
Centre (KY)	R	Rutgers (NJ)	L
Chicago, U. of (IL)	M	▲Scripps (CA)	S
Claremont McKenna (CA)	R	▲Smith (MA)	R
Colby (ME)	R	South, U. of the (TN)	R
Colgate (NY)	R	Southwestern (TX)	R
Colorado Col.	R	Stanford (CA)	M
Columbia (NY)	M	Swarthmore (PA)	R
Connecticut Col.	R	Texas A&M	XL
Connecticut, U. of	XL	Texas, U. of (Austin)	XL
Dallas, U. of (TX)	R	Trinity (TX)	R
Dartmouth (NH)	M	Tufts (MA)	M
Davidson (NC)	M	Tulane (LA)	M
DePauw (IN)	R	Union (NY)	R
Dickinson (PA)	R	U.S. Air Force Academy (CO)	M
Drew (NJ)	R	U.S. Military Academy (NY)	M
Duke (NC)	M	U.S. Naval Academy (MD)	M
Emory (GA)	M	Ursinus (PA)	R
Florida, U. of	XL	Vanderbilt (TN)	M
Franklin & Marshall (PA)	R	Villanova (PA)	M
Furman (SC)	R	Virginia, U. of	L
Georgetown (DC)	M	■Wabash (IN)	S
George Washington (DC)	M	Wake Forest (NC)	M
Grinnell (IA)	R	Washington & Lee (VA)	R
Hamilton (NY)	R	▲Wellesley (MA)	R
Harvard (MA)	M	Wesleyan (CT)	R
Holy Cross (MA)	R	Whitman (WA)	R
Illinois, U. of	XL	Willamette (OR)	R
Johns Hopkins (MD)	M	William & Mary (VA)	M
Kenyon (OH)	R	Williams (MA)	R
Lehigh (PA)	M	Yale (CT)	M
Macalester (MN)	R	Yeshiva (NY)	R
MIT (MA)	M		
Miami, U. of (OH)	L		

POLITICAL SCIENCE continues next page

POLITICAL SCIENCE, continued

GROUP II
Very Selective

▲Agnes Scott (GA) .... S
Albany (SUNY)(NY) L
Albertson (ID) .... S
Albion (MI) .... R
Alma (MI) .... R
Arcadia (PA)..................................... R
Auburn (AL) L
Austin (TX) .... R
Belmont (TN) .... R
Bethany (WV) .... S
Bradley (IL) .... M
California, U. of (Davis) L
California, U. of (Riverside) L
California, U. of (Santa Barbara) L
Catholic U. (DC) .... M
Clark (MA) .... R
Clemson (SC) L
Colorado State L
College of Charleston (SC) L
Cornell College (IA) .... R
Creighton (NE) .... M
Dayton, U. of (OH) .... M
Delaware, U. of L
Denison (OH) .... R
DePaul (IL) L
Drake (IA) .... M
Elon (NC) .... R
Florida International L
George Mason (VA) L
Georgia, U. of Xl
Gonzaga (WA) .... R
Grove City (PA) .... R
Guilford (NC)..................................... R
Hampden-Sydney (VA) .... S
Hawaii, U. of L
Hillsdale (MI).................................... R
Hobart & William Smith (NY) .... R
Hofstra (NY)..................................... M
Hope (MI)... R
Howard (DC) .... M
Illinois College .... S
Illinois, U. of (Chicago)..................... L
Iowa, U. of....................................... XL
James Madison (VA).......................... M
John Carroll (OH) .... R
Kansas, U. of L
Knox (IL)... R
Lake Forest (IL) .... R
Lipscomb (TN) .... R

Manhattan (NY) .... M
Manhattanville (NY).......................... R
Marist (NY) .... M
Marquette (WI) .... M
Maryland, U. of XL
Maryland, U. of (Baltimore County) .... M
Massachusetts, U. of L
Millersville (PA) .... M
Minnesota, U. of XL
Minnesota, U. of (Morris).................. R
Missouri, U. of (St. Louis) .... M
North Carolina (Charlotte) L
North Central (IL) .... R
Oglethorpe (GA)............................... S
Ohio State XL
Ohio U. L
Ohio Wesleyan................................. R
Oklahoma City U. .... R
Oklahoma, U. of XL
Oklahoma State L
Oregon, U. of L
Pittsburgh, U. of (PA)....................... L
Portland, U. of (OR).......................... R
Presbyterian (SC) .... R
Providence (RI) .... M
Puget Sound (WA) .... R
Purchase (SUNY)(NY) .... R
Randolph Macon (VA) .... R
Redlands, U. of (CA) .... R
Richard Stockton (NJ) .... M
Ripon (WI) .... S
Roanoke (VA).................................... R
St. Bonaventure (NY) .... R
St. Cloud (MN) L
St. John's (MN) .... R
St. John's (NY) L
St. Joseph's (PA) .... R
St. Lawrence (NY) .... R
St. Mary's College of Maryland .... R
San Diego, U. of (CA) .... M
Santa Clara U. (CA)........................... M
Siena (NY).. R
Skidmore (NY) .... R
South Carolina................................. L
Spring Hill (AL) .... R
Stonehill (MA) .... R
Stony Brook (SUNY)(NY) L

GROUP II continues next page

POLITICAL SCIENCE, continued

GROUP II, continued

Susquehanna (PA) .... R
▲ Sweet Briar (VA) .... S
Syracuse (NY) L
Tennessee, U. of XL
▲ Trinity (DC) .... S
Utah, U. of L
Vermont, U. of L
Washington & Jefferson (PA).............. R
Webster (MO) .... R
Westchester (PA) .... M
Western Washington U. .... R

Westminster (MO) .... S
Westminster (UT) .... R
Wheaton (MA) .... R
Wilberforce (OH) .... S
Winthrop (SC) .... M
Wisconsin, U. of XL
Wittenberg (OH) .... R
Wofford (SC) .... R
Wooster, College of the (OH) .... R
Wyoming, U. of L

GROUP III
Selective

Adrian (MI) .... R
Albright (PA) .... R
Appalachian State (NC) L
Arizona State XL
Azusa Pacific (CA) .... R
Baker (KS) .... R
Baldwin-Wallace (OH) .... R
Ball State (IN) L
Belmont Abbey (NC) .... S
▲ Bennett (NC) .... S
Bridgewater (MA) .... M
Brockport (SUNY)(NY) .... M
California State U. (Chico) L
California State U. (Fullerton) L
California State U. (Long Beach) L
California State U. (Northridge) L
California State U. (Sacramento) ...... M
California State U. (San Marcos) ...... M
California State U. (Stanislaus) .... M
Campbell (NC) .... R
Carthage (WI) .... R
▲ Chatham (PA)..................................... S
Christopher Newport (VA) .... M
City College (CUNY)(NY) L
▲ Converse (SC) .... S
Eastern Connecticut .... M
Eastern Kentucky L
Eastern Michigan L
Gardner-Webb (NC) .... S
Grambling (LA).................................. M

Hartwick (NY)..................................... R
Heidelburg (OH) .... S
Illinois State L
John Jay (CUNY)(NY) .... M
Kutztown (PA)..................................... M
Lock Haven (PA) .... M
Louisiana State XL
Louisville (KY) L
▲ Mary Baldwin (VA) .... S
Massachusetts, U. of (Boston)........... M
Mercyhurst (PA).................................. R
Michigan State...................................XL
Mt. St. Mary's (MD) .... R
▲ Pine Manor (MA) .... S
Radford (VA) .... M
Rhode Island, U. of L
St. Mary's (TX) .... R
South Dakota, U. of .... M
Southern Connecticut .... M
Southern Illinois U. (Carbondale) L
Southern Illinois U. (Edwardsville) L
Southwest Missouri L
▲ Spelman (GA) .... R
Suffolk (MA) .... R
Texas, U. of (Arlington) L
Utah State L
Virginia Wesleyan .... R
Westfield (MA) .... M
Whittier (CA) .... R
Wisconsin, U. of (Milwaukee) L

PRE-LAW

Author's Note: *Law School Associations usually recommend that a student choose a major dependent upon one's own individual intellectual interests and upon "the quality of undergraduate education" provided by various departments and colleges. The following recommended colleges have been taken primarily from our recommended departments in English, Economics, and Political Science.*

• ─────── GROUP I ─────── •
Most Selective

Albany (SUNY) (NY)	L	Duke (NC)	M
Allegheny (PA)	R	Emory (GA)	M
American U. (DC)	M	Florida, U. of	XL
Amherst (MA)	R	Franklin & Marshall (PA)	R
Bard (NY)	R	Furman (SC)	R
▲ Barnard (NY)	R	Georgetown (DC)	M
Bates (ME)	R	George Washington (DC)	M
Binghamton (SUNY) (NY)	L	Gettysburg (PA)	R
Boston Col. (MA)	L	Grinnell (IA)	R
Boston U. (MA)	L	Hamilton (NY)	R
Bowdoin (ME)	R	Harvard (MA)	M
Brandeis (MA)	R	Haverford (PA)	S
Brown (RI)	M	Holy Cross (MA)	R
▲ Bryn Mawr (PA)	S	Illinois, U. of (Chicago)	L
Bucknell (PA)	M	Illinois, U. of (Urbana-Champaign)	XL
Buffalo (SUNY) (NY)	L	Illinois Wesleyan	R
California, U. of (Berkeley)	XL	Iowa, U. of	XL
California, U. of (Los Angeles)	XL	Johns Hopkins (MD)	M
California, U. of (San Diego)	L	Kalamazoo (MI)	R
Carleton (MN)	R	Kenyon (OH)	R
Carnegie Mellon (PA)	M	Lafayette (PA)	R
Case Western Reserve (OH)	M	Macalester (MN)	R
Centre (KY)	R	Maryland, U. of (Baltimore County)	M
Chicago, U. of (IL)	M	MIT (MA)	M
Claremont McKenna (CA)	R	Miami, U. of (OH)	L
Clark (MA)	R	Michigan, U. of	XL
Clarkson (NY)	M	Middlebury (VT)	R
Colby (ME)	R	▲ Mount Holyoke (MA)	R
Colgate (NY)	R	Muhlenberg (PA)	R
Colorado Col.	R	New College (FL)	S
Columbia (NY)	M	New Jersey, College of	M
Connecticut Col.	R	North Carolina, U. of	L
Dallas, U. of (TX)	R	Northwestern (IL)	M
Dartmouth (NH)	M	Notre Dame (IN)	M
Davidson (NC)	R	Oberlin (OH)	R
DePauw (IN)	R	Occidental (CA)	R
Dickinson (PA)	R	Pennsylvania, U. of	L
Drew (NJ)	R		

GROUP I continues next page

Enrollment Code

■ *Men Only* **S = Small (less than 1000 students)** **R = Moderate (1000-3000 students)** **M = Medium (3000-8000 students)**
▲ *Women Only* **L = Large (8000-20,000 students)** **XL = Extra Large (over 20,000 students)**

PRE-LAW, continued

GROUP I, Continued

Pitzer (CA)	S
Pomona (CA)	R
Princeton (NJ)	M
Providence (RI)	M
Reed (OR)	R
Rhodes (TN)	R
Richmond, U. of (VA)	M
Rice (TX)	R
Richmond, U. of (VA)	M
Rochester, U. of (NY)	M
Rutgers (NJ)	L
Sarah Lawrence (NY)	R
Skidmore (NY)	R
▲ Smith (MA)	R
South, U. of the (TN)	R
Southwestern (TX)	R
Stanford (CA)	M
St. Olaf (MN)	R
Swarthmore (PA)	R
Trinity (CT)	R
Trinity (TX)	R
Tufts (MA)	M
Tulane (LA)	M
Union (NY)	R
Vanderbilt (TN)	M
Vassar (NY)	R
Villanova (PA)	M
Virginia, U. of	L
■ Wabash (IN)	S
Wake Forest (NC)	M
Washington & Lee (VA)	R
Washington U. (MO)	M
▲ Wellesley (MA)	R
Wesleyan U. (CT)	R
Wheaton (IL)	R
Whitman (WA)	R
Williams (MA)	R
Wisconsin, U. of	XL
Worcester Poly. Inst. (MA)	R
Yale (CT)	M

GROUP II
Very Selective

▲ Agnes Scott (GA)	S
Alabama, U. of	L
Albertson (ID)	S
Albion (MI)	R
Alfred (NY)	R
Alma (MI)	R
Arcadia (PA)	R
Arizona, U. of	XL
Augsburg (MN)	R
Augustana (IL)	R
Baylor (TX)	R
Belmont (TN)	R
Bennington (VT)	S
Birmingham-Southern (AL)	R
Bradley (IL)	M
Brigham Young (UT)	XL
Butler (IN)	R
California, U. of (Davis)	L
California, U. of (Irvine)	L
California, U. of (Riverside)	L
California, U. of (Santa Barbara)	L
Calvin (MI)	M
Catholic (DC)	R
Chapman (CA)	R
City College (CUNY)(NY)	L
Clark (MA)	R
Columbia Col. (SC)	R
Connecticut, U. of	XL
Cornell Col. (IA)	R
Creighton (NE)	M
Dayton, U. of (OH)	M
Delaware, U. of	L
Denison (OH)	R
Denver, U. of (CO)	M
DePaul (IL)	L
Drake (IA)	M
Drury (MO)	R
Evansville (IN)	R
Elizabethtown (PA)	R
Flagler (FL)	R
Fordham (NY)	L
George Mason (VA)	L
Georgetown College (KY)	R
Georgia, U. of	XL
Gonzaga (WA)	R
Goucher (MD)	R
Grand Valley (MI)	L

GROUP II continues next page

PRE-LAW, continued

•• ━━━━━━━━━━━━━━━━━━━ **GROUP II,** continued ━━━━━━━━━━ ••

Guilford (NC) .... R	Ohio U. L
Hamline (MN) .... R	Ohio Wesleyan .... R
■ Hampden-Sydney (VA) .... S	Oklahoma City U. .... R
Hartwick (NY) .... R	Oklahoma, U. of XL
Hendrix (AR) .... R	Oneonta (SUNY) (NY) .... M
Hiram (OH) .... R	Oregon, U. of L
Hobart & Wm. Smith (NY) .... R	Oswego (SUNY)(NY) .... M
Hofstra (NY) .... M	Pittsburgh, U. of (PA) L
Hope (MI) .... R	Portland State (OR) L
Howard (DC) .... M	Presbyterian (SC) .... R
Hunter (CUNY) (NY) L	Principia (IL) .... S
Illinois College .... S	Puget Sound (WA) .... R
Illinois, U. of (Chicago) L	Purchase (SUNY) (NY) .... R
Indiana (PA) L	Queens (NC) .... S
James Madison (VA) L	Randolph-Macon (VA) .... R
Juniata (PA) .... R	▲ Randolph-Macon Woman's Col. (VA) .... S
Kansas State L	Redlands, U. of (CA) .... R
Knox (IL) .... R	Ripon (WI) .... S
Lake Forest (IL) .... R	Rutgers (Camden) (NJ) .... M
LaSalle (PA) .... M	▲ Salem College (NC) .... S
Lawrence (WI) .... R	Salisbury State (MD) .... M
Loras (IA) .... R	San Diego, U. of .... M
Loyola (LA) .... R	San Francisco, U. of (CA) .... M
Loyola (MD) .... M	Santa Clara U. (CA) .... R
Manhattan (NY) .... M	▲ Scripps (CA) .... S
Marietta (OH) .... R	Seton Hall (AL) .... M
Marquette (WI) .... M	Siena (NY) .... R
Maryland, U. of XL	South Carolina, U. of L
Massachusetts, U. of L	South Dakota, U. of .... M
Mercyhurst (PA) .... R	Spring Hill (AL) .... R
Michigan State XL	St. Bonaventure (NY) .... R
Michigan, U. of (Dearborn) ...... M	St. Cloud (MN) L
Millersville (PA) .... M	St. John's (MN) .... R
Millsaps (MS) .... S	St. Lawrence (NY) .... R
Minnesota, U. of XL	▲ St. Mary's Col. (IN) .... R
Minnesota, U. of (Morris) .... R	Stetson (FL) .... R
Mississippi, U. of L	Stonehill (MA) .... R
Nebraska, U. of L	Stony Brook (SUNY) (NY) L
New Hampshire, U. of L	▲ Sweet Briar (VA) .... S
North Carolina, U. of (Charlotte) L	Syracuse (NY) L
North Carolina, U. of (Wilmington) L	▲ Trinity (DC) .... S
North Carolina State L	Tuskegee (AL) .... M
North Central (IL) .... R	Ursinus (PA) .... R
Oglethorpe (GA) .... S	
Ohio State XL	*GROUP II continues next page*

| PRE-LAW, continued |

GROUP II, continued

Vermont, U. of L
Virginia Commonwealth U. L
Virginia Military Inst. .... R
Warren Wilson (NC) .... S
Washington & Jefferson (PA)............. R
Washington, U. of................................XL
Wells (NY) .... S
West Chester (PA) .... M

Western Washington U. L
Westminster Col. (MO)........................ S
Westmont (CA) .... R
Wheaton (MA) .... R
Wilberforce (OH) .... S
Wittenberg (OH) .... R
Wofford (SC) .... R
Wooster (OH) .... R

GROUP III
Selective

Adrian (MI) .... R
Albright (PA) .... R
Arkansas, U. of...................................... L
Baldwin-Wallace (OH) .... R
Belmont Abbey (NC) .... S
▲ Bennett (NC) .... S
Bethany (WV) .... S
California State U. (Channel Islands) ... R
California State U. (Long Beach) L
California State U. (Monterey Bay) .... R
California State U. (Northridge) L
Campbell (NC)...................................... R
▲ Chatham (PA)..................................... S
Chestnut Hill (PA) .... S
Emerson (MA) .... R
Fairleigh Dickinson (NJ) .... M
Fisk (TN)... S
Florida A&M .... M
Fort Lewis (CO) .... M
Gwynedd-Mercy (PA) .... S
Hawaii, U. of... L
Heidelberg (OH) .... S
▲ Hollins (VA).. S
Illinois State.. L
Longwood (VA)..................................... R
Louisiana-Lafayette L

Louisiana State XL
Lynchburg (VA) .... R
Massachusetts, U. of (Boston)........... M
Mount St. Joseph (OH) .... R
Mount St. Mary's (MD) .... R
Niagara (NY)... R
Radford (VA)... M
Rhode Island, U. of............................. L
Roanoke (VA).. R
Rockford (IL) .... S
▲ Rosemont (PA) .... S
San Francisco State (CA) L
Seattle U. (WA) .... R
Southwest Missouri L
▲ Spelman (GA) .... R
St. Anselm (NH) .... R
St. Mary's (TX) .... R
▲ Stephens (MO) .... S
Temple (PA) L
Tennessee, U. of XL
Utah, U. of... L
Virginia Wesleyan .... R
Whittier (CA) .... R
Wilson (PA) .... S
Wisconsin, U. of (Milwaukee) L
Wyoming, U. of.................................... L

Enrollment Code		
■ *Men Only*	S = Small (less than 1000 students) R = Moderate (1000-3000 students)	M = Medium (3000-8000 students)
▲ *Women Only*	L = Large (8000-20,000 students) XL = Extra Large (over 20,000 students)	

PRE-MED/PRE-DENTAL

Author's Note: In addition to general college requirements and requirements of their major department, premedical and predental students must usually pass with a good grade the following: general chemistry, zoology, organic chemistry, general biology, English composition or literature, and general physics.

Other required or highly recommended courses are: advanced biology, psychology or sociology, physical chemistry, calculus, and quantitative chemistry. Of course, the wise path to follow is to consult the exact course requirements of the school you expect to apply to. The recommended colleges below are taken primarily from our recommended departments in biology and chemistry.

GROUP I
Most Selective

Albany (SUNY) (NY) L	Furman (SC) .... R
Allegheny (PA) .... R	Geneseo (SUNY) (NY) .... M
American U. (DC) .... M	Georgetown (DC) .... M
Amherst (MA) .... R	Gettysburg (PA) .... R
Bates (ME) .... R	Grinnell (IA) .... R
Binghamton (SUNY) (NY) L	Hamilton (NY) .... R
Boston Col. (MA) L	Harvard (MA) .... M
Bowdoin (ME) .... R	Harvey Mudd (CA) .... S
Brandeis (MA) .... R	Haverford (PA) .... S
Brown (RI) .... M	Holy Cross (MA) .... R
▲ Bryn Mawr (PA) .... S	Illinois, U. of (Urbana-Champaign) XL
Bucknell (PA) .... M	Illinois Wesleyan .... R
Buffalo (SUNY) (NY) L	Iowa State XL
California Inst. of Tech. .... S	Iowa, U. of XL
California, U. of (Berkeley) XL	Johns Hopkins (MD) .... M
California, U. of (Los Angeles) XL	Kalamazoo (MI) .... R
California, U. of (San Diego) L	Kenyon (OH) .... R
Carleton (MN) .... R	Knox (IL) .... R
Carnegie-Mellon (PA) .... M	Lafayette (PA) .... R
Case Western Reserve U. (OH) .... M	Lawrence (WI) .... R
Centre (KY) .... R	Macalester (MN) .... R
Chicago, U. of (IL) .... M	Miami, U. of (FL) L
Citadel, The (SC) .... R	Miami, U. of (OH) L
Claremont McKenna (CA) .... R	MIT (MA) .... M
Clark (MA) .... R	Michigan, U. of XL
Colby (ME) .... R	Middlebury (VT) .... R
Colgate (NY) .... R	▲ Mount Holyoke (MA) .... R
Colorado Col. .... R	New College (FL) .... S
Colorado School of Mines .... R	New Jersey, College of .... M
Columbia (NY) .... M	North Carolina, U. of L
Cornell (NY) L	Northwestern (IL) .... M
Dallas, U. of (TX) .... R	Notre Dame (IN) .... M
Dartmouth (NH) .... M	Oberlin (OH) .... R
Davidson (NC) .... R	Occidental (CA) .... R
DePauw (IN) .... R	Pitzer (CA) .... S
Dickinson (PA) .... M	Pomona (CA) .... R
Drew (NJ) .... R	Princeton (NJ) .... M
Duke (NC) .... R	Puget Sound (WA) .... R
Emory (GA) .... M	Reed (OR) .... R
Fairfield (CT) .... M	Rhodes (TN) .... R
Florida, U. of XL	Rice (TX) .... R
Franklin & Marshall (PA) .... R	

GROUP I continues next page

PRE-MED/PRE-DENTAL, continued

GROUP I, continued

Richmond, U. of (VA)	R
Rochester, U. of (NY)	M
Rutgers (NJ)	L
Skidmore (NY)	R
▲ Smith (MA)	R
South, U. of the (TN)	R
Southwestern (TX)	R
Stanford (CA)	M
Stetson (FL)	R
St. Mary's College of Maryland	R
St. Olaf (MN)	R
Swarthmore (PA)	S
Texas, U. of (Austin)	XL
Trinity (CT)	R
Trinity (TX)	R
Tufts (MA)	M
Tulane (LA)	M
Union (NY)	R
Ursinus (PA)	R
Vanderbilt (TN)	M
Vassar (NY)	R
Villanova (PA)	M
Virginia, U. of	L
■ Wabash (IN)	S
Wake Forest (NC)	M
Washington & Lee (VA)	M
Washington U. (MO)	M
▲ Wellesley (MA)	R
Wesleyan (CT)	R
Wheaton (IL)	R
Whitman (WA)	R
Willamette (OR)	R
William & Mary (VA)	M
Williams (MA)	R
Yale (CT)	M
Yeshiva (NY)	R

GROUP II
Very Selective

▲ Agnes Scott (GA)	S
Alabama, U. of	l
Albertson (ID)	S
Albion (MI)	R
Albright (PA)	R
Alma (MI)	R
Arizona State	XL
Arizona, U. of	XL
Augustana (SD)	M
Austin (TX)	R
Baylor (TX)	M
Berry (GA)	R
Bethany (WV)	S
Birmingham-Southern (AL)	R
Brigham Young (UT)	XL
Butler (IN)	R
California, U. of (Davis)	L
California, U. of (Irvine)	L
California, U. of (Riverside)	L
California, U. of (Santa Barbara)	L
California, U. of (Santa Cruz)	M
Canisius (NY)	M
Carroll (WI)	R
Chapman (CA)	R
City College (CUNY)(NY)	L
College of Charleston (SC)	L
Columbia Col. (SC)	R
Colorado, U. of	L
Concordia (MN)	R
Connecticut, U. of	XL
Cornell (IA)	R
Creighton (NE)	M
Dayton, U. of (OH)	M
Delaware, U. of	L
DePaul (IL)	L
Denison (OH)	R
Denver, U. of (CO)	M
Duquesne (PA)	M
Earlham (IN)	R
Eckerd (FL)	R
Erskine (SC)	S
Evansville (IN)	R
Florida State	L
Fordham (NY)	M
Franklin (IN)	S
Georgia, U. of	XL
Gonzaga (WA)	R
Guilford (NC)	R
Hamline (MN)	R

GROUP II continues next page

Enrollment Code

■ *Men Only*
▲ *Women Only*

S = Small (less than 1000 students)   R = Moderate (1000-3000 students)   M = Medium (3000-8000 students)
L = Large (8000-20,000 students)   XL = Extra Large (over 20,000 students)

PRE-MED/PRE-DENTAL, continued

GROUP II, continued

■ Hampden-Sydney (VA) .... S
  Hendrix (AR) .... R
  Hiram (OH) .... R
  Hobart & Wm. Smith (NY) .... R
  Hofstra (NY) .... M
▲ Hollins (VA) .... S
  Hood (MD) .... S
  Hope (MI) .... R
  Houghton (NY) .... S
  Houston Baptist (TX) .... R
  Howard (DC) .... M
  Huntingdon (AL) .... S
  Illinois, U. of (Chicago) L
  Indiana U. XL
  Ithaca Col. (NY) .... M
  James Madison (VA) L
  Juniata (PA) .... R
  Kansas, U. of L
  Kansas State L
  Kentucky, U. of L
  Knox (IL) .... R
  Lake Forest (IL) .... R
  Lewis & Clark (OR) .... R
  Lipscomb (TN) .... R
  Loyola (IL) .... M
  Loyola (LA) .... R
  Loyola (MD) .... M
  Lycoming (PA) .... R
  Marquette (WI) .... M
  Mary Washington (VA) .... M
  Massachusetts, U. of L
  McDaniel (MD) .... R
  Michigan State XL
  Michigan, U. of (Dearborn) .... M
  Millsaps (MS) .... R
  Minnesota, U. of (Morris) .... R
  Mississippi State L
  Monmouth (IL) .... S
  Moravian (PA) .... R
  Morningside (IA) .... S
  Muhlenberg (PA) .... R
  Nebraska Wesleyan .... R
  Nevada, U. of (Reno) L
  New Hampshire, U. of L
  New York U. L
  North Carolina, U. of (Charlotte) L
  North Central (IL) .... R
  Ohio State XL
  Ohio Wesleyan .... R
  Oregon, U. of L

  Pacific Lutheran (OR) .... R
  Pacific University (OR) .... R
  Pennsylvania State XL
  Pittsburgh, U. of (PA) L
  Presbyterian (SC) .... R
  Randolph-Macon (VA) .... R
▲ Randolph-Macon Woman's Col. (VA) .... S
  Redlands, U. of (CA) .... R
  Regis (CO) .... R
  Richard Stockton (NJ) .... M
  Ripon (WI) .... S
  San Diego, U. of (CA) .... M
  San Francisco, U. of (CA) .... M
  Scranton, U. of (PA) .... M
▲ Scripps (CA) .... S
  Seton Hall (NJ) .... M
  Siena (NY) .... R
  Spring Hill (AL) .... R
  St. John's (MN) .... R
  St. Joseph's U. (PA) .... R
  St. Louis (MO) .... M
  St. Louis Col. of Pharmacy (MO) .... S
  St. Scholastica (MN) .... R
  St. Thomas, U. of (MN) .... S
  St. Thomas, U. of (TX) .... R
  Stetson (FL) .... R
  Stony Brook (SUNY) (NY) L
  Susquehanna (PA) .... R
  Tennessee, U. of XL
  Texas A&M XL
  Transylvania (KY) .... S
  Truman State (MO) .... M
  Tuskegee (AL) .... M
  Utah, U. of L
  Valparaiso U. (IN) .... M
  Vermont, U. of L
  Washington College (MD) .... S
  Washington & Jefferson (PA) .... R
  Washington, U. of XL
  Wells (NY) .... S
  Westminster (MO) .... S
  Westminster (PA) .... R
  Westmont (CA) .... R
  Wheaton (MA) .... R
  Winona State U. (MN) .... M
  Wisconsin, U. of XL
  Wittenberg (OH) .... R
  Wofford (SC) .... R
  Wooster (OH) .... R
  Wyoming, U. of L

PRE-MED/PRE-DENTAL, continued

GROUP III
Selective

American International (MA) .... R	Kentucky Wesleyan .... S
Benedictine (IL) .... R	Louisiana-Lafayette L
▲ Bennett (NC) .... S	Louisiana State XL
Blackburn (IL) .... S	Lynchburg (VA) .... R
Brooklyn Col. (SUNY) (NY) L	Mount St. Joseph (OH) .... R
California State U. (Channel Islands) .... R	Mount St. Mary's (MD) .... R
California State U. (Fullerton) L	Nova Southeastern (FL) .... R
California State U. (Monterey Bay) .... R	Rider (NJ) .... R
California State U. (San Jose) L	▲ Spelman (GA) .... R
Carroll (MT) .... R	St. Mary's (TX) .... R
Carson-Newman (TN) .... R	St. Vincent (PA) .... R
Delaware Valley (PA) .... R	South Dakota, U. of .... M
Dillard (LA) .... R	Temple (PA) L
East Carolina (NC) L	Texas, U. of (San Antonio) L
Elmhurst (IL) .... R	Thomas More (KY) .... R
Florida A&M .... M	Virginia Commonwealth L
Florida Southern .... R	Virginia Wesleyan .... R
Freed-Hardeman (TN) .... R	Walla Walla (WA) .... R
Gardner-Webb (NC) .... R	Wartburg (IA) .... R
Heidelberg (OH) .... S	Wayne State (MI) L
Ind.U.-Purdue U.-Indianapolis (IN) .. L	Wilkes (PA) .... R
Jacksonville (FL) .... R	Xavier U. of Louisiana .... R

PSYCHOLOGY

━━━━━━━━━━━━━━━━━━━━━━ **GROUP I** ━━━━━━━━━━━━━━━━━━━━━━
Most Selective

Allegheny (PA)	R	Johns Hopkins (MD)	M
Amherst (MA)	R	Kenyon (OH)	R
Bard (NY)	R	Lafayette (PA)	R
▲ Barnard (NY)	R	Lehigh (PA)	M
Bates (ME)	R	Macalester (MN)	R
Binghamton (SUNY) (NY)	L	Miami U. (OH)	L
Boston U. (MA)	L	Michigan, U. of	XL
Brandeis (MA)	R	▲ Mount Holyoke (MA)	R
▲ Bryn Mawr (PA)	S	New College (FL)	S
Bucknell (PA)	M	New Jersey, College of	M
Buffalo (SUNY)(NY)	L	New York U.	L
California, U. of (Berkeley)	XL	North Carolina, U. of	L
California, U. of (Los Angeles)	XL	Northwestern (IL)	M
California, U. of (San Diego)	L	Notre Dame, U of (IN)	M
Carleton (MN)	R	Pennsylvania, U. of	L
Carnegie-Mellon (PA)	M	Pitzer (CA)	S
Case Western Reserve U. (OH)	M	Pomona (CA)	S
Centre (KY)	R	Reed (OR)	R
Chicago, U. of (IL)	M	Richmond, U. of (VA)	R
Claremont McKenna (CA)	R	Rhodes (TN)	R
Clarkson (NY)	M	Rochester, U. of (NY)	M
Colby (ME)	R	Rutgers (NJ)	L
Colgate (NY)	R	▲ Scripps (CA)	S
Colorado College	R	▲ Simmons (MA)	R
Columbia (NY)	M	Skidmore (NY)	R
Connecticut Col.	R	▲ Smith (MA)	R
Dallas, U. of (TX)	R	Southwestern (TX)	R
Dartmouth (NH)	M	Stanford (CA)	M
Davidson (NC)	R	St. Mary's College of Maryland	R
DePauw (IN)	R	St. Olaf (MN)	R
Dickinson (PA)	R	Swarthmore (PA)	R
Drew (NJ)	R	Tufts (MA)	M
Duke (NC)	M	Tulane (LA)	M
Emory (GA)	M	Union (NY)	R
Franklin & Marshall (PA)	R	Vanderbilt (TN)	M
Furman (SC)	R	Vassar (NY)	R
Georgetown (DC)	M	Virginia, U. of	L
George Washington (DC)	M	■ Wabash (IN)	S
Georgia Institute of Tech.	L	Wake Forest (NC)	M
Gettysburg (PA)	R	Washington U. (MO)	M
Grinnell (IA)	R	Wesleyan (CT)	R
Gustavus Adolphus (MN)	R	Wheaton (IL)	R
Harvard (MA)	M	Whitman (WA)	R
Haverford (PA)	S	Willamette (OR)	R
Holy Cross (MA)	R	Williams (MA)	R
Illinois, U. of (Urbana-Champaign)	XL	Yale (CT)	M
Illinois Wesleyan	R	Yeshiva (NY)	M
James Madison (VA)	L		

PSYCHOLOGY, continued

GROUP II
Very Selective

Adelphi (NY)	M	Elmira (NY)	R
▲ Agnes Scott (GA)	S	Elon (NC)	R
Alabama, U. of	L	Fairfield (CT)	M
Albany (SUNY) (NY)	L	Fairmont (WV)	M
Albright (PA)	R	Flagler (FL)	R
Alfred (NY)	R	Florida Atlantic	L
Alma (MI)	R	Florida Inst. of Tech.	R
Arizona State	XL	Florida International	L
Arizona, U. of	XL	Florida State	L
Belmont (TN)	R	George Mason (VA)	L
Beloit (WI)	R	Georgia State	`L
Berry (GA)	R	Grand Valley (MI)	L
Bethany (WV)	S	Guilford (NC)	R
Birmingham-Southern (AL)	R	Hamline (MN)	R
Brigham Young (UT)	XL	Hampton (VA)	M
Cal. Poly State U. (SLO)	L	Hanover (IN)	R
California, U. of (Irvine)	L	Hendrix (AR)	R
California, U. of (Merced)	R	Herbert Lehman (CUNY) (NY)	L
California, U. of (Riverside)	L	Hobart & Wm. Smith (NY)	R
California, U. of (Santa Barbara)	L	Hood (MD)	S
California, U. of (Santa Cruz)	M	Hope (MI)	R
Carroll (WI)	R	Houghton (NY)	S
Catholic (DC)	R	Houston, U. of (TX)	L
Central Florida, U. of	L	Hunter (CUNY) (NY)	L
Chapman (CA)	R	Illinois, U. of (Chicago)	L
Cincinnati, U. of	L	Indiana U.	XL
Clark (MA)	R	Iowa, U. of	XL
Coe (IA)	R	John Carroll (OH)	R
College of Charleston (SC)	L	Kansas, U. of	L
Colorado State	L	Kean (NJ)	M
Colorado, U. of	L	Kentucky, U. of	L
Concordia (MN)	R	Lake Forest (IL)	R
Connecticut, U. of	XL	LaSalle (PA)	M
Cornell Col. (IA)	R	Lebanon Valley (PA)	R
Creighton (NE)	M	LeMoyne (NY)	R
Delaware, U. of	L	Loras (IA)	R
Denison (OH)	R	Louisiana State U.	L
Denver, U. of (CO)	M	Loyola (IL)	M
DePaul (IL)	L	Luther (IA)	R
Dubuque, U. of (IA)	S	Lycoming (PA)	R
Earlham (IN)	R	Maine, U. of	L
Eastern Michigan	L		

GROUP II continues next page

PSYCHOLOGY, continued

GROUP II, continued

Manhattanville (NY)	R	Rockhurst (MO)	R
Marist (NY)	M	Rollins (FL)	R
Marquette (WI)	R	Salisbury State (MD)	M
Maryville (TN)	S	San Francisco, U. of (CA)	M
Mary Washington (VA)	M	Santa Clara, U. of (CA)	M
Massachusetts, U. of	L	Shepherd (WV)	M
Mercer (GA)	R	Siena (NY)	R
Merrimack (MA)	R	Southern California	L
Michigan State	XL	St. Lawrence (NY)	R
Millersville (PA)	M	St. Mary's College (CA)	R
▲ Mills (CA)	S	St. Thomas, U. of (TX)	R
Minnesota, U. of (Morris)	R	Stetson (FL)	R
Minnesota, U. of	XL	Stonehill (MA)	R
Missouri, U. of	XL	Stony Brook (SUNY) (NY)	L
Missouri, U. of (Kansas City)	M	Susquehanna (PA)	R
Missouri, U. of (St. Louis)	M	▲ Sweet Briar (VA)	S
Moravian (PA)	R	Syracuse (NY)	L
Morningside (IA)	S	Texas, U. of (Austin)	XL
Muhlenberg (PA)	R	Towson (MD)	L
Nebraska Wesleyan	R	Transylvania (KY)	R
Nevada, U. of (Las Vegas)	L	Tulsa, U. of (OK)	R
New Paltz (SUNY) (NY)	M	Valparaiso U. (IN)	M
New Mexico, U. of	L	Vermont, U of	L
Newman U. (KS)	S	Virginia Tech.	L
North Carolina (Asheville)	R	Virginia, U. of	L
North Carolina, U. of (Charlotte)	L	Washington College (MD)	S
North Carolina, U. of (Wilmington)	L	Washington & Jefferson (PA)	R
Northeastern (MA)	L	Washington, U. of	XL
Ohio State	XL	Webster (MO)	R
Ohio U.	L	Wells (NY)	S
Ohio Wesleyan	R	West Florida, U. of	M
Oklahoma City U.	R	Western Michigan	L
Oklahoma, U. of	XL	Western Washington U.	R
Oklahoma State	L	Westminster (MO)	S
Oregon, U. of	L	Westminster (UT)	R
Oswego (SUNY) (NY)	M	Westmont (CA)	R
Pace (NY)	M	Wheaton (MA)	R
Pittsburgh, U. of (PA)	L	Whitworth (WA)	R
Portland State (OR)	L	Winthrop (SC)	M
Queens (CUNY) (NY)	L	Wisconsin, U. of	XL
Randolph-Macon (VA)	R	Wittenberg (OH)	R
▲ Randolph-Macon Woman's Col. (VA)	S	Wofford (SC)	R
Roanoke (VA)	R	Xavier (OH)	R

PSYCHOLOGY continues next page

PSYCHOLOGY, continued

GROUP III
Selective

Alabama, U. of (Birmingham)	M
Alaska Pacific	S
▲ Alverno (WI)	R
American International (MA)	R
Aquinas (MI)	R
Arcadia (PA)	R
Arkansas, U. of	L
Averett (VA)	S
Baker (KS)	R
Baldwin-Wallace (OH)	R
Ball State (IN)	L
▲ Bay Path (MA)	R
Bethel (MN)	R
Biola (CA)	R
Blackburn (IL)	S
Bridgewater (MA)	M
Bridgewater (VA)	R
Brockport (SUNY)(NY)	M
Caldwell (NJ)	S
California (PA)	M
California Lutheran	R
California State U. (Bakersfield)	M
California State U. (Channel Islands)	R
California State U. (Chico)	L
California State U. (Dominguez Hills)	M
California State U. (Long Beach)	L
California State U. (Los Angeles)	L
California State U. (Northridge)	L
California State U. (Sacramento)	M
California State U. (San Bernardino)	M
California State U. (San Marcos)	M
California State U. (Stanislaus)	M
Canisius (NY)	M
Carson-Newman (TN)	R
Carthage (WI)	R
Castleton State (VT)	R
▲ Cedar Crest (PA)	S
Central Connecticut	M
Central Michigan	L
Central Washington	L
Chaminade (HI)	R
Chapman (CA)	R
Coker (SC)	S
Colorado, U. of (Colorado Springs)	M
Colorado, U. of (Denver)	M
Delaware State	R
Dominican (CA)	S
Dominican (IL)	S
D'Youville (NY)	R
East Carolina	L
Eastern Connecticut	M
Eastern Illinois	L
Edgewood (WI)	S
Elmhurst (IL)	R
Fitchburg (MA)	R
Framingham (MA)	M
Franciscan U. of Steubenville (OH)	R
George Fox (OR)	R
▲ Hollins (VA)	S
Holy Names (CA)	S
John Jay College (CUNY)(NY)	M
▲ Judson (AL)	S
Keene State (NH)	R
Kentucky Wesleyan	S
Liberty (VA)	R
Lindenwood (MO)	S
Long Island U. (C.W.Post)(NY)	M
Longwood (VA)	R
Lyndon State(VT)	R
Lyon (AR)	S
Maine, U. of (Farmington)	R
Manchester (IN)	R
Marshall (WV)	L
▲ Mary Baldwin (VA)	S
Marymount (VA)	R
Massachusetts, U. of (Dartmouth)	M
Mercy (NY)	M
▲ Meredith (NC)	R
Middle Tennessee	L
Millersville (PA)	M
Minnesota State U. (Moorhead)	M
Minnesota, U. of (Duluth)	L

GROUP III continues next page

PSYCHOLOGY, continued

GROUP III, continued

Molloy (NY)	R	St. Scholastica (MN)	R
Montclair State (NJ)	M	St. Thomas Aquinas (NY)	R
Muskingum (OH)	R	St. Vincent (PA)	R
New Hampshire, U. of	L	Salem State (MA)	M
North Carolina (Greensboro)	M	Seton Hall (NJ)	M
Northeastern State (OK)	L	Siena Heights (MI)	S
Northern Arizona	L	Shippensburg (PA)	M
Northwestern (IA)	R	Simpson (IA)	R
Northwestern (MN)	R	Sonoma State (CA)	M
Nyack (NY)	R	South Dakota, U. of	M
Oakland City U. (IN)	R	Southern Connecticut	M
Oklahoma Baptist	R	Southern Illinois U. (Carbondale)	L
Otterbein (OH)	R	Springfield (MA)	R
Ozarks, College of the (MO)	R	▲Stephens (MO)	S
Palm Beach Atlantic (FL)	R	Taylor (IN)	R
▲Pine Manor (MA)	S	Texas A&M (Corpus Christi)	M
Point Park (PA)	R	Texas, U. of (San Antonio)	L
Potsdam (SUNY)(NY)	R	Texas, U. of (Tyler)	R
Purchase (SUNY) (NY)	R	Texas Wesleyan	R
Regis (CO)	R	Virginia Commonwealth U.	L
Rhode Island College	M	Virginia Wesleyan	R
Rockford (IL)	S	Western Kentucky	L
Roger Williams (RI)	M	Western New England (MA)	R
Roosevelt (IL)	R	Westfield (MA)	M
▲Rosemont (PA)	S	Wheeling Jesuit (WV)	R
Sacred Heart (CT)	R	Wilkes (PA)	R
St. Ambrose (IA)	R	William Paterson (NJ)	M
St. Anselm (NH)	R	Wilson (PA)	S
St. Edward's (TX)	M	Wisconsin, U. of (Green Bay)	M
St. Francis (NY)	R	Wisconsin, U. of (Stout)	M
St, John's (NY)	L	Worcester State (MA)	M
St. Joseph's (IN)	S	Wyoming, U. of	L
St. Joseph's (NY)	R	Xavier University of Louisiana	R
St. Martin's (WA)	S	York (NE)	S
St. Mary (KS)	S		

RELIGIOUS STUDIES

GROUP I
Most Selective

▲ Barnard (NY) .... R
Bates (ME) .... R
Boston College (MA) L
Bowdoin (ME) .... R
Brown (RI) .... M
California, U. of (Berkeley) XL
Carleton (MN) .... R
Case Western Reserve (OH) .... M
Centre (KY) .... R
Chicago, U. of (IL) .... M
Claremont McKenna (CA) .... R
Colby (ME) .... R
Colgate (NY) .... R
Columbia (NY) .... M
Dartmouth (NH) .... M
Davidson (NC) .... R
DePauw (IN) .... R
Dickinson (PA) .... R
Drew (NJ) .... R
Duke (NC) .... M
Emory (GA) .... M
Furman (SC) .... R
Georgetown (DC) .... M
Grinnell (IA) .... R
Gustavus Adolphus (MN) .... R
Hamilton (NY) .... R
Haverford (PA) .... S
Holy Cross (MA) .... R
Kenyon (OH) .... R

Lawrence (WI) .... R
Macalester (MN) .... R
North Carolina, U. of L
Northwestern (IL) .... M
Notre Dame (IN) .... M
Oberlin (OH) .... R
Occidental (CA) .... R
Pittsburgh, U. of (PA) L
Pomona (CA) .... R
Princeton (NJ) .... M
Rhodes (TN) .... R
Richmond, U. of (VA) .... R
Rutgers (NJ) L
St. Joseph's (PA) .... R
St. Olaf (MN) .... R
South, U. of the (TN) .... R
Southwestern (TX) .... R
Stanford (CA) .... M
Trinity (CT) .... R
Virginia, U. of L
■ Wabash (IN) .... S
Wake Forest (NC) .... M
▲ Wellesley (MA) .... R
Wesleyan (CT) .... R
Wheaton (IL) .... R
Willamette (OR) .... R
William & Mary (VA) .... M
Wisconsin Lutheran .... S
Yale (CT) .... M

RELIGIOUS STUDIES continues next page

Enrollment Code

■ *Men Only*	S = Small (less than 1000 students)	R = Moderate (1000-3000 students)	M = Medium (3000-8000 students)
▲ *Women Only*	L = Large (8000-20,000 students)	XL = Extra Large (over 20,000 students)	

RELIGIOUS STUDIES, continued

GROUP II
Very Selective

Alaska Pacific	S	Loyola (LA)	R
Arizona State	XL	Luther (IA)	R
Asbury (KY)	R	Lycoming (PA)	R
Augustana (SD)	R	Marquette)WI)	M
Austin (TX)	R	Master's (CA)	R
Baylor (TX)	M	Muhlenberg (PA)	R
Belmont (TN)	R	Newman U. (KS)	S
Bethany (WV)	S	North Carolina (Charlotte)	L
Bethel (IN)	R	Oklahoma City U.	R
Bethel (MN)	M	Pacific Lutheran (WA)	R
Birmingham-Southern (AL)	R	Portland, U. of (OR)	R
Brigham Young (UT)	XL	Presbyterian (SC)	R
Bryan (TN)	S	Roanoke (VA)	R
Bryn Athyn (PA)	S	Rockhurst (MO)	R
California, U. of (Santa Barbara)	L	Rollins (FL)	R
Capital (OH)	R	Rowan (NJ)	M
Catholic U. (DC)	M	St. Bonaventure (NY)	R
Central (IA)	R	St. Edward's (TX)	M
Christendom (VA)	S	St. John's (MN)	R
Christian Brothers (TN)	R	St. Louis U. (MO)	M
Concordia (CA)	R	▲ St. Mary's College (IN)	R
Creighton (NE)	M	St. Mary's (MN)	R
Denver, U. of (CO)	M	St. Scholastica (MN)	R
DePaul (IL)	L	St. Thomas (MN)	R
Detroit Mercy (MI)	M	St. Thomas, U. of (TX)	R
Drury (MO)	R	Sanford (AL)	R
Duquesne (PA)	M	San Diego, U. of (CA)	M
Earlham (IN)	R	Santa Clara U. (CA)	M
Eckerd (FL)	R	Southern Methodist (TX)	L
Elizabethtown (PA)	R	Stetson (FL)	R
Florida State	L	Stony Brook (SUNY) (NY)	L
Fordham (NY)	M	Syracuse (NY)	L
Gonzaga (WA)	R	Tennessee, U. of	XL
Gordon (MA)	R	Texas Christian U.	M
Guilford (NC)	R	Union (NE)	R
Harding (AR)	M	Valparaiso U. (IN)	M
Hendrix (AR)	R	Vermont, U. of	L
Hiram (OH)	R	Wartburg (IA)	R
Houghton (NY)	S	Westmont (CA)	R
Iowa, U. of	XL	Whitworth (WA)	R
John Carroll (OH)	R	Wittenberg (OH)	R
LaSalle (PA)	M	Wofford (SC)	R
Lipscomb (TN)	R	Wooster (OH)	R
Loras (IA)	R	Xavier (OH)	R

RELIGIOUS STUDIES, continued

GROUP III
Selective

Abilene Christain (TX) .... M	Mississippi College .... R
Andrews (MI) .... R	■ Morehouse (GA) .... R
Aquinas (MI) .... R	Muskingum (OH) .... R
Benedictine (KS) .... R	Northwestern (IA) .... S
Brescia (KY) .... S	Northwestern (MN) .... R
California State U. (Chico) L	Nyack (NY) .... R
California State U. (Fullerton) L	Oakland City U. (IN) .... R
California State U. (Long Beach) L	Oklahoma Baptist .... R
Carthage (WI) .... R	Olivet Nazarene (IL) .... R
Chaminade (HI) .... R	Ouachita Baptist (AR) .... R
Concordia (NE) .... R	Regis (CO) .... R
Cumberland (KY) .... R	St. Ambrose (IA) .... R
De Sales (PA) .... S	▲ St. Catherine (MN) .... R
Doane (NE) .... S	St, John's (NY) L
Dordt (IA) .... R	Saint Peter's (NJ) .... R
Eastern Mennonite (VA) .... R	St. Vincent (PA) .... R
Franciscan U. of Steubenville (OH) .... R	Seton Hall (NJ) .... M
Freed-Hardeman (TN) .... R	Silver Lake (WI) .... S
George Fox (OR) .... R	Simpson (IA) .... R
Hardin-Simmons (TX) .... R	Southern Nazarene (OK) .... R
John Brown (AR) .... R	Southwest Baptist (MO) .... R
Kentucky Wesleyan .... R	Taylor (IN) .... R
King (TN) .... S	Texas Lutheran .... R
Liberty (VA) .... R	Union University (TN) .... R
Louisiana College .... R	Virginia Commonwealth U. L
Louisiana State XL	Virginia Wesleyan .... R
Marywood (PA) .... R	Wheeling Jesuit (WV) .... R
Mercyhurst (PA) .... R	York (NE) .... S
Milligan (TN) .... S	

SOCIOLOGY

GROUP I
Most Selective

Amherst (MA) .... R	Grinnell (IA) .... R
Bard (NY) .... R	Harvard (MA) .... M
▲ Barnard (NY) .... R	Holy Cross (MA) .... R
Binghamton (SUNY)(NY) .... M	Illinois, U. of (Urbana-Champaign) XL
Boston College (MA) L	Johns Hopkins (MD) .... M
Bowdoin (ME) .... R	Kalamazoo (MI) .... R
▲ Bryn Mawr (PA) .... S	Lycoming (PA) .... R
Bucknell (PA) .... M	Michigan, U. of XL
California, U. of (Berkeley) XL	North Carolina, U. of L
California, U. of (Los Angeles) XL	Northwestern (IL) .... M
Chicago, U. of (IL) .... M	Notre Dame (IN) .... M
Clarkson (NY) .... M	Oberlin (OH) .... R
Colorado College .... R	Pennsylvania, U. of L
Columbia (NY) .... M	Pitzer (CA) .... S
Connecticut College .... R	Pomona (CA) .... R
Dartmouth (NH) .... M	Princeton (NJ) .... M
DePauw (IN) .... R	Southwestern (TX) .... R
Emory (GA) .... M	Stanford (CA) .... M
Florida, U. of XL	Trinity (TX) .... R
Franklin & Marshall (PA) .... R	Virginia, U. of L
Geneseo (SUNY)(NY) .... M	Wheaton (IL) .... R
Georgetown (DC) .... M	Willamette (OR) .... R
George Washington (DC) .... M	Yale (CT) .... M
Gettysburg (PA) .... S	

SOCIOLOGY, continued

GROUP II
Very Selective

Albany (SUNY) (NY)	L
Arizona, U. of	XL
Asbury (KY)	R
Augsburg (MN)	R
Belmont (TN)	R
Beloit (WI)	R
Brigham Young (UT)	XL
Brown (RI)	M
California, U. of (Santa Barbara)	L
Catholic (DC)	R
Cincinnati, U. of (OH)	L
City College (CUNY)(NY)	L
Clemson(SC)	L
College of Charleston (SC)	L
Colorado, U. of	L
Concordia (MN)	R
Connecticut, U. of	XL
Cornell Col. (IA)	R
Covenant (GA)	S
Dayton, U. of (OH)	M
Denison (OH)	R
Denver, U. of (CO)	M
Drake (IA)	M
Earlham (IN)	R
Florida International	L
Georgetown College (KY)	R
Gordon (MA)	R
Hamline (MN)	R
Hanover (IN)	R
Hendrix (AR)	R
Hofstra (NY)	M
▲Hollins (VA)	S
Howard (DC)	M
Illinois College	S
Indiana U.	XL
Iowa, U. of	XL
Iowa State	XL
James Madison (VA)	M
Knox (IL)	R
Lake Forest (IL)	R
Lebanon Valley (PA)	R
Lewis & Clark (OR)	R
Manhattanville (NY)	R
McDaniel (MD)	R

Merrimack (MA)	R
Minnesota, U. of	XL
Mississippi State	L
Moravian (PA)	R
■ Morehouse (GA)	R
Mount Mercy (IA)	S
New College (FL)	S
New Mexico, U. of	L
North Carolina (Asheville)	R
North Carolina, U. of (Wilmington)	L
North Texas	L
Oklahoma State	L
Oregon, U. of	L
Pace (NY)	M
Portland State (OR)	L
Principia (IL)	S
Puget Sound (WA)	R
Queens (CUNY)(NY)	L
Regis (CO)	R
Roanoke (VA)	R
Rutgers (Camden) (NJ)	M
▲Salem Col. (NC)	S
San Diego State U. (CA)	XL
▲Simmons (MA)	R
St. Lawrence (NY)	R
St. Mary's Col. (CA)	R
South Dakota School of Mines	R
Stony Brook (SUNY)(NY)	L
Syracuse (NY)	L
Towson (MD)	L
▲Trinity (DC)	S
Washington State	L
Washington, U. of	XL
Wells (NY)	S
Westminster (PA)	R
Western Washington U.	L
Wheaton (MA)	R
Winona State U. (MN)	M
Wisconsin, U. of	XL
Wisconsin, U. of (Stevens Point)	M
Wofford (SC)	R
Wooster (OH)	R

SOCIOLOGY continues next page

SOCIOLOGY, continued

GROUP III
Selective

Adrian (MI)	R	Massachusetts, U. of (Boston)	M
Akron, U. of (OH)	L	Massachusetts, U. of (Dartmouth)	M
Albright (PA)	R	Michigan State	XL
Augusta (GA)	M	Minnesota, U. of (Duluth)	M
Belmont Abbey (NC)	S	Montana, U. of	M
Benedictine (KS)	R	π Mount St. Joseph (OH)	R
Biola (CA)	R	Nevada, U. of (Reno)	L
Bridgewater (VA)	R	New Orleans (LA)	L
Bridgewater State (MA)	M	Northern Colorado	L
California State U. (Fresno)	L	Northern Illinois	L
California State U. (East Bay)	M	Northern Michigan	M
California State U. (Fullerton)	L	Old Dominion (VA)	L
California State U. (Los Angeles)	L	Quincy (IL)	R
California State U. (Northridge)	L	St. Anselm (NH)	R
California State U. (Sacramento)	M	▲ St. Catherine (MN)	R
California State U. (San Bernardino)	M	St. John's (NY)	L
California State U. (San Marcos)	M	St. Mary's U. of San Antonio (TX)	R
Castleton State (VT)	R	St. Rose (NY)	R
Central Connecticut	M	Salem State (MA)	M
Coker (SC)	S	San Francisco State (CA)	L
Doane (NE)	S	Shaw (NC)	R
D'Youville (NY)	R	Shippensburg (PA)	M
Eastern (PA)	R	Simpson (IA)	R
Eastern Connecticut	M	Sonoma State (CA)	M
Eastern Michigan	L	South Alabama	M
Fisk (TN)	S	Southern Connecticut	M
Fort Hays (KS)	M	Southern Oregon State U.	M
Framingham State (MA)	M	Southwest Missouri	L
Gardner-Webb (NC)	S	▲ Spelman (GA)	R
George Fox (OR)	R	Suffolk (MA)	R
Georgia State	L	Tarleton State (TX)	M
Grambling (LA)	M	Temple (PA)	L
Hartwick (NY)	R	Virginia Wesleyan	R
Johnson C. Smith (NC)	R	Wagner (NY)	R
Kean (NJ)	M	West Chester (PA)	M
Indiana (PA)	L	Western Connecticut State	M
Indiana U.-Purdue U.-Indianapolis (IN)	L	Western Illinois	L
Lamar (TX)	M	Western Kentucky	L
Lenoir-Rhyne (NC)	R	Western Michigan	L
Louisville (KY)	L	Whitman (WA)	R
Lynchburg (VA)	R	William Paterson (NJ)	M
Manchester (IN)	R	Wilson (PA)	S
▲ Mary Baldwin (VA)	S	Wisconsin, U. of (LaCrosse)	L
Mass. Col. of Lib. Arts. (N. Adams)	R		

ZOOLOGY

GROUP I
Most Selective

California, U. of (Berkeley) XL
Cornell (NY) L
Florida, U. of XL
Miami, U. of (OH) L

Michigan, U. of XL
North Carolina, U. of L
Pennsylvania State XL
Wisconsin, U. of XL

GROUP II
Very Selective

Albertson (ID) .... S
Arizona State XL
Brigham Young (UT) XL
California, U. of (Davis) L
California, U. of (Santa Barbara) L
Clemson (SC) L
Connecticut, U. of XL
Georgia, U. of L
Hawaii, U. of L
Indiana U. XL
Iowa State XL
Kansas, U. of L
Kentucky, U. of XL

Maryland, U. of XL
Massachusetts, U. of L
North Carolina State L
North Central (IL) .... R
Ohio Wesleyan .... R
Ohio U. L
Oklahoma, U. of XL
Oswego (SUNY)(NY) .... M
Texas A&M XL
Texas, U. of (Austin) XL
Vermont, U. of L
Washington State L
Washington, U. of XL

GROUP III
Selective

Cal. Poly. State U. (Pomona) L
California State U. (San Jose) L
Colorado State L
Eastern Illinois L
Howard (DC) .... M
Louisiana-Lafayette L
Louisiana State XL
Montana, U. of .... M

Oregon State L
San Jose State (CA) L
Southeastern Oklahoma State .... M
Southern Illinois U. (Carbondale) L
Tennessee, U. of XL
Weber State (UT) L
Wyoming, U. of L

SECTION TWO

MISCELLANEOUS MAJORS

AFRICANA STUDIES

Albany (SUNY) (NY)
Bates (ME)
Bowling Green (OH)
Brooklyn (CUNY) (NY)
California, U. of (Berkeley)
California, U. of (Santa Barbara)
Chicago, U. of (IL)
City (CUNY)(NY)
Coe (IA)
Columbia (NY)
Connecticut, U. of
Denison (OH)
Duke (NC)
Earlham (IN)
Eastern Illinois
Emory (GA)
Franklin & Marshall (PA)
Harvard (MA)
Howard (DC)
Illinois, U. of (Chicago)
Loyola Marymount (CA)
Luther (IA)
Mercer (GA)

Nebraska, U. of (Omaha)
New York U.
North Carolina (Chapel Hill)
Northwestern (IL)
Oberlin (OH)
Ohio State U.
Pennsylvania, U. of
Pittsburgh, U. of (PA)
Princeton (NJ)
Portland State (OR)
Rutgers (NJ)
San Diego State (CA)
San Francisco State (CA)
Stanford (CA)
Stony Brook (SUNY)(NY)
Toledo, U. of (OH)
Vassar (NY)
Washington U. (MO)
▲Wellesley (MA)
Wesleyan (CT)
Wooster (OH)
Wisconsin, U. of
Yale (CT)

ALTERNATIVE COLLEGES (see page ix)

Antioch (OH)
Atlantic, College of the (ME)
Berea (WV)
Deep Springs (CA)
Eugene Lang (NY)
Evergreen (WA)
Goddard (VT)
Hampshire (MA)
Marlboro (VT)
New College (FL)

New School U.-Eugene Lang Coll. (NY)
Prescott (AZ)
St. John's (MD) (NM)
Shimer (IL)
Simon's Rock (MA)
Sterling (VT)
Thomas Aquinas (CA)
Unity (ME)
Warren Wilson (NC)

ANIMAL SCIENCES

Arizona, U. of
Arkansas, U. of
Auburn (AL)
Berry (GA)
Brigham Young (UT)
Cal Poly (Pomona)
Cal Poly (SLO)
Cal State U. (Fresno)

California, U. of (Davis)
Clemson (SC)
Colorado State
Connecticut, U. of
Cornell (NY)
Delaware Valley (PA)

■ *Men Only*
▲ *Women Only*

ANIMAL SCIENCES continues next page

ANIMAL SCIENCES, continued

Delaware, U. of
Florida, U. of
Georgia U. of
Hampshire (MA)
Hawaii, U. of
Idaho, U. of
Illinois, U. of
Iowa State
Kansas State
Kentucky, U. of
Louisiana State U.
Maine, U. of
Maryland, U. of
Massachusetts, U. of
Michigan State
Minnesota, U. of
Mississippi State
Missouri, U. of
Montana, U. of (Bozeman)
Nebraska, U. of
Nevada, U of (Reno)
New Hampshire, U. of
New Mexico State
North Carolina State

North Dakota State U.
Ohio State
Oklahoma State
Oregon State
Ozarks, College of the (MO)
Pennsylvania State
Purdue (IN)
Rhode Island, U. of
Rutgers (NJ)
South Dakota State
Southern Illinois (Carbondale)
Southwest Missouri
Tarleton State (TX)
Tennessee
Texas A&M
Texas A&M (Kingsville)
Texas Tech
Utah State
Vermont, U. of
Virginia Poly
Washington State
West Virginia U.
Wisconsin, U.of
Wyoming, U. of

APPLIED MATHEMATICS

American (DC)
Auburn (AL)
▲ Barnard (NY)
Boston U. (MA)
Brown (RI)
Cal Tech
California, U. of (Berkeley)
California, U. of (Los Angeles)
California, U. of (San Diego)
Carnegie-Mellon (PA)
Case Western (OH)
Chicago, U. of (IL)
Clarkson (NY)
Colgate (NY)
Colorado, U. of
Columbia (NY)
Connecticut, U. of
Florida State
George Washington (DC)
Georgia Tech
Harvard (MA)
Idaho, U. of
Illinois Inst. of Tech

Lehigh (PA)
Michigan, U. of
Missouri, U. of (Rolla)
New Jersey Inst of Tech.
Northwestern (IL)
Pittsburgh, U. of (PA)
Pitzer (CA)
Rice (TX)
Rochester, U. of (NY)
Rutgers (NJ)
San Jose State (CA)
Stony Brook (SUNY)(NY)
Tulane (LA)
Tulsa (OK)
Virginia, U. of
Wake Forest (NC)
Washington U. (MO)
Western Michigan
Western Washington
Wisconsin
Worcester Poly (MA)
Yale (CT)

■ *Men Only*
▲ *Women Only*

ARCHAEOLOGY

Baylor (TX)
Boston U. (MA)
Bowdoin (ME)
Brown (RI)
▲ Bryn Mawr (PA)
Cornell (NY)
Dartmouth (NH)
Dickinson (PA)
Evansville (IN)
Florida State
George Washington (DC)
Hamilton (NY)
Harvard (MA)
Haverford (PA)
Hunter (CUNY) (NY)
Kent State (OH)
Maryland, U. of
π Mary Washington, U. of (VA)

Michigan, U. of
Missouri, U. of
North Carolina, U. of (Greensboro)
New York U.
Oberlin (OH)
Rhode Island College
Texas, U. of
Virginia
Washington & Lee (VA)
Washington U. (MO)
▲ Wellesley (MA)
Wesleyan (CT)
West Florida
Wheaton (IL)
Wisconsin (La Crosse)
Wooster (OH)
Yale (CT)

π *Classical Archeology*

ART THERAPY

Alverno (WI)
Anna Maria (MA)
Arcadia (PA)
Art Institute of Chicago (IL)
Avila (MO)
Barat (IL)
Bowling Green (OH)
Brescia (KY)
Capital U. (OH)
Carlow (PA)
▲ Cedar Crest
▲ Converse (SC)
▲ Edgewood (WI)
Emporia State (KS)
Harding (AR)
Indianapolis, U. of

Lesley (MA)
Long Island U. (CW Post)(NY)
Marygrove (MI)
Marian Col. of Fond du Lac (WI)
▲ Meredith (NC)
Millikin (IL)
Pittsburg (KS)
Russell Sage (NY)
Santa Fe, Col. of (NM)
▲ Seton Hill (PA)
South Illinois (Edwardsville)
Spring Hill (AL)
Springfield (MA)
St. Thomas Aquinas (NY)
Wisconsin (Superior)

■ *Men Only*
▲ *Women Only*

ATMOSPHERIC SCIENCES

Albany (SUNY) (NY)
Arizona, U. of
Brockport (SUNY) (NY)
California (PA)
California, U. of (Davis)
Cornell (NY)
Embry-Riddle (FL)
Florida Inst. of Tech.
Florida State
Hawaii
Iowa State
Kansas
Lyndon State (VT)
Metropolitan State (CO)
Millersville (PA)
Nebraska
North Carolina State
North Dakota, U. of
Northern Illinois

Northland (WI)
Oklahoma, U. of
Oneonta (SUNY) (NY)
Pennsylvania State
Purdue (IN)
San Francisco State (CA)
San Jose State (CA)
St. Louis University (MO)
South Alabama
Stony Brook (SUNY)(NY)
Texas A&M
Utah, U. of
Valparaiso (IN)
Washington, U. of
Western Illinois
Western Connecticut
Wilkes-Barre (PA)
Wisconsin, U. of
Wisconsin, U. of (Milwaukee)

AUDIOLOGY/SPEECH/LANGUAGE THERAPY

Abilene Christian (TX)
Adelphi (NY)
Akron, U. of (OH)
Andrews (MI)
Arizona
Arizona State
Auburn (AL)
Ball State (IN)
Boston U.
Buffalo (SUNY) (NY)
California State U. (East Bay)
California State U. (Fresno)
California State U. (San Marcos)
Clarion (PA)
Colorado
East Tennessee
East Stroudsburg (PA)
Eastern Illinois
Eastern Washington
Elmira (NY)
Florida
Florida State
Fontbonne (MO)
Geneseo (SUNY) (NY)
Geneva (PA)
George Washington (DC)

Hardin-Simmons (TX)
Hawaii
Hofstra (NY)
Illinois, U. of
Iowa, U. of
James Madison (VA)
Kansas
Kean (NJ)
Longwood (VA)
Loyola (MD)
Maine, U. of
Maryville (TN)
Michigan State
Minnesota, U. of
Misericordia, College (PA)
Mississippi U. of Women
Montevallo (AL)
Moorhead (MN)
Nazareth (NY)
Nebraska
New Hampshire, U. of
New Paltz (SUNY) (NY)
No. Colorado
No. Iowa
No. Michigan
Oklahoma

■ *Men Only*
▲ *Women Only*

AUDIOLOGY / SPEECH / LANGUAGE THERAPY continues
next page

AUDIOLOGY/SPEECH/LANGUAGE THERAPY, continued

Pace (NY)
Plattsburg (SUNY) (NY)
Portland State (OR)
Purdue (IN)
Richard Stockton (NJ)
Rhode Island
St. John's (NY)
St. Louis U. (MO)
S. Alabama
S. Dakota, U. of
S. Florida
Science and Arts of Oklahoma
Southeastern Louisiana
Syracuse (NY)

Tennessee
Texas
Texas (Dallas)
Texas Christian
Towson (MD)
Tulsa (OK)
Utah State
Washington, U. of
Wayne State (MI)
Western Michigan
Western Washington
Worcester State (MA)
Wisconsin
Wyoming

AVIATION MANAGEMENT

Aeronautics, College of (NY)
Alaska, U. of (Anchorage)
Auburn (AL)
Central Missouri
Daniel Webster (NH)
Dowling (NY)
Dubuque, U. of (IA)
Eastern Kentucky
Eastern Michigan
Embry-Riddle (FL)
Fairmont (WV)
Farmingdale (SUNY)(NY)
Florida Inst. of Tech.
Hampton (VA)
Henderson (AR)

Jacksonville (FL)
Lewis (IL)
Lynn (FL)
Metropolitan State (CO)
Minnesota State U. (Mankato)
New Haven (CT)
North Dakota, U. of
Purdue (IN)
Robert Morris (PA)
Rocky Mountain (MT)
St. Francis (NY)
St. Louis (MO)
Southern Illinois U.
Tarleton State (TX)

AVIATION SCIENCE

Andrews (MI)
Averett (VA)
Baylor (TX)
Bowling Green (OH)
Daniel Webster (NH)
Dowling (NY)
Embry-Riddle (FL)
Fairmont (WV)
Florida Inst. of Tech.
Geneva (PA)
Georgia Institute of Technology
Grace (NE)
Hampton (VA)
Henderson State (AR)
Illinois, U. of
Kansas State
Kent State (OH)
Lewis (IL)

Metropolitan State (CO)
Minnesota State U. (Mankato)
North Dakota, U. of
Ohio State
Ohio University
Oklahoma State
Purdue (IN)
Rocky Mountain (MT)
St. Cloud State (MN)
St. Louis U. (MO)
Salem State (MA)
Salem-Teikyo (WV)
San Jose State (CA)
Southern Illinois
Walla Walla (WA)
Western Michigan
Westminster (UT)

■ *Men Only*
▲ *Women Only*

Aviation - Human Factors

BIOMEDICAL ENGINEERING

California, U. of (Berkeley)
California, U. of (Davis)
California, U. of (Santa Cruz)
Cornell (NY)
Duke (NC)
Johns Hopkins (MD)

North Carolina, U. of
Pennsylvania, U. of
Southern California
Stanford (CA)
Wisconsin, U. of
Wright State (OH)

BIOPHYSICS

Brown (RI)
Buffalo (SUNY)(NY)
California, U. of (Irvine)
California, U. of (San Diego)
Centenary (LA)
Chicago U. of (IL)
Columbia (NY)
Connecticut, U. of
Geneseo (SUNY)(NY)
■ Hampden-Sydney (VA)
Hampshire (MA)
Harvard (MA)
Houston, U. of (TX)
Illinois Institute of Tech.

Illinois, U. of
Iowa State
Johns Hopkins (MD)
Michigan, U. of
Oregon State
Pennsylvania, U. of
Pitzer (CA)
Rensselaer (NY)
St. Bonaventure (NY)
Scranton, U. of (PA)
Suffolk (MA)
Temple (PA)
Walla Walla (WA)
Washington U. (MO)

CERAMICS

Alfred (NY)
Arcadia (PA)
Bennington (VT)
Bowling Green (OH)
Cleveland Institute of Art (OH)
Colorado State
East Carolina (NC)
Hartford, U. of (CT)
Kansas City Art Institute (MO)
Maryland Inst. College of Art
Massachusetts College of Art

Miami (FL)
Montevallo (AL)
Moore (PA)
North Texas
Oklahoma, U. of
Rhode Island School of Design
San Jose State (CA)
Syracuse (NY)
Temple (PA)
Washington, U. of

■ *Men Only*
▲ *Women Only*

CINEMATOGRAPHY/FILM STUDIES/VIDEO PRODUCTION

* Arts, U. of the (PA)
Bard (NY)
Bennington (VT)
Bowling Green (OH)
Boston U. (MA)
Brooklyn (CUNY) (NY)
Brown (RI)
California College of Arts & Crafts
California State U. (Long Beach)
California, U. of (Berkeley)
California, U. of (Irvine)
California, U. of (Los Angeles)
California, U. of (Santa Barbara)
California, U. of (Santa Cruz)
California Institute of the Arts
Central Florida
Chapman (CA)
Chicago, U. of (IL)
Claremont-McKenna (CA)
Clark (MA)
Cogswell (CA)
Colgate (NY)
Columbia (Hollywood)(CA)
Colorado State
Colorado, U. of
Columbia (IL)
Columbia (NY)
Columbus Coll. of Art & Design (OH)
Denison (OH)
DeSales (PA)
Eastern Washington
Emerson (MA)
Emory (GA)
Evergreen (WA)
Florida
Florida State
Georgia State
Hampshire (MA)
Hofstra (NY)
**▲Hollins
Howard (DC)
Hunter (CUNY) (NY)
Iowa
Ithaca (NY)

Kansas
Loyola-Marymount (CA)
Massachusetts College of Art
Memphis (TN)
Michigan
New Orleans, U. of (LA)
New York U.
North Carolina, U. of (Greensboro)
North Carolina, U. of (Wilmington)
North Carolina State
North Texas
Northern Michigan
Northwestern (IL)
Oberlin (OH)
Oklahoma
Pennsylvania State
Pittsburgh, U. of (PA)
Pitzer (CA)
Point Park (PA)
Purchase (SUNY) (NY)
Purdue (IN)
Rhode Island College
Rhode Island School of Design
Rochester Inst. of Tech. (NY)
Rochester, U. of (NY)
San Francisco Art Institute (CA)
San Francisco State (CA)
Santa Fe (NM)
Sarah Lawrence (NY)
Southern California
Southern Methodist (TX)
Syracuse (NY)
Temple (PA)
Texas Christian
Texas, U. of
Toledo (OH)
Towson (MD)
Visual Arts, School of (NY)
Wayne State (MI)
Webster (MO)
Wesleyan (CT)
Wisconsin (Milwaukee)
Woodbury (CA)

and Writing for Media Performance

**Film and Photography*

■ *Men Only*
▲ *Women Only*

COMPUTER ENGINEERING

Alabama, U. of (Huntsville)
Arkansas, U. of
Arizona, U. of
Arizona State
Auburn (AL)
Binghamton (SUNY)(NY)
California, U. of (Berkeley)
California, U. of (Davis)
California, U. of (Los Angeles)
California, U. of (San Diego)
California, U. of (Santa Cruz)
California Poly. (SLO)
California State U. (Long Beach)
Carnegie-Mellon (PA)
Case Western Reserve (OH)
Central Florida
Clarkson (NY)
Clemson (SC)
Colorado, U. of
Columbia (NY)
Cornell (NY)
Drexel (PA)
Florida Atlantic
Florida Inst. of Tech.
Florida State
Florida, U. of
George Mason (VA)
George Washington (DC)
Georgia Tech.
Gonzaga (WA)
Harvey Mudd (CA)
Illinois, U. of
Illinois, U. of (Chicago)
Iowa State
Johns Hopkins (MD)
Kansas, U. of
Kansas State
Lehigh (PA)

Louisville, U. of (KY)
Marquette (WI)
Maryland, U. of
Maryland, U. of (Baltimore Co.)
Massachusetts, U. of (Dartmouth)
MIT (MA)
Michigan, U. of
Michigan State
Michigan Tech.
Milwaukee Sch. of Engin. (WI)
New Jersey Inst. of Tech.
New Mexico, U. of
North Carolina State
Northwestern (IL)
Notre Dame (IN)
Ohio State
Oklahoma, U. of
Pennsylvania State
Pennsylvania, U. of
Pittsburgh, U. of (PA)
Princeton (NJ)
Purdue (IN)
Rensselaer (NY)
Rochester Inst. of Tech. (NY)
Rose-Hulman (IN)
San Jose State (CA)
South Florida
Stony Brook (SUNY)(NY)
Texas A&M
Texas, U. of (Arlington)
Tulane (LA)
Union (NY)
Utah, U. of
Vanderbilt (TN)
Virginia Poly Tech.
Washington, U. of
Washington U. (MO)
Wright State (OH)

■ *Men Only*
▲ *Women Only*

COMPUTER GRAPHICS

Allegheny (PA)
American (DC)
Andrews (MI)
Arts, U. of the (PA)
Central Oklahoma
Champlain (VT)
Cogswell (CA)
Columbia (IL)
Columbus College of Art &
    Design (OH)
Dominican (IL)
Dubuque (IA)
E. Michigan
Embry-Riddle (FL)
Fashion Institute of Tech. (NY)
Huntingdon (AL)

Jacksonville (FL)
LaSalle (PA)
Lewis (IL)
Loyola Marymount (CA)
Monmouth (NJ))
New York Institute of Tech.
Pratt Institute (NY)
Purdue (IN)
Ringling (FL)
Rochester Institute of Tech (NY)
Springfield (MA)
Syracuse (NY)
Taylor (IN)
Tampa (FL)
Woodbury (CA)

CREATIVE WRITING

▲Agnes Scott (GA)
Alabama, U. of
Albertson (ID)
Allegheny (PA)
Arizona, U. of
Bard (NY)
Belhaven (MS)
Belmont (TN)
Beloit (WI)
Bennington (VT)
Bowling Green (OH)
* Briar Cliff (IA)
California Institute of the Arts
California, U. of (Riverside)
Carlow (PA)
Carnegie Mellon (PA)
Chapman (CA)
Columbia (NY)
Creighton (NE)
Dana (NE)
Dominican (CA)
East Carolina (NC)
Eastern Kentucky
Eckerd (FL)
Emerson (MA)
Florida State
Grand Valley (MI)
Hamilton (NY)
▲Hollins (VA)

Iowa
Kenyon (OH)
Knox (IL)
* Lafayette (PA)
Lewis-Clark State (ID)
Linfield (OR)
Long Island U. (Southampton)(NY)
Lycoming (PA)
Maine (Farmington)
Michigan, U. of
New Paltz (SUNY)(NY)
New School U. (Lang) (NY)
North Carolina (Wilmington)
Oberlin (OH)
Oregon, U. of
Pacific U. (OR)
Pittsburgh, U. of (PA)
Redlands (CA)
St. Andrews (NC)
San Francisco State (CA)
Santa Fe, College of (NM)
Sarah Lawrence (NY)
▲Stephens (MO)
Susquehanna (PA)
▲Sweet Briar (VA)
Wheaton (MA)
Wichita State (KS)

■ *Men Only*
▲ *Women Only*

* *Writing Major*
# *English & Creative Writing*

CRIMINAL JUSTICE

Adelphi (NY)
Alaska, U. of (Anchorage)
Albany (SUNY) (NY)
Anna Maria (MA)
Arizona, U. of
Bloomsburg (PA)
Bowling Green (OH)
Brockport (SUNY) (NY)
Buena Vista (IA)
California State U. (Bakersfield)
California State U. (Fresno)
California State U. (Fullerton)
California State U. (Long Beach)
California State U. (Los Angeles)
California State U. (Sacramento)
California State U. (San Bernardino)
California, U. of (Irvine)
Castleton (VT)
Central Missouri
Chadron State (NE)
Chaminade (HI)
Columbia (MO)
Dayton, U. of (OH)
Delaware, U. of
Dillard (LA)
East Tennessee
Eastern Kentucky
Eastern Washington
Edinboro (PA)
Elmira (NY)
Fairmont State (WV)
Florida Gulf Coast U.
Florida International
Florida Southern
Florida State
Gannon (PA)
George Washington (DC)
Georgia State
Grambling (LA)
Grand Valley (MI)
Great Falls, U. of (MT)
Guilford (NC)
Hamline (MN)
\# ■ Hampden-Sydney (VA)
Hannibal-La Grange (MO)
Hardin-Simmons (TX)
Illinois (Chicago)

Indiana
Iona (NY)
Jacksonville State (AL)
John Jay (CUNY) (NY)
Juniata (PA)
Kentucky Wesleyan
Lindenwood (MO)
Long Island U. (C.W. Post)(NY)
Longwood (VA)
Loras (IA)
Lycoming (PA)
Madonna (MI)
Mansfield (PA)
Marist (NY)
Marshall (WV)
Maryland
Massachusetts State College
 (Westfield)
Mercy (NY)
Mercyhurst (PA)
Michigan State
Minnesota State U. (Mankato)
Minnesota State U. (Moorhead)
Missouri, U. of (St. Louis)
Mitchell (CT)
Mount Mercy (IA)
Nebraska, U. of (Omaha)
New Haven (CT)
New Mexico State
North Carolina (Charlotte)
North Carolina Wesleyan
North Florida
North Michigan
Northeastern (MA)
Northeastern State (OK)
Norwich (VT)
Ohio Northern
Pittsburgh (Bradford)
Portland, U. of (OR)
Potsdam (SUNY) (NY)
Quinnipiac (CT)
Radford (VA)
Regis (CO)

\# *Military Leadership and*
National Security Studies

■ *Men Only*
▲ *Women Only*

CRIMINAL JUSTICE continues next page

CRIMINAL JUSTICE, continued

Richard Stockton (NJ)
Richmond (VA)
Roanoke (VA)
Roger Williams (RI)
Rowan (NJ)
Sacred Heart (CT)
Saginaw Valley (MI)
St. Ambrose (IA)
St. Anselm (NH)
St. Cloud (MN)
St. Edward's (TX)
St. Francis (NY)
St. John's (NY)
St. Leo (FL)
Salem State (MA)
Salve Regina-The Newport College (RI)
Sam Houston State (TX)
San Diego State (CA)
San Jose State (CA)
Seton Hall (NJ)
Simpson (IA)

South Dakota, U. of
South Florida
Southern Illinois U.
    (Carbondale)
Southern Oregon
Southwest Texas
Tarleton State (TX)
Texas (Tyler)
Toledo (OH)
Washburn (KS)
Weber State (UT)
Western Carolina (NC)
Western Connecticut
Western Illinois
West Virginia Wesleyan
Wilmington (OH)
Wisconsin (Milwaukee)
Wisconsin (Platteville)
York (PA)
Youngstown State (OH)

■ *Men Only*
▲ *Women Only*

DESIGN/COMMERCIAL ART

Alfred (NY)
Art Center College of Design (CA)
Arts, U. of the (PA)
Brenau (GA)
Brigham Young (UT)
California College of Arts & Crafts
California Inst. of the Arts
California Poly (SLO)
California, U. of (Davis)
Carnegie Mellon (PA)
Carthage (WI)
Central Oklahoma
Champlain (VT)
Chowan (NC)
Cincinnati, U. of (OH)
Cleveland Institute of Art (OH)
Columbia (IL)
Columbus College of Art & Design (OH)
Cornish (WA)
Creighton (NE)
Drake (IA)
Dubuque (IA)
Edgewood (WI)
Endicott (MA)
Fashion Inst. of Tech. (NY)
Flagler (FL)
Florida A&M
Fort Hays (KS)
Grand Valley (MI)
Illinois, U. of
Iowa State
Kansas City Art Institute (MO)
Kean (NJ)

Kendall Coll. of Art & Design (MI)
Kent State (OH)
Long Island U. (C.W. Post)(NY)
Lyndon State (VT)
Maryland Institute - College of Art
Maryland, U. of
Maryville (MO)
Massachusetts College of Art
Massachusetts, U. of (Dartmouth)
Memphis College of Art
Milliken (IL)
Montserrat (MA)
Moore (PA)
Moravian (PA)
Morningside (IA)
New York Inst.of Technology
North Carolina State
Ohio State
Otis College of Art and Design (CA)
Parsons School of Design (NY)
Rhode Island School of Design
Ringling (FL)
Rochester Inst. of Tech. (NY)
* Roger Williams (RI)
St. Mary's (MN)
San Jose State (CA)
Southern Illinois U.
Texas Christian
Visual Arts, School of (NY)

* Graphic Design Communications

■ Men Only
▲ Women Only

EAST ASIAN STUDIES

Bates (ME)
Berea (KY)
Binghamton (SUNY) (NY)
▲ Bryn Mawr (PA)
Bucknell (PA)
California, U. of (Davis)
California, U. of (Los Angeles)
California, U. of (San Diego)
Chicago, U. of (IL)
Coe (IA)
Colgate (NY)
Colorado College
Columbia (NY)
Connecticut College
Cornell (NY)
Denison (OH)
Denver, U. of (CO)
DePauw (IN)
Furman (SC)
George Washington (DC)
Hamilton (NY)
Hamline (MN)
Harvard (MA)
Hawaii, U. of
Illinois, U. of
Indiana
Kansas, U. of
Lawrence (WI)
Lehigh (PA)

Lewis & Clark (OR)
Macalester (MN)
Manhattanville (NY)
Maryland, U. of
Middlebury (VT)
North Central (IL)
Oberlin (OH)
Ohio State
Oregon, U. of
Pennsylvania, U. of
Pomona (CA)
Puget Sound (WA)
Redlands (CA)
Reed (OR)
Rutgers (NJ)
Sarah Lawrence (NY)
Stanford (CA)
Ursinus (PA)
Utah, U. of
Vassar (NY)
Washington & Lee (VA)
Washington U. (MO)
Washington, U. of
▲ Wellesley (MA)
Wesleyan (CT)
Western Washington
Westmont (CA)
Wisconsin, U. of
Wittenberg (OH)

E-COMMERCE

Bellevue (NE)
California State U.
    (Monterey Bay)
Carnegie Mellon (PA)
Castleton State (VT)
Champlain (VT)
Christopher Newport (VA)
Clarkson (NY)
DePaul (IL)
Emory (GA)

Jacksonville State (AL)
▲ Judson (AL)
Northwestern Oklahoma
Old Dominion (VA)
San Jose State (CA)
Scranton (PA)
Seattle U. (WA)
Southern Alabama
Thomas (ME)
Utah State

■ *Men Only*
▲ *Women Only*

ENTOMOLOGY

Auburn (AL)
California State U.
(Stanislaus)
California, U. of (Davis)
California, U. of (Riverside)
Colorado State
Cornell (NY)
Delaware, U. of
Florida A & M
Florida, U. of
Georgia, U. of
Harvard (MA)
Hawaii, U. of
Idaho, U. of
Illinois, U. of

Iowa State
Maine, U. of
Michigan State
North Carolina State
Ohio State
Oklahoma State
Oregon State
Purdue (IN)
Rutgers (NJ)
San Jose State (CA)
Texas A & M
Utah State
Washington State
Wisconsin, U. of

ENTREPRENEUR STUDIES

American (DC)
American International (MA)
Arizona, U. of
Babson (MA)
Baylor (TX)
Black Hills State U. (SD)
Bradley (IL)
Brown (RI)
Buena Vista (IA)
California State U.
(San Bernardino)
California, U. of (Riverside)
Canisius (NY)
Case Western Reserve (OH)
Catawba (NC)
Central Connecticut
Chowan (NC)
Colorado State
Columbia College (SC)
Connecticut, U. of
Creighton (NE)
Dayton (OH)
Duquesne (PA)
Eastern Michigan
Fairleigh Dickinson (NJ)
Ferris State U. (MI)
Florida State
Gannon (PA)
Gonzaga (WA)
Hampton (VA)
Hartford, U. of (CT)
Hawaii Pacific
Hofstra (NY)
Houston, U. of (TX)
Illinois
Indiana

Juniata (PA)
Louisiana State U.
Lourdes (OH)
Lyndon State (VT)
Lynn (FL)
Maryland, U. of
Miami (FL)
Middle Tennessee
Mississippi U. for Women
Muhlenberg (PA)
New Mexico
Northeastern (MA)
North Carolina (Greensboro)
North Dakota
North Texas
Ohio University
Oklahoma, U. of
Palm Beach Atlantic (FL)
Pennsylvania, U. of
Reinhardt (GA)
Rensselaer (NY)
St. Mary's (TX)
▲Seton Hill (PA)
Syracuse (NY)
Virginia Commonwealth
Washington & Jefferson (PA)
Washington State
Waynesburg (PA)
Western Carolina (NC)
Wheeling Jesuit (WV)
Wichita State (KS)
Winthrop (SC)
Wyoming
Xavier (LA)
Xavier (OH)

■ *Men Only*
▲ *Women Only*

ENVIRONMENTAL STUDIES

Adelphi (NY)
Alaska Pacific
Albion (MI)
Alfred (NY)
Allegheny (PA)
Antioch (OH)
Atlantic, College of the (ME)
Bates (ME)
Berry (GA)
Bethel (KS)
Bowdoin (ME)
Brenau (GA)
Briar Cliff (IA)
Brockport (SUNY)(NY)
Brown (RI)
California State U. (Channel Islands)
California, U. of (Davis)
California, U. of (Merced)
California, U. of (Riverside)
California, U. of
      (Santa Barbara)
California, U. of (Santa Cruz)
Carleton (MN)
Carroll (WI)
Case Western Reserve
Centenary (LA)
Central (IA)
Chestnut Hill (PA)
Chicago, U. of (IL)
Claremont McKenna (CA)
Clark (MA)
Clarkson (NY)
Colby (ME)
Colgate (NY)
Colorado, U. of
Connecticut College
Connecticut, U. of
Dartmouth (NH)
Davis & Elkins (WV)
Delaware Valley (PA)
Denison (OH)
Denver, U. of (CO)
DePaul (IL)
Dickinson (PA)
Doane (NE)
Dordt (IA)
Drake (IA)

Dubuque (IA)
Duke (NC)
Earlham (IN)
Eastern Connecticut
Eastern Kentucky
Eckerd (FL)
Elizabethtown (PA)
Endicott (MA)
Evergreen State (WA)
Florida Gulf Coast
Florida, U. of
Florida Institute of Tech.
George Fox (OR)
Georgetown College (KY)
Georgia
Green Mountain (VT)
Harvard (MA)
Hawaii Pacific
Idaho
Johnson State (VT)
Juniata (PA)
Lake Forest (IL)
Linfield (OR)
Long Island U. (C.W. Post)(NY)
Loyola (IL)
Lynchburg (VA)
Lyndon (VT)
Macalester (MN)
Marietta (OH)
Maritime College (SUNY)(NY)
Maryville (MO)
Michigan, U. of
Michigan State
Middlebury (VT)
Minnesota, U. of
Monmouth (IL)
Montreat (NC)
Moravian (PA)
Nebraska, U. of
Nevada, U. of (Reno)
New Hampshire, U. of
New Mexico Inst. of Min. & Tech.
π New Mexico State
North Carolina (Asheville)

π *Environmental & Occupational Health*

ENVIRONMENTAL STUDIES *continues next page*

ENVIRONMENTAL STUDIES, continued

North Carolina (Greensboro)
Northland (WI)
* Northwestern (IA)
Oberlin (OH)
Ohio Wesleyan
Oregon Inst. of Tech.
Oregon State
Pacific U. (OR)
Pennsylvania State
Pennsylvania, U. of
Pittsburgh (Bradford)
Pittsburgh, U. of (PA)
Pitzer (CA)
Plattsburgh (SUNY)(NY)
Portland State (OR)
Prescott (AZ)
Purchase (SUNY) (NY)
Ramapo (NJ)
Randolph-Macon (VA)
Rensselaer (NY)
Rhode Island, U. of
Richard Stockton (NJ)
Ripon (WI)
Rochester Inst. of Tech. (NY)
Rocky Mountain (MT)
Rutgers (NJ)
Sacred Heart (CT)
St. Anselm (NH)
St. John's (NY)
St. Lawrence (NY)
St. Michael's (VT)
St. Norbert (WI)
Salisbury State (MD)

Santa Fe, College of (NM)
Sarah Lawrence (NY)
Shepherd (WV)
South, U. of the (TN)
South Florida
Southwestern (TX)
Stanford (CA)
Stockton State (NJ)
SUNY College of Env.
    Sci. & Forestry
Susquehanna (PA)
Tarleton State (TX)
Unity (ME)
Utah State
Valparaiso (IN)
Vermont, U. of
Virginia, U. of
Warren Wilson (NC)
Washington State
Washington, U. of
Wesleyan (CT)
Western Washington
West Virginia Wesleyan
Westfield State (MA)
Westminster (MO)
Whitman (WA)
Wilson (PA)
Wisconsin
Wisconsin (Green Bay)
Worcester Poly (MA)
Yale (CT)
Akron, U. of (OH)

* *Environmental Science*

EQUESTRIAN STUDIES

Averett (VA)
Centenary (NJ)
Colorado State
Delaware Valley (PA)
Findlay (OH)
▲ Judson (AL)
Lake Erie (OH)
Otterbein (OH)
Puerto Rico, U. of
    (Rio Piedras)

Rocky Mountain (MT)
St. Andrews (NC)
Salem-Teikyo (WV)
▲ Stephens (MO)
Truman State (MO)
Virginia Intermont
William Woods (MO)
Wilson (PA)

■ *Men Only*
▲ *Women Only*

EXERCISE SCIENCE/WELLNESS/MOVEMENT

Abilene Christian (TX)
Adelphi (NY)
Adrian (MI)
Alma (MI)
Austin (TX)
Ball State (IN)
* Belhaven (MS)
Bloomsburg (PA)
Bluffton (OH)
Boston U.
Bridgewater (VA)
Buena Vista (IA)
Cal Poly (SLO)
California State U. (Fresno)
California State U. (Fullerton)
California State U.
  (Long Beach)
California State U.
  (San Bernardino)
California State U.
  (San Marcos)
Carthage (WI)
Castleton (VT)
Central (IA)
Chapman (CA)
Colby-Sawyer (NH)
Colorado, U. of
Concordia (NE)
Connecticut, U. of
Cumberland (KY)
Dayton (OH)
DePauw (IN)
Drury (MO)
Eastern Nazarene (MA)
Evansville (IN)
Fitchburg (MA)
Florida Atlantic
Fort Lewis (CO)
Georgetown (KY)
George Washington (DC)
Gordon (MA)
Greensboro (NC)
Houston (TX)
Humboldt State (CA)
High Point (NC)
Idaho, U. of
Illinois, U. of (Chicago)

▲Immaculata (PA)
James Madison (VA)
Kennesaw State (GA)
Lipscomb (TN)
Linfield (OR)
Lynchburg (VA)
Massachusetts, U. of
▲Meredith (NC)
Miami U. (OH)
Millersville (PA)
Mississippi U. for Women
Nevada, U. of (Las Vegas)
New Hampshire, U. of
North Texas
Northeastern Illinois
Otterbein (OH)
Pacific U. (OR)
Pittsburgh, U. of (PA)
Puget Sound (WA)
▲St. Catherine (MN)
San Francisco State (CA)
Schreiner (TX)
Shaw (NC)
Slippery Rock (PA)
Southwestern (TX)
Southwest Texas State
Springfield (MA)
Stetson (FL)
Tampa, U. of (FL)
Tennessee, U. of
Texas A&M (Corpus Christi)
Texas A&M (Kingsville)
Toledo (OH)
Transylvania (KY)
Texas Lutheran
Texas Women's
Utah
Westfield (MA)
Willamette (OR)
Western State College of
  Colorado
Western Maryland
Whitworth (WA)
Willamette (OR)
Wyoming

■ *Men Only*
▲ *Women Only*

* Exercise Science and
Sports Medicine

FASHION DESIGN / MERCHANDISING

Albright (PA)
Auburn (AL)
Baylor (TX)
Bowling Green (OH)
Brenau (GA)
California College of
    Arts & Crafts
California State U. (Fresno)
California State U.
    (Sacramento)
Central Washington
Champlain (VT)
Cincinnati (OH)
Colorado State
Columbus College of Art &
    Design (OH)
Delaware, U. of
Dominican (IL)
Drexel (PA)
Florida State
Framingham (MA)
Eastern Michigan
Hawaii, U. of
High Point (NC)
Illinois, U. of

Indiana (PA)
Iowa State
Kansas State
Kent State (OH)
Kentucky, U. of
Lasell (MA)
Lynn (FL)
▲Meredith (NC)
New Hampshire College
North Carolina (Greensboro)
Oklahoma State
Oregon State
Pratt (NY)
Rhode Island School of Design
Rhode Island, U. of
▲Stephens (MO)
Tarleton State (TX)
Texas Christian
Virginia Commonwealth U.
Washington State
Wisconsin, U. of
Wisconsin, U. of (Stout)

 # Especially Interior Design

FORENSIC SCIENCES / TECHNOLOGY

▲Bay Path (MA)
Bemidji State (MN)
Central Florida
▲Cedar Crest (PA)
Chaminade (HI)
Defiance (OH)
Duquesne (PA)
Eastern Kentucky
Eastern Washington
Edinboro (PA)
Florida Gulf Coast U.
* Guilford (NC)

Hamline (MN)
John Jay (CUNY)(NY)
Kansas State
Marygrove (MI)
Miami, U. of (FL)
Mississippi, U. of
New Haven, U. of (CT)
St. Scholastica (MN)
**Towson (MD)
Virginia Commonwealth U.
West Virginia

Forensic Biology
** *Forensic Chemistry*

■ *Men Only*
▲ *Women Only*

GENETICS

Ball State (IN)
California, U. of (Berkeley)
California, U. of (Davis)
California, U. of (Irvine)
California, U. of (Los Angeles)
Carnegie Mellon (PA)
▲ Cedar Crest (PA)
Chicago, U. of (IL)
Connecticut, U. of
Cornell (NY)
Florida State
Fredonia (SUNY)(NY)
Georgia, U. of
Harvard (MA)
Illinois, U. of
Illinois, U. of (Chicago)

Iowa State
Kansas
Maryland, U. of
Minnesota
Ohio State
Ohio Wesleyan
Otterbein (OH)
Purdue (IN)
Rochester, U. of (NY)
Rutgers (NJ)
Texas A & M
Vermont, U. of
Washington State
Western Kentucky
Wisconsin, U. of

GERONTOLOGY/GERIATRIC SERVICES

Alfred (NY)
Arkansas, U. of (Pine Bluff)
Bethune-Cookman (FL)
California (PA)
California State U. (Sacramento)
Case Western (OH)
Central Washington
Florida Gulf Coast U.
Fort Hays (KS)
Gwynedd-Mercy (PA)
Kent State (OH)
King's (PA)
Langston (OK)
Lindenwood (VA)
Lourdes (OH)
Madonna (MI)
Massachusetts (Boston)
Mount St. Mary's (CA)
\# Mount St. Joseph (OH)

North Carolina (Greensboro)
North Colorado
North Texas
Oneonta (SUNY)(NY)
Quinnipiac (CT)
Roosevelt (IL)
Richard Stockton (NJ)
St. Mary's (CA)
San Diego State (CA)
Scranton (PA)
Shaw (NC)
South Florida
Southern California
Southwest Missouri
Springfield (MA)
Stephen F. Austin (TX)
Wagner (NY)
Washburn (KS)
Weber State (UT)

\# Also, Aging Services Administration
/ Social Work

HEALTH SERVICES ADMINISTRATION

Alfred (NY)
Appalachian State (NC)
Arcadia (PA)
Arizona
Detroit Mercy (MI)
Eastern Michigan
Eastern Washington
Herbert Lehman (CUNY)(NY)
James Madison (VA)
Kentucky
Madonna (MI)
▲ Mary Baldwin (VA)
Michigan (Dearborn)
Missouri, U. of
Mount Mercy (IA)
North Carolina
(Chapel Hill)

Northeastern (MA)
Oregon State
Pennsylvania State
Providence College (RI)
Quinnipiac (CT)
Saint Scholastica (MN)
Scranton (PA)
South Dakota, U. of
Springfield (MA)
Stonehill (MA)
Utah, U. of
Washburn (KS)
Washington, U. of
Wisconsin (Eau Claire)

HISPANIC STUDIES/LATIN AMERICAN STUDIES

American (DC)
Arizona, U. of
Assumption (MA)
Austin (TX)
California, U. of (Berkeley)
California, U. of
(Santa Barbara)
California, U. of
(Santa Cruz)
California State
(Long Beach)
Chicago, U. of (IL)
City (CUNY) (NY)
Connecticut College
Connecticut, U. of
DePaul (IL)
Flagler (FL)
Gettysburg (PA)
George Fox (OR)
Hunter (CUNY)(NY)
Johns Hopkins (MD)
Loyola Marymount (CA)
Michigan, U. of
Minnesota (Morris)
▲ Mount Holyoke (MA)

New Mexico, U. of
North Carolina
Northern Colorado
Northridge State (CA)
Northwestern (IL)
Pomona (CA)
Rice (TX)
Rollins (FL)
Rutgers (NJ)
San Diego State (CA)
San Francisco State (CA)
▲ Scripps (CA)
▲ Smith (MA)
Sonoma State (CA)
Stetson (FL)
Texas, U. of
Tulane (LA)
Virginia, U. of
Washington, U. of
Wheaton (MA)
Whittier (CA)
Willamette (OR)
Wisconsin, U. of
Wisconsin (Eau Claire)

■ *Men Only*
▲ *Women Only*

HORTICULTURE

Auburn (AL)
Arkansas, U. of
Berry (GA)
Brigham Young (UT)
Cal Poly (Pomona)
Cal Poly (San Luis Obispo)
California, U. of (Davis)
* California, U. of (Riverside)
Christopher Newport
Clemson (SC)
Colorado State
Connecticut, U. of
Cornell (NY)
Delaware Valley (PA)
Delaware, U. of
* Dordt (IA)
Florida, U. of
• Florida Southern
Georgia, U. of
Hawaii, U. of
Idaho, U. of
Illinois, U. of
Iowa State
Kansas State
Maine, U. of
Maryland, U. of
Michigan State
Mississippi State

Missouri, U. of
Montana State (Bozeman)
Nebraska, U. of
New Hampshire, U. of
North Carolina State
North Dakota State
Northwest Missouri
Ohio State
Oklahoma State
Oregon State
Pennsylvania State
Purdue (IN)
Rhode Island, U. of
Rutgers (NJ)
South Dakota State
Southwest Missouri
Tarleton (TX)
Temple (PA)
Tennessee Tech
Tennessee, U. of
Texas A & M
Texas Tech
Utah State
Vermont, U. of
Virginia Poly
Washington State
Washington, U. of
Wisconsin, U. of

Plant Science
• *And Citrus*

■ *Men Only*
▲ *Women Only*

HOTEL AND RESTAURANT MANAGEMENT

Ashland (OH)
Auburn (AL)
Berea (KY)
Bowling Green (OH)
Cal Poly (Pomona)
Central Florida
Champlain (VT)
Colorado State
Cornell (NY)
Delaware
Denver, U. of (CO)
Endicott (MA)
Fairleigh Dickinson (NJ)
Florida International U.
Florida State
Georgia Southern
* Green Mountain (VT)
Georgia State
Houston, U. of (TX)
Illinois, U. of
Indiana (PA)
Iowa State
Kansas State
Lasell (MA)
• Lyndon State (VT)
Massachusetts, U. of
Michigan State
Missouri, U. of
Nebraska
Nevada (Las Vegas)
New Hampshire College

New Hampshire, U. of
New Haven (CT)
New Mexico State
New Orleans, U. of (LA)
New York University
Niagara (NY)
North Dakota State
Northern Arizona
Northern Michigan
North Texas
Oklahoma State
Ozarks (MO)
Penn State
Plattsburgh (SUNY)(NY)
Purdue (IN)
Rochester Inst. of Tech. (NY)
Roosevelt (IL)
Siena Heights (MI)
South Carolina, U. of
South Dakota State U.
Southern Illinois
     (Carbondale)
Southern New Hampshire, U. of
Texas A&M (Kingsville)
Texas Tech.
Virginia Poly. Inst.
Washington State
Western Illinois
Western Kentucky
Widener (PA)
Wisconsin (Stout)

* *Resort Mangement*

• *Ski Resort Management*

Restaurant and Food Management

HUMAN RESOURCES MANAGEMENT

American (DC)
Baylor (TX)
Birmingham-Southern (AL)
Boston College (MA)
Bowling Green (OH)
Briar Cliff (IA)
Cabrini (PA)
Cal. Poly. State U.
     (Pomona)
Cal. State (Los Angeles)
DeSales (PA)
Duquesne (PA)
Florida State
Hastings (NE)
Hawaii Pacific
Holy Names (CA)
Houston (TX)
Indiana (PA)
Loras (IA)
LeMoyne (NY)
Lindenwood (MO)
Lipscomb (TN)
Marietta (OH)
Michigan State

Muhlenberg (PA)
Nevada, U. of (Las Vegas)
New Mexico, U. of
Northeastern (MA)
Oakland (MI)
Ohio State
Ohio University
Oklahoma, U. of
Point Park (PA)
Puerto Rico, U. of
     (Rio Piedras)
Rider (NJ)
Rockhurst (MO)
St. Leo (FL)
St. Mary's (TX)
Southwestern (KS)
Tarleton State (TX)
Utah State
Washington U. (MO)
Western Illinois
Wichita State (KS)
Widener (PA)
Wisconsin (Oshkosh)

INDUSTRIAL ARTS

Auburn (AL)
Berea (KY)
California (PA)
π California State U. (Fresno)
Cal. Poly. (Pomona)
Central Michigan
Cincinnati, U. of (OH)
Clemson (SC)
Colorado State
Ferris State (MI)
Fitchburg (MA)
Florida A & M
Idaho
Indiana State
Iowa State
Louisiana State U.

Millersville (PA)
Montclair (NJ)
Nebraska, U. of
New Mexico, U. of
North Carolina State
Northern Colorado
Northern Illinois
Oklahoma State
Oswego (SUNY) (NY)
Pittsburgh, U. of (PA)
Purdue (IN)
Southern Illinois
Texas A&M
Western Michigan
Wisconsin, U. of (Stout)
Wyoming

π *Also Construction Management*

INDUSTRIAL DESIGN

Alfred (NY)
Appalachian State (NC)
Arizona State
Arts, U. of the (PA)
Auburn (AL)
Brigham Young (UT)
California College of
   Arts & Crafts
California State U.
   (Long Beach)
Carnegie-Mellon (PA)
Cincinnati, U of (OH)
Georgia Inst. of Tech.
Illinois, U. of (Chicago)
Illinois, U. of
Kansas, U. of
Kent State (OH)
Metropolitan State (CO)

Michigan, U. of
North Carolina State
Pratt (NY)
Pittsburgh, U. of (PA)
Purdue (IN)
Rhode Island School
   of Design
Rochester Inst. of Tech. (NY)
San Houston State (TX)
San Jose State (CA)
Syracuse (NY)
Tufts (MA)
Virginia Poly
Washington U. (MO)
Western Michigan
Western Washington
Washington, U. of

INTERIOR DESIGN

Adrian (MI)
Akron, U. of (OH)
Alabama, U. of
Arcadia (PA)
Arizona State
Arkansas, U. of
Auburn (AL)
Bayor (TX)
Boston Architectural Center (MA)
Bowling Green (OH)
Bridgeport, U. of (CT)
California State U. (Fresno)
California State U.
   (Sacramento)
Centenary (NJ)
Central Michigan
Central Washington
Chaminade (HI)
Cincinnati, U. of (OH)
Cleveland Inst. of Art (OH)
Colorado State U.
Columbia College (IL)
Columbus College of Art &
   Design (OH)
Cornell (NY)
Drexel (PA)
Eastern Kentucky
Eastern Michigan
Fairmont (WV)
Fashion Inst. of Tech. (NY)
Ferris State (MI)
Florida, U. of

Florida International
Florida State
George Washington (DC)
Georgia, U. of
Georgia Southern
High Point (NC)
Houston, U. of (TX)
Howard (DC)
Idaho, U. of
Indiana U.
Iowa State
Kansas State
Kansas, U. of
Kean (NJ)
Kent State (OH)
Kentucky, U. of
Louisiana State
Louisiana, U. of (Lafayette)
Louisville, U. of (KY)
Maryland Inst. of Art
Miami (OH)
Michigan State
Michigan, U. of
Minnesota, U. of
Mississippi, U. of
Moore (PA)
Mt. Ida (MA)
Mt. St. Joseph (OH)
Murray State (KY)
Nevada, U. of (Las Vegas)

■ *Men Only*
▲ *Women Only*

INTERIOR DESIGN continues next page

INTERIOR DESIGN, continued

Nevada, U. of (Reno)
New Haven, U. of (CT)
NY Sch. of Interior Design
North Carolina (Greensboro)
North Dakota State U.
Northern Iowa
Ohio State
Ohio U.
Oklahoma, U. of
Oregon State
Parsons (NY)
Pratt Institute (NY)
Ringling Sch. of Art &
   Design (FL)
Rochester Inst. of Tech. (NY)
▲Salem (NC)
San Diego State (CA)
San Jose State
Seattle Pacific (WA)

South Dakota State U.
Southern Illinois (Carbondale)
Suffolk (MA)
Syracuse (NY)
Tennessee Tech. U
Tennessee, U. of
Texas A&M (Kingsville)
Texas Christian
Texas, U. of
Ursuline (OH)
Utah State
Virginia Commonwealth
Visual Arts, Sch. of (NY)
West Virginia, U. of
Western Carolina
Western Kentucky
Western Michigan
William Woods (MO)
Wisconsin, U. of

INTERNATIONAL RELATIONS/STUDIES

▲Agnes Scott (GA)
American U. (DC)
+ Arcadia (PA)
Austin (TX)
☎ Babson (MA)
π Belmont Abbey (NC)
Beloit (WI)
● Bentley (MA)
Bethany (WV)
☎ Bethune-Cookman (FL)
Boston U. (MA)
Bradley (IL)
Brown (RI)
☎ Bryant (RI)
▲Bryn Mawr (PA)
Bucknell (PA)
☎ Butler (IN)
☎ Caldwell (NJ)
California State U. (Chico)
California State U.
   (Long Beach)
California, U. of (Davis)
++ Carthage (WI)
π Central (IA)
▲Chatham (PA)
City (CUNY) (NY)
Claremont McKenna (CA)
●● Clark (MA)
Colby (ME)
Colgate (NY)
Colorado
Connecticut College
☎ Cornell (IA)

Davidson (NC)
Dayton (OH)
Denison (OH)
☎ Denver, U. of (CO)
DePaul (IL)
☎ Dickinson (PA)
Dominican (CA)
☎ Drake (IA)
π D'Youville (NY)
✪ Earlham (IN)
Eckerd (FL)
☎ Elizabethtown (PA)
☎ Elmira (NY)
Emory (GA)
Evansville (IN)
☎ Florida International
George Mason (VA)
+ George Washington (DC)
+ Georgetown (DC)
π Georgia
Georgia Tech.
Goucher (MD)
Grand Valley (MI)
Hamline (MN)
☎ Hawaii
+ Hawaii Pacific
☎ Hiram (OH)
☎ Husson (ME)
Johns Hopkins (MD)
Juniata (PA)

INTERNATIONAL RELATIONS
continues next page

INTERNATIONAL RELATIONS/STUDIES, continued

☎ Illinois
Indiana
Iowa, U. of
Kalamazoo (MI)
★ Kansas State
Kenyon (OH)
Knox (IL)
Lehigh (PA)
☎ Lenoir-Rhyne (NC)
Lewis & Clark (OR)
Linfield (OR)
Loras (IA)
Macalester (MN)
Maine (Farmington)
Manhattanville (NY)
▲ Mary Baldwin (VA)
☎ Marygrove (MI)
Massachusetts, U. of
▲ Meredith (NC)
Miami, U. of (FL)
☎ Michigan, U. of
Middlebury (VT)
++ Minnesota, U. of
☎ Minnesota State U. (Mankato)
**Mississippi, U. of
☎ Moravian (PA)
Mt. Holyoke (MA)
Mt. St. Mary's (MD)
Muhlenberg (PA)
Nebraska
North Carolina (Chapel Hill)
π Northeastern (MA)
Oglethorpe (GA)
Ohio U.
Ohio Wesleyan
π Oklahoma City U.
Pacific, U. of the (CA)
Pennsylvania, U. of
Pepperdine (CA)
Pittsburgh, U. of
Pitzer (CA)
Pomona (CA)
Princeton (NJ)
Providence (RI)
++ Puget Sound (WA)
▲ Randolph-Macon
    Woman's Col. (VA)
Redlands (CA)
Richmond (VA)
Rhodes (TN)
☎ Rochester Inst. of Tech. (NY)
San Diego, U. of (CA)

++ San Diego State (CA)
Scranton, U. of (PA)
▲ Scripps (CA)
☎ South Carolina, U. of
☎ Southern California, U. of
Southwestern (TX)
Spring Hill (AL)
☎ St. Andrews (NC)
▲ St. Catherine (MN)
☎ St. Louis U. (MO)
☎ St. Mary's (MN)
St. Mary's (TX)
St. Michael's (VT)
☎ St. Norbert (WI)
St. Olaf (MN)
☎ St. Peter's (NJ)
▲ Stephens (MO)
☎ Stetson (FL)
▲ Sweet Briar (VA)
☎ Texas A&M (Kingsville)
▲ Trinity (DC)
Tufts (MA)
Tulane (LA)
U. S. Military Academy (NY)
Vassar (NY)
Virginia Poly. Institute
Virginia Wesleyan
Washington College (MD)
Washington, U. of
☎▲ Wesleyan (GA)
Westminster (MO)
π Westmont (CA)
☎ Westminster (UT)
Wheaton (MA)
Wheeling Jesuit (WV)
Whittier (CA)
William & Mary (VA)
William Jewell (MO)
Wilson (PA)
Wisconsin, U. of
Wisconsin (Oshkosh)
Wyoming, U. of

Global Studies
★ *International Economics*
☎ *International Business*
★ *International Marketing*
✪ *Peace & Global Studies*
** *Also, International Business*
++ *International Political Economy*
● *International Culture and Economy*
●● *Also, Global Environmental Studies*
π *International Business and Global Affairs*
+ *International Relations, also International Business*

JAPANESE STUDIES

Bucknell (PA)
California, U. of (Los Angeles)
California, U. of (Santa Barbara)
Case Western Reserve (OH)
DePaul (IL)
Dillard (LA)
Earlham (IN)
Georgetown (DC)
Hawaii, U. of
Linfield (OR)
Macalester (MN)
Michigan, U. of

Minnesota, U. of
North Central (IL)
Oberlin (OH)
Oregon, U. of
Pacific, U. of the (CA)
San Francisco State (CA)
Sarah Lawrence (NY)
Stanford (CA)
Swarthmore (PA)
Washington, U. of
Washington U. (MO)
Willamette (OR)

JAZZ

Alabama
Arizona State
Arizona, U. of
Auburn (AL)
Augustana (IL)
Bennington College (VT)
Berklee College of Music (MA)
Bowling Green (OH)
California Institute of the Arts
California State U. (Fullerton)
California State U. (Los Angeles)
California State U. (Northridge)
Cincinnati
Delaware
Denver, U. of
DePaul U. (IL)
Duquesne U. (PA)
Elmhurst (IL)
Five Towns College (NY)
Florida Atlantic
Georgia State
Hampshire College (MA)
Hartford (CT)
Idaho
Iowa
Indiana U.
Indiana U. (PA)
* Johns Hopkins (MD)
Knox (IL)
Long Island U. (Brooklyn)(NY)
Loyola U. (New Orleans) (LA)
Manhattan School of
   Music (NY)
Mannes College of Music (NY)

Marlboro College (VT)
Miami (FL)
Michigan State
Middle Tennessee
Minnesota (Duluth)
Minnesota
New England Conservatory
   of Music (MA)
New York U. (NY)
North Florida
North Texas
Oberlin College (OH)
Ohio State U. (OH)
Rochester (NY)
Rowan (NJ)
Rutgers (NJ)
San Diego State (CA)
Shenandoah U. (VA)
South Florida
Southern California
Southwest Texas State
Temple U. (PA)
Tennessee
Texas (Arlington)
Virginia Commonwealth
Washington, U. of
Webster U. (MO)
Western Maryland
Western Michigan U.
Western Washington
Westfield State (MA)
William Patterson (NJ)

■ *Men Only*
▲ *Women Only*

* *Jazz Performance*

LINGUISTICS

Alaska, U. of (Fairbanks)
Arizona, U. of
Beloit (WI)
Boston U. (MA)
Brown (RI)
Buffalo (SUNY) (NY)
California State U. (Fresno)
California, U. of (Berkeley)
California, U. of (Los Angeles)
California, U. of (San Diego)
California, U. of
      (Santa Barbara)
California, U. of (Santa Cruz)
Chicago, U. of (IL)
Clemson (SC)
Colorado, U. of
Connecticut, U. of
Cornell (NY)
Florida State
Florida, U. of
Georgetown (DC)
Georgia, U. of
Harvard (MA)
Illinois, U. of
Indiana U.
Iowa, U. of
Kansas, U. of
Kentucky, U. of
Lawrence (WI)
Maryland, U. of
Massachusetts, U. of
MIT (MA)

Michigan, U. of
Minnesota, U. of
Mississippi, U. of
New Mexico, U. of
New York U.
North Carolina, U. of
Northeastern (MA)
Ohio State U.
Oklahoma, U. of
Oregon, U. of
Pennsylvania, U. of
Pittsburgh, U. of (PA)
Pitzer (CA)
Pomona (CA)
Portland State (OR)
Queens (CUNY) (NY)
Rice (TX)
Rochester, U. of
Rutgers (NJ)
San Jose State (CA)
▲Scripps (CA)
Southern California, U. of
Southern Maine, U. of
Stanford (CA)
Tennessee, U. of
Texas, U. of
Tulane (LA)
Virginia, U. of
Washington, U. of
▲Wellesley (MA)
Wisconsin, U. of
Yale (CT)

■ *Men Only*
▲ *Women Only*

MARINE SCIENCE

Alaska Pacific
American (DC)
Atlantic, College of the (ME)
Barry (FL)
Brown (RI)
California State U.
    (Long Beach)
California State U. (Stanislaus)
California, U. of (San Diego)
California, U. of
    (Santa Barbara)
California, U. of (Santa Cruz)
Coastal Carolina (SC)
College of Charleston (SC)
Eckerd (FL)
Fairleigh Dickinson (NJ)
Florida Inst. of Technology
Hawaii Pacific
Idaho, U. of
Jacksonville U. (FL)
▲ Judson (AL)
Juniata (PA)
Kutztown (PA)
Long Island U.
    (Southampton)(NY)

Maine, U. of
Maine, U. of (Machias)
Maine Maritime
★ Maritime College (SUNY)(NY)
Miami, U. of (FL)
North Carolina, U. of
    (Wilmington)
Northern Michigan
Rhode Island, U. of
Richard Stockton (NJ)
Roger Williams (RI)
Samford (AL)
South Alabama
π South Carolina
South Florida
Southwest Texas State
Spring Hill (AL)
Tampa, U. of (FL)
Texas A&M
Texas A&M (Galveston)
U.S. Coast Guard Academy (CT)
Unity (ME)
Washington, U. of
West Florida

π *Also, Oceanography*

★ *and Marine Environmental Science*

MEDICAL TECHNOLOGY

Alabama, U. of (Birmingham)
Alaska, U. of (Anchorage)
American International (MA)
Avila (MO)
Barry (FL)
Bowling Green (OH)
Bradley (IL)
Briar Cliff (IA)
Buffalo (SUNY) (NY)
Carroll (WI)
Cincinnati (OH)
Connecticut
East Tennessee
Edgewood (WI)
Elon (NC)
Fairmont (WV)
Florida Atlantic
Florida International
Gwynedd-Mercy (PA)
▲ Hood (MD)
Houston (TX)
Humboldt (CA)
Loma Linda (CA)
▲ Mary Baldwin (VA)
Massachusetts, U. of (Boston)
Mercy (NY)

Miami U. (OH)
Michigan
Michigan State
Midwestern State (TX)
Minnesota, U. of
Minnesota State U. (Mankato)
North Carolina (Greensboro)
Pacific U. (OR)
Pittsburgh (PA)
St. Leo (FL)
St. Mary's (NE)
▲ St. Mary's (IN)
Salisbury (MD)
Sciences, U. of the (PA)
Scranton (PA)
Springfield (MA)
Stetson (FL)
Suffolk (MA)
Texas
Texas A&M (Corpus Christi)
Thomas More (KY)
Tuskegee (AL)
Virginia Commonwealth
Washington, U. of
Western Connecticut
Wisconsin, U. of

MIDDLE EASTERN STUDIES

Arizona, U. of
Arkansas, U. of
Barnard (NY)
Brandeis (MA)
Brigham Young (UT)
Brown (RI)
California, U. of
    (Berkeley)
California, U. of
    (Los Angeles)
California, U. of
    (Santa Barbara)
Chicago, U. of
Columbia (NY)
Connecticut, U. of
Cornell (NY)
Emory (GA)
Florida State
Fordham (NY)
George Washington (DC)

Hampshire (MA)
Harvard (MA)
Indiana, U. of
Johns Hopkins (MD)
Lycoming (PA)
Massachusetts, U. of
Michigan, U. of
Minnesota, U. of
New York U.
Princeton (NJ)
Rutgers (NJ)
Southwest Texas State
Texas, U. of
Toledo, U. of (OH)
U.S. Military Academy (NY)
Utah, U. of
Washington, U. of
Washington U (MO)
Wooster (OH)
Yale (CT)

■ *Men Only*
▲ *Women Only*

MORTUARY SCIENCE/FUNERAL SERVICES

Central Oklahoma
Cincinnati Coll. of Mort. Sci.
π District of Columbia, U. of the
π Ferris State (MI)
Gannon (PA)
π Lynn (FL)

Minnesota, U. of
Mount Ida (MA)
Point Park (PA)
Southern Illinois
St. John's (NY)
Wayne State (MI)

π *Two Year Only*

MUSIC THERAPY

Alabama, U. of
Alverno (WI)
Anna Maria (MA)
Arizona State
Augsburg (MN)
Baldwin-Wallace (OH)
Berklee Coll. of Music (MA)
Charleston Southern (SC)
Colorado State
Dayton (OH)
Drury (MO)
Duquesne (PA)
East Carolina (NC)
Eastern Michigan (MI)
Elizabethtown (PA)
Evansville (IN)
Florida State
Fredonia (SUNY)(NY)
Georgia
Howard (DC)
Immaculata (PA)
Incarnate Word (TX)
Iowa
Kansas
Loyola (LA)
Mansfield (PA)

Maryville, U. of
(St. Louis)(MO)
Miami, U. of (FL)
Michigan State
Minnesota
Mississippi U. for Women
Montclair (NJ)
Nazareth (NY)
New Paltz (SUNY)(NY)
North Dakota, U. of
Ohio U.
Pacific, U. of the (CA)
Queens (NC)
Shenandoah (VA)
Slippery Rock (PA)
Southern Methodist (TX)
Southwestern Oklahoma
Temple (PA)
Texas Women's
Utah State
Wartburg (IA)
Western Illinois
Western Michigan
Wisconsin, U. of (Eau Claire)
Wisconsin, U. of (Oshkosh)
Wooster (OH)

■ *Men Only*
▲ *Women Only*

MUSICAL THEATER

Adrian (MI)
American Academy of
    Dramatic Arts (NY)
Arizona, U. of
Baldwin-Wallace (OH)
California State (Fullerton)
Carnegie Mellon (PA)
Catholic U. (DC)
Central Florida
Central Michigan
Central Oklahoma
Cincinnati, U. of (OH)
Coastal Carolina (SC)
Elmhurst (IL)
Elon (NC)
Florida
Florida State
Fredonia (SUNY)(NY)
Illinois Wesleyan
James Madison (VA)
Miami, U. of (FL)
Muhlenberg (PA)

North Colorado
Northwestern (IL)
New York U.
Oklahoma, U. of
Otterbein (OH)
Point Park (PA)
Rochester, U. of (NY)
Russell Sage (NY)
Santa Clara (CA)
Sarah Lawrence (NY)
Southern Illinois U.
    (Carbondale)
Southwest Missouri State
Syracuse (NY)
Texas Christian
Trinity (CT)
West Virginia Wesleyan
Weber State (UT)
Western Illinois
Western Michigan
Wilkes (PA)
Wisconsin (Stevens Point)

NAVAL ARCHITECTURE

California Maritime
    Academy
Michigan, U. of
New Orleans, U. of (LA)
SUNY Maritime College (NY)
Texas A&M (Galveston)

U.S. Coast Guard Academy (CT)
U.S. Merchant Marine
    Academy (NY)
U.S. Naval Academy (MD)
Webb Institute (NY)

NEUROSCIENCE

Allegheny (PA)
Amherst (MA)
Baldwin-Wallace (OH)
Bowling Green (OH)
Bowdoin (ME)
Brown (RI)
California, U. of
    (Los Angeles)
Carthage (WI)
Central Michigan
Claremont McKenna (CA)
Colby (ME)
Colgate (NY)
Colorado College
Connecticut, U. of
Dickinson (PA)
Drake (IA)
Drew (NJ)

Emory (GA)
Florida State
Harvey Mudd (CA)
Macalester (MN)
Michigan
Muskingum (OH)
New College (FL)
Northwestern (IL)
Oberlin (OH)
Pittsburgh (PA)
Pitzer (CA)
Pomona (CA)
Regis (CO)
Rochester, U. of (NY)
▲Scripps (CA)
Texas, U. of (Dallas)
Ursinus (PA)
Wesleyan (CT)

■ *Men Only*
▲ *Women Only*

NUTRITIONAL SCIENCE

Alabama, U. of
Andrews (MI)
Arizona, U. of
Auburn (AL)
Ball State (IN)
Boston U. (MA)
Bridgewater (VA)
Cal Poly (SLO)
California, U. of (Berkeley)
California, U. of (Davis)
Case Western Reserve (OH)
Chapman (CA)
Clemson (SC)
Colorado State
Connecticut, U. of
Cornell (NY)
Delaware
Dominican (IL)
Florida, U. of
Framingham State (MA)
Georgia, U. of
Hawaii, U. of
Illinois
Kansas State
Long Island U.
   (C.W. Post)(NY)
Marygrove (MI)
Marywood (PA)
Minnesota, U. of
Mississippi State
Missouri, U. of

Nebraska, U. of
New Hampshire, U. of
New York Inst. of Tech.
North Carolina, U. of
North Carolina, U. of
   (Greensboro)
Ohio State
Oklahoma State
Oregon State
Pittsburgh, U. of (PA)
Rhode Island, U. of
Purdue (IN)
Rutgers (NJ)
▲Sage Colleges
   (Russell Sage)(NY)
St. John's/St. Benedict (MN)
St. Louis U. (MO)
San Jose State
Seattle Pacific (WA)
▲Simmons (MA)
Tennessee Tech
Tennessee, U. of
Texas A&M
Texas A&M (Kingsville)
Texas Tech
Virginia Poly
Viterbo (WI)
Winthrop (SC)
Wisconsin, U. of
Wisconsin, U. of (Stout)

OCCUPATIONAL THERAPY

American International (MA)
▲ Bay Path (MA)
Boston U. (MA)
Brenau (GA)
Buffalo (SUNY) (NY)
Cleveland State (OH)
Colorado State
Dominican (CA)
Eastern Carolina
Eastern Kentucky
Elizabethtown (PA)
Findlay (OH)
Florida Gulf Coast
Florida, U. of
Gannon (PA)
Illinois (Chicago)
I.U.- P.U.- Indianapolis (IN)
Kansas, U. of
Maryville (St. Louis)(MO)
McKendree (IL)
Minnesota, U. of
Missouri
New England, U. of (ME)
New Hampshire, U. of
New Mexico, U. of
Newman (KS)
New York Inst. of Tech.
North Carolina, U. of
North Dakota, U. of
Ohio State
Penn State
Pittsburgh, U. of (PA)

Puget Sound (WA)
St. Ambrose (IA)
▲ St. Catherine (MN)
St. Louis U. (MO)
▲ St. Mary (NE)
St. Scholastica (MN)
Salem State (MA)
San Jose State (CA)
Sciences, U. of the (PA)
Scranton (PA)
South Dakota
Southern California
Stony Brook (SUNY)(NY)
Temple (PA)
Texas A&M (Corpus Christi)
▲ Texas Woman's
Texas U. of (Health Sci.Ctr.-
    San Antonio)
Towson (MD)
Tuskegee (AL)
Utica College (NY)
Washington U. (MO)
Washington, U. of
Wayne State (MI)
Western Michigan
Wisconsin, U. of
Wisconsin, U. of
    (La Crosse)
Wisconsin, U. of
    (Milwaukee)
Worcester State (MA)
Xavier (OH)

ORTHOTICS / PROSTHETICS

California State
    (Dominguez Hills)
Florida International

Texas, U. of, S.W. Med Ctr.
    (Dallas)
Washington, U. of

PARKS AND RECREATION SERVICES

π Alaska Pacific
Alderson-Broaddus (WV)
Arizona State
Aurora (IL)
Bowling Green (OH)
Cal. Poly. State U. (Pomona)
Cal. Poly. State U. (SLO)
California State U.
   (Dominguez Hills)
California State U. (Fresno)
California State U.
   (Los Angeles)
California State U.
   (Northridge)
California State U.
   (Sacramento)
Catawba (NC)
Central Michigan
Clemson (SC)
Colorado State
Connecticut
Florida International
Florida State
Franklin (IN)
Georgia State
Georgia, U. of
Gordon (MA)
\# Green Mountain (VT)
Idaho
Illinois State
Illinois, U. of
Indiana U.
Kansas State
Kean (NJ)
Lock Haven (PA)
• Lyndon (VT)
Maine, U. of
Mankato State (MN)

Maryland, U. of
Mesa State (CO)
Michigan State
Minnesota
Minnesota State U. (Mankato)
Missouri
Montana
Nevada (Reno)
New York U.
North Carolina (Greensboro)
North Carolina State
Northern Arizona
Northern Iowa
π Northland (WI)
Ohio U.
Pfeiffer (NC)
Pittsburgh (Bradford)
Purdue (IN)
San Diego State (CA)
San Jose State (CA)
Science & Arts of Oklahoma
Shepherd (WV)
Slippery Rock (PA)
Southern Conneccticut
Southwest Missouri
Springfield College (MA)
Taylor (IN)
Texas A&M
Virginia Wesleyan
West Virginia U.
Western Carolina (NC)
Western State College of
   Colorado
Western Washington
Wingate (NC)
Winona State (MN)
Wisconsin (LaCrosse)

π *Outdoor Studies*
\# *Resort Management*
• *Also Ski Resort Management*

PEACE AND CONFLICT STUDIES

American (DC)
Bethel (KS)
Bluffton (OH)
California, U. of (Berkeley)
Chapman (CA)
π Clark (MA)
Colgate (NY)
DePauw (IN)
Earlham (IN)
Eastern Mennonite (PA)
Goshen (IN)
Guilford (NC)
Hamline (MN)
Hampshire (MA)
Juniata (PA)
Kent State (OH)

Manchester (IN)
Manhattan (NY)
Missouri, U. of
Molloy (NY)
Mount St. Clair (IA)
North Carolina, U. of
Northland (WI)
Norwich (VT)
Quincy (IL)
St. Benedict/St. John's (MN)
St. Thomas (MN)
Washington, U. of
▲ Wellesley (MA)
Whitworth (WA)
Youngstown State (OH)

π Also Global Environmental Studies

PHOTOJOURNALISM

Boston U. (MA)
Indiana U.
Missouri, U. of
Montana, U. of
Northern Illinois U.
Ohio U.

Rochester Inst. of Tech. (NY)
St. Edward's (TX)
San Jose State (CA)
Southern Illinois
Texas
Western Kentucky

 # Photocommunications

■ *Men Only*
▲ *Women Only*

PHYSICAL EDUCATION

Alderson-Broaddus (WV)
Asbury (KY)
Augsburg (MN)
Baker (KS)
Bemidji State (MN)
Berea (KY)
Berry (GA)
Bethany (WV)
Blackburn (IL)
Bridgewater (MA)
Brockport (SUNY) (NY)
Castleton (VT)
Chowan (NC)
Coe (IA)
Colorado, U. of
Colorado State
Cornell (IA)
Cortland State (NY)
Dana (NE)
Davis & Elkins (WV)
Denison (OH)
Doane (NE)
East Stroudsburg (PA)
Elon (NC)
Eureka (IL)
Faulkner (AL)
Florida Southern
Florida State
Florida, U. of
Franklin (IN)
Georgia, U. of
Goshen (IN)
Graceland (IA)
Grambling (LA)
Hamline (MN)
Hanover (IN)
Hardin-Simmons (TX)
Illinois College
Illinois, U. of (Chicago)
Indiana (PA)
Iowa, U. of
Ithaca (NY)
Jacksonville (FL)
Jamestown (ND)
Johnson C. Smith (NC)
Kansas State
Kansas, U. of
Kean (NJ)

Kennesaw State (GA)
Kentucky Wesleyan
King (TN)
Lebanon Valley (PA)
LeTourneau (TX)
Longwood (VA)
Linfield (OR)
Luther (IA)
Maine, U. of
McPherson (KS)
Michigan State
Monmouth (IL)
Nebraska, U. of
Nevada (Reno)
North Carolina, U. of
Norwich (VT)
Occidental (CA)
Ohio U.
Oregon State
Otterbein (OH)
Ozarks (MO)
Pacific U. (OR)
Pennsylvania State
Peru State (NE)
Plymouth State (NH)
Puerto Rico, U. of
   (Mayaguez)
Purdue (IN)
Rockford (IL)
St. Leo (FL)
Skidmore (NY)
Slippery Rock (PA)
South Florida, U. of
Springfield (MA)
Sterling (KS)
Texas, U. of
Union (TN)
Ursinus (PA)
Walsh (OH)
Washington State
Western Illinois
Western Washington
Westmont (CA)
West Virginia U.
William & Mary (VA)
Wisconsin (LaCrosse)
Wisconsin, U. of

■ *Men Only*
▲ *Women Only*

PHYSICAL THERAPY

American International (MA)
Azusa Pacific (CA)
Barry (FL)
Boston University (MA)
Bowling Green (OH)
Bradley (IL)
Buffalo (SUNY) (NY)
California State U. (Fresno)
California State U.
   (Sacramento)
Clarke (IA)
Clarkson (NY)
Connecticut, U. of
Dayton (OH)
D'Youville (NY)
Daemen (NY)
Duquesne (PA)
Evansville (IN)
Fairmont State (WV)
Florida Gulf Coast U.
Florida International
Florida, U. of
Grambling (LA)
Grand Valley (MI)
Hartford (CT)
Houston, U. of (TX)
Hunter (CUNY) (NY)
Huntington (AL)
Husson (ME)
Illinois (Chicago)
Indiana State
I.U.-P.U.- Indianapolis (IN)
Ithaca (NY)
Kentucky, U. of
Lebanon Valley (PA)
Louisiana-Lafayette
Louisville, U. of (KY)
Manhattan (NY)
Maryville (St. Louis) (MO)

Miami, U. of (FL)
Midwestern State (TX)
Minnesota, U. of
Missouri, U. of
Mount St. Joseph (OH)
Mt. St. Mary's (CA)
Nazareth (NY)
Nebraska, U. of
Nevada (Reno)
New England, U. of (ME)
New Mexico, U. of
New York Inst. of Tech.
North Dakota, U. of
Northeastern (MA)
Northern Illinois
Ohio State U.
Ohio University
Pacific (OR)
Pittsburgh, U. of (PA)
Regis (CO)
Russell Sage (NY)
St. Francis (PA)
St. Louis U. (MO)
Saint Scholastica (MN)
Sciences, U. of the (PA)
Scranton, U. of (PA)
Slippery Rock (PA)
Springfield College (MA)
Texas Southern
Texas U. of (Health Sci.Ctr.-
   San Antonio)
Toledo (OH)
Utah
Washington U. (MO)
Waynesburg (PA)
West Virginia U.
Western Carolina (NC)
Wisconsin, U. of

■ *Men Only*
▲ *Women Only*

PHYSICIAN ASSISTANT

Alderson-Broaddus (WV)
Augsburg (MN)
Butler (IN)
Daeman (NY)
DeSales (PA)
D'Youville (NY)
East Carolina
Gannon (PA)
George Washington (DC)
High Point (NC)
Hofstra (NY)
Howard (DC)
Idaho State
Kentucky
King's (PA)
Miami, U. of (FL)
New York Inst. of Tech.

Nova Southeastern (FL)
Pace (NY)
Pacific (OR)
Rochester Inst. of Tech. (NY)
Rocky Mountain (MT)
St. Francis (NY)
St. Francis (PA)
St. Louis (MO)
Sciences, U. of the (PA)
▲Seton Hill (PA)
South Dakota
Southern California
Springfield (MA)
Stony Brook (SUNY)(NY)
Union (NE)
Wichita State (KS)
Wisconsin

PRE-VETERINARY

Arkansas, U. of
Auburn (AL)
California, U. of (Davis)
Cal. Poly. State U.
    (San Luis Obispo)
Clemson (SC)
Colorado State
Delaware Valley (PA)
Elmhurst (IL)
Evansville, U. of (IN)
Fort Lewis (CO)
Georgia, U. of
▲Hollins (VA)
Humboldt State (CA)
Idaho, U. of
Iowa State
Juniata (PA)
Kansas State
Lawrence (WI)
Louisiana-Lafayette
Loyola (CA)
MacMurray (IL)
Maryland, U. of
Michigan State
Minnesota, U. of
Montana, U. of
Moravian (PA)
π Mount Ida (MA)
Murray State (KY)
Muskingum (OH)

Nebraska, U. of
Nevada, U. of (Reno)
New Hampshire, U. of
New Mexico State
Northland (WI)
Oklahoma State
Purdue (IN)
Rhode Island, U. of
▲Russell Sage
    (The Sage Colleges)(NY)
▲Salem (NC)
South Dakota State U.
Southern Mississippi, U. of
Susquehanna (PA)
Tennessee, U. of
Texas A & M
Tuskegee (AL)
Utah State
Vermont, U. of
Virginia Wesleyan
Warren Wilson (NC)
Washington & Jefferson (PA)
Washington State
West Virginia Wesleyan
Wilmington (OH)
Wingate (NC)
Winona State (MN)
Wyoming, U. of

■ *Men Only*
▲ *Women Only*

π *Veterinary Technician*

PUBLIC HEALTH

American (DC)
Baylor (TX)
Bethel (MN)
Brown (RI)
Central Oklahoma
Central State (OH)
Central Washington
Delaware State
Dillard (LA)
Florida State
Hofstra (NY)
Holy Family (PA)
Idaho, U. of
Indiana U.
Ind. U.-Pur U.-Ind U. (IN)
Johns Hopkins(MD)
Kansas, U. of
Kent State (OH)
Moorhead State (MN)
New Mexico State
New Orleans, U. of (LA)
Northern Illinois

Ohio U.
Purdue (IN)
Richard Stockton (NJ)
Rutgers (NJ)
St. Cloud (MN)
St. Joseph's (NY)
Salem-Teikyo (WV)
San Francisco State (CA)
San Jose State (CA)
▲ Simmons (MA)
Southern Connecticut State
Texas Women's
Utah State
Virginia Commonwealth
West Chester (PA)
Western Illinois
Western Kentucky
Western Michigan
Western Washington
Wisconsin (Eau Claire)
Worcester State (MA)

RANGE MANAGEMENT

Brigham Young (UT)
California, U. of
    (Berkeley)
California, U. of (Davis)
Colorado State
Eastern Oregon
Humboldt State (CA)
Idaho, U. of
Montana State (Bozeman)
Nebraska, U. of
New Mexico State U.
North Dakota State U.

Oregon State U.
South Dakota State U.
Stephen F. Austin State U. (TX)
Tarleton State (TX)
Texas A&M
Texas A&M (Kingsville)
Texas Christian
Texas Tech.
Utah State
Washington State
Wyoming, U. of

■ *Men Only*
▲ *Women Only*

SOCIAL AND REHABILITATION SERVICES

Arizona, U. of
Assumption (MA)
Boston U. (MA)
California State U.
   (Los Angeles)
Gustavus Adolphus (MN)
Iowa, U. of
Louisiana State
Maine (Farmington)
Marshall (WV)
Montana, U. of
Northern Colorado
North Texas

Ohio State
Seattle (WA)
South Florida, U. of
Southern Mississippi
Springfield College (MA)
Texas, U. of (Austin)
Virginia Commonwealth
Wartburg (IA)
West Virginia Wesleyan
Wilberforce (OH)
Wisconsin
Wright State (OH)

SOCIAL WORK

Adelphi (NY)
Alabama, U. of
Alaska, U. of (Anchorage)
Alaska, U. of (Fairbanks)
Andrews (MI)
Arizona State
Arkansas, U. of
Ashland (OH)
Augsburg (MN)
Azusa Pacific (CA)
Ball State (IN)
Barry (FL)
Baylor (TX)
Belmont (TN)
Bemidji State (MN)
▲ Bennett (NC)
Bethany (KS)
Bethany (WV)
Bethel (KS)
Boise State (ID)
Brescia (KY)
Brigham Young (UT)
Brockport (SUNY) (NY)
Buena Vista (IA)
California (PA)
California (Berkeley)
California State U. (Chico)
California State U. (Fresno)
California State U. (Fullerton)
California State U.
   (Los Angeles)
California State U.
   (Sacramento)

California State U.
   (San Bernardino)
Carroll (WI)
Castleton (VT)
Catholic (DC)
Clarke (IA)
Colorado State
Connecticut, U. of
Creighton (NE)
Cumberland (KY)
Dana (NE)
David Lipscomb (TN)
Dillard (LA)
Eastern Michigan
Eastern Nazarene (MA)
Eastern Washington
Elizabethtown (PA)
Elmira (NY)
Elms (MA)
Ferris State (MI)
Florida Atlantic
Florida International
Florida State
Fort Hays (KS)
Franciscan U. of Steubenville (OH)
Fredonia (SUNY) (NY)
Georgia State
Georgia U. of
Gordon (MA)
Hawaii Pacific
Hood (MD)
Hope (MI)

■ *Men Only*
▲ *Women Only*

SOCIAL WORK continues next page

SOCIAL WORK, continued

Humboldt State (CA)
Illinois, U. of
Illinois, U. of (Chicago)
Indiana
Indiana U.-Purdue U.-
  Indianapolis (IN)
Iowa, U. of
Juniata (PA)
Kansas State
Kansas, U. of
Kean (NJ)
Kentucky
Lindenwood (MO)
Lipscomb (TN)
Longwood (VA)
Loras (IA)
Lourdes (OH)
Madonna (MI)
Maine, U. of
Manchester (IN)
Marquette (WI)
Marshall (WV)
▲ Mary Baldwin (VA)
Marygrove (MI)
Maryland (Baltimore Co.)
▲ Meredith (NC)
Michigan State
Michigan, U. of
Middle Tennessee
Millersville (PA)
Minnesota State U.
  (Moorhead)
Missouri, U. of
Mount St. Joseph (OH)
Nazareth (NY)
Nevada, U. of (Las Vegas)
Nevada, U. of (Reno)
New Mexico State
New York University
Niagara (NY)
North Carolina (Greensboro)
North Carolina (Pembroke)
North Carolina State
Northern Iowa
Northwestern State (LA)
Pittsburgh, U. of (PA)
Portland, U. of (OR)
Presentation (SD)
Providence (RI)
Radford (VA)

Rhode Island College
Richard Stockton (NJ)
Rochester Inst. of Tech. (NY)
Rockford (IL)
Sacred Heart (CT)
Saginaw Valley (MI)
▲ St. Catherine (MN)
St. Edward's (TX)
St. Leo (FL)
St. Louis (MO)
St. Olaf (MN)
St. Scholastica (MN)
St. Thomas (MN)
Salem State (MA)
Salisbury State (MD)
San Francisco State (CA)
Shepherd (WV)
Shippensburg U. of (PA)
South Connecticut
South Florida, U. of
Southern Connecticut
Tarleton State (TX)
Tennessee, U. of
Texas A&M (Kingsville)
Texas, U. of (Arlington)
Texas, U. of (Austin)
Texas Women's
Utah State
Valparaiso (IN)
Vermont, U. of
Walla Walla (WA)
Warren Wilson (NC)
Wartburg (IA)
Washburn (KS)
Washington U. (MO)
Washington, U. of
Wayne State (MI)
West Florida
Western Carolina (NC)
Western Maryland
Western Michigan
Western New England (MA)
William Woods (MO)
Winona State (MN)
Winthrop (SC)
Wisconsin, U. of
Wisconsin, U. of
  (Milwaukee)
Wyoming, U. of

■ *Men Only*
▲ *Women Only*

SPECIAL EDUCATION

Alabama, U. of
Alderson-Broaddus (WV)
American International (MA)
Arizona State
Arizona, U. of
Arkansas
Auburn (AL)
Augustana (SD)
Bemidji State (MN)
π Bethel (IN)
Boston U. (MA)
Brenau (GA)
Bridgewater State (MA)
California State (Fresno)
π California State
   (Northridge)
Central (CT)
Clarke (IA)
Clarion (PA)
Connecticut, U. of
▲Converse (SC)
Culver-Stockton (MO)
Curry (MA)
Dana (NE)
Delaware State
Doane (NE)
Eastern Kentucky
Eastern Michigan
Edinboro (PA)
Emporia State (KS)
π Flagler (FL)
Florida Gulf Coast
Florida, U. of
Fontbonne (MO)
Fort Hays (KS)
Geneseo (SUNY) (NY)
Georgia Southwestern
Georgia, U. of
Gonzaga (WA)
Hartford (CT)
Hofstra (NY)
Holy Names (CA)
Hood (MD)
Idaho, U. of
Illinois State
Indiana U.
Juniata (PA)
Kansas State
Kansas Wesleyan
Kean (NJ)
Keene (NH)
Kentucky, U. of
Kutztown (PA)
Landmark College (VT)

Lasell (MA)
Lesley (MA)
Lindenwood (MO)
Loras (IA)
Louisiana State U.
Lyndon State (VT)
Maine, U. of (Farmington)
Marygrove (MI)
Maryland, U. of
Miami, U. of (FL)
Michigan State
Michigan, U. of
Millersville (PA)
Montana State (Billings)
Muskingum (OH)
Nebraska, U. of
Nebraska, U. of (Omaha)
New Mexico State
Nevada, U. of (Las Vegas)
Nevada, U. of (Reno)
North Florida
North Texas
Northern Colorado, U. of
Northern Illinois
Northern Iowa
Oklahoma, U. of
Old Dominion (VA)
Pennsylvania State
Peru State (NE)
Presbyterian (SC)
Providence (RI)
Quincy (IL)
Rhode Island College
Rowan (NJ)
St. Cloud (MN)
St. Elizabeth (NJ)
▲St. Joseph (CT)
St. Louis U. (MO)
St. Martin's (WA)
Silver Lake (WI)
▲Simmons (MA)
Southern Connecticut
Southern Florida
Southern Illinois U.
   (Carbondale)
Southern Utah
Tennessee, U. of
Texas, U. of
▲Trinity (DC)
Utah State
Utah, U. of
Vanderbilt (TN)

■ *Men Only*
▲ *Women Only*

π *Also Deaf Studies*
SPECIAL ED. continues next page

SPECIAL EDUCATION, continued

Walsh (OH)
West Chester (PA)
West Florida
Western Carolina
Western Washington
Westfield (MA)
Wisconsin, U. of

Wisconsin, U. of (Eau Claire)
Wisconsin, U. of (Milwaukee)
Wisconsin, U. of (Oshkosh)
Winona (MN)
Wittenberg (OH)
Wyoming, U. of
Xavier (LA)

SPORTS MEDICINE/ATHLETIC TRAINING

Alderson-Broaddus (WV)
Alfred (NY)
Baldwin Wallace (OH)
Ball State (IN)
Belmont Abbey (NC)
Boise State (ID)
Bryan (TN)
California (PA)
California Lutheran
Canisius (NY)
Carthage (WI)
Castleton (VT)
Catawba (NC)
Charleston, College of (SC)
Charleston, U. of (WV)
Chowan (NC)
Clarke (IA)
Coe (IA)
Colby-Sawyer (NH)
Colorado State
Connecticut, U. of
East Stroudsburg (PA)
Eastern Nazarene (MA)
Elon (NC)
Endicott (MA)
Eureka (IL)
Evansville (IN)
Florida Southern
Florida State
Gardner-Webb (NC)
George Fox (OR)
Gustavus Adolphus (MN)
Heidelberg (OH)
High Point (NC)
Illinois (Chicago)
Indiana U.
James Madison (VA)
LaSell (MA)
Lees-McCrae (NC)
Lindenwood (MO)
Linfield (OR)
Lipscomb (TN)
Lynchburg (VA)
Manchester (IN)
Manhattan (NY)

Marietta (OH)
McKendree (IL)
Merrimack (MA)
Mercyhurst (PA)
Minnesota State U. (Mankato)
Missouri Baptist
Mount Union (OH)
Neumann (PA)
Nevada, U. of (Las Vegas)
New Mexico State
North Dakota
Northeastern (MA)
Northwestern (IA)
Norwich (VT)
Ohio Northern
Ohio State
Otterbein (OH)
Palm Beach Atlantic (FL)
Pepperdine (CA)
Quincy (IL)
Quinnipiac (CT)
Roanoke (VA)
St. Andrews (NC)
Samford (AL)
Slippery Rock (PA)
Southern Maine
Southwest Missouri
Southwest Texas State
Springfield (MA)
Sterling (KS)
Taylor (IN)
Texas (Arlington)
Towson (MD)
Tusculum (TN)
Tulsa (OK)
Union (TN)
Waynesburg (PA)
West Virginia Wesleyan
West Chester (PA)
Whitworth (WA)
William Woods (MO)
Wilmington (OH)
Wingate (NC)
Xavier (OH)

■ *Men Only*
▲ *Women Only*

SPORTS SCIENCES / MANAGEMENT

Alabama, U. of
Alderson-Broaddus (WV)
Arizona State
Averett (VA)
Belmont Abbey (NC)
Bemidji (MN)
Berry (GA)
Bowling Green (OH)
Briar Cliff (IA)
Buena Vista (IA)
Cabrini (PA)
Carthage (WI)
Castleton (VT)
Central Washington
Chowan (NC)
✳ Coastal Carolina (SC)
Colby-Sawyer (NH)
Concordia (CA)
Connecticut, U. of
Dallas, U. of (TX)
Eastern Connecticut
Elon (NC)
Endicott (MA)
Faulkner (AL)
Flagler (FL)
Florida Southern
Florida, U. of
Guilford (NC)
High Point (NC)
Husson (ME)
Idaho, U. of
Incarnate Word (TX)
Indiana U.
Ithaca (NY)
Kansas, U. of
Kentucky Wesleyan
Knox (IL)
Liberty (VA)
Louisville (KY)
Lynchburg (VA)
Lynn (FL)
MacMurray (IL)
Malone (OH)
Marian (WI)
Massachusetts, U. of
Michigan, U. of
Millersville (PA)

Misericordia (PA)
Mississippi U. for Women
Missouri Baptist
Mount Union (OH)
\# Nebraska, U. of
Neumann (PA)
North Carolina State
North Michigan
Ohio Northern
Ohio State
Oklahoma
Oregon, U. of
Pfeiffer (NC)
Richmond (VA)
Robert Morris (PA)
Rutgers (NJ)
Seton Hall (NJ)
Shepherd (WV)
Simpson (IA)
South Carolina, U. of
Southern New Hampshire, U. of
Springfield (MA)
St. Ambrose (IA)
St. John's (NY)
St. Leo (FL)
St. Olaf (MN)
St. Thomas U. (FL)
Stetson (FL)
Southwest Baptist (MO)
Tampa, U. of (FL)
Tarleton State (TX)
Taylor (IN)
Temple (PA)
Tennessee
Texas Christian
Towson (MD)
Tulsa (OK)
Union (TN)
West Virginia U.
Western Carolina
Western New England (MA)
Wingate (NC)
Xavier (OH)

■ *Men Only*
▲ *Women Only*

\# *PGA Golf Management*
✳ *Professional Golf Management*

URBAN STUDIES

Akron, U. of (OH)
Albany (SUNY)(NY)
Aquinas (MI)
Augsburg (MN)
▲ Barnard (NY)
Boston U. (MA)
Brown (RI)
▲✪ Bryn Mawr (PA)
California State U. (Northridge)
California, U. of (San Diego)
★ Cal Poly State U. (SLO)
Canisius (NY)
Cincinnati, U. of (OH)
Cleveland State (OH)
College of Charleston (SC)
Columbia (NY)
Connecticut College
Connecticut, U. of
Cornell (NY)
David Lipscomb (TN)
DePaul (IL)
Eastern Washington
Elmhurst (IL)
Florida International
Florida, U. of
Furman (SC)
Georgia State
Grambling (LA)
Hamline (MN)
Hampshire (MA)
Harvard (MA)
Hunter (CUNY)(NY)
Illinois (Chicago)
Indiana State
Lehigh (PA)
Lipscomb (TN)
Loyola Marymount (CA)
Macalester (MN)

Malone (OH)
Manhattan (NY)
Maryland, U. of
Minnesota, U. of
π Minnesota State U. (Mankato)
■ Morehouse (GA)
Mount Mercy (IA)
Nebraska, U. of
New York U.
Northwestern (IL)
Ohio State
Pennsylvania, U. of
Pittsburgh, U. of (PA)
★★ Portland State (OR)
Rockford (IL)
Rutgers (NJ)
St. Louis (MO)
St. Peter's (NJ)
San Francisco State U. (CA)
Shippensburg (PA)
Stanford (CA)
Tampa, U. of (FL)
Towson State (MD)
Trinity (TX)
Vanderbilt (TN)
Vassar (NY)
Virginia Commonwealth
Virginia Poly
Washington U. (MO)
Wayne State (MI)
Western Washington
π Westfield State (MA)
Wisconsin, U. of
  (Green Bay)
Wittenberg (OH)
Wooster (OH)
Worcester State (MA)
Wright State (OH)

π *Regional Planning*
★ *City & Regional Planning*
★★ *Community Development*
✪ *Growth and Structure of Cities*

■ *Men Only*
▲ *Women Only*

VOICE

Ball State (IN)
Bucknell (PA)
Catholic (DC)
Chapman (CA)
Cincinnati, U. of (OH)
Cleveland Inst. of Music (OH)
Connecticut College
Florida Southern
Florida State
Fredonia (SUNY)(NY)
Furman (SC)
Illinois, U. of
Illinois Wesleyan
Ithaca (NY)
Indiana U.
Julliard (NY)
Kansas, U. of
Manhattan Sch. of Music (NY)
Mannes (NY)
Miami, U. of (FL)

Michigan, U. of
New Hampshire, U. of
New York U.
Northwestern (IL)
Nyack (NY)
Ohio U.
Pacific Lutheran (WA)
Palm Beach Atlantic (FL)
Rice (TX)
Rider (Westminster) (NJ)
Roosevelt (IL)
Samford (AL)
San Francisco Conserv. of
   Music (CA)
Southern California
Syracuse (NY)
Temple (PA)
Tulsa, U. of (OK)
Weber State (UT)

WILDLIFE/WILDLANDS MANAGEMENT

Alaska (Fairbanks)
Arizona, U. of
Auburn (AL)
Ball State (IN)
Brevard (NC)
California, U. of (Davis)
Clemson (SC)
Colorado State
Connecticut, U. of
Cornell (NY)
Eastern Kentucky
Eastern New Mexico
Florida, U. of
Frostburg State (MD)
Georgia, U. of
π Grand Valley (MI)
Humboldt State (CA)
Idaho, U. of
Kansas State
Louisiana State
Maine, U. of
Massachusetts, U. of
Michigan State
Michigan, U. of
Mississippi State
Missouri, U. of
Montana, U. of
Nebraska, U. of

New Hampshire, U. of
New Mexico State
North Carolina State
Ohio State
Oklahoma State
Oregon State
Penn State
Purdue (IN)
Rhode Island, U. of
Rutgers (NJ)
South Dakota State
Tarleton State (TX)
Tennessee Tech
Tennessee, U. of
Texas A&M
Texas Tech.
Unity (ME)
Utah State
Vermont, U. of
Virginia Poly Tech
Washington State
Washington, U. of
West Virginia, U. of
Wisconsin, U. of
Wisconsin, U. of
   (Stevens Point)
Wyoming, U. of

■ *Men Only*
▲ *Women Only*

π *Natural Resources Management*

WOMEN'S STUDIES

▲Agnes Scott (GA)
Antioch (OH)
Arizona State
Arizona, U. of
▲Barnard (NY)
Bates (ME)
Beloit (WI)
Berea (WV)
Bowling Green (OH)
Brandeis (MA)
Brown (RI)
Cal Poly State U. (Pomona)
California State U. (Fresno)
California State U.
  (Long Beach)
California, U. of (Berkeley)
California, U. of (Davis)
California, U. of (Riverside)
California, U. of
  (Santa Barbara)
California, U. of (Santa Cruz)
Carleton (MN)
Colby (ME)
Colorado College
Colorado, U. of
Connecticut College
Connectut, U. of
Dartmouth (NH)
Delaware, U. of
Denver, U. of (CO)
DePauw (IN)
Drew (NJ)
Duke (NC)
Emory (GA)
Florida, U. of
Florida International
Florida State
Franklin & Marshall (PA)
Goucher (MD)
Harvard (MA)
Hawaii, U. of
Hobart & William Smith (NY)
▲Hollins (VA)
Iowa State
Kansas, U. of
Kansas State
Kalamazoo (MI)
Louisville (KY)
Macalester (MN)
Maine, U. of
Maryland, U. of
Massachusetts, U. of

Michigan, U. of
Middlebury (VT)
▲Mills (CA)
Missouri, U. of
▲Mt. Holyoke (MA)
Nebraska, U. of
Nevada, U. of (Las Vegas)
Nevada, U. of (Reno)
New College (FL)
Northwestern (IL)
Ohio State
Oklahoma, U. of
Oregon, U. of
Pennsylvania, U. of
Pittsburgh, U. of (PA)
Pitzer (CA)
Portland State (OR)
Regis (CO)
Rhode Island, U. of
Rice (TX)
Rochester, U. of (NY)
▲Rosemont (PA)
Rutgers (NJ)
San Francisco State (CA)
Sarah Lawrence (NY)
▲Scripps (CA)
▲Simmons (MA)
Skidmore (NY)
▲Smith (MA)
Southern California
Southern Maine
Southwestern (TX)
▲Spelman (GA)
Stanford (CA)
Syracuse (NY)
Towson (MD)
Vassar (NY)
Washington State
Washington U. (MO)
Washington, U. of
▲Wellesley (MA)
Wells (NY)
Wesleyan (CT)
West Chester (PA)
Wheaton (MA)
Wisconsin, U. of
Wisconsin, U. of
  (Milwaukee)
Wooster (OH)
Wyoming, U. of
Yale (CT)

■ *Men Only*
▲ *Women Only*

SECTION THREE

AVERAGE SAT-1/
EXPECTED AVERAGE NEW SAT-1/
ACT TOTALS
RECOMMENDED MAJORS

ABILENE CHRISTIAN UNIVERSITY (TX) .... acu.edu **1080/1620/23**
Art, Bus Admin, Chem, Nurs, Reli Stu

ADELPHI COLLEGE (NY) .... adelphi.edu **1100/1650/24**
Ed, Nurs, Physics, Psych

ADRIAN COLLEGE (MI) .... adrian.edu **1035/1550/22**
Art, Bus Admin, Comp Sci, Ed, English, Math, Poli Sci, Pre-Law, Soc

AGNES SCOTT COLLEGE (GA) .... agnesscott.edu **1210/1810/27**
Art, Bio, Bus Admin, Classics, Econ, English, For Lang, Hist, Math, Physics, Poli Sci, Pre-Law, Pre-Med/Pre-Dental, Psych

AKRON, UNIVERSITY OF (OH) .... uakron.edu **1000/1500/21**
Bus Admin, Chem, Drama, Ed, Engine, Hist, Home Ec, Nurs, Soc

ALABAMA, UNIVERSITY OF (AL) .... ua.edu **1105/1660/24**
Amer St, Anthro, Art, Bot, Bus Admin, Communic, Drama, Engine, English, For Lang, Geol, Hist, Music, Philo, Pre-Law, Pre-Med/Pre-Dental, Psych

ALABAMA, UNIVERSITY OF (BIRMINGHAM) .... uab.edu **1040/1560/22**
Bus Admin, Chem, Comp Sci, Drama, Engine, English, Nurs, Philo, Psych

ALABAMA, UNIVERSITY OF (HUNTSVILLE) .... uah.edu **1150/1725/25**
Bus Admin, Chem, Communic, Comp Sci, Engine, English, Math, Nurs, Philo

ALASKA PACIFIC UNIVERSITY (AK) .... alaskapacific.edu **1070/1605/23**
Bus Admin, Ed, Music, Psych, Reli Stu

ALASKA, UNIVERSITY OF (ANCHORAGE) (AK) .. uaa.alaska.edu **1000/1545/21**
Art, Bus Admin, Econ, Ed

ALASKA, UNIVERSITY OF (FAIRBANKS) (AK) .... uaf.edu **1030/1545/22**
Anthro, Bio, Bus Admin, Drama, Engine, Geol, Nurs

ALBANY COLLEGE OF PHARMACY (NY) .... acp.edu **1140/1715/25**
Pharm

ALBERTSON COLLEGE OF IDAHO (ID) .... albertson.edu **1135/1700/25**
Bio, Bus Admin, Chem, Ed, English, Hist, Math, Music, Poli Sci, Pre-Law, Pre-Med/Pre-Dental, Zoo

ALBION COLLEGE (MI) .... albion.edu **1130/1695/25**
Econ, English, Hist, Math, Philo, Poli Sci, Pre-Law, Pre-Med/Pre-Dental,

ALBRIGHT COLLEGE (PA) .... albright.edu **1040/1560/22**
Art, Biochem, Bio, Bus Admin, Poli Sci, Pre-Law, Pre-Med/Pre-Dental, Psych, Soc

ALDERSON-BROADDUS COLLEGE (WV) .... ab.edu **1000/1500/21**
Bus Admin, Ed, Music, Nurs

ALFRED UNIVERSITY (NY) .... alfred.edu **1160/1895/26**
Art, Bio, Bus Admin, Chem, Comp Sci, Ed, Engine, English, Hist, Pre-Law, Psych

ALLEGHENY COLLEGE (PA) .... alleg.edu **1195/1795/26**
Bio, Chem, Comp Sci, Drama, Econ, English, For Lang, Geol, Hist, Philo,
Physics, Pre-Law, Pre-Med/Pre-Dental, Psych

ALMA COLLEGE (MI) .... alma.edu **1140/1710/25**
Art, Bio, Bus Admin, Chem, Communic, Comp Sci, Ed, English, Hist,
Poli Sci, Pre-Law, Pre-Med/Pre-Dental, Psych

ALVERNO COLLEGE (WI) .... alverno.edu **1000/1500/21**
Bio, Communic, Bus Admin, Ed, English, Nurs, Psych

AMERICAN ACADEMY OF DRAMATIC ARTS (NY) ..... aada.org **1205/1810/27**
Drama

AMERICAN INTERNATIONAL COLLEGE (MA) .... aic.edu **1000/1500/21**
Bus Admin, Pre-Med/Pre-Dental, Psych

AMERICAN UNIVERSITY (DC) .... american.edu **1260/1890/27**
Amer St, Anthro, Art, Bus Admin, Econ, Communic, Hist, Math,
Poli Sci, Pre-Law, Pre-Med/Pre-Dental

AMHERST COLLEGE (MA) .... amherst.edu **1420/2130/31**
Amer St, Astro, Bio, Chem, Classics, Drama, Econ, English, Geol, Hist,
Philo, Physics, Poli Sci, Pre-Law, Pre-Med/Pre-Dental, Psych, Soc

ANDERSON UNIVERSITY (IN) .... anderson.edu **1080/1620/23**
Ed, Music

ANDREWS UNIVERSITY (MI) .... andrews.edu **1050/1575/22**
Arch, Chem, Music, Nurs, Reli Stu

ANNA MARIA COLLEGE (MA) .... annamaria.edu **1000/1500/21**
Art, Bus Admin, Music

APPALACHIAN STATE UNIVERSITY (NC) .... appstate.edu **1120/1680/24**
Bus Admin, Communic, Ed, English, Hist, Poli Sci

AQUINAS COLLEGE (MI) .... aquinas.edu **1060/1590/23**
Art, Bio, Chem, English, Psych, Reli Stu

ARCADIA UNIVERISTY (PA) .... arcadia.edu **1050/1575/22**
Art, Bio, Chem, Comp Sci, Ed, English, Math, Poli Sci, Pre-Law, Psych

ARIZONA, UNIVERSITY OF (AZ) .... arizona.edu **1105/1655/24**
Ag, Amer St, Anthro, Arch, Art, Astro, Bio, Bus Admin, Chem, Communic, Drama,
Ed, Engine, English, Forest, For Lang, Geol, Hist, Nurs, Pharm, Philo, Pre-Law,
Pre-Med/Pre-Dental, Psych, Soc

ARIZONA STATE UNIVERSITY (AZ) .... asu.edu **1102/1650/23**
Anthro, Arch, Art, Biochem, Bio, Bus Admin, Communic, Comp Sci,
Drama, Ed, Engine, English, For Lang, Geog, Geol, Hist, Math, Music,
Nurs, Physics, Poli Sci, Pre-Med/Pre-Dental, Psych, Reli Stu, Zoo

ARKANSAS, UNIVERSITY OF (AR) ....uark.edu **1163/1750/25**
Ag, Anthro, Arch, Bus Admin, Communic, Comp Sci, Econ, Ed, Engine,
English, Hist, Music, Physics, Pre-Law, Psych

ART CENTER COLLEGE OF DESIGN (CA) .... artcenter.edu **1100/1650/24**
Art

ART INSTITUTE OF CHICAGO (IL) .... artic.edu/saic **1100/1650/24**
Art

ARTS, UNIVERSITY OF THE (PA) .... uarts.edu **1060/1590/23**
Art, Drama, Music

ASBURY COLLEGE (KY) .... asbury.edu **1150/1725/25**
Art, Bus Admin, Communic, Ed, Music, Philo, Reli Stu, Soc

ASHLAND UNIVERSITY (OH) .... ashland.edu **1040/1560/22**
Bus Admin, Chem, Ed

ASSUMPTION COLLEGE (MA) .... assumption.edu **1080/1620/23**
Bus Admin, Econ, Ed, English, Hist, Philo

AUBURN UNIVERSITY (AL) ....auburn.edu **1120/1680/24**
Ag, Arch, Art, Bus Admin, Communic, Comp Sci, Econ, Ed, Engine, English, Forest, Hist, Math, Pharm, Physics, Poli Sci,

AUGSBURG COLLEGE (MN) ....augsburg.edu **1080/1620/23**
Bus Admin, Communic, Comp Sci, Ed, English, Physics, Pre-Law, Soc

AUGUSTA STATE UNIVERSITY (GA) .... aug.edu **1000/1500/21**
English, Soc

AUGUSTANA COLLEGE (IL) .... augustana.edu **1180/1770/26**
Art, Bio, Bus Admin, Ed, English, Music, Pre-Law

AUGUSTANA COLLEGE (SD) .... augie.edu **1120/1680/24**
Bio, Chem, Ed, English, Music, Pre-Med/Pre-Dental, Reli Stu

AUSTIN COLLEGE (TX) .... austincollege.edu **1210/1810/26**
Biochem, Bio, Bus Admin, Chem, Ed, Hist, Philo, Poli Sci, Pre-Med/Pre-Dental, Reli Stu

AVERETT UNIVERSITY (VA) .... averett.edu **1000/1500/21**
Bus Admin, Ed, Math, Psych

AVILA UNIVERSITY (MO) ....avila.edu **1050/1575/22**
Bus Admin, Ed, Nurs

AZUSA PACIFIC (CA) .... apu.edu **1000/1500/21**
Bio, Bus Admin, English, Music, Nurs, Poli Sci

BABSON COLLEGE (MA) .... babson.edu **1240/1850/28**
Bus Admin, Econ

BAKER UNIVERSITY (KS) .... bakeru.edu **1080/1620/23**
Bio, Bus Admin, Comp Sci, Ed, Music, Nurs, Poli Sci, Psych

BALDWIN-WALLACE COLLEGE (OH) .... bw.edu **1080/1620/23**
Bus Admin, Chem, Comp Sci, Econ, Ed, English, Hist, Math, Music, Poli Sci, Pre-Law, Psych

BALL STATE UNIVERSITY (IN) .... bsu.edu **1040/1560/22**
Anthro, Art, Bio, Botany, Communic, Comp Sci, Ed, Geog, Math, Nurs, Physics, Poli Sci, Psych

BARD COLLEGE (NY) .... bard.edu **1300/1980/29**
Art, Drama, English, For Lang, Hist, Music, Pre-Law, Psych, Soc

BARNARD COLLEGE (NY) .... barnard.edu **1330/2000/30**
*Anthro, Arch, Art Hist, Biochem, Bio, Chem, Classics, Drama, Econ, Engine, English,
For Lang, Geol, Hist, Math, Music, Nurs, Philo, Physics, Poli Sci, Pre-Law, Psych, Reli Stu, Soc*

BARRY UNIVERSITY (FL) .... barry.edu **1000/1500/21**
Bio, Bus Admin, Drama, Ed, Nurs

BATES COLLEGE (ME) .... bates.edu **1350/2020/30**
*Art, Bio, Chem, Econ, English, For Lang, Geol, Hist, Math, Philo, Physics, Poli Sci, Pre-Law,
Pre-Med/Pre-Dental, Psych, Rel Stu*

BAYLOR UNIVERSITY (TX) .... baylor.edu **1170/1755/26**
*Bus Admin, Chem, Classics, Drama, Ed, Engine, English, Hist, Math,
Music, Nurs, Pre-Law, Pre-Med/Pre-Dental, Reli Stu*

BAY PATH COLLEGE (MA) .... baypath.edu **1010/1515/21**
Bus Admin, Psych

BELHAVEN COLLEGE (MS) .... belhaven.edu **1130/1700/24**
Art, Bus Admin, Comp Sci, Drama, Ed, Music

BELLARMINE UNIVERSITY (KY) .... bellarmine.edu **1140/1710/26**
Bus Admin, Econ, Ed, English, Hist, Math, Nurs, Philo

BELMONT ABBEY COLLEGE (NC) .... belmontabbeycollege.edu **1020/1565/22**
Bus Admin, Poli Sci, Pre-Law, Soc

BELMONT UNIVERSITY (TN) .... belmont.edu **1120/1680/24**
*Art, Bio, Bus Admin, Ed, English, Math, Music, Nurs, Philo, Poli Sci,
Pre-Law, Psych, Reli Stu, Soc*

BELOIT COLLEGE (WI) .... beloit.edu **1250/1875/28**
Anthro, Biochem, Bio, Classics, Drama, Econ, English, For Lang, Hist, Geol, Music, Physics, Psych, Soc

BEMIDJI STATE UNIVERSITY (MN) .... bemidji.msus.edu **1040/1555/22**
Chem, Communic, Comp Sci, Ed, Geog

BENEDICTINE COLLEGE (KS) .... benedictine.edu **1030/1545/22**
Astro, Bus Admin, Chem, Comp Sci, Drama, Music, Philo, Reli Stu, Soc

BENEDICTINE UNIVERSITY (IL) .... ben.edu **1030/1545/22**
Bio, Bus Admin, Comp Sci, Pre-Med/Pre-Dental

BENNETT COLLEGE (NC) .... bennett.edu **1000/1500/21**
Bus Admin, Comp Sci, Ed, Math, Poli Sci, Pre-Law, Pre-Med/Pre-Dental

BENNINGTON COLLEGE (VT) .... bennington.edu **1225/1845/29**
Drama, English, Music, Pre-Law

BENTLEY COLLEGE (MA) .... bentley.edu **1170/1755/26**
Bus Admin, Econ

BEREA COLLEGE (KY) .... berea.edu **1095/1645/24**
Ag, Bio, Bus Admin, Chem, Econ, Ed, English, Home Ec, Music, Nurs

BERKLEE COLLEGE OF MUSIC (MA) .... berklee.edu **1100/1650/24**
Music

BERRY COLLEGE (GA) .... berry.edu **1150/1725/25**
Bio, Bus Admin, Chem, Ed, English, Forest, Pre-Med/Pre-Dental, Psych

BETHANY COLLEGE (KS) bethany2b.edu **1080/1620/23**
Chem, Ed, Music

BETHANY COLLEGE (WV) .... bethanycollege.edu **1040/1560/22**
*Bio, Chem, Communic, Drama, Econ, Ed, English, For Lang, Music,
Physics, Poli Sci, Pre-Law, Pre-Med/Pre-Dental, Psych, Reli Stu*

BETHEL COLLEGE (IN) .... bethel-in.edu **1060/1590/23**
Ed, English, Music, Nurs, Philo, Reli Stu

BETHEL COLLEGE (KS) .... bethelks.edu **1100/1650/24**
Ed, Music, Nurs

BETHEL COLLEGE (MN) .... bethel.edu **1160/1740/26**
Biochem, Bio, Bus Admin, Ed, Nurs, Philo, Psych, Reli Stu

BIOLA UNIVERSITY (CA) .... biola.edu **1120/1680/24**
Ed, Philo, Psych, Soc

BIRMINGHAM-SOUTHERN COLLEGE (AL) .... bsc.edu **1185/1775/26**
*Art, Bio, Bus Admin, Chem, Drama, Ed, English, Hist, Math, Music, Pre-Law,
Pre-Med/Pre-Dental, Psych, Reli Stu*

BLACKBURN COLLEGE (IL) .... blackburn.edu **1000/1500/21**
Bio, Bus Admin, Ed, Pre-Med/Pre-Dental, Psych

BLOOMSBURG UNIVERSITY (PA) .... bloomu.edu **1040/1560/22**
Art, Bus Admin, Chem, Comp Sci, Ed, Geog, Geol, Nurs

BLUFFTON COLLEGE (OH) .... bluffton.edu **1070/1600/23**
Bus Admin, Chem, Ed, Math, Music

BOISE STATE UNIVERSITY (ID) .... boisestate.edu **1070/1600/23**
Art, Bus Admin, Drama, Ed, Engine, Geol, Hist, Math, Nurs

BOSTON ARCHITECTURAL CENTER (MA) .... the-bac.edu **1100/1650/24**
Arch

BOSTON COLLEGE (MA) .... bc.edu **1320/1980/30**
*Art, Bio, Bus Admin, Chem, Communic, Comp Sci, Drama, Econ, English, For Lang,
Hist, Music, Nurs, Philo, Poli Sci, Pre-Law, Pre-Med/Pre-Dental, Reli Stu, Soc*

BOSTON CONSERVATORY OF MUSIC (MA).. bostonconservatory.edu **1050/1575/22**
Music

BOSTON UNIVERSITY (MA) .... bu.edu **1299/1950/29**
*Anthro, Art, Art Hist, Astro, Bio, Bus Admin, Chem, Communic, Drama, Econ, Ed,
Engine, For Lang, Geog, Hist, Math, Music, Philo, Physics, Poli Sci, Pre-Law, Psych*

BOWDOIN COLLEGE (ME) .... bowdoin.edu **1360/2040/31**
*Anthro, Art Hist, Biochem, Bio, Chem, Classics, Econ, English, For Lang, Geol,
Hist, Math, Music, Philo, Poli Sci, Pre-Law, Pre-Med/Pre-Dental, Reli Stu, Soc*

BOWLING GREEN STATE UNIVERSITY (OH) .... bgsu.edu **1030/1550/22**
Amer St, Art, Bus Admin, Ed, Geol, Math, Music, Philo

BRADLEY UNIVERSITY (IL) .... bradley.edu **1175/1660/26**
*Art, Bus Admin, Chem, Comp Sci, Econ, Ed, Engine, English, Nurs,
Physics, Poli Sci, Pre-Law*

BRANDEIS UNIVERSITY (MA) .... brandeis.edu **1350/2025/30**
*Amer St, Anthro, Biochem, Bio, Chem, Comp Sci, Drama, Econ, English, Hist, Math,
Music, Physics, Poli Sci, Pre-Law, Pre-Med/Pre-Dental, Psych*

BRENAU UNIVERSITY (GA) .... brenau.edu **1020/1580/22**
Drama, Music

BRESCIA UNIVERSITY (KY) .... brescia.edu **1020/1580/22**
Art, Bus Admin, Ed, English, Reli Stu

BRIAR CLIFF UNIVERSITY (IA) .... briarcliff.edu **1040/1550/22**
Art, Bio, Bus Admin, English, Hist, Math, Music, Nurs

BRIDGEWATER COLLEGE (VA) .... bridgewater.edu **1010/1510/22**
Bus Admin, Hist, Music, Psych, Soc

BRIDGEWATER STATE COLLEGE (MA) .... bridgew.edu **1030/1550/22**
Communic, Ed, Geog, Hist, Poli Sci, Psych, Soc

BRIGHAM YOUNG UNIVERSITY (UT) .... byu.edu **1200/1800/26**
*Art, Astro, Bus Admin, Chem, Econ, Ed, Engine, English, For Lang, Geol,
Home Ec, Music, Pre-Law, Pre-Med, Reli Stu, Psych, Zoo*

BROWN UNIVERSITY (RI) .... brown.edu **1440/2130/32**
*Amer St, Anthro, Art, Art Hist, Bio, Biochem, Chem, Classics, Comp Sci, Econ, Engine, English,
For Lang, Geol, Hist, Philo, Poli Sci, Physics, Pre-Law, Pre-Med/Pre-Dental, Reli Stu, Soc*

BRYAN COLLEGE (TN) .... bryan.edu **1100/1650/24**
Communic, Ed, Hist, Music, Reli Stu

BRYANT UNIVERSITY (RI) .... bryant.edu **1100/1640/24**
Bus Admin, Comp Sci, Math

BRYN ATHYN COLL. OF THE NEW CHURCH (PA) newchurch.edu/college **1150/1725/25**
English, Hist, Reli Stu

BRYN MAWR COLLEGE (PA) .... brynmawr.edu **1310/1970/29**
*Art, Art Hist, Astro, Bio, Chem, Classics, Econ, English, For Lang,
Geol, Hist, Math, Physics, Pre-Law, Pre-Med/Pre-Dental, Psych, Soc*

BUCKNELL UNIVERSITY (PA) .... bucknell.edu **1330/1990/30**
*Bio, Bus Admin, Chem, Comp Sci, Drama, Econ, Ed, Engine, English, Hist, Math, Music,
Philo, Pre-Law, Pre-Med/Pre-Dental, Psych, Soc*

BUENA VISTA UNIVERSITY (IA) .... bvu.edu **1080/1620/23**
Bus Admin, Communic, Comp Sci, Ed

BUTLER UNIVERSITY (IN) .... butler.edu **1180/1760/26**
*Art, Bus Admin, Chem, Communic, Comp Sci, Drama, Ed, Engine, Music, Pharm,
Pre-Law, Pre-Med/Pre-Dental*

CALDWELL COLLEGE (NJ) .... caldwell.edu **1000/1500/21**
Bus Admin, Ed, Psych

CALIFORNIA COLLEGE OF ARTS AND CRAFTS (CA) ..ccac-art.edu **1070/1610/23**
Arch, Art

CALIFORNIA INSTITUTE OF TECHNOLOGY (CA) . caltech.edu **1520/2220/34**
Astro, Bio, Chem, Engine, Geol, Math, Physics, Pre-Med/Pre-Dental

CALIFORNIA INSTITUTE OF THE ARTS (CA) .... calarts.edu **1100/1650/24**
Art, Drama, Music

CALIFORNIA, UNIVERSITY OF, AT
    BERKELEY .... berkeley.edu **1350/2020/30**
    Anthro, Arch, Biochem, Bio, Bot, Bus Admin, Chem, Comp Sci, Engine,
    English, For Lang, Geog, Geol, Hist, Math, Music, Philo, Poli Sci, Physics,
    Pre-Law, Pre-Med/Pre-Dental, Psych, Reli Stu, Soc, Zoo
    DAVIS .... ucdavis.edu **1250/1875/28**
    Ag, Anthro, Art, Bio, Biochem, Bot, Chem, Econ, Engine, English, Geol,
    Hist, Physics, Poli Sci, Pre-Law, Pre-Med/Pre-Dental, Zoo
    IRVINE... uci.edu **1260/1890/28**
    Art, Bio, Chem, Comp Sci, Drama, Engine, English, Math, Physics, Pre-Law,
    Pre-Med/Pre-Dental, Psych
    LOS ANGELES .... ucla.edu **1350/2020/30**
    Anthro, Art Hist, Bio, Biochem, Bus Admin, Chem, Communic, Comp Sci, Drama,
    Econ, Engine, English, For Lang, Hist, Math, Music, Philo, Poli Sci, Pre-Law,
    Pre-Med/Pre-Dental, Psych, Soc
    MERCED .... ucmerced.edu **1100/1650/24**
    Art, Bio, Comp Sci, Econ, Engine, Hist, Psych
    RIVERSIDE .... ucr.edu **1140/1710/25**
    Ag, Art Hist, Biochem, Bio, Bot, Bus Admin, Drama, Ed, Engine, Hist,
    Math, Music, Poli Sci, Pre-Law, Pre-Med/Pre-Dental, Psych
    SAN DIEGO .... ucsd.eu **1330/1990/29**
    Amer St, Biochem, Bio, Chem, Communic, Comp Sci, Drama, Econ, Engine,
    Math, Music, Physics, Poli Sci, Pre-Law, Pre-Med/Pre-Dental, Psych
    SANTA BARBARA...............................ucsb.edu **1250/1875/28**
    Art, Art Hist, Bio, Bus Admin, Chem, Classics, Comp Sci, Ed, Econ, Engine,
    For Lang, Geog, Geol, Music, Philo, Physics, Poli Sci, Pre-Law,
    Pre-Med/Pre-Dental, Psych, Reli Stu, Soc, Zoo
    SANTA CRUZ ....ucsc.edu **1199/1800/27**
    Amer St, Anthro, Art Hist, Bio, Chem, Comp Sci, Econ, English, Hist,
    Math, Music, Physics, Pre-Med/Pre-Dental, Psych

CALIFORNIA LUTHERAN UNIVERSITY (CA) .... clunet.edu **1099/1640/24**
Bus Admin, Communic, Ed, Psych

CALIFORNIA MARITIME ACADEMY (CA) .... csum.edu **1030/1540/22**
Bus Admin, Engine

CALIFORNIA POLYTECHNIC U. AT POMONA (CA) csupomona.edu **1000/1500/21**
Ag, Arch, Bio, Bus Admin, Comp Sci, Engine, Physics, Zoo

CALIFORNIA POLYTECHNIC U. AT SAN LUIS OBISPO (CA) calpoly.edu **1220/1830/27**
Ag, Arch, Bio, Biochem, Bus Admin, Comp Sci, Communic, Engine, English, Math,
Physics, Psych

CALIFORNIA STATE UNIVERSITY, AT:

BAKERSFIELD .... csubak.edu **1000/1500/21**
Bus Admin, Econ, Ed, English, Geol, Nurs, Psych

CHANNEL ISLANDS (CAMARILLO)(CA) .... csuci.edu **1000/1500/21**
Art, Bio, Bus Admin, Econ, Ed, English, Hist, Math, Pre-Law,
Pre-Med/Pre-Dental, Psych

CHICO .... csuchico.edu **1060/1590/23**
Ag, Anthro, Bio, Chem, Comp Sci, Econ, Geog, Geol, Nurs, Poli Sci, Psych, Reli Stu

DOMINGUEZ HILLS .... csudh.edu **1000/1500/21**
Bus Admin, Chem, Math, Nurs, Philo, Physics, Psych

EAST BAY .... csueb.edu **1000/1500/21**
Art, Bus Admin, Comp Sci, Econ, English, Geol, Hist, Music, Soc

FRESNO .... csufresno.edu **1000/1500/21**
Ag, Amer St, Art, Bus Admin, Chem, Ed, Engine, English, Home Ec,
Music, Nurs, Philo, Soc

FULLERTON .... fullerton.edu **1000/1500/21**
Amer St, Anthro, Bus Admin, Chem, Communic, Engine, English, Hist,
Music, Nurs, Poli Sci, Pre-Med/Pre-Dental, Soc

LONG BEACH .... csulb.edu **1000/1500/21**
Anthro, Art, Art Hist, Chem, Classics, Communic, Drama, Econ, Hist, Music,
Poli Sci, Pre-Law, Psych

LOS ANGELES .... calstatela.edu **1000/1500/21**
Art, Bus Admin, Ed, Engine, Nurs, Psych, Soc

MONTEREY BAY .... scumb.edu **1000/1500/21**
Art, Bio, Comp Sci, Ed, English, Math, Pre-Law, Pre-Med/Pre-Dental

NORTHRIDGE .... csun.edu **1000/1500/21**
Art, Art Hist, Bus Admin, Comp Sci, Communic, Drama, Econ, Engine,
English, Geog, Music, Philo, Physics, Poli Sci, Pre-Law, Psych, Soc

SACRAMENTO .... csus.edu **1000/1500/21**
Anthro, Bus Admin, Communic, Comp Sci, Drama, Ed, Engine, English,
For Lang, Geol, Home Ec, Music, Poli Sci, Psych, Soc

SAN BERNARDINO .... csusb.edu **1000/1500/21**
Art, Bus Admin, Communic, Comp Sci, Ed, Psych, Soc

SAN JOSE .... sjsu.edu **1060/1590/23**
Art, Bus Admin, Chem, Communic, Comp Sci, Math, Music, Nurs,
Physics, Pre-Med/Pre-Dental, Zoo

SAN MARCOS .... csusm.edu **1000/1500/21**
Bus Admin, Chem, Comp Sci, Ed, Hist, Poli Sci, Psych, Soc

STANISLAUS .... csustan.edu **1000/1500/21**
Bus Admin, Comp Sci, Ed, Poli Sci, Psych

CALIFORNIA UNIVERSITY OF PENNSYLVANIA (PA) . cup.edu **1000/1500/21**
Chem, Ed, English, Nurs, Psych

CALVIN COLLEGE (MI) .... calvin.edu **1190/1770/26**
Ed, Engine, English, For Lang, Hist, Nurs, Philo, Physics, Pre-Law

CAMPBELL UNIVERSITY (NC) .... campbell.edu **1040/1550/22**
Bus Admin, English, Hist, Pharm, Poli Sci, Pre-Law

CANISIUS COLLEGE (NY) .... canisius.edu **1100/1640/24**
Bio, Bus Admin, Communic, Comp Sci, Ed, English, Hist, Pre-Med/Pre-Dental, Psych

CAPITAL UNIVERSITY (OH) .... capital.edu **1080/1620/23**
Bus Admin, Chem, Communic, Comp Sci, Ed, Hist, Music, Nurs, Reli Stu

CARLETON COLLEGE (MN) .... carleton.edu **1370/2050/31**
Amer St, Bio, Chem, Classics, Comp Sci, Drama, Econ, English, For Lang, Geol, Hist, Math, Music, Philo, Physics, Poli Sci, Pre-Law, Pre-Med/Pre-Dental, Psych, Reli Stu

CARNEGIE MELLON UNIVERSITY (PA) .... cmu.edu **1360/2040/30**
Arch, Art, Bus Admin, Chem, Comp Sci, Drama, Econ, Engine, English, Hist, Math, Music, Philo, Physics, Pre-Law, Pre-Med/Pre-Dental, Psych

CARROLL COLLEGE (MT) .... carroll.edu **1090/1630/24**
Bio, Chem, Comp Sci, Engine, Hist, Math, Nurs, Philo, Pre-Med/Pre-Dental

CARROLL COLLEGE (WI) .... cc.edu **1100/1650/24**
Art, Chem, Comp Sci, Ed, Nurs, Pre-Med/Pre-Dental, Psych

CARSON-NEWMAN COLLEGE (TN) .... cn.edu **1075/1605/23**
Chem, Ed, English, Hist, Music, Nurs, Pre-Med/Pre-Dental, Psych

CARTHAGE COLLEGE (WI) .... carthage.edu **1090/1630/24**
Bus Admin, For Lang, Geog, Music, Physics, Poli Sci, Psych, Reli Stu

CASE WESTERN RESERVE UNIVERSITY (OH) .... cwru.edu **1350/2025/30**
Amer St, Anthro, Art, Art Hist, Astro, Biochem, Bio, Bus Admin, Chem, Classics, Comp Sci, Drama, Econ, Engine, Hist, Math, Music, Nurs, Physics, Pre-Law, Pre-Med/Pre-Dental, Psych, Reli Stu

CASTLETON STATE COLLEGE (VT) .... castleton.edu **1000/1500/21**
Art, Bus Admin, Communic, Ed, Psych, Soc

CATAWBA COLLEGE (NC) .... catawba.edu **1000/1500/21**
Bus Admin, Comp Sci, Drama, Ed

CATHOLIC UNIVERSITY OF AMERICA (DC) .... cua.edu **1165/1755/26**
Arch, Classics, Drama, Engine, English, For Lang, Music, Nurs, Philo, Physics, Poli Sci, Pre-Law, Psych, Reli Stu, Soc

CEDAR CREST COLLEGE (PA) .... cedarcrest.edu **1080/1620/23**
At, Bio, Nurs, Psych

CEDARVILLE UNIVERSITY (OH) .... cedarville.edu **1160/1730/25**
Bus Admin, Ed, Music, Nurs

CENTENARY COLLEGE OF LOUISIANA (LA) ...... centenary.edu **1180/1765/26**
Art, Bio, Bus Admin, Chem, Ed, English, Geol, Music

CENTRAL ARKANSAS, UNIVERSITY OF (AR) .... uca.edu **1070/1600/23**
Bus Admin, Nurs

CENTRAL COLLEGE (IA) .... central.edu **1108/1660/24**
Bio, Chem, Comp Sci, Ed, English, For Lang, Music, Philo, Reli Stu

CENTRAL CONNECTICUT STATE UNIVERSITY (CT) ccsu.edu **1000/1500/21**
Bus Admin, Ed, Engine, Geog, Hist, Music, Psych, Soc

CENTRAL FLORIDA, UNIVERSITY OF (FL) .... ucf.edu **1160/1735/26**
Bus Admin, Comp Sci, Communic, Drama, Engine, English, Music, Philo, Physics, Psych

CENTRAL MICHIGAN UNIVERSITY (MI) ....cmich.edu **1050/1570/22**
Bio, Communic, Drama, Ed, English, Home Ec, Geog, Music, Psych

CENTRAL MIISSOURI STATE UNIVERSITY (MO) ..... cmsu.edu **1000/1500/21**
Communic, Econ, Nurs

CENTRAL OKLAHOMA, UNIVERSITY OF (OK) .... ucok.edu **1000/1500/21**
Bus Admin, Econ, Ed, Music

CENTRAL WASHINGTON UNIVERSITY .... cwu.edu **1000/1500/21**
Anthro, Bus Admin, Chem, English, Geog, Music, Psych

CENTRE COLLEGE (KY) .... centre.edu **1220/1825/27**
Art, Biochem, Bio, Chem, Classics, Econ, Ed, English, For Lang, Hist, Philo,
Physics, Poli Sci, Pre-Law, Pre-Med/Pre-Dental, Psych, Reli Stu

CHAMINADE UNIVERSITY OF HONOLULU (HI) . chaminade.edu **1000/1500/21**
Bus Admin, Ed

CHAMPLAIN COLLEGE (VT) .... champlain.edu **1000/1500/21**
Bus Admin, Comp Sci

CHAPMAN UNIVERSITY (CA) .... chapman.edu **1190/1780/26**
Art Hist, Bus Admin, Communic, Econ, Music, Pre-Law, Pre-Med/Pre-Dental, Psych

CHARLESTON, COLLEGE OF (SC) .... cofc.edu **1180/1770/26**
Bio, Bus Admin, Chem, Communic, Drama, Ed, For Lang, Geol, Math, Poli Sci,
Pre-Med/Pre-Dental, Psych, Soc

CHARLESTON SOUTHERN UNIVERSITY (SC) .... csuniv.edu **1070/1600/23**
Comp Sci, Ed, English, Music

CHARLESTON, UNIVERSITY OF (WV) .... uchaswv.edu **1000/1500/21**
Hist, Nurs

CHATHAM COLLEGE (PA) .... chatham.edu **1080/1610/23**
Art, Bio, Bus Admin, Communic, English, Hist, Poli Sci, Pre-Law

CHESTNUT HILL COLLEGE (PA) .... chc.edu **1000/1500/21**
Ed, English, Pre-Law

CHEYNEY UNIVERSITY OF PENNSYLVANIA (PA) .. cheney.edu **1000/1500/21**
Ed

CHICAGO, UNIVERSITY OF (IL) .... uchicago.edu **1400/2100/34**
Amer St, Anthro, Art, Art Hist, Biochem, Bio, Chem, Classics, Comp Sci,
Econ, English, For Lang, Geog, Geol, Hist, Math, Music, Philo, Physics,
Poli Sci, Pre-Law, Pre-Med/Pre-Dental, Psych, Reli Stu, Soc

CHOWAN COLLEGE (NC) .... chowan.edu **900/1350/20**
Art, Bus Admin, Comp Sci, English

CHRISTIAN BROTHERS UNIVERSITY (TN) .... cbu.edu **1100/1650/24**
Bus Admin, Ed, Engine, Reli Stu

CHRISTENDOM COLLEGE (VA) .... christendom.edu **1199/1790/26**
Hist, Philo, Reli Stu

CHRISTOPHER NEWPORT UNIVERSITY (VA) .... cnu.edu **1150/1725/25**
Bus Admin, Comp Sci, English, Math, Music, Philo, Physics, Poli Sci

CINCINNATI, UNIVERSITY OF (OH) .... uc.edu **1060/1590/23**
Arch, Art, Bus Admin, Classics, Ed, Engine, English, Hist, Math, Music, Nurs, Pharm, Psych, Soc

CITADEL, THE (SC) .... citadel.edu **1070/1600/23**
Bus Admin, Chem, Ed, Engine, English, Pre-Law

CLAREMONT MCKENNA COLLEGE (CA) .... mckenna.edu **1400//2100/31**
Bio, Bus Admin, Chem, Econ, English, Hist, Philo, Poli Sci, Pre-Law,
Pre-Med/Pre-Dental, Psych, Reli Stu

CLARK ATLANTA UNIVERSITY (GA) .... cau.edu **1000/1500/21**
Bus Admin, Comp Sci, Ed, Math, Physics

CLARK UNIVERSITY (MA) .... clarku.edu **1180/1770/26**
Bio, Biochem, Bus Admin, Chem, Communic, Econ, English, For Lang,
Geog, Music, Physics, Poli Sci, Pre-Law, Pre-Med/Pre-Dental, Psych

CLARKE COLLEGE (IA) .... clarke.edu **1100/1650/24**
Art, Art Hist, Bio, Chem, Communic, Comp Sci, Drama, Ed, Music, Nurs, Philo

CLARKSON UNIVERSITY (NY) .... clarkson.edu **1200/1800/26**
Bio, Biochem, Bus Admin, Chem, Comp Sci, Engine, Math, Physics, Pre-Law, Psych, Soc

CLEMSON UNIVERSITY (SC) .... clemson.edu **1195/1785/26**
Ag, Arch, Bio, Bus Admin, Chem, Comp Sci, Econ, Ed, Engine, English,
Forest, For Lang, Physics, Poli Sci, Soc, Zoo

CLEVELAND INSTITUTE OF ART (OH) .... cia.edu **1080/1620/23**
Art

CLEVELAND INSTITUTE OF MUSIC (OH) .... cim.edu **1220/1840/27**
Music

COASTAL CAROLINA (SC) .... coastal.edu **1040/1560/22**
Art, Bus Admin, Comp Sci, Ed, Philo

COE COLLEGE (IA) .... coe.edu **1150/1720/25**
Art, Bio, Bus Admin, Chem, Drama, Ed, English, Hist, Music, Nurs, Physics, Psych

COGSWELL POLYTECHNIC COLLEGE (CA) ....cogswell.edu **1000/1500/21**
Comp Sci, Engine

COKER COLLEGE (SC) .... coker.edu **1000/1500/21**
Art, Bus Admin, Drama, Ed, Music, Psych, Soc

COLBY COLLEGE (ME) .... colby.edu **1330/2000/29**
Art, Bio, Bus Admin, Chem, Econ, English, For Lang, Math, Music,
Physics, Poli Sci, Pre-Law, Pre-Med/Pre-Dental, Psych, Soc, Reli Stu

COLBY-SAWYER COLLEGE (NH) .... colby-sawyer.edu **1010/1510/21**
Nurs

COLGATE UNIVERSITY (NY) .... colgate.edu **1340/2000/30**
Art, Art Hist, Bio, Chem, Classics, Comp Sci, Drama, Econ, English,
For Lang, Geog, Geol, Hist, Math, Philo, Poli Sci, Pre-Law,
Pre-Med/Pre-Dental, Psych, Reli Stu

COLORADO COLLEGE (CO) .... coloradocollege.edu **1250/1870/28**
*Anthro, Art, Art Hist, Bio, Chem, Drama, Econ, English, Geol, Hist,
Math, Philo, Poli Sci, Pre-Law, Pre-Med/Pre-Dental, Psych, Soc*

COLORADO, UNIVERSITY OF (CO) .... colorado.edu **1165/1758/25**
*Anthro, Astro, Bio, Biochem, Bus Admin, Chem, Communic, Econ, Engine, English,
Hist, Geog, Geol, Math, Music, Nurs, Physics, Pre-Med/Pre-Dental, Psych, Soc*

COLORADO, UNIVERSITY OF (COLORADO SPRINGS) . uccs.edu **1060/1590/23**
Anthro, Bus Admin, Comp Sci, Ed, Engine, Geog, Nurs, Physics, Psych

COLORADO, UNIVERSITY OF (DENVER) .... cudenver.edu **1060/1590/23**
Art, Bio, Bus Admin, Comp Sci, Math, Psych

COLORADO SCHOOL OF MINES (CO) .... mines.edu **1240/1860/28**
Comp Sci, Econ, Engine, Geol, Math, Physics, Pre-Med/Pre-Dental

COLORADO STATE UNIVERSITY (CO) .... colostate.edu **1110/1660/24**
Ag, Anthro, Art, Art Hist, Bot, Bus Admin, Comp Sci, Engine, Forest, Geol, Poli Sci, Psych, Zoo

COLUMBIA COLLEGE (IL) .... colum.edu **1000/1500/21**
Art Hist, Communic, Drama

COLUMBIA COLLEGE (MO) .... ccis.edu **1000/1500/21**
Art, Bus Admin

COLUMBIA COLLEGE (SC) .... columbia.college.sc.edu **1020/1530/22**
Bio, Bus Admin, Drama, Ed, Pre-Law, Pre-Med/Pre-Dental, Psych

COLUMBIA UNIV./BARNARD COLL. (NY) .columbia.edu   **1400/2100/31; 1330/2000/30**
*Anthro, Arch, Art Hist, Biochem, Bio, Chem, Classics, Drama, Econ, Engine,
English, For Lang, Geol, Hist, Math, Music, Philo, Physics, Poli Sci,
Pre-Law, Pre-Med/Pre-Dental, Psych, Reli Stu, Soc*

CONCORDIA COLLEGE-MOORHEAD (MN) .... cord.edu **1120/1680/24**
*Bio, Bus Admin, Chem, Ed, English, For Lang, Math, Music,
Pre-Med/Pre-Dental, Psych, Reli Stu, Soc*

CONCORDIA UNIVERSITY (NE) .... cune.edu **1070/1600/23**
Bus Admin, Ed, Reli Stu

CONCORDIA UNIVERSITY (CA) .... cui.edu **1040/1560/22**
Bus Admin, Music, Reli Stu

CONNECTICUT, UNIVERSITY OF (CT) .... uconn.edu **1185/1775/26**
*Ag, Art, Biochem, Bio, Bot, Bus Admin, Communic, Econ, Ed, Engine, Forest, Hist,
Home Ec, Nurs, Poli Sci, Pharm, Pre-Law, Pre-Med/Pre-Dental, Psych, Soc, Zoo*

CONNECTICUT COLLEGE (CT) .... conncoll.edu **1270/1900/28**
*Anthro, Art, Art Hist, Biochem, Bio, Bot, Chem, Classics, Drama,
Econ, Ed, English, For Lang, Hist, Math, Music, Philo, Poli Sci,
Pre-Law, Pre-Med/Pre-Dental, Psych, Soc*

CONVERSE COLLEGE (SC) .... converse.edu **1080/1620/23**
Art, Chem, Drama, Ed, Music, Poli Sci

THE COOPER UNION (NY) .... cooper.edu **1460/2190/34**
Arch, Art, Engine

CORNELL COLLEGE (IA) .... cornell-iowa.edu **1200/1800/26**
Art, Bio, Econ, Ed, English, Geol, Hist, Philo, Poli Sci, Pre-Law, Pre-Med/Pre-Dental, Psych, Soc

CORNELL UNIVERSITY (NY) .... cornell.edu **1380/2070/31**
Ag, Arch, Art, Astro, Biochem, Bio, Bot, Chem, Comp Sci, Drama, Econ, Engine, English, Hist, Philo, Physics, Pre-Med/Pre-Dental, Zoo

CORNISH COLLEGE OF THE ARTS (WA) .... cornish.edu **1100/1650/24**
Art, Drama, Music

COVENANT COLLEGE (GA) ....covenant.edu **1185/1775/26**
Hist, Music, Soc

CREIGHTON UNIVERSITY (NE) .... creighton.edu **1195/1795/26**
Art, Bio, Bus Admin, Chem, Classics, Communic, Drama, Ed, Music, Nurs, Pharm, Philo, Physics, Poli Sci, Pre-Law, Pre-Med/Pre-Dental, Psych, Reli Stu

CULVER-STOCKTON COLLEGE (MO) .... culver.edu **1000/1500/21**
Art, Bus Admin

CUMBERLAND COLLEGE (KY) .... cumber.edu **1050/1575/22**
Chem, Ed, Hist, Music, Reli Stu

CURTIS INSTITUTE OF MUSIC (PA) .... curtis.edu **1100/1650/24**
Music

DAEMEN COLLEGE (NY) .... daemen.edu **1000/1500/21**
Bio, Bus Admin, Ed, English, Nurs

DALLAS, UNIVERSITY OF (TX) .... udallas.edu **1200/1800/26**
Art, Bio, Biochem, Classics, Comp Sci, Drama, Econ, Ed, English, For Lang, Hist, Philo, Poli Sci, Pre-Law, Pre-Med/Pre-Dental, Psych

DANA COLLEGE (NE) .... dana.edu **1020/1530/22**
Art, Communic, Drama, Ed, English, Music

DARTMOUTH COLLEGE (NH) .... dartmouth.edu **1435/2150/32**
Anthro, Art, Bio, Chem, Classics, Comp Sci, Drama, Econ, Engine, English, For Lang, Geog, Geol, Hist, Math, Physics, Poli Sci, Pre-Law, Pre-Med/Pre-Dental, Psych, Reli Stu, Soc

DAVIDSON COLLEGE (NC) .... davidson.edu **1360/2040/31**
Bio, Chem, Drama, Econ, English, Hist, Math, Philo, Poli Sci, Pre-Law, Pre-Med/Pre-Dental, Psych, Reli Stu

DAYTON, UNIVERSITY OF (OH) .... udayton.edu **1170/1755/26**
Bus Admin, Communic, Ed, Engine, Geol, Music, Poli Sci, Pre-Law, Pre-Med/Pre-Dental, Soc

DELAWARE STATE UNIVERSITY .... dsc.edu **1000/1500/21**
Hist, Psych

DELAWARE, UNIVERSITY OF (DE) .... udel.edu **1180/1770/26**
Art, Art Hist, Bio, Bot, Bus Admin, Chem, Communic, Econ, Ed, Engine, English, Hist, Nurs, Poli Sci, Pre-Law, Pre-Med/Pre-Dental, Psych

DELAWARE VALLEY COLLEGE (PA) .... devalcol.edu **1020/1530/22**
Ag, Bio, Bus Admin, Chem, Pre-Med/Pre-Dental

DENISON UNIVERSITY (OH) .... denison.edu **1210/1810/27**
Art, Art Hist, Bio, Biochem, Comp Sci, Drama, Econ, English, Geol, Hist,
Music, Philo, Physics, Poli Sci, Pre-Law, Pre-Med/Pre-Dental, Psych, Soc

DENVER, UNIVERSITY OF (CO) .... du.edu **1120/1690/24**
Art, Art Hist, Bio, Bus Admin, Chem, Communic, Comp Sci, Engine, English,
Geog, Hist, Music, Physics, Pre-Law, Pre-Med/Pre-Dental, Psych, Reli Stu, Soc

DePAUL UNIVERSITY (IL) .... depaul.edu **1150/1725/25**
Amer St, Bus Admin, Chem, Communic, Comp Sci, Drama, Ed, English, Geog,
Hist, Math, Music, Philo, Poli Sci, Pre-Law, Pre-Med/Pre-Dental, Psych, Reli Stu

DePAUW UNIVERSITY (IN) .... depauw.edu **1240/1860/27**
Art, Biochem, Bio, Bus Admin, Chem, Communic, Comp Sci, Econ, English, For Lang, Hist,
Music, Philo, Physics, Poli Sci, Pre-Law, Pre-Med/Pre-Dental, Psych, Reli Stu, Soc

DeSALES UNIVERSITY (PA) .... desales.edu **1085/1625/24**
Bio, Chem, Drama, English, Philo, Reli Stu

DETROIT MERCY, UNIVERSITY OF (MI) .... udmercy.edu **1100/1650/24**
Arch, Engine, Nurs, Philo, Reli Stu

DICKINSON COLLEGE (PA) .... dickinson.edu **1275/1958/29**
Bio, Comp Sci, Ed, English, For Lang, Hist, Math, Physics, Poli Sci, Pre-Law,
Pre-Med/Pre-Dental, Psych, Reli Stu

DILLARD UNIVERSITY (LA) .... dillard.edu **1030/1540/22**
Bio, Bus Admin, Ed, Nurs, Pre-Med/Pre-Dental

DOANE COLLEGE (NE) .... doane.edu **1075/1610/23**
Bio, Bus Admin, Ed, English, Philo, Physics, Reli Stu, Soc

DOMINICAN UNIVERSITY OF CALIFORNIA (CA) ... dominican.edu **1010/1510/21**
Ed, Nurs, Psych

DOMINICAN UNIVERSITY (IL) .... dom.edu **1070/1600/23**
Bus Admin, Psych

DORDT COLLEGE (IA) .... dordt.edu **1130/1690/25**
Ag, Art, Ed, Engine, English, Reli Stu

DRAKE UNIVERSITY (IA) .... drake.edu **1190/1780/26**
Art, Astro, Bio, Bus Admin, Chem, Communic, Drama, Econ, Ed, English,
For Lang, Hist, Music, Pharm, Poli Sci, Pre-Law, Soc

DREW UNIVERSITY (NJ) .... drew.edu **1230/1840/27**
Art, Chem, Classics, Drama, Econ, English, For Lang, Hist, Poli Sci, Pre-Law,
Pre-Med/Pre-Dental, Psych, Reli Stu

DREXEL UNIVERSITY (PA) .... drexel.edu **1160/1740/25**
Arch, Comp Sci, Engine

DRURY UNIVERSITY (MO) .... drury.edu **1130/1690/25**
Ag, Arch, Bio, Ed, English, Music, Pre-Law, Reli Stu

DUBUQUE, UNIVERSITY OF (IA) .... dbq.edu **1070/1600/23**
Bus Admin, Communic, English, Ed, Psych

DUKE UNIVERSITY (NC) .... duke.edu **1440/2160/31**
Anthro, Bio, Bot, Chem, Classics, Econ, Engine, English, Hist, Math, Nurs, Philo, Poli Sci,
Pre-Law, Pre-Med/Pre-Dental, Psych, Reli Stu

DUQUESNE UNIVERSITY (PA) .... duq.edu **1115/1665/24**
Bio, Bus Admin, Chem, Classics, Communic, Ed, Music, Nurs, Pharm, Pre-Med/Pre-Dental, Reli Stu

D'YOUVILLE COLLEGE (NY) .... dyc.edu **1060/1590/23**
Bio, Ed, English, Nurs, Psych, Soc

EARLHAM COLLEGE (IN) .... earlham.edu **1225/1845/27**
Anthro, Astro, Bio, Chem, Ed, English, For Lang, Geol, Math, Philo, Pre-Med/Pre-Dental,
Psych, Reli Stu, Soc

EAST CAROLINA UNIVERSITY (NC) .... ecu.edu **1080/1620/23**
Art, Art Hist, Econ, Ed, Engine, Hist, Math, Music, Nurs, Pre-Med/Pre-Dental, Psych

EAST CENTRAL STATE UNIVERSITY (OK) .... ecok.edu **1000/1500/21**
Ed, English

EAST STROUDSBURG UNIVERSITY (PA) .... esu.edu **1000/1500/21**
Bio, Comp Sci

EAST TENNESSEE STATE UNIVERSITY (TN) .... etsu.edu **1030/1540/22**
Art, Bio, Bus Admin, Communic, Econ, English, Hist, Math, Nurs, Philo

EASTERN COLLEGE (PA) .... eastern.edu **1090/1630/24**
Bus Admin, Nurs, Soc

EASTERN CONNECTICUT STATE UNIVERSITY (CT) easternct.edu **1040/1560/22**
Amer St, Art Hist, Bio, Bot, Bus Admin, Communic, Comp Sci, Econ, Ed, Hist, Math,
Poli Sci, Psych, Soc

EASTERN ILLINOIS UNIVERSITY (IL) .... eiu.edu **1030/1540/22**
Art, Bot, Bus Admin, Ed, English, Home Ec, Psych, Zoo

EASTERN KENTUCKY UNIVERSITY (KY) .... eku.edu **1000/1500/21**
Communic, Ed, Nurs, Poli Sci

EASTERN MENNONITE UNIVERSITY (VA) .... emu.edu **1070/1600/23**
Ed, Nurs, Reli Stu

EASTERN MICHIGAN UNIVERSITY (MI) .... emich.edu **1010/1510/21**
Bus Admin, Chem, Comp Sci, Ed, English, Hist, Music, Nurs, Physics, Poli Sci, Psych

EASTERN NAZARENE COLLEGE (MA) .... enc.edu **1000/1500/21**
Bus Admin, English

EASTERN OREGON UNIVERSITY (OR) .... eou.edu **1000/1500/21**
Bio, Bus Admin, Ed, English, Nurs

EASTERN WASHINGTON UNIVERSITY (WA) .... ewu.edu **1000/1500/21**
Chem, Econ, English, For Lang, Geol, Math, Nurs

ECKERD COLLEGE (FL) .... eckerd.edu **1140/1715/25**
Bio, Bus Admin, Comp Sci, English, For Lang, Pre-Med/Pre-Dental, Reli Stu

EDGEWOOD COLLEGE (WI) .... edgewood.edu **1040/1560/22**
Art, Ed, Nurs

EDINBORO UNIVERSITY OF PENNSYLVANIA (PA) .... edinboro.edu **1000/1500/21**
Art, Art Hist, Ed, English, Geog, Geol, Philo, Physics

ELIZABETHTOWN COLLEGE (PA) .... etown.edu **1120/1680/24**
Bio, Bus Admin, Ed, English, Pre-Law, Reli Stu

ELMHURST COLLEGE (IL) .... elmhurst.edu **1050/1575/22**
Bio, Chem, Ed, Geog, Music, Nurs, Physics, Pre-Med/Pre-Dental, Psych

ELMIRA COLLEGE (NY) .... elmira.edu **1130/1700/25**
Bus Admin, Ed, Hist, Nurs, Psych

ELMS COLLEGE (MA) .... elms.edu **1020/1530/22**
Ed, Nurs

ELON UNIVERSITY (NC) .... elon.edu **1170/1755/26**
Bio, Bus Admin, Communic, Drama, Ed, Philo, Poli Sci, Psych

EMBRY-RIDDLE AERONAUTICAL UNIVERSITY (FL) emu.edu **1110/1660/24**
Comp Sci, Engine

EMERSON COLLEGE (MA) .... emerson.edu **1195/1795/26**
Drama, English, Pre-Law

EMMANUEL COLLEGE (MA) .... emmanuel/edu **1040/1560/22**
Art, Bio

EMORY & HENRY COLLEGE (VA) .... ehc.edu **1020/1530/22**
Bus Admin, For Lang

EMORY UNIVERSITY (GA) .... emory.edu **1350/2025/30**
Amer St, Anthro, Art Hist, Bio, Bus Admin, Chem, Classics, Econ, English, For Lang, Hist, Nurs, Poli Sci, Pre-Law, Pre-Med/Pre-Dental, Psych, Reli Stu, Soc

EMPORIA STATE UNIVERSITY (KS) .... emporia.edu **1040/1560/22**
Art, Chem, Ed, Geol, Nurs

ENDICOTT COLLEGE (MA) .... endicott.edu **1050/1575/22**
Art, Bus Admin, Communic

ERSKINE COLLEGE (SC) .... erskine.edu **1120/1680/24**
Bio, Bus Admin, Ed, Hist, Pre-Med/Pre-Dental

EUREKA COLLEGE (IL) .... eureka.edu **1090/1635/24**
Bus Admin, Comp Sci, Ed, English

EVANSVILLE, UNIVERSITY OF (IN) .... evansville.edu **1140/1710/25**
Comp Sci, Drama, Music, Nurs, Physics, Pre-Med/Pre-Dental

FAIRFIELD UNIVERSITY (CT) .... fairfield.edu **1190/1780/26**
Bio, Bus Admin, Communic, Math, Nurs, Physics, Pre-Med/Pre-Dental, Psych

FAIRLEIGH DICKINSON (NJ) .... fdu.edu **1000/1500/21**
Art, Bus Admin, English, Pre-Law

FAIRMONT STATE COLLEGE (WV) .... fscwv.edu **1000/1500/21**
Bus Admin, Ed, Hist, Nurs, Psych

FAULKNER UNIVERSITY (AL) .... faulkner.edu **1000/1500/21**
Bus Admin

FERRIS STATE UNIVERSITY (MI) .... ferris.edu **1000/1500/21**
Bus Admin, Comp Sci, Nurs, Pharm

FISK UNIVERSITY (TN) .... fisk.edu **1010/1510/21**
Bus Admin, Math, Physics, Pre-Law, Soc

FITCHBURG STATE COLLEGE (MA) .... fsc.edu **1020/1530/22**
Bio, Communic, Ed, Hist, Nurs, Psych

FIVE TOWNS COLLEGE (NY) .... ftc.edu **1000/1500/21**
Music

FLAGLER COLLEGE (FL) .... flagler.edu **1100/1650/24**
Bus Admin, Communic, Ed, Pre-Law, Psych

FLORIDA, UNIVERSITY OF (FL) .... ufl.edu **1260/1890/28**
Ag, Anthro, Arch, Art, Astro, Bot, Bus Admin, Classics, Communic, Drama, Engine, English, Forest, For Lang, Geol, Hist, Math, Music, Nurs, Pharm, Philo, Physics, Poli, Sci, Pre-Law, Pre-Med/Pre-Dental, Soc, Zoo

FLORIDA A&M (FL) .... famu/edu **1000/1500/21**
Arch, Bus Admin, Communic, Ed, Engine, English, Pharm, Physics, Pre-Law, Pre-Med/Pre-Dental

FLORIDA ATLANTIC UNIVERSITY (FL) .... fau.edu **1050/1575/22**
Bus Admin, Ed, Engine, Hist, Math, Psych

FLORIDA GULF COAST UNIVERSITY (FL) .... fgcu.edu **1040/1560/22**
Bus Admin, Comp Sci, Ed, English, Nurs

FLORIDA INSTITUTE OF TECHNOLOGY (FL) .... fit.edu **1100/1650/24**
Astro, Bio, Biochem, Bus Admin, Chem, Communic, Comp Sci, Engine, Physics, Psych

FLORIDA INTERNATIONAL UNIVERSITY (FL) .... fiu.edu **1150/1725/25**
Arch, Art, Bio, Bus Admin, Ed, Engine, Geog, Nurs, Poli Sci, Psych, Soc

FLORIDA SOUTHERN COLLEGE (FL) .... flsouthern.edu **1050/1575/22**
Bio, Chem, Communic, Drama, Ed, Music, Pre-Med/Pre-Dental

FLORIDA STATE UNIVERSITY (FL) .... fsu.edu **1160/1740/25**
Amer St, Art, Art Hist, Bus Admin, Chem, Classics, Comp Sci, Drama, Econ, Ed, English, Hist, Home Ec, Music, Philo, Physics, Pre-Med/Pre-Dental, Psych, Reli Stu

FONTBONNE UNIVERSITY (MO) .... fontbonne.edu **1050/1575/22**
Art, Communic, Drama, Ed, Math

FORDHAM UNIVERSITY (NY) .... fordham.edu **1180/1770/26**
Classics, Communic, Drama, English, Philo, Pre-Law, Pre-Med/Pre-Dental, Reli Stu

FORT HAYS STATE UNIVERSITY (KS) .... fhsu.edu **1050/1575/22**
Art, Ed, English, Music, Nurs, Philo, Soc

FORT LEWIS COLLEGE (CO) .... fortlewis.edu **1000/1500/21**
Anthro, Art, Bio, English, Geol, Physics, Pre-Law

FRAMINGHAM STATE COLLEGE (MA) .... framingham.edu **1040/1560/22**
Bio, Biochem, Bus Admin, Chem, Econ, Ed, Psych

FRANCISCAN UNIVERSITY OF STEUBENVILLE (OH) franuniv.edu **1110/1660/24**
English, Nurs, Philo, Psych, Reli Stu

FRANKLIN COLLEGE (IN) .... franklincollege.edu **1050/1575/23**
Communic, Drama, Ed, Pre-Med

FRANKLIN & MARSHALL COLLEGE (PA) .... fandm.edu **1255/1880/28**
Amer Stu, Bio, Bus Admin, Chem, Econ, English, For Lang, Geol, Physics,
Poli Sci, Pre-Law, Pre-Med/Pre-Dental, Psych, Soc

FREED-HARDEMAN UNIVERSITY (TN) .... fhu.edu **1080/1620/23**
Bus Admin, Ed, Pre-Med/Pre-Dental, Reli Stu

FRIENDS UNIVERSITY (KS) .... friends.edu **1050/1575/22**
Ed, English, Music

FROSTBURG STATE UNIVERSITY (MD) .... frostburg.edu **1015/1520/21**
Art, Bus Admin, Comp Sci, Ed, Geog, Philo

FURMAN UNIVERSITY (SC) .... furman.edu **1265/1900/28**
Art, Bio, Bus Admin, Chem, Comp Sci, Econ, Geol, Hist, Music, Poli Sci, Pre-Law,
Pre-Med/Pre-Dental, Psych, Reli Stu

GANNON UNIVERSITY (PA) .... gannon.edu **1060/1640/23**
Bus Admin, Chem, Engine, Nurs

GARDNER-WEBB UNIVERSITY (NC) .... gardner-webb.edu **1040/1560/23**
Bus Admin, Comp Sci, Poli Sci, Pre-Med/Pre-Dental, Soc

GENEVA COLLEGE (PA) .... geneva.edu **1100/1650/24**
Communic, Ed, Engine

GEORGETOWN COLLEGE (KY) .... georgetowncollege.edu **1080/1620/23**
Bio, Bus Admin, Chem, Communic, Ed, English, Hist, Pre-Law, Soc

GEORGETOWN UNIVERSITY (DC) .... georgetown.edu **1380/2070/31**
Amer St, Anthro, Art Hist, Biochem, Bio, Bus Admin, Chem, Classics, Econ, English, For Lang,
Hist, Nurs, Philo, Physics, Poli Sci, Pre-Law, Pre-Med/Pre-Dental, Psych, Reli Stu, Soc

GEORGE FOX UNIVERSITY (OR) .... georgefox.edu **1120/1680/24**
Art, Bio, Bus Admin, Ed, Psych, Reli Stu, Soc

GEORGE MASON UNIVERSITY (VA) .... gmu.edu **1120/1680/24**
Amer St, Anthro, Art Hist, Bus Admin, Communic, Comp Sci, Drama,
Econ, English, Math, Nurs, Philo, Physics, Poli Sci, Psych, Pre-Law

GEORGE WASHINGTON UNIVERSITY (DC) .... gwu.edu **1260/1890/28**
Amer St, Anthro, Art Hist, Bus Admin, Chem, Comp Sci, Drama, Econ, Engine,
Geog, Hist, Philo, Poli Sci, Pre-Law, Psych, Soc

GEORGIA, UNIVERSITY OF (GA) .... uga.edu **1195/1780/26**
Ag, Art Hist, Astro, Bio, Biochem, Chem, Classics, Communic, Drama, Econ, Ed,
English, For Lang, Forest, Geog, Hist, Home Ec, Music, Pharm, Philo, Poli Sci, Pre-Law,
Pre-Med/Pre-Dental, Psych, Zoo

GEORGIA INSTITUTE OF TECHNOLOGY (GA) ....gatech.edu **1330/1990/30**
Arch, Bus Admin, Chem, Comp Sci, Econ, Engine, Hist, Math, Physics, Psych

GEORGIA SOUTHERN UNIVERSITY (GA) .... gasou.edu **1050/1575/22**
Art, Bus Admin, Ed, Hist, Home Ec, Nurs

GEORGIA SOUTHWESTERN STATE UNIVERSITY (GA) ... gsw.edu **1000/1500/21**
Ed, English, Nurs

GEORGIA STATE UNIVERSITY (GA) .... gsu.edu **1060/1590/23**
Astro, Bio, Bus Admin, Chem, Communic, Comp Sci, Econ, Ed, Math, Music,
Nurs, Philo, Physics, Psych, Soc

GETTYSBURG COLLEGE (PA) .... gettysburg.edu **1260/1890/28**
Bio, Bus Admin, Communic, Drama, Econ, English, Hist, Pre-Law, Pre-Med/Pre-Dental, Psych, Soc

GONZAGA UNIVERSITY (WA) ....gonzaga.edu **1190/1780/26**
Bio, Bus Admin, Chem, Communic, Ed, Engine, English, Hist, Philo, Poli Sci, Pre-Law,
Pre-Med/Pre-Dental, Reli Stu

GORDON COLLEGE (MA) .... gordon.edu **1199/1800/26**
Art, Bio, Ed, English, Music, Reli Stu, Soc

GOSHEN COLLEGE (IN) .... goshen.edu **1170/1755/26**
English, Music, Nurs, Physics

GOUCHER COLLEGE (MD) .... goucher.edu **1170/1755/26**
Art, Bus Admin, Chem, Comp Sci, Drama, Ed, English, Hist, Pre-Law

GRACELAND UNIVERSITY (IA) .... graceland.edu **1001/1500/21**
Bus Admin, Ed, Hist, Nurs

GRAMBLING STATE UNIVERSITY (LA) .... gram.edu **1000/1500/21**
Bus Admin, Ed, Nurs, Poli Sci, Soc

GREAT FALLS, UNIVERSITY OF (MT) .... ugf.edu **1000/1500/21**
Comp Sci, Ed

GRAND VALLEY STATE UNIVERSITY (MI) .... gvsu.edu **1080/1620/23**
Anthro, Art, Drama, Engine, English, For Lang, Pre-Law, Psych

GREEN MOUNTAIN COLLEGE (VT) .... greenmtn.edu **1000/1500/21**
Bus Admin

GREENSBORO COLLEGE (NC) .... gborocollege.edu **1000/1500/21**
Drama, Ed

GRINNELL COLLEGE (IA) .... grinnell.edu **1334/2000/30**
Anthro, Bio, Chem, Classics, Comp Sci, Econ, English, For Lang, Hist, Math,
Physics, Poli Sci, Pre-Law, Pre-Med/Pre-Dental, Psych, Reli Stu, Soc

GROVE CITY COLLEGE (PA) .... gcc.edu **1270/1900/28**
Bio, Bus Admin, Econ, Ed, Engine, English, Poli Sci

GUILFORD COLLEGE (NC) .... guilford.edu **1130/1700/25**
*Art, Bio, Bus Admin, Econ, Ed, English, Geol, Hist, Physics, Poli Sci,
Pre-Law, Pre-Med/Pre-Dental, Psych, Reli Stu*

GUSTAVUS ADOLPHUS COLLEGE (MN) .... gustavus.edu **1220/1830/27**
Bio, Bus Admin, Chem, Classics, Ed, English, For Lang, Geol, Hist, Music, Nurs, Physics, Psych, Reli Stu

GWYNEDD-MERCY COLLEGE (PA) .... gmc.edu **1000/1500/21**
Bio, Communic, English, Nurs, Pre-Law

HAMILTON COLLEGE (NY) .... hamilton.edu **1320/1980/30**
*Bio, Chem, Comp Sci, Drama, Econ, English, Geol, Hist, Philo, Physics,
Poli Sci, Pre-Law, Pre-Med/Pre-Dental, Reli Stu*

HAMLINE UNIVERSITY (MN) .... hamline.edu **1120/1680/24**
Anthro, Art, Bio, Chem, Ed, English, Hist, Physics, Pre-Law, Pre-Med/Pre-Dental, Psych, Soc

HAMPDEN-SYDNEY COLLEGE (VA) .... hsc.edu **1140/1710/25**
Bio, Classics, Econ, English, Hist, Poli Sci, Pre-Law, Pre-Med/Pre-Dental

HAMPTON UNIVERSITY (VA) .... hamptonu.edu **1030/1545/24**
Bus Admin, Psych

HANNIBAL-LA GRANGE COLLEGE (MO) .... hlg.edu **1000/1500/21**
Ed, Music

HANOVER COLLEGE (IN) .... hanover.edu **1130/1700/25**
Bus Admin, Communic, Drama, Ed, English, Hist, Philo, Physics, Psych, Soc

HARDIN-SIMMONS UNIVERSITY (TX) .... hsutx.edu **1020/1530/22**
Bio, Communic, Econ, Ed, Music, Nurs, Reli Stu

HARDING UNIVERSITY (AR) .... harding.edu **1120/1680/24**
Bus Admin, Ed, Music, Nurs, Reli Stu

HARTFORD, UNIVERSITY OF (CT) .... hartford.edu **1060/1600/23**
Bus Admin, Drama, Engine, Music

HARTWICK COLLEGE (NY) .... hartwick.edu **1115/1675/24**
Bus Admin, Geol, Music, Nurs, Poli Sci, Pre-Law, Soc

HARVARD UNIVERSITY (MA) .... harvard.edu **1485/2230/33**
*Amer St, Anthro, Art, Art Hist, Astro, Biochem, Bio, Chem, Classics, Comp Sci, Econ,
English, For Lang, Geol, Hist, Math, Music, Philo, Physics, Poli Sci, Pre-Law,
Pre-Med/Pre-Dental, Psych, Soc*

HARVEY MUDD COLLEGE (CA) .... hmc.edu **1450/2175/32**
Bio, Chem, Comp Sci, Engine, Math, Physics, Pre-Med/Pre-Dental

HASTINGS COLLEGE (NE) .... hastings.edu **1070/1600/23**
Bus Admin, Communic, Ed, Hist, Music, Physics

HAVERFORD COLLEGE (PA) .... haverford.edu **1380/2080/31**
*Art, Astro, Bio, Chem, Econ, English, For Lang, Hist, Philo, Physics, Pre-Law,
Pre-Med/Pre-Dental, Psych, Reli Stu*

HAWAII, UNIVERSITY OF (HI) ....uhm.hawaii.edu **1090/1635/24**
Ag, Amer St, Anthro, Art, Astro, Bot, Drama, For Lang, Poli Sci, Pre-Law, Zoo

HAWAII PACIFIC UNIVERSITY (HI) ....hpu.edu **1050/1575/22**
Bus Admin, Communic, Comp Sci, Econ, Nurs, Pre-Med/Pre-Dental

HEIDELBERG COLLEGE (OH) .... heidelberg.edu **1050/1575/22**
Bio, Bus Admin, Econ, Ed, Hist, Music, Poli Sci, Pre-Law, Pre-Med/Pre-Dental

HENDERSON STATE UNIVERSITY (AR) ....hsu.edu **1030/1545/22**
Bus Admin, Ed, Nurs

HENDRIX COLLEGE (AR) ....hendrix.edu **1240/1860/28**
*Bio, Bus Admin, Chem, Comp Sci, Econ, English, Math, Physics, Pre-Law,
Pre-Med/Pre-Dental, Psych, Reli Stu, Soc*

HIGH POINT UNIVERSITY (NC) ....highpoint.edu **1030/1550/22**
Comp Sci

HILLSDALE COLLEGE (MI) ....hillsdale.edu **1190/1790/26**
Amer St, Bus Admin, Ed, Hist, Poli Sci

HIRAM COLLEGE (OH) .... hiram.edu **1140/1710/25**
Bio, Chem, Comp Sci, Ed, English, Hist, Math, Music, Pre-Law, Pre-Med/Pre-Dental, Reli Stu

HOBART & WILLIAM SMITH COLLEGE (NY) ....hws.edu **1190/1790/26**
Amer Stu, Bio, Chem, Econ, English, Hist, Poli Sci, Pre-Law, Pre-Med/Pre-Dental, Psych

HOFSTRA UNIVERSITY (NY) ....hofstra.edu **1130/1700/25**
*Anthro, Art, Bus Admin, Communic, Drama, Music, Poli Sci, Pre-Law, Pre-Med/Pre-Dental,
Soc*

HOLLINS UNIVERSITY (VA) ....hollins.edu **1140/1710/25**
*Art, Art Hist, Chem, Drama, English, For Lang, Hist, Pre-Law,
Pre-Med/Pre-Dental, Soc, Psych*

HOLY CROSS, COLLEGE OF THE (MA) ....holycross.edu **1300/1950/29**
*Bio, Chem, Classics, Econ, English, For Lang, Hist, Math, Philo, Physics,
Poli Sci, Pre-Law, Pre-Med/Pre-Dental, Psych, Reli Stu, Soc*

HOLY NAMES UNIVERSITY (CA) ....hnu.edu **1000/1500/21**
Bio, Ed, Music, Nurs, Psych

HOOD COLLEGE (MD) ....hood.edu **1100/1650/24**
Bio, Bus Admin, Ed, Hist, Philo, Pre-Med/Pre-Dental, Psych

HOPE COLLEGE (MI) ....hope.edu **1185/1770/26**
Bio, Chem, Geol, Music, Poli Sci, Pre-Law, Pre-Med/Pre-Dental, Psych

HOUGHTON COLLEGE (NY) ....houghton.edu **1160/1740/25**
Art, Bio, Chem, Ed, Music, Pre-Med/Pre-Dental, Psych, Reli Stu

HOUSTON BAPTIST UNIVERSITY (TX) ....hbu.edu **1040/1560/23**
Bio, Chem, Pre-Med/Pre-Dental

HOUSTON, UNIVERSITY OF (TX) ....uh.edu **1060/1590/23**
Arch, Art, Bus Admin, Communic, Engine, Music, Psych

HOWARD UNIVERSITY (DC) .... howard.edu **1060/1590/23**
Arch, Bus Admin, Communic, Engine, English, Nurs, Poli Sci, Pre-Law, Pre-Med/Pre-Dental, Soc, Zoo

HUMBOLDT STATE UNIVERSITY (CA) .... humboldt.edu **1060/1590/23**
Anthro, Art, Bot, Forest, Geog, Geol, Zoo

HUNTINGDON COLLEGE (AL) .... huntingdon.edu **1120/1680/24**
Chem, Ed, Music, Pre-Med/Pre-Dental

HUNTINGTON COLLEGE (IN) .... huntcol.edu **1050/1575/22**
Ed

HUSSON COLLEGE (ME) .... husson.edu **1000/1500/21**
Bus Admin, Comp Sci, Ed, Nurs

IDAHO, UNIVERSITY OF (ID) .... uidaho.edu **1105/1665/24**
Ag, Arch, Bus Admin, Communic, Comp Sci, Engine, Forest, Geol, Music, Physics

IDAHO STATE UNIVERSITY (ID) .... isu.edu **1000/1500/21**
Nurs, Pharm

ILLINOIS, UNIVERSITY OF, AT:
        URBANA-CHAMPAIGN .... uiuc.edu **1270/1900/28**
        Ag, Anthro, Arch, Astro, Bus Admin, Chem, Communic, Comp Sci, Drama, Ed, Engine,English, Forest, For Lang, Hist, Math, Music, Nurs, Pharm, Physics, Poli Sci, Pre-Law, Pre-Med/Pre-Dental, Psych, Soc
        CHICAGO .... uic.edu **1100/1650/24**
        Arch, Art, Art Hist, Bio, Bus Admin, Classics, Econ, Engine, English, For Lang, Hist, Math, Music, Nurs, Pharm, Philo, Poli Sci, Pre-law, Pre-Med/Pre-Dental, Psych

ILLINOIS COLLEGE (IL) .... ic.edu **1130/1695/25**
Bio, Bus Admin, Communic, Comp Sci, Econ, Ed, English, For Lang, Hist, Math, Poli Sci, Pre-Law, Soc

ILLINOIS INSTITUTE OF TECHNOLOGY (IL) .... iit.edu **1280/1920/29**
Arch, Engine, Math

ILLINOIS STATE UNIVERSITY (IL) .... ilstu.edu **1060/1590/23**
Drama, Ed, Poli Sci, Pre-Law

ILLINOIS WESLEYAN UNIVERSITY (IL) .... iwu.edu **1270/1900/28**
Bio, Chem, Drama, English, Music, Nurs, Physics, Pre-Law, Pre-Med/Pre-Dental, Psych

IMMACULATA UNIVERSITY (PA) .... immaculata.edu **1000/1500/21**
Bus Admin, Nurs

INDIANA STATE UNIVERSITY (IN) .... indstate.edu **1000/1500/21**
Art, Bus Admin, Communic, Drama, Ed, Geog, Music, Physics

INDIANA UNIVERSITY (IN) .... indiana.edu **1100/1665/24**
Bio, Bus Admin, Chem, Communic, Drama, Ed, For Lang, Geog, Geol, Hist, Music, Nurs, Pre-Med/Pre-Dental, Psych, Soc, Zoo

INDIANA UNIVERSITY OF PENNSYLVANIA .... iup.edu **1150/1725/25**
Anthro, Art, Art Hist, Biochem, Bio, Bus Admin, Communic, Ed, Geog, Hist, Math, Music, Nurs, Philo, Physics, Soc

INDIANA U./PURDUE U./INDIANAPOLIS (IN) ....iupui.edu **1000/1500/21**
Econ, Ed, Engine, Nurs, Soc

INDIANA INSTITUTE OF TECHNOLOGY (IN) .... indtech.edu **1050/1575/22**
Bus Admin

IONA COLLEGE (NY) .... iona.edu **1010/1515/21**
Bus Admin

IOWA, UNIVERSITY OF .... uiowa.edu **1160/1740/25**
Amer St, Anthro, Art, Astro, Biochem, Bus Admin, Communic, Comp Sci, Drama, Ed, Engine, English, For Lang, Music, Nurs, Pharm, Physics, Poli Sci, Pre-Law, Pre-Med/Pre-Dental, Psych, Reli Stu

IOWA STATE UNIVERSITY (IA) .... iastate.edu **1160/1740/25**
Ag, Arch, Art, Bio, Bus Admin, Chem, Comp Sci, Econ, Ed, Engine, English, Forest, Home Ec, Philo, Physics, Pre-Med/Pre-Dental, Soc, Zoo

ITHACA COLLEGE (NY) .... ithaca.edu **1183/1770/26**
Biochem, Bus Admin, Chem, Communic, Music, Pre-Med/Pre-Dental

JACKSONVILLE STATE (AL) .... jsu.edu **1000/1500/21**
Comp Sci, Ed, Nurs

JACKSONVILLE UNIVERSITY (FL) .... ju.edu **1070/1600/23**
Art, Bio, Bus Admin, Communic, Drama, Music, Nurs, Physics, Pre-Med/Pre-Dental

JAMES MADISON UNIVERSITY (VA) .... jmu.edu **1170/1755/26**
Art, Bus Admin, Ed, Communic, Comp Sci, Drama, For Lang, Music, Poli Sci, Pre-law, Pre-Med/Pre-Dental, Psych, Soc

JAMESTOWN COLLEGE (ND) .... jc.edu **1050/1575/22**
Comp Sci, Ed, English, Nurs

JOHN BROWN UNIVERSITY (AR) .... jbu.edu **1100/1650/24**
Music, Reli Stu

JOHN CARROLL UNIVERSITY (OH) .... jcu.edu **1140/1700/25**
Bus Admin, Communic, English, Philo, Poli Sci, Psych, Reli Stu

JOHNS HOPKINS UNIVERSITY (MD) .... jhu.edu **1400/2100/31**
Amer St, Anthro, Art Hist, Bio, Chem, Classics, Comp Sci, Engine, Geog, Hist, Music, Nurs, Philo, Physics, Poli Sci, Pre-Law, Pre-Med/Pre-Dental, Psych, Soc

JOHNSON C. SMITH (NC) .... jcsu.edu **1000/1500/21**
Communic, Soc

JOHNSON STATE COLLEGE (VT) .... jsc.vsc.edu **1000/1500/21**
Drama, Ed, English, Music

JUDSON COLLEGE (AL) .... judson.edu **1030/1540/22**
Art, Bus Admin, Communic, Ed, English, Music, Psych

JUILLIARD SCHOOL(NY) ....juilliard.edu **1120/1680/24**
Drama, Music

JUNIATA COLLEGE (PA) .... juniata.edu **1170/1755/26**
Art, Bio, Bus Admin, Chem, Communic, Ed, English, Geol, Hist, Pre-Law, Pre-Med/Pre-Dental

KALAMAZOO COLLEGE (MI) .... kzoo.edu **1300/1950/28**
Amer St, Bio, Chem, Classics, Econ, English, For Lang, Hist, Physics, Pre-Law, Pre-Med/Pre-Dental, Soc

KANSAS CITY ART INSTITUTE (MO) .... kcai.edu **1050/1575/22**
Art

KANSAS, UNIVERSITY OF (KS) .... ukans.edu **1100/1650/24**
Anthro, Arch, Art, Art Hist, Astro, Bio, Chem, Communic, Drama, Econ, Engine, For Lang, Geog, Hist, Pharm, Poli Sci, Pre-Med/Pre-Dental, Psych, Zoo

KANSAS STATE UNIVERSITY (KS) .... ksu.edu **1100/1650/24**
Ag, Arch, Art, Bio, Biochem, Bus Admin, Communic, Comp Sci, Drama, Ed, Engine, English, For Lang, Geog, Hist, Home Ec, Math, Music, Philo, Physics, Pre-Law, Pre-Med/Pre-Dental

KANSAS WESLEYAN UNIVERSITY (KS) .... kwu.edu **1050/1575/22**
Comp Sci, Ed, Nurs

KEAN UNIVERSITY (NJ) .... kean.edu **1010/1510/21**
Ed, Psych, Soc

KEENE STATE COLLEGE (NH) .... keene.edu **1000/1500/21**
Art, Communic, Drama, Ed, English, Geog, Music, Psych

KENNESAW STATE UNIVERSITY (GA) .... kennesaw.edu **1090/1635/24**
Bus Admin, Chem, English, Hist, Nurs

KENT STATE UNIVERSITY (OH) .... kent.edu **1030/1545/22**
Arch, Art, Communic, Comp Sci, Ed, Music, Nurs, Physics

KENTUCKY, UNIVERSITY OF (KY) .... uky.edu **1130/1700/25**
Ag, Arch, Bio, Bus Admin, Classics, Communic, Ed, Engine, English, Hist, Music, Pharm, Pre-Med/Pre-Dental, Psych, Zoo

KENTUCKY WESLEYAN COLLEGE (KY) .... kwc.edu **1030/1540/22**
Bio, Bus Admin, Chem, Communic, Ed, English, Hist, Pre-Med/Pre-Dental, Psych, Reli Stu

KENYON COLLEGE (OH) .... kenyon.edu **1320/1980/30**
Anthro, Art, Bio, Chem, Classics, Drama, Econ, English, Hist, Math, Music, Philo, Physics, Poli Sci, Pre-Law, Pre-Med/Pre-Dental, Psych, Reli Stu

KETTERING UNIVERSITY (MI) .... kettering.edu **1220/1830/27**
Engine

KING COLLEGE (TN) .... king.edu **1100/1650/24**
Ed, English, Nurs, Reli Stu

KING'S COLLEGE (PA) .... kings.edu **1040/1560/22**
Bio, Bus Admin, Chem

KNOX COLLEGE (IL) .... knox.edu **1250/1875/28**
Anthro, Art, Bio, Biochem, Chem, Drama, English, Hist, Math, Music, Physics, Poli Sci, Pre-Law, Pre-Med/Pre-Dental, Soc

KUTZTOWN UNIVERSITY (PA) .... kutztown.edu **1000/1500/21**
Art, Ed, Hist, Poli Sci

LAFAYETTE COLLEGE (PA) .... lafayette.edu **1300/1950/29**
Anthro, Art, Bio, Bus Admin, Chem, Comp Sci, Econ, Engine, English, Geol, Hist,
Pre-Law, Pre-Med/Pre-Dental, Psych

LAKE FOREST COLLEGE (IL) .... lfc.edu **1150/1725/25**
Art, Art Hist, Bio, Chem, Econ, Ed, English, For Lang, Hist, Music, Poli Sci,
Pre-Law, Pre-Med/Pre-Dental, Psych, Soc

LAMAR UNIVERSITY (TX) .... lamar.edu **1000/1500/21**
Ed, Engine, Geol, Soc

LAMBUTH UNIVERSITY (TN) .... lambuth.edu **1035/1550/22**
Art, Bio, Ed, Hist

LA SALLE UNIVERSITY (PA) .... lasalle.edu **1100/1650/24**
Bus Admin, Chem, Comp Sci, English, Math, Pre-Law, Reli Stu, Psych

LASELL COLLEGE (MA) .... lasell.edu **1000/1500/21**
Bus Admin, Ed

LA VERNE, UNIVERSITY OF (CA) .... ulv.edu **1010/1510/21**
Bus Admin, Ed

LAWRENCE UNIVERSITY (WI) .... lawrence.edu **1250/1875/28**
Art, Bio, Chem, Drama, English, For Lang, Hist, Music, Philo, Physics,
Pre-Law, Pre-Med/Pre-Dental, Reli Stu

LEBANON VALLEY COLLEGE OF PENNSYLVANIA (PA) . lvc.edu **1108/1660/24**
Art, Bus Admin, Math, Music, Nurs, Psych, Soc

LEHIGH UNIVERSITY (PA) .... lehigh.edu **1300/1950/29**
Arch, Biochem, Bio, Bus Admin, Chem, Comp Sci, Econ, Engine, English,
Geol, Hist, Math, Physics, Poli Sci, Psych

LEMOYNE COLLEGE (NY) .... lemoyne.edu **1100/1650/24**
Bio, Bus Admin, Communic, Drama, English, Psych

LENOIR-RHYNE COLLEGE (NC) .... lrc.edu **1020/1530/22**
Bus Admin, Soc

LESLEY UNIVERSITY (MA) .... lesley.edu **1045/1570/22**
Bus Admin, Ed

LETOURNEAU COLLEGE (TX) .... letu.edu **1150/1725/25**
Bus Admin, Ed, Engine

LEWIS & CLARK COLLEGE (OR) .... lclark.edu **1240/1860/28**
Bio, Biochem, Bus Admin, Communic, Drama, English, For Lang, Physics,
Pre-Med/Pre-Dental, Soc

LEWIS-CLARK STATE COLLEGE (ID) .... lcsc.edu **1000/1500/21**
Art, Bio, Chem, Communic, Ed, English, Math, Nurs

LIBERTY UNIVERSITY (VA) .... liberty.edu **1030/1550/22**
Communic, Comp Sci, Ed, Hist, Nurs, Psych, Reli Stu

LINDENWOOD UNIVERSITY (MO) .... lindenwood.edu **1080/1620/23**
Art, Bus Admin, Drama, Ed, Psych

LINFIELD COLLEGE (OR) .... linfield.edu **1100/1650/24**
Bio, Bus Admin, Chem, Econ, Ed, For Lang, Hist, Physics

LIPSCOMB UNIVERSITY (TN) .... lipscomb.edu **1125/1690/25**
Bio, Bus Admin, Chem, Ed, Engine, English, Nurs, Poli Sci, Pre-Med/Pre-Dental, Reli Stu

LOCK HAVEN UNIVERSITY (PA) .... lhup.edu **1000/1500/21**
Art, Bio, Chem, Ed, Hist, Music, Poli Sci

LONG ISLAND UNIVERSITY (BROOKLYN) (NY) .... liu.edu **1000/1500/21**
Chem, English, Nurs

LONG ISLAND UNIVERSITY (C.W.POST) (NY) .... liu.edu **1050/1575/22**
Art, Bio, Bus Admin, Chem, Drama, Ed, English, Psych

LONGWOOD UNIVERSITY (VA) .... lwc.edu **1080/1620/23**
Bus Admin, Drama, Ed, English, Music, Pre-Law, Psych

LORAS COLLEGE (IA) .... loras.edu **1085/1625/23**
Art, Bio, Bus Admin, Chem, Communic, Econ, Ed, English, Hist, Philo, Physics, Pre-Law, Psych, Reli Stu

LOUISIANA COLLEGE (LA) .... lacollege.edu **1050/1575/22**
Ed, English, Music, Nurs, Reli Stu

LOUISIANA-LAFAYETTE, UNIVERSITY OF (LA) . louisiana.edu **1040/1560/22**
Art, Bio, Bus Admin, Chem, Comp Sci, Ed, Engine, English, Geol, Math, Music, Nurs, Physics, Pre-Med/Pre-Dental, Zoo

LOUISIANA STATE UNIVERSITY (LA) .... lsu.edu **1095/1640/24**
Ag, Anthro, Arch, Art, Astro, Biochem, Bot, Chem, Communic, Econ, Engine, English, Geog, Geol, Hist, Math, Music, Philo, Physics, Poli Sci, Pre-Law, Pre-Med/Pre-Dental, Psych, Reli Stu, Zoo

LOUISVILLE, UNIVERSITY OF (KY) .... louisville.edu **1020/1530/22**
Bus Admin, Chem, Engine, Music, Poli Sci, Soc

LOWELL, UNIVERSITY OF MASSACHUSETTS AT (MA) .....uml.edu **1085/1625/23**
Art Hist, Bus Admin, Comp Sci, Engine, Math, Music, Physics

LOYOLA COLLEGE (MD) .... loyola.edu **1200/1800/26**
Bio, Bus Admin, Communic, Engine, Pre-Law, Pre-Med/Pre-Dental

LOYOLA MARYMOUNT UNIVERSITY (CA) .... lmu.edu **1145/1720/25**
Art, Bus Admin, Communic, Engine

LOYOLA UNIVERSITY OF CHICAGO (IL) .... luc.edu **1150/1725/25**
Bio, Communic, Drama, Hist, Music, Nurs, Philo, Physics, Pre-Med/Pre-Dental, Psych

LOYOLA UNIVERSITY OF NEW ORLEANS (LA) .... loyno.edu **1230/1840/27**
Bio, Bus Admin, Chem, Comp Sci, Communic, Econ, English, Hist, Music, Philo, Pre-Law, Pre-Med/Pre-Dental, Reli Stu

LUTHER COLLEGE (IA) .... luther.edu **1170/1750/25**
Anthro, Bio, Bus Admin, Ed, English, Hist, Music, Nurs, Psych, Reli Stu

LYCOMING COLLEGE (PA) .... lycoming.edu **1140/1710/25**
Art, Astro, Bio, Chem, English, Philo, Pre-Med/Pre-Dental, Psych, Reli Stu

LYNCHBURG COLLEGE (VA) .... lynchburg.edu   **1030/1545/22**
Bio, Communic, Math, Pre-Law, Pre-Med/Pre-Dental, Soc

LYNDON STATE COLLEGE (VT) .... lsc.vsc.edu   **1000/1500/21**
Bio, Communic, English, Psych

LYON COLLEGE (AR) .... lyon.edu   **1150/1725/25**
Drama, Ed, English, For Lang, Math, Psych

MACALESTER COLLEGE (MN) .... macalester.edu   **1340/2000/30**
*Anthro, Art, Bio, Chem, Classics, Communic, Drama, Econ, English, For Lang,
Geog, Hist, Philo, Physics, Poli Sci, Pre-Law, Pre-Med/Pre-Dental, Psych, Reli Stu*

MacMURRAY COLLEGE (IL) .... mac.edu   **1000/1500/21**
Nurs

MAINE, UNIVERSITY OF (ME) .... umaine.edu   **1090/1630/24**
*Ag, Biochem, Bot, Bus Admin, Chem, Communic, Comp Sci, Drama, Econ,
Engine, Forest, Music, Nurs, Philo, Psych*

MAINE, UNIVERSITY OF (FARMINGTON) (ME) . umf.maine.edu   **1070/1605/23**
Bus Admin, Ed, Geog, Psych

MALONE COLLEGE (OH) .... malone.edu   **1080/1620/23**
Bus Admin, Math, Nurs

MANCHESTER COLLEGE (IN) .... manchester.edu   **1000/1500/21**
Bus Admin, Ed, Psych, Soc

MANHATTAN COLLEGE (NY) .... manhattan.edu   **1130/1700/25**
Bus Admin, Ed, Engine, Poli Sci, Pre-Law

MANHATTAN SCHOOL OF MUSIC (NY) .... msmnyc.edu   **1100/1650/24**
Music

MANHATTANVILLE COLLEGE (NY) .... manhattanville.edu   **1080/1620/23**
Art, Art Hist, Bus Admin, Drama, Econ, Ed, English, Hist, Music, Poli Sci, Psych, Soc

MANNES SCHOOL OF MUSIC (NEW SCHOOL U.) (NY) mannes.edu   **1100/1650/24**
Music

MANSFIELD UNIVERSITY OF PENNSYLVANIA (PA) mnsfld.edu   **1000/1500/21**
Chem, Communic, Ed, English, For Lang, Geog, Philo, Physics

MARIETTA COLLEGE (OH) .... marietta.edu   **1085/1625/23**
Art, Bus Admin, Engine, English, Physics, Pre-Law

MARIST COLLEGE (NY) .... marist.edu   **1160/1740/25**
Bio, Bus Admin, Comp Sci, Communic, Poli Sci, Psych

MARQUETTE UNIVERSITY (WI) .... marquette.edu   **1160/1740/25**
*Bio, Bus Admin, Chem, Communic, Comp Sci, English, Engine, Hist,
Nurs, Philo, Poli Sci, Pre-Law, Pre-Med/Pre-Dental, Psych, Reli Stu*

MARSHALL UNIVERSITY (WV) .... marshall.edu   **1040/1560/22**
Bus Admin, Chem, Communic, Econ, Ed, Nurs, Psych

MARY BALDWIN COLLEGE (VA) .... mbc.edu **1060/1590/23**
Art, Bus Admin, Chem, Communic, Drama, Hist, Physics, Poli Sci, Psych, Soc

MARYGROVE COLLEGE (MI) .... marygrove.edu **1000/1500/21**
Comp Sci

MARYLAND INSTITUTE-COLLEGE OF ART (MD) ...... mica.edu **1140/1710/25**
Art

MARYLAND, UNIVERSITY OF (MD) .... maryland.edu **1230/1840/27**
*Ag, Anthro, Arch, Astro, Bot, Bus Admin, Communic, Comp Sci, Econ, Ed, Engine,
Hist, Music, Pharm, Philo, Physics, Poli Sci, Pre-Law, Zoo*

MARYLAND, UNIVERSITY OF (BALTIMORE COUNTY) (MD) umbc.edu **1230/1840/27**
Amer St, Art, Chem, Classics, Comp Sci, Drama, Econ, Nurs, Physics, Poli Sci, Pre-Law

MARYMOUNT MANHATTAN COLLEGE (NY) .... mmm.edu **1030/1550/22**
Art, Communic, Drama

MARYMOUNT UNIVERSITY (VA) .... marymount.edu **1000/1500/21**
Nurs, Psych

MARYVILLE COLLEGE (TN) .... maryvillecollege.edu **1080/1620/23**
Bio, Chem, Music, Psych

MARYVILLE UNIVERSITY-ST. LOUIS (MO) .... maryville.edu **1110/1650/24**
Art, Ed, Nurs

MARY WASHINGTON, UNIVERSITY OF (VA) ....umw.edu **1210/1815/27**
Amer St, Bio, Bus Admin, Chem, Comp Sci, Econ, English, Geog, Hist, Pre-Med/Pre-Dental, Psych

MARYWOOD UNIVERSITY (PA) .... marywood.edu **1030/1540/22**
Art, Ed, Home Ec, Music Reli Stu

MASSACHUSETTS, UNIVERSITY OF (MA) .... umass.edu **1160/1740/25**
*Astro, Bus Admin, Chem, Communic, Comp Sci, Econ, Engine, English,
Hist, Nurs, Poli Sci, Pre-Law, Pre-Med/Pre-Dental, Psych, Zoo*

MASSACHUSETTS, UNIVERSITY OF (BOSTON) (MA). umb.edu **1060/1600/23**
*Amer St, Bus Admin, Classics, English, Geog, Hist, Music, Nurs, Philo, Physics,
Poli Sci, Pre-Law, Psych, Soc*

MASSACHUSETTS, UNIV. OF (DARTMOUTH) (MA) .... umassd.edu **1070/1605/23**
Art, Chem, Engine, Nurs, Psych, Soc

MASSACHUSETTS COLLEGE OF ART (MA) .... massart.edu **1080/1620/23**
Art

MASSACHUSETTS COLL. OF LIBERAL ARTS (NO. ADAMS)(MA) mcla.mass.edu **1060/1600/23**
Bus Admin, Communic, Ed, English, Philo, Physics, Soc

MASSACHUSETTS COLLEGE OF PHARMACY (MA) .... mcp.edu **1040/1560/22**
Pharm

MASSACHUSETTS INSTITUTE OF TECHNOLOGY (MA) ... mit.edu **1480/2215/33**
*Arch, Astro, Biochem, Bio, Bus Admin, Chem, Comp Sci, Econ, Engine,
Geol, Math, Physics, Poli Sci, Pre-Law, Pre-Med/Pre-Dental*

MASSACHUSETTS MARITIME ACADEMY (MA) .... mma.edu **1040/1560/22**
Engine

MASSACHUSETTS STATE COLLEGE SYSTEM (MA) **1020/1530/22**
Ed

MASTER'S COLLEGE, THE (CA) .... masters.edu **1010/1520/21**
Bus Admin, Communic, English, Reli Stu

McDANIEL COLLEGE (MD) .... mdc.edu **1130/1700/25**
Bio, Bio Chem, Bus Admin, Drama, Ed, Music, Pre-Med/Pre-Dental, Soc

McKENDREE COLLEGE (IL) .... mckendree.edu **1120/1680/24**
Bio, Chem, Comp Sci, Hist, Nurs

McMURRY UNIVERSITY (TX) .... mcm.edu **1000/1500/21**
Bus Admin, Nurs

McPHERSON COLLEGE (KS) .... mcpherson.edu **1000/1500/21**
Art, Drama, Ed

MEMPHIS COLLEGE OF ART (TN) ....mca.edu **1000/1500/21**
Art

MEMPHIS, UNIVERSITY OF (TN) .... memphis.edu **1060/1590/23**
Art, Communic, Ed, Engine, English, Music, Nurs

MERCER UNIVERSITY (GA) .... mercer.edu **1160/1740/25**
Bus Admin, Econ, Ed, Engine, English, Music, Pharm, Psych

MEREDITH COLLEGE (NC) .... meredith.edu **1050/1575/22**
Bio, Bus Admin, English, Music, Psych

MERCY COLLEGE (NY) .... mercynet.edu **1000/1500/21**
Nurs, Psych

MERCYHURST COLLEGE (PA) .... mercyhurst.edu **1080/1620/23**
Anthro, Art, Bus Admin, English, Poli Sci, Pre-Law, Reli Stu

MERRIMACK COLLEGE (MA) ....merrimack.edu **1080/1620/23**
Bus Admin, English, Psych, Soc

MESSIAH COLLEGE (PA) .... messiah.edu **1175/1760/26**
Art, Bus Admin, Ed, Engine, English, Philo

MIAMI UNIVERSITY (OH) .... muohio.edu **1210/1810/27**
Arch, Bot, Bus Admin, Econ, Ed, English, Hist, Music, Poli Sci, Pre-Law, Pre-Med/Pre-Dental, Psych, Zoo

MIAMI, UNIVERSITY OF (FL) .... miami.edu **1210/1810/27**
Arch, Bio, Biochem, Communic, Drama, Ed, Hist, Music, Pre-Med/Pre-Dental

MICHIGAN, UNIVERSITY OF (MI) .... umich.edu **1290/1932/29**
Amer St, Anthro, Arch, Art, Art Hist, Astro, Bot, Bus Admin, Chem, Classics, Communic, Comp Sci, Econ, Ed, Engine, English, Forest, For Lang, Geog, Hist, Math, Music, Nurs, Pharm, Philo, Physics, Poli Sci, Pre-Law, Pre-Med/Pre-Dental, Psych, Soc, Zoo

MICHIGAN, UNIVERSITY OF (DEARBORN) (MI) .... umd.umich.edu **1090/1635/24**
Bus Admin, Chem, Comp Sci, Econ, Engine, Math, Physics, Pre-Law, Pre-Med/Pre-Dental

MICHIGAN STATE UNIVERSITY (MI) .... msu.edu **1120/1680/24**
Ag, Biochem, Bio, Bot, Bus Admin, Chem, Communic, Econ, Ed, Engine, English, Forest, Geog, Hist, Home Ec, Math, Music, Poli Sci, Pre-Law, Pre-Med/Pre-Dental, Psych, Soc

MICHIGAN TECHNOLOGICAL UNIVERSITY (MI) .... mtu.edu **1190/1775/26**
Bus Admin, Engine, Forest, Geol

MIDDLEBURY COLLEGE (VT) .... middlebury.edu **1400/2100/31**
Art, Bio, Classics, Drama, Econ, English, For Lang, Geog, Hist, Physics, Poli Sci, Pre-Law, Pre-Med/Pre-Dental

MIDDLE TENNESSEE STATE UNIVERSITY (TN) .... mtsu.edu **1050/1575/22**
Bus Admin, Ed, English, Hist, Psych

MIDWESTERN STATE UNIVERSITY (TX) .... mwsu.edu **1000/1500/21**
Nurs

MILLERSVILLE UNIV. OF PENNSYLVANIA (PA) ..... millersville.edu **1060/1590/23**
Art, Bio, Bus Admin, Chem, Comp Sci, Econ, Ed, English, Hist, Poli Sci, Physics, Pre-Law, Psych

MILLIGAN COLLEGE (TN) .... milligan.edu **1070/1600/23**
Bio, Bus Admin, Chem, Communic, Ed, Hist, Nurs, Philo, Psych, Reli Stu

MILLIKIN UNIVERSITY (IL) .... millikin.edu **1080/1620/23**
Art, Drama, Ed, Music

MILLS COLLEGE (CA) .... mills.edu **1150/1725/25**
Art, Communic, Ed, For Lang, Music, Psych

MILLSAPS COLLEGE (MS) .... millsaps.edu **1185/1775/26**
Bio, Bus Admin, Chem, Classics, Comp Sci, Drama, English, Geol, Hist, Math, Music, Pre-Law, Pre-Med/Pre-Dental

MILWAUKEE SCHOOL OF ENGINEERING (WI) .... msoe.edu **1185/1770/26**
Arch, Engine, Nurs

MINNESOTA STATE UNIVERSITY (MANKATO) (MN) ... mnsu.edu **1010/1520/21**
Astro, Comp Sci, Drama, Engine

MINNESOTA STATE UNIVERSITY (MOORHEAD) (MN) mnstate.edu **1040/1560/22**
Art, Bio, Ed, Music, Physics, Psych

MINNESOTA, UNIVERSITY OF (MN) .... umn.edu **1180/1770/26**
Ag, Amer St, Art Hist, Biochem, Bus Admin, Communic, Drama, Econ, Ed, Engine, For Lang, Forest, Geog, Geol, Hist, Music, Nurs, Pharm, Philo, Poli Sci, Pre-Law, Psych, Soc

MINNESOTA, UNIVERSITY OF (DULUTH) (MN) ...... d.umn.edu **1070/1600/23**
Art, Bio, Communic, Comp Sci, Ed, Engine, Geol, Music, Psych, Soc

MINNESOTA, UNIVERSITY OF (MORRIS) (MN) .... mrs.umn.edu **1140/1710/25**
Bio, Chem, Comp Sci, Ed, English, For Lang, Geol, Hist, Philo, Poli Sci, Pre-Law, Pre Med/Pre-Dental, Psych

COLLEGE MISERICORDIA (PA) .... miseri.edu **1010/1515/21**
Biochem, Bio, Bus Admin, Chem, Communic, Ed, English, Hist, Nurs

MISSISSIPPI COLLEGE (MS) ....mc.edu **1095/1645/24**
Bus Admin, Ed, Music, Nurs, Reli Stu

MISSISSIPPI STATE UNIVERSITY (MS) .... msstate.edu **1090/1635/24**
Ag, Arch, Biochem, Bus Admin, Comp Sci, Ed, Engine, Forest, Pre-Med/Pre-Dental, Soc

MISSISSIPPI, UNIVERSITY OF (MS) .... olemiss.edu **1090/1635/24**
Bus Admin, Communic, Ed, Engine, English, Pharm, Physics, Pre-Law

MISSISSIPPI UNIVERSITY FOR WOMEN (MS) .... muw.edu **1115/1670/24**
Bus Admin, Ed, English, Nurs

MISSOURI BAPTIST COLLEGE (MO) .... mobap.edu **1000/1500/21**
Ed

MISSOURI SOUTHERN STATE UNIVERSITY (MO) ..... mssc.edu **1000/1500/21**
Bio, Bus Admin, Communic, Ed

MISSOURI, UNIVERSITY OF (MO) .... missouri.edu **1165/1750/25**
Ag, Art Hist, Biochem, Bus Admin, Communic, Engine, English, Forest, Hist, Nurs, Psych

MISSOURI, UNIVERSITY OF (KANSAS CITY) (MO) ... umkc.edu **1100/1650/24**
Art, Art Hist, Bus Admin, Chem, Communic, Comp Sci, Econ, English, Hist, Music, Pharm, Psych

MISSOURI, UNIVERSITY OF (ROLLA) (MO) .... umr.edu **1230/1840/27**
Bio, Chem, Comp Sci, Engine, Hist

MISSOURI, UNIVERSITY OF (ST. LOUIS) .... umsl.edu **1080/1620/23**
Bus Admin, Communic, Ed, Nurs, Philo, Poli Sci, Psych

MOBILE, UNIVERSITY OF (AL) .... umobile.edu **1050/1575/24**
Bio, Bus Admin, Comp Sci, Ed, Music, Nurs

MOLLOY COLLEGE (NY) .... molloy.edu **1010/1515/21**
Nurs, Psych

MONMOUTH COLLEGE (IL) .... monm.edu **1070/1610/23**
Bio, Bus Admin, Chem, Econ, Ed, Pre-Med/Pre-Dental

MONMOUTH UNIVERSITY (NJ) .... monmouth.edu **1040/1560/22**
Art, Bus Admin, Communic, Comp Sci, Music

MONTANA TECH OF THE UNIV. OF MONTANA (MT) ... mtech.edu **1100/1650/24**
Comp Sci, Engine, Math, Nurs

MONTANA, UNIVERSITY OF (MT) ....umt.edu **1080/1620/23**
Astro, Bot, Bus Admin, Classics, Communic, Comp Sci, Drama, Ed, English, Forest, Music, Pharm, Soc, Zoo

MONTANA STATE UNIVERSITY (BILLINGS) (MT) . msubillings.edu **1000/1500/21**
Art, Ed, Math

MONTANA STATE UNIVERSITY (MT) .... montana.edu **1090/1630/24**
Ag, Arch, Art, Comp Sci, Econ, Engine, For Lang, Forest, Nurs, Physics

MONTCLAIR STATE (NJ) .... montclair.edu **1100/1650/24**
Art, Bus Admin, Classics, Ed, English, Home Ec, Psych

MONTEVALLO, UNIVERSITY OF (AL) .... montevallo.edu **1020/1530/22**
Art, Communic, Ed, English, Home Ec, Music

MONTSERRAT COLLEGE OF ART (MA) .... montserrat.edu **1000/1500/21**
Art

MONTREAT COLLEGE (NC) .... montreat.edu **1050/1570/22**
Bus Admin

MOORE COLLEGE OF ART (PA) .... moore.edu **1050/1570/22**
Art

MORAVIAN COLLEGE (PA) .... moravian.edu **1125/1685/25**
*Art, Biochem, Bus Admin, Communic, Comp Sci, Ed, Music, Nurs,
Pre-Med/Pre-Dental, Psych, Soc*

MOREHOUSE COLLEGE (GA) ....morehouse.edu **1080/1620/23**
Bus Admin, Comp Sci, Hist, Reli Stu, Soc

MORGAN STATE UNIVERSITY (MD) .... morgan.edu **1000/1500/21**
Arch, Bio, Engine

MORNINGSIDE COLLEGE (IA) .... morningside.edu **1050/1575/22**
Art, Bio, Communic, Ed, Music, Nurs, Pre-Med/Pre-Dental, Psych

MOUNT HOLYOKE COLLEGE (MA) .... mtholyoke.edu **1290/1950/29**
*Art Hist, Astro, Biochem, Bio, Chem, Drama, Econ, English, For Lang, Geol, Hist,
Math, Poli Sci, Pre-Law, Pre-Med/Pre-Dental, Psych*

MOUNT MERCY COLLEGE (IA) .... mtmercy.edu **1095/1645/24**
Bio, Bus Admin, Ed, English, Nurs, Philo, Soc

MOUNT ST. JOSEPH, COLLEGE OF (OH) ....msj.edu **1020/1530/22**
*Art, Bio, Bus Admin, Chem, Comp Sci, Ed, English, Math, Music, Nurs,
Pre-Law, Pre-Med/Pre-Dental, Soc*

MOUNT ST. MARY'S COLLEGE (CA) .... msmc.la.edu **1060/1590/23**
Bio, Bus Admin, Music, Nurs

MOUNT ST. MARY'S COLLEGE (MD) .... msmary.edu **1080/1620/23**
Bus Admin, Ed, Poli Sci, Pre-Law, Pre-Med/Pre-Dental

MOUNT ST. MARY COLLEGE (NY) .... msmc.edu **1020/1530/22**
Nurs

MOUNT UNION COLLEGE (OH) .... muc.edu **1050/1575/22**
Bus Admin, Comp Sci, Ed

MUHLENBERG COLLEGE (PA) .... muhlenberg.edu **1225/1840/26**
*Art, Bio, Biochem, Bus Admin, Communic, Drama, English, Hist, Math, Philo, Pre-Law,
Pre-Med/Pre-Dental, Psych, Reli Stu*

MURRAY STATE UNIVERSITY (KY) .... murraystate.edu **1070/1600/23**
Ag, Art, Bio, Chem, Communic, Comp Sci, Ed, English, Hist, Math, Music, Nurs

MUSEUM OF FINE ARTS, SCHOOL OF THE (MA) ..... smfa.edu **1070/1600/23**
Art

MUSKINGUM COLLEGE (OH) .... muskingum.edu **1070/1610/23**
Bus Admin, Chem, Communic, Comp Sci, Ed, Geol, Hist, Music, Physics, Psych, Reli Stu

NAZARETH COLLEGE OF ROCHESTER (NY) .... naz.edu **1135/1700/25**
Bio, Bus Admin, Ed, English, For Lang

NEBRASKA, UNIVERSITY OF (NE) .... unl.edu **1130/1700/25**
*Ag, Arch, Astro, Bus Admin, Communic, Econ, Ed, Engine, For Lang, Home Ec,
Music, Physics, Pre-Law*

NEBRASKA, UNIVERSITY OF (KEARNEY) (NE) .... unk.edu **1040/1560/22**
Bus Admin, Econ

NEBRASKA, UNIVERSITY OF (OMAHA) (NE) ...... unomaha.edu **1050/1575/22**
Bus Admin, Comp Sci, Ed

NEBRASKA WESLEYAN UNIVERSITY (NE) .... nebrwesleyan.edu **1110/1660/24**
Bio, Chem, Pre-Med/Pre-Dental, Psych

NEVADA, UNIVERSITY OF, AT:
      LAS VEGAS .... unlv.edu **1020/1530/22**
      *Anthro, Arch, Art, Bus Admin, Drama, Ed, Engine, English, Hist,
      Music, Nurs, Psych*
      RENO .... unr.edu **1040/1560/22**
      *Ag, Biochem, Bus Admin, Communic, Comp Sci, Ed, Engine,
      English, Geol, Music, Nurs, Physics, Pre-Med/Pre-Dental, Soc*

NEW COLLEGE OF FLORIDA (FL) .... ncf.edu **1320/1990/30**
*Anthro, Bio, Chem, English, Math, Philo, Physics, Pre-Law,
Pre-Med/Pre-Dental, Psych, Soc*

NEW ENGLAND CONSERVATORY (MA) newenglandconservatory.edu **1100/1650/24**
Music

NEW HAMPSHIRE, UNIVERSITY OF (NH) .... unh.edu **1115/1675/24**
*Ag, Bio, Bus Admin, Chem, Communic, Drama, Ed, Engine, English,
Hist, Music, Philo, Physics, Pre-Med/Pre-Dental, Pre-Law, Psych*

NEW JERSEY, COLLEGE OF (NJ) .... tcnj.edu **1250/1875/28**
Art, Ed, Engine, English, Math, Nurs, Pre-Law, Pre-Med/Pre-Dental, Psych

NEW JERSEY INSTITUTE OF TECHNOLOGY (NJ) .... njit.edu **1150/1725/25**
Arch, Comp Sci, Engine

NEWMAN UNIVERSITY (KS) .... newmanu.edu **1030/1545/22**
Bus Admin, Math, Psych, Reli Stu

NEW MEXICO INST. OF MINING & TECHNOLOGY (NM) .. nmt.edu **1200/1800/26**
Chem, Comp Sci, Engine, Geol, Physics

NEW MEXICO STATE UNIVERSITY (NM) .... nmsu.edu **1030/1545/22**
Ag, Anthro, Bio, Bus Admin, Chem, Comp Sci, Ed, Engine, English, Hist, Math

NEW MEXICO, UNIVERSITY OF (NM) .... unm.edu **1080/1620/23**
*Amer St, Anthro, Art, Bio, Bus Admin, Drama, Econ, Ed, Engine,
For Lang, Geol, Hist, Nurs, Pharm, Psych, Soc*

NEW ORLEANS, UNIVERSITY OF (LA) .... uno.edu **1050/1575/22**
Bus Admin, Ed, English, Engine, Geog, Hist, Physics, Soc

NEW SCHOOL UNIV. (EUGENE LANG COLL.) (NY) ..newschool.edu **1200/1800/26**
Drama, Ed, English

NEW YORK, CITY UNIVERSITY OF, AT
    BARUCH COLLEGE .... baruch.cuny.edu **1080/1620/23**
Bus Admin, Comp Sci, Econ
    BROOKLYN COLLEGE .... brooklyn.cuny.edu **1020/1530/22**
Bio, Chem, Comp Sci, Drama, Ed, Geol, Philo, Physics, Pre-Med/Pre-Dental
    CITY COLLEGE .... ccny.cuny.edu **1030/1545/22**
Anthro, Arch, Art Hist, Chem, Ed, Econ, Engine, English, Hist, Philo,
Physics, Poli Sci, Pre-Law, Pre-Med/Pre-Dental, Soc
    HERBERT LEHMAN COLLEGE .... lehmman.cuny.edu **1000/1500/21**
Ed, For Lang, Philo, Psych
    HUNTER COLLEGE .... hunter.cuny.edu **1050/1575/22**
Anthro, Art, Art Hist, Bio, Chem, Classics, Communic, Comp Sci, Drama, Ed,
English, Geog, Nurs, Pre-Law, Psych
    JOHN JAY COLL. OF CRIMINAL JUSTICE . jjay.cuny.edu **1000/1500/21**
Poli Sci, Psych
    QUEENS COLLEGE .... qc.edu **1040/1560/22**
Anthro, Art Hist, Comp Sci, Econ, Ed, English, Music, Philo, Psych, Soc

NEW YORK INSTITUTE OF TECHNOLOGY (NY) .... nyit.edu **1100/1650/24**
Arch, Engine

NEW YORK, STATE UNIVERSITY OF, AT
    ALBANY .... albany.edu **1170/1755/26**
Anthro, Art, Art Hist, Bio, Bus Admin, Chem, Comp Sci, Econ, For Lang, Geol,
Math, Philo, Physics, Poli Sci, Pre-Law, Pre-Med/Pre-Dental, Psych, Soc
    BINGHAMTON .... binghamton.edu **1235/1850/27**
Anthro, Art, Art Hist, Bio, Biochem, Bus Admin, Chem, Comp Sci,
Drama, English, Engine, For Lang, Geol, Hist, Math, Music, Nurs,
Philo, Physics, Poli Sci, Pre-Law, Pre-Med/Pre-Dental, Psych, Soc
    BROCKPORT, COLLEGE AT .... brockport.edu **1050/1575/22**
Bus Admin, Communic, Comp Sci, Drama, Geol, Hist, Nurs, Poli Sci, Psych
    BUFFALO .... buffalo.edu **1170/1755/26**
Amer St, Anthro, Arch, Art, Bus Admin, Chem, Classics, Ed, Engine, English,
Geog, Hist, Math, Music, Nurs, Pharm, Pre-Law, Pre-Med/Pre-Dental, Psych
    FREDONIA, COLLEGE AT .... fredonia.edu **1120/1680/24**
Amer St, Bus Admin, Communic, Ed, English, Hist, Music
    GENESEO, COLLEGE AT .... geneseo.edu **1262/1890/28**
Bio, Biochem, Bus Admin, Ed, Geol, Music, Philo, Physics, Pre-Med/Pre-Dental, Soc
    MARITIME COLLEGE .... sunymaritime.edu **1040/1560/22**
Engine
    NEW PALTZ, COLLEGE AT .... newpaltz.edu **1130/1700/25**
Bus Admin, Communic, Ed, Engine, English, For Lang, Geog, Philo, Psych
    ONEONTA, COLLEGE AT ....oneonta.edu **1080/1620/23**
Econ, Ed, English, Geog, Geol, Home Ec, Music, Philo, Pre-Law
    OSWEGO, COLLEGE AT .... oswego.edu **1090/1635/24**
Bio, Bus Admin, Communic, Comp Sci, Ed, English, Pre-Law, Psych, Zoo
    PLATTSBURGH, COLLEGE AT .... plattsburgh.edu **1060/1590/23**
Anthro, Bus Admin, Communic, Geol, Nurs
    POTSDAM, COLLEGE AT .... potsdam.edu **1060/1590/23**
Art, Bus Admin, Comp Sci, Ed, Math, Music, Psych

NEW YORK, STATE UNIVERSITY OF, AT (*Continued*)
      PURCHASE, COLLEGE AT .... purchase.edu   **1090/1635/24**
      Art, Communic, Drama, English, Music, Poli Sci, Pre-Law, Psych
      STONY BROOK .... sunysb.edu   **1170/1755/26**
      Anthro, Art Hist, Astro, Biochem, Bio, Chem, Comp Sci, Engine, English, For Lang, Geo, Hist, Music, Philo, Physics, Poli Sci, Pre-Law, Pre-Med/Pre-Dental, Psych, Reli Stu, Soc

NEW YORK UNIVERSITY (NY) ....nyu.edu   **1340/2000/30**
Art, Art Hist, Bus Admin, Classics, Communic, Drama, Econ, For Lang, Math, Music, Nurs, Philo, Physics, Pre-Med/Pre-Dental, Psych

NIAGARA UNIVERSITY (NY) .... niagara.edu   **1055/1580/23**
Bus Admin, Drama, English, Pre-Law

NICHOLS STATE UNIVERSITY (LA) .... nichols.edu   **1000/1500/21**
Bio, Chem, Ed, Nurs

NORTH CAROLINA SCHOOL OF THE ARTS (NC) ......ncarts.edu   **1130/1700/25**
Drama, Music

NORTH CAROLINA, UNIVERSITY OF, AT
      ASHEVILLE ....unca.edu   **1167/1750/26**
      Art, Classics, Ed, Hist, Psych, Soc
      CHAPEL HILL .... unc.edu   **1280/1920/28**
      Amer St, Anthro, Art Hist, Bio, Bot, Bus Admin, Chem, Classics, Communic, Drama, Ed, English, For Lang, Hist, Nurs, Pharm, Poli Sci, Pre-Law, Pre-Med/Pre-Dental, Reli Stu, Soc
      CHARLOTTE .... uncc.edu   **1100/1650/24**
      Bus Admin, Chem, Engine, For Lang, Geog, Nurs, Poli Sci, Pre-Law, Pre-Med/Pre-Dental, Psych, Reli Stu
      GREENSBORO .... uncg.edu   **1050/1575/22**
      Art, Bus Admin, Classics, Communic, Comp Sci, Drama, Ed, Music, Nurs, Psych
      PEMBROKE... uncp.edu   **1000/1500/21**
      Bio, Bus Admin, Communic
      WILMINGTON.. uncwil.edu   **1100/1650/24**
      Bio, Bus Admin, Chem, English, Pre-Law, Psych, Soc

NORTH CAROLINA STATE UNIVERSITY (NC) .... ncsu.edu   **1200/1800/26**
Ag, Arch, Astro, Bot, Chem, Econ, Engine, Forest, Math, Physics, Pre-Law, Zoo

NORTH CENTRAL COLLEGE (IL) .... noctrl.edu   **1120/1680/24**
Bio, Bus Admin, Chem, Communic, Comp Sci, Poli Sci, Pre-Law, Pre-Med/Pre-Dental, Zoo

NORTH DAKOTA STATE UNIVERSITY (ND)...... ndsu.nodak.edu   **1100/1650/24**
Ag, Arch, Ed, Engine, Pharm

NORTH DAKOTA, UNIVERSITY OF (ND) .... und.nodak.edu   **1070/1600/23**
Art, Bio, Bus Admin, Chem, Communic, Ed, Engine, English, Nurs

NORTH FLORIDA, UNIVERSITY OF (FL)........................ unf.edu   **1150/1725/25**
Bus Admin, Communic, Comp Sci, Ed, Math, Music, Nurs

NORTH GEORGIA COLLEGE (GA) .... ngcsu.edu   **1080/1620/23**
Bus Admin

NORTH TEXAS, UNIVERSITY OF (TX) .... unt.edu   **1085/1625/23**
Communic, Music, Soc

NORTHEASTERN ILLINOIS UNIVERSITY (IL) .... neiu.edu **1000/1500/21**
Comp Sci, Ed, English

NORTHEASTERN STATE UNIVERSITY (OK) .... nsuok.edu **1000/1500/21**
Ed, English, Math, Psych

NORTHEASTERN UNIVERSITY (MA) .... neu.edu **1220/1830/27**
Arch, Bus Admin, Comp Sci, Engine, English, Hist, Pharm, Philo, Psych

NORTHERN ARIZONA (AZ) .... nau.edu **1050/1575/22**
Astro, Bot, Bus Admin, Ed, Forest, Psych

NORTHERN COLORADO, UNIVERSITY OF .... unco.edu **1060/1590/23**
Bus Admin, Econ, Ed, Hist, Music, Nurs, Soc

NORTHERN ILLINOIS UNIVERSITY (IL) .... niu.edu **1050/1575/22**
Art, Bio, Biochem, Bus Admin, Chem, Communic, Ed, Engine, Home Ec, Geol, Nurs, Physics, Philo

NORTHERN IOWA, UNIVERSITY OF (IA) .... uni.edu **1080/1620/23**
Art, Bus Admin, Ed

NORTHERN KENTUCKY UNIVERSITY (KY) .... nku.edu **1000/1500/21**
Bus Admin, Communic, Ed, English

NORTHERN MICHIGAN UNIVERSITY (MI) .... nmu.edu **1090/1635/24**
Art, Bio, Chem, Comp Sci, Ed, English, Math, Nurs, Physics, Soc

NORTHLAND COLLEGE (WI) .... northland.edu **1100/1650/24**
Bio, Geol

NORTHWESTERN COLLEGE (IA) .... nwciowa.edu **1110/1660/24**
Bio, Chem, Drama, Ed, English, For Lang, Hist, Music, Physics, Reli Stu

NORTHWESTERN COLLEGE (MN) .... nwc.edu **1100/1660/24**
Bus Admin, Ed, Music, Psych, Reli Stu

NORTHWESTERN STATE UNIV. OF LOUISIANA (LA) .... nsula.edu **1000/1500/21**
Bus Admin, Comp Sci, Ed, Hist, Music, Nurs, Pharm

NORTHWESTERN UNIVERSITY (IL) .... northwestern.edu **1398/2095/31**
Amer Stu, Anthro, Astro, Chem, Classics, Communic, Drama, Econ, Engine, English, Hist, Math, Music, Poli Sci, Pre-Law, Pre-Med/Pre-Dental, Psych, Reli Stu, Soc

NORTHWOOD UNIVERSITY (MI) .... northwood.edu **1000/1500/21**
Bus Admin

NORWICH UNIVERSITY (VT) .... norwich.edu **1060/1590/23**
Arch

NOTRE DAME, UNIVERSITY OF (IN) .... nd.edu **1360/2040/31**
Anthro, Arch, Bus Admin, Chem, Engine, English, For Lang, Hist, Math, Poli Sci, Philo, Physics, Pre-Med/Pre-Dental, Pre-Law, Psych, Reli Stu, Soc

NOVA SOUTHEASTERN UNIVERSITY (FL) .... nova.edu **1050/1575/22**
Bus Admin, Pre-Med/Pre-Dental

NYACK COLLEGE (NY) .... nyackcollege.edu **1000/1500/21**
Bus Admin, Ed, Music, Psych, Reli Stu

OAKLAND CITY UNIVERSITY (IN).. oak.edu **1000/1500/21**
Bus Admin, Ed, Psych, Reli Stu

OAKLAND UNIVERSITY (MI) .... oakland.edu **1040/1560/22**
Bus Admin, Chem, Communic, Comp Sci, Econ, Engine, Nurs

OBERLIN COLLEGE (OH)...oberlin.edu **1350/2030/30**
Art Hist, Bio, Chem, Classics, English, Hist, Math, Music, Philo, Physics, Pre-Law,
Pre-Med/Pre-Dental, Reli Stu, Soc

OCCIDENTAL COLLEGE (CA) .... oxy.edu **1260/1890/28**
Bio, Chem, Econ, Ed, Drama, Math, Physics, Poli Sci, Pre-Law, Pre-Med/Pre-Dental, Reli Stu

OGLETHORPE UNIVERSITY (GA) .... ogelthorpe.edu **1210/1820/27**
Bio, Bus Admin, Econ, English, Poli Sci, Pre-Law

OHIO NORTHERN UNIVERSITY (OH)............................ onu.edu **1140/1710/24**
Bio, Biochem, Bus Admin, Chem, Engine, Nurs, Pharm

OHIO STATE UNIVERSITY (OH) .... osu.edu **1150/1725/25**
Ag, Arch, Art, Biochem, Bus Admin, Chem, Drama, Econ, Ed, Engine, English, For Lang, Geog,
Hist, Math, Nurs, Pharm, Philo, Physics, Poli Sci, Pre-Law, Pre-Med/Pre-Dental, Psych

OHIO UNIVERSITY (OH) ....ohiou.edu **1100/1650/24**
Art, Bot, Bus Admin, Communic, Drama, Ed, Engine, English, Hist, Math, Music,
Physics, Pre-Law, Psych, Zoo

OHIO WESLEYAN UNIVERSITY (OH) ....owu.edu **1210/1820/27**
Bio, Bot, Chem, Communic, Econ, Poli Sci, Pre-Med/Pre-Dental, Pre-Law, Psych

OKLAHOMA BAPTIST UNIVERSITY (OK) ....okbu.edu **1130/1690/25**
Ed, English, Music, Nurs, Psych, Reli Stu

OKLAHOMA CHRISTIAN UNIVERSITY (OK) .... ocu.edu **1080/1620/23**
Bio, English

OKLAHOMA CITY UNIVERSITY (OK) ....okcu.edu **1080/1620/23**
Bio, Bus Admin, Communic, Comp Sci, Drama, English, Music, Nurs, Poli Sci, Pre-Law,
Psych, Reli Stu

OKLAHOMA, UNIVERSITY OF (OK)............................. ou.edu **1170/1750/26**
Anthro, Arch, Astro, Bus Admin, Chem, Classics, Communic, Drama, Econ, Ed, Engine,
English, Geog, Geol, Hist, Poli Sci, Pre-Law, Psych, Zoo

OKLAHOMA STATE UNIVERSITY (OK).................... okstate.edu **1120/1680/24**
Ag, Bio, Botany, Bus Admin, Drama, Ed, Engine, English, Forest, Geog, Geol, Music,
Physics, Poli Sci, Psych, Soc, Zoo

OLD DOMINION UNIVERSITY (VA) .... odu.edu **1050/1575/22**
Art, Bus Admin, Econ, Engine, Soc

OLIN COLLEGE OF ENGINEERING (MA) .... olin.edu **1490/2220/34**
Engine

OLIVET NAZARENE UNIVERSITY (IL) .... olivet.edu **1100/1650/24**
Ed, Nurs, Reli Stu

ORAL ROBERTS UNIVERSITY (OK) ....oru.edu **1060/1590/23**
Bus Admin, Ed, Music, Nurs

OREGON, UNIVERSITY OF (OR) .... uoregon.edu **1100/1650/24**
*Anthro, Arch, Art, Art Hist, Bus Admin, Chem, Communic, Comp Sci, Ed, English,
For Lang, Geog, Math, Music, Poli Sci, Pre-Law, Pre-Med/Pre-Dental, Psych, Soc*

OREGON INSTITUTE OF TECHNOLOGY (OR) ....oit.edu **1040/1560/22**
Bus Admin, Engine

OREGON STATE UNIVERSITY (OR) .... orst.edu **1080/1620/23**
Ag, Biochem, Bot, Econ, Engine, Forest, Hist, Home Ec, Philo, Physics, Zoo

OTIS ART INSTITUTE/PARSONS (CA) .... otisart.edu **1000/1500/21**
Art

OTTERBEIN COLLEGE (OH) .... otterbein.edu **1080/1620/23**
Art, Chem, Drama, English, Music, Psych

OUACHITA BAPTIST UNIVERSITY (AR) .... obu.edu **1090/1630/24**
Ed, Music, Reli Stu

OZARKS, COLLEGE OF THE (MO) .... cofo.edu **1060/1590/23**
Ag, Art, Bus Admin, Comp Sci, Ed, Math, Philo, Physics, Psych

PACE UNIVERSITY (NY) .... pace.edu **1100/1650/24**
Bus Admin, Comp Sci, Nurs, Psych, Soc

PACIFIC LUTHERAN UNIVERSITY (WA) .... plu.edu **1120/1680/24**
Bio, Bus Admin, Comp Sci, Ed, Music, Nurs, Pre-Med/Pre-Dental, Reli Stu

PACIFIC OAKS COLLEGE (CA) .... pacificoaks.edu **1100/1650/24**
Ed, Home Ec

PACIFIC UNIVERSITY (OR) .... pacificu.edu **1110/1660/24**
Bio, Bus Admin, Comp Sci, English, For Lang, Physics, Pre-Med/Pre-Dental

PACIFIC, UNIVERSITY OF THE (CA) .... uop.edu **1160/1740/25**
Art, Bus Admin, Ed, Engine, Music, Pharm

PALM BEACH ATLANTIC COLLEGE (FL) .... pbac.edu **1060/1600/23**
Bus Admin, Ed, Pharm, Psych

PARSONS SCHOOL OF DESIGN (NY) .... parsons.edu **1100/1650/24**
Art

PENNSYLVANIA ACAD. OF THE FINE ARTS (PA) .... pafa.edu **1000/1500/21**
Art

PENNSYLVANIA, UNIVERSITY OF (PA) .... upenn.edu **1420/2130/32**
*Amer St, Anthro, Art, Art Hist, Astro, Biochem, Bus Admin, Classics, Econ, Engine,
English, For Lang, Geol, Hist, Math, Nurs, Philo, Physics, Poli Sci, Pre-Law, Psych, Soc*

PENNSYLVANIA STATE UNIV. (ERIE)(PA) .... pserie.psu.edu **1060/1590/23**
Bus Admin, English, Math, Physics

PENNSYLVANIA STATE UNIVERSITY (PA).................. psu.edu **1240/1860/28**
Ag, Arch, Astro, Biochem, Bot, Bus Admin, Chem, Communic, Comp Sci, Ed, Engine, Forest, Geog, Nurs, Pre-Med/Pre-Dental, Zoo

PEPPERDINE UNIVERSITY (CA) .... pepperdine.edu **1220/1830/27**
Bio, Bus Admin, Communic, Comp Sci, For Lang

PERU STATE COLLEGE (NE)....................................... peru.edu **1000/1500/21**
Bus Admin, Ed, Music

PHILADELPHIA BIBLICAL UNIVERSITY (PA)...............pbu.edu **1070/1600/23**
Ed, Music

PHILADELPHIA UNIVERSITY (PA) .... philau.edu **1070/1600/23**
Bus Admin

PINE MANOR COLLEGE (MA) .... pmc.edu **900/1350/19**
Amer St, Art Hist, Bio, Bus Admin, Communic, Nurs, Poli Sci, Psych

PITTSBURG STATE UNIVERSITY (KS).................... pittstate.edu **1000/1500/21**
Bus Admin, Ed, Music

PITTSBURGH, UNIVERSITY OF (PA)........................... pitt.edu **1200/1800/26**
Anthro, Art Hist, Astro, Biochem, Bus Admin, Chem, Classics, Communic, Comp Sci, Ed, Engine, English, For Lang, Hist, Math, Nurs, Pharm, Philo, Physics, Poli Sci, Pre-Law, Pre-Med/Pre-Dental, Psych, Reli Stu

PITTSBURGH, UNIV. OF (BRADFORD) (PA)............ upb.pitt.edu **1040/1560/22**
Bio, Comp Sci, Nurs

PITTSBURGH, UNIV. OF (GREENSBURG) (PA) ..... pitt.edu/~upg **1070/1600/23**
Anthro, Bus Admin, English, Hist

PITTSBURGH, UNIV. OF (JOHNSTOWN) (PA)   pitt.edu/~upjweb **1040/1560/22**
Bus Admin, Comp Sci, Ed, Engine

PITZER COLLEGE (CA) .... pitzer.edu **1230/1850/27**
Anthro, Bio, English, Hist, Pre-Med/Pre-Dental, Pre-Law, Psych, Soc

PLYMOUTH STATE COLLEGE (NH) .... plymouth.edu **1000/1500/21**
Ed, English

POINT LOMA NAZARENE UNIVERSITY (CA) .... ptloma.edu **1120/1680/24**
Bus Admin, Ed, Home Ec, Nurs

POINT PARK COLLEGE (PA)... ppc.edu **1020/1530/22**
Bio, Drama, English, Psych

POLYTECHNIC UNIVERSITY OF NEW YORK (NY) ....poly.edu **1200/1800/26**
Engine

POMONA COLLEGE (CA) .... pomona.edu **1450/2175/32**
Amer St, Anthro, Art Hist, Bio, Chem, Econ, English, For Lang, Geol, Hist, Math, Music, Philo, Physics, Poli Sci, Pre-Law, Pre-Med/Pre-Dental, Psych, Reli Stu, Soc

PORTLAND STATE UNIVERSITY (OR) .... pdx.edu **1030/1545/22**
Art, Bus Admin, Comp Sci, English, For Lang, Music, Pre-Law, Psych, Soc

PORTLAND, UNIVERSITY OF (OR) .... up.edu **1140/1710/25**
Bus Admin, Chem, Ed, Engine, Hist, Nurs, Philo, Poli Sci, Reli Stu

PRATT INSTITUTE (NY) .... pratt.edu **1140/1710/25**
Arch

PRESBYTERIAN COLLEGE (SC) .... presby.edu **1150/1725/25**
Bio, Bus Admin, English, Physics, Poli Sci, Pre-Law, Pre-Med/Pre-Dental, Reli Stu

PRESENTATION COLLEGE (SD) .... presentation.edu **1000/1500/21**
Bus Admin, Nurs

PRINCETON UNIVERSITY (NJ) .... princeton.edu **1480/2220/33**
*Arch, Art Hist, Bio, Biochem, Chem, Classics, Comp Sci, Drama, Econ,
Engine, English, For Lang, Geol, Hist, Math, Music, Philo, Physics, Poli Sci,
Pre-Law, Pre-Med/Pre-Dental, Reli Stu*

PRINCIPIA COLLEGE (IL) .... prin.edu/college **1150/1725/25**
Anthro, Art, Bus Admin, Ed, English, Philo, Pre-Law, Soc

PROVIDENCE COLLEGE (RI) .... providence.edu **1210/1815/27**
Bio, Bus Admin, Chem, Ed, English, Hist, Philo, Poli Sci, Pre-Law

PUERTO RICO, UNIV. OF (PR) .... upr.clu.edu **1100/1650/24**
Bus Admin, Ed

PUERTO RICO, UNIV. OF (CAYEY) (PR) ..... wwwcuc.upr.clu.edu **1000/1500/21**
Bio, Bus Admin, Chem, Ed

PUERTO RICO, UNIV. OF (MAYAGUEZ) (PR) .... uprm.edu **1170/1750/26**
Chem, Engine, For Lang, Math

PUGET SOUND, UNIVERSITY OF (WA) .... ups.edu **1250/1875/28**
Bio, Bus Admin, Chem, Econ, English, Music, Poli Sci, Pre-Law, Pre-Med/Pre-Dental, Soc

PURDUE UNIVERSITY (IN) .... purdue.edu **1150/1725/25**
Ag, Biochem, Bot, Bus Admin, Chem, Engine, Forest, Geol, Nurs, Pharm

QUEENS COLLEGE (NC) .... queens.edu **1140/1710/25**
Bus Admin, English, Hist, Music, Pre-Law

QUINCY UNIVERSITY (IL) .... quincy.edu **1050/1575/22**
Bus Admin, Hist, Soc

QUINNIPIAC UNIVERSITY (CT) .... quinnipiac.edu **1110/1670/24**
Bus Admin, Communic, Comp Sci

RADFORD UNIVERSITY (VA) .... radford.edu **1000/1500/21**
Bus Admin, Ed, Geog, Poli Sci, Pre-Law

RAMAPO COLLEGE OF NEW JERSEY (NJ) .... ramapo.edu **1050/1575/22**
Bus Admin, Comp Sci, Hist

RANDOLPH-MACON COLLEGE (VA) .... rmc.edu **1115/1675/24**
Bio, Bus Admin, Econ, English, Poli Sci, Pre-Law, Pre-Med/Pre-Dental, Psych

RANDOLPH-MACON WOMAN'S COLLEGE (VA) .... rmwc.edu **1150/1725/25**
Art, Bio, Classics, Communic, English, Pre-Law, Pre-Med/Pre-Dental, Psych

REDLANDS, UNIVERSITY OF (CA) .... redlands.edu **1125/1690/25**
Art, Bus Admin, Ed, English, Music, Poli Sci, Pre-Law, Pre-Med/Pre-Dental

REED COLLEGE (OR) .... reed.edu **1370/1960/31**
Art Hist, Bio, Chem, Econ, English, For Lang, Hist, Math, Philo, Physics,
Pre-Law, Pre-Med/Pre-Dental, Psych

REGIS COLLEGE (MA) .... regiscollege.edu **1000/1500/21**
Communic, English

REGIS UNIVERSITY (CO) .... regis.edu **1090/1640/24**
Bus Admin, Communic, Comp Sci, Ed, Hist, Nurs, Philo, Pre-Med/Pre-Dental,
Psych, Reli Stu, Soc

REINHARDT COLLEGE (GA) .... reinhardt.edu **1000/1500/21**
Bio, Bus Admin, Communic

RENSSELAER POLYTECHNIC INSTITUTE (NY) .... rpi.edu **1310/1975/29**
Arch, Bio, Bus Admin, Chem, Comp Sci, Engine, Geol, Math, Physics

RHODE ISLAND COLLEGE (RI) .... ric.edu **1000/1500/21**
Bio, Econ, Ed, Hist, Music, Philo, Psych

RHODE ISLAND SCHOOL OF DESIGN (RI) .... risd.edu **1225/1838/27**
Arch, Art

RHODE ISLAND, UNIVERSITY OF (RI) .... uri.edu **1100/1650/24**
Anthro, Bio, Communic, Comp Sci, Engine, English, Music, Nurs, Pharm, Poli Sci, Pre-Law

RHODES COLLEGE (TN) .... rhodes.edu **1300/1950/29**
Art, Bio, Bus Admin, Chem, Classics, Econ, English, For Lang, Hist, Music,
Philo, Physics, Poli Sci, Pre-Law, Pre-Med/Pre-Dental, Psych, Reli Stu

RICE UNIVERSITY (TX) .... rice.edu **1420/2130/32**
Anthro, Arch, Biochem, Bio, Chem, Comp Sci, Engine, English, Hist,
Math, Music, Physics, Pre-Law, Pre-Med/Pre-Dental

RICHARD STOCKTON COLL. OF NEW JERSEY (NJ) ... stockton.edu **1132/1700/25**
Bus Admin, Chem, Econ, Philo, Physics, Poli Sci, Pre-Med/Pre-Dental

RICHMOND, UNIVERSITY OF (VA) .... richmond.edu **1290/1940/29**
Bio, Bus Admin, Chem, English, Hist, Poli Sci, Pre-Law, Pre-Med/Pre-Dental, Reli Stu

RIDER UNIVERSITY (NJ) .... rider.edu **1040/1560/22**
Amer St, Bio, Bus Admin, Chem, Communic, Comp Sci, Ed, Music, Pre-Med/Pre-Dental

RIPON COLLEGE (WI) .... ripon.edu **1150/1725/25**
Bio, Biochem, Bus Admin, Chem, Econ, English, Hist, Poli Sci, Pre-Law, Pre-Med/Pre-Dental

ROANOKE COLLEGE (VA) .... roanoke.edu **1117/1675/24**
Art, Bio, Bus Admin, Chem, English, Hist, Math, Music, Poli Sci, Pre-Law, Psych, Reli Stu, Soc

ROBERT MORRIS COLLEGE (PA) .... robert-morris.edu **1000/1500/21**
Bus Admin, Comp Sci, Communic, Ed, English

ROCHESTER, UNIVERSITY OF (NY) .... rochester.edu **1340/2010/30**
Art, Art Hist, Biochem, Bio, Chem, Comp Sci, Econ, Engine, For Lang, Geol, Hist, Music,
Nurs, Philo, Physics, Poli Sci, Pre-Law, Pre-Med/Pre-Dental, Psych

ROCHESTER INSTITUTE OF TECHNOLOGY (NY) .... rit.edu **1230/1840/27**
Bio, Bus Admin, Chem, Comp Sci, Engine, Math, Physics

ROCKFORD COLLEGE (IL) .... rockford.edu **1080/1620/23**
Art, Bio, Bus Admin, Drama, English, Nurs, Pre-Law, Psych

ROCKHURST UNIVERSITY (MO) .... rockhurst.edu **1110/1665/24**
Bus Admin, Chem, Ed, Math, Nurs, Psych, Reli Stu

ROCKY MOUNTAIN COLLEGE (MT) .... rocky.edu **1060/1590/22**
Art, Drama, Ed, English, Music

ROGER WILLIAMS UNIVERSITY (RI) .... rwu.edu **1080/1620/23**
Arch, Bus Admin, Communic, Ed, Engine, Psych

ROLLINS COLLEGE (FL) .... rollins.edu **1160/1740/25**
Chem, Classics, Drama, English, Physics, Psych, Reli Stu

ROOSEVELT UNIVERSITY (IL) .... roosevelt.edu **1060/1590/23**
Bus Admin, Communic, Comp Sci, Music, Psych

ROSE-HULMAN INST. OF TECHNOLOGY (IN) .rose-hulman.edu **1330/2000/30**
Chem, Comp Sci, Econ, Engine, Math, Physics

ROSEMONT COLLEGE (PA) .... rosemont.edu **1020/1530/22**
Art, Art Hist, English, For Lang, Hist, Pre-Law, Psych

ROWAN UNIVERSITY (NJ) .... rowan.edu **1170/1755/26**
Art, Bus Admin, Communic, Ed, Engine, Hist, Music, Philo, Physics, Reli Stu

RUSSELL SAGE COLL. (THE SAGE COLLEGES) (NY) ...... sage.edu **1060/1600/23**
Nurs

RUTGERS UNIVERSITY (NJ) .... rutgers.edu **1210/1810/27**
Ag, Anthro, Art Hist, Biochem, Bio, Bus Admin, Chem, Drama, Econ, Ed, Engine, English, For Lang, Hist, Music, Pharm, Philo, Physics, Poli Sci, Pre-Law, Pre-Med/Pre-Dental, Psych, Reli Stu

RUTGERS UNIVERSITY (CAMDEN) (NJ) .... rutgers.edu **1100/1650/24**
Comp Sci, English, Hist, Pre-Law, Soc

SACRED HEART UNIVERSITY (CT) .... sacredheart.edu **1060/1590/23**
Biochem, Bus Admin, Psych

SAGINAW VALLEY STATE UNIVERSITY (MI) .... svsu.edu **1000/1500/21**
Ed, Nurs

ST. AMBROSE UNIVERSITY (IA) .... sau.edu **1030/1545/22**
Bus Admin, Communic, Comp Sci, Ed, Hist, Nurs, Philo, Psych, Reli Stu

ST. ANDREWS PRESBYTERIAN COLLEGE (NC) .... sapc.edu **1000/1500/21**
Biochem, Bus Admin, Ed, Philo

ST. ANSELM COLLEGE (NH) .... anselm.edu **1120/1680/24**
Classics, Econ, English, For Lang, Nurs, Pre-Law, Psych, Soc,

ST. BONAVENTURE UNIVERSITY (NY) .... sbu.edu **1060/1590/23**
Bus Admin, Communic, Ed, English, Philo, Poli Sci, Pre-Law, Reli Stu

ST. CATHERINE, COLLEGE OF (MN) .... stkate.edu **1100/1650/24**
Bus Admin, Ed, English, Music, Nurs, Philo, Reli Stu, Soc

ST. CLOUD STATE UNIVERSITY (MN) .... stcloudstate.edu **1020/1530/22**
Communic, Comp Sci, Ed, Philo, Poli Sci, Pre-Law

ST. EDWARD'S UNIVERSITY (TX) .... stedwards.edu **1080/1620/23**
Art, Bus Admin, Communic, Comp Sci, Drama, Ed, English, Psych, Reli Stu

ST. FRANCIS COLLEGE (NY) .... stfranciscollege.edu **1010/1515/21**
Bus Admin, Psych

ST. JOHN FISHER COLLEGE (NY) .... sjfc.edu **1065/1600/23**
Bus Admin, Communic

ST. JOHN'S UNIVERSITY (NY) .... stjohns.edu **1080/1620/23**
Bus Admin, Chem, Pharm, Philo, Poli Sci, Psych, Reli Stu, Soc

SAINT JOHN'S UNIV./COLL. OF SAINT BENEDICT (MN) .... csbsju.edu **1170/1755/26**
Bio, Bus Admin, Chem, Classics, Comp Sci, Econ, Ed, Hist, Nurs, Philo,
Physics, Poli Sci, Pre-Law, Pre-Med/Pre-Dental, Reli Stu

SAINT JOSEPH COLLEGE (CT) .... sjc.edu **1000/1500/21**
Ed

ST. JOSEPH'S COLLEGE (IN) .... saintjoe.edu **1020/1530/22**
Bus Admin, Ed, Psych

ST. JOSEPH'S COLLEGE (ME) .... sjcme.edu **1000/1500/21**
Ed, Nurs

ST. JOSEPH'S COLLEGE (NY) .... sjcny.edu **1080/1620/23**
Bus Admin, Comp Sci, Ed, Hist, Math, Psych

SAINT JOSEPH'S UNIVERSITY (PA) .... sju.edu **1220/1830/27**
Bus Admin, English, Hist, Poli Sci, Pre-Med/Pre-Dental, Reli Stu

ST. LAWRENCE UNIVERSITY (NY) .... stlawu.edu **1160/1740/25**
Econ, English, Geol, Poli Sci, Pre-Law, Psych, Soc

ST. LOUIS COLLEGE OF PHARMACY (MO) .... stlcop.edu **1180/1770/26**
Pharm, Pre-Med/Pre-Dental

SAINT LOUIS UNIVERSITY (MO) .... slu.edu **1190/1790/26**
Bio, Bus Admin, Chem, Communic, Ed, Engine, English, Nurs, Philo, Pre-Med/Pre-Dental, Reli Stu

SAINT MARTIN'S COLLEGE (WA) .... stmartin.edu **1000/1500/21**
Bus Admin, Ed, Engine, Psych

SAINT MARY, COLLEGE OF (NE) .... csm.edu **1050/1575/22**
Comp Sci, Ed, Nurs

SAINT MARY, UNIVERSITY OF (KS) .... stmary.edu **1010/1515/21**
Comp Sci, Ed, English, Psych

SAINT MARY'S COLLEGE (IN) .... saintmarys.edu **1130/1700/25**
Art, Bus Admin, Communic, Ed, English, Nurs, Philo, Pre-Law, Reli Stu

SAINT MARY'S COLLEGE OF CALIFORNIA (CA) .. stmarys-ca.edu **1100/1650/24**
Bus Admin, Ed, Psych, Soc

ST. MARY'S COLLEGE OF MARYLAND (MD) .... smcm.edu **1275/1915/28**
Anthro, Bio, Econ, English, Hist, Math, Music, Poli Sci, Pre-Med/Pre-Dental, Psych

ST. MARY'S UNIVERSITY OF MINNESOTA (MN) .... smumn.edu **1070/1600/23**
Bus Admin, Chem, Communic, Comp Sci, Drama, Ed, Hist, Philo, Reli Stu

ST. MARY'S UNIVERSITY (TX) .... stmarytx.edu **1070/1600/23**
Bus Admin, English, Poli Sci, Pre-Law, Pre-Med/Pre-Dental, Soc

SAINT MICHAEL'S COLLEGE (VT) .... smcvt.edu **1115/1670/24**
Bio, Bus Admin, Chem, Communic, Ed

SAINT NORBERT COLLEGE (WI) .... snc.edu **1130/1700/25**
Bio, Bus Admin, Communic, Comp Sci, Ed, English, Hist

SAINT OLAF COLLEGE (MN) .... stolaf.edu **1260/1890/28**
Amer St, Art, Bio, Chem, Classics, Drama, Econ, English, Hist, Math, Music, Nurs, Philo, Physics, Pre-Law, Pre-Med/Pre-Dental, Psych, Reli Stu

SAINT PETER'S COLLEGE (NJ) .... stpeters.edu **1000/1500/21**
English, Reli Stu

SAINT ROSE, COLLEGE OF (NY) .... strose.edu **1080/1620/23**
Art, Bus Admin, Ed, Soc

ST. SCHOLASTICA, COLLEGE OF (MN) .... css.edu **1140/1710/25**
Bio, Bus Admin, Chem, Comp Sci, Ed, English, Nurs, Pre-Med/Pre-Dental, Psych, Reli Stu

SAINT THOMAS AQUINAS COLLEGE (NY) .... stac.edu **1030/1545/22**
Ed, Psych

SAINT THOMAS, UNIVERSITY OF (MN) .... stthomas.edu **1145/1720/25**
Bus Admin, Chem, Communic, Econ, Ed, Geol, Philo, Reli Stu

SAINT THOMAS, UNIVERSITY OF (TX) .... stthom.edu **1140/1710/25**
Chem, Philo, Pre-Med/Pre-Dental, Psych, Reli Stu

ST. VINCENT COLLEGE (PA) .... stvincent.edu **1090/1635/24**
Bio, Bus Admin, Chem, Pre-Med/Pre-Dental, Psych, Reli Stu

SALEM COLLEGE (NC) .... salem.edu **1120/1680/24**
Art, Art Hist, Bus Admin, Econ, English, Pre-Law, Soc

SALEM STATE COLLEGE (MA) .... sscmass.edu **1000/1500/21**
Art, Chem, Comp Sci, Drama, Ed, Geog, Geol, Hist, Nurs, Psych, Soc

SALISBURY UNIVERSITY (MD) .... ssu.edu **1125/1675/24**
Ed, English, Geog, Philo, Pre-Law, Psych

SAMFORD UNIVERSITY (AL) .... samford.edu **1140/1700/25**
Bus Admin, Communic, Music, Nurs, Pharm, Reli Stu

SAN DIEGO STATE UNIVERSITY (CA) .... sdsu.edu **1100/1650/24**
Art, Art Hist, Astro, Bus Admin, Chem, Communic, Ed, Engine, English, Geog, Geol, Hist, Nurs, Soc

SAN DIEGO, UNIVERSITY OF (CA) .... sandiego.edu **1180/1780/26**
Bus Admin, Math, Nurs, Poli Sci, Pre-Law, Pre-Med/Pre-Dental, Reli Stu

SAN FRANCISCO ART INSTITUTE (CA) .... sfai.edu **1000/1510/21**
Art

SAN FRANCISCO CONSERVATORY OF MUSIC (CA) .. sfcm.edu **1160/1750/25**
Music

SAN FRANCISCO, UNIVERSITY OF (CA) .... usfca.edu **1095/1650/24**
Bus Admin, Econ, Nurs, Pre-Law, Pre-Med/Pre-Dental, Psych

SAN FRANCISCO STATE UNIVERSITY (CA) .... sfsu.edu **1000/1510/21**
Anthro, Astro, Communic, Drama, English, Hist, Pre-Law, Soc

SAN JOSE STATE UNIVERSITY (CA) .... sjsu.edu **1060/1600/23**
*Art, Bus Admin, Chem, Communic, Comp Sci, Engine, Math, Music, Nurs, Physics,
Pre-Med/Pre-Dental, Zoo*

SANTA CLARA UNIVERSITY (CA) .... scu.edu **1240/1860/27**
*Bus Admin, Communic, Comp Sci, Engine, English, Hist, Music, Philo, Physics,
Poli Sci, Pre-Law, Psych, Reli Stu*

SANTA FE, COLLEGE OF (NM) .... csf.edu **1110/1660/24**
Art, Drama, Ed

SARAH LAWRENCE COLLEGE (NY) .... slc.edu **1240/1860/28**
Amer St, Art, Art Hist, Drama, English, Geog, Hist, Music, Pre-Law

SCHOOL OF THE ART INSTITUTE OF CHICAGO (IL) .. saic.ed **1100/1660/24**
Art

SCHREINER UNIVERSITY (TX) .... schreiner.edu **1000/1500/21**
Bus Admin, English

SCIENCES IN PHILADELPHIA, UNIV. OF THE (PA) ...... usip.edu **1120/1680/24**
Bio, Biochem, Bus Admin, Chem, Comp Sci, Pharm

SCRANTON, UNIVERSITY OF (PA) .... scranton.edu **1140/1700/25**
Bio, Bus Admin, Communic, Pre-Med/Pre-Dental

SCRIPPS COLLEGE (CA) .... scrippscol.edu **1330/2000/30**
*Art, Art Hist, Bio, Classics, Drama, English, For Lang, Music, Poli Sci, Pre-Law, Pre-Med/
Pre-Dental, Psych*

SEATTLE PACIFIC UNIVERSITY (WA) .... spu.edu **1170/1760/26**
Bio, Chem, Drama, Ed, Engine, English, Nurs

SEATTLE UNIVERSITY (WA) .... seattleu.edu **1120/1680/24**
Bus Admin, Chem, Drama, Econ, Engine, English, Hist, Math, Nurs, Philo, Pre-Law

SETON HALL UNIVERSITY (NJ) .... shu.edu **1100/1650/24**
Bus Admin, Communic, Ed, Nurs, Philo, Pre-Law, Pre-Med/Pre-Dental, Psych, Reli Stu

SETON HILL COLLEGE (PA) .... setonhill.edu **1000/1500/21**
Art, Drama, Music

SHAW UNIVERSITY (NC) .... shawuniversity.edu **1010/1510/21**
Bus Admin, Soc

SHAWNEE STATE UNIVERSITY (OH) .... shawnee.edu **1000/1500/21**
Art, Ed

SHENANDOAH UNIVERSITY (VA) ....su.edu **1010/1510/21**
Music, Nurs

SHEPHERD COLLEGE (WV) .... shepherd.edu **1000/1500/21**
Art, Bus Admin, Chem, Ed, English, Hist, Music, Psych

SHIPPENSBURG UNIVERSITY (PA) .... ship.edu **1070/1600/23**
Bio, Bus Admin, Chem, Comp Sci, Econ, Ed, English, Hist, Physics, Psych, Soc

SHORTER COLLEGE (GA) .... shorter.edu **1050/1575/22**
Chem, Ed, Music

SIENA COLLEGE (NY) ....siena.edu **1115/1675/24**
Bio, Biochem, Bus Admin, Chem, Poli Sci, Pre-Law, Pre-Med/Pre-Dental, Psych

SIENA HEIGHTS UNIVERSITY (MI)................... sienaheights.edu **1000/1500/21**
Art, Psych

SILVER LAKE COLLEGE (WI) .... sl.edu **1000/1500/21**
Bus Admin, Ed, Reli Stu

SIMMONS COLLEGE (MA) .... simmons.edu **1100/1650/24**
Bus Admin, Communic, Ed, Math, Nurs, Psych, Soc

SIMPSON COLLEGE (IA) .... simpson.edu **1120/1680/24**
Bus Admin, Ed, Math, Music, Psych, Reli Stu, Soc

SKIDMORE COLLEGE (NY) .... skidmore.edu **1300/1950/29**
Amer St, Anthro, Art, Art Hist, Bio, Biochem, Bus Admin, Chem, Classics, Drama, Ed, English, For Lang, Geol, Music, Philo, Poli Sci, Pre-Law, Pre-Med/Pre-Dental, Psych

SLIPPERY ROCK UNIVERSITY (PA) ....sru.edu **1000/1500/21**
Communic, Drama, Ed, English, For Lang, Music

SMITH COLLEGE (MA) .... smith.edu **1270/1910/28**
Amer St, Anthro, Art, Art Hist, Bio, Econ, Engine, English, For Lang, Geol, Hist, Music, Philo, Physics, Poli Sci, Pre-Law, Pre-Med/Pre-Dental, Psych

SONOMA STATE UNIVERSITY (CA) .... sonoma.edu **1030/1545/22**
Anthro, Art Hist, Bus Admin, Chem, Geog, Music, Nurs, Physics, Psych, Soc

SOUTH, UNIVERSITY OF THE (TN) .... sewanee.edu **1230/1845/27**
Amer St, Anthro, Bio, Chem, Econ, Drama, English, Forest, For Lang, Geol, Hist, Poli Sci, Physics, Pre-Law, Pre-Med/Pre-Dental, Reli Stu

SOUTH ALABAMA, UNIVERSITY OF (AL) .... usouthal.edu **1060/1590/23**
Bio, Bus Admin, Communic, English, For Lang, Nurs, Philo, Soc

SOUTH CAROLINA, UNIVERSITY OF (SC) .... sc.edu **1120/1680/24**
Bus Admin, Communic, Comp Sci, Drama, Ed, Engine, English, For Lang, Geog, Geol, Hist, Nurs, Pharm, Physics, Poli Sci, Pre-Law

SOUTH DAKOTA, UNIVERSITY OF (SD) .... usd.edu   **1050/1575/22**
Art, Bio, Bus Admin, English, Hist, Music, Nurs, Poli Sci, Pre-law, Pre-Med/Pre-Dental, Psych

SOUTH DAKOTA SCHOOL OF MINES AND TECH. (SD) .... sdsmt.edu   **1120/1680/24**
Engine, Geol, Math, Physics

SOUTH DAKOTA STATE UNIVERSITY (SD) .... sdstate.edu   **1060/1590/23**
Econ, Engine, Math, Nurs, Pharm, Soc

SOUTH FLORIDA, UNIVERSITY OF (FL) .... usf.edu   **1060/1590/23**
Amer St, Anthro, Bus Admin, Chem, Drama, Ed, Engine, For Lang, Music, Nurs, Philo

SOUTHEAST MISSOURI STATE UNIV. (MO) .... semo.edu   **1040/1560/22**
Bus Admin, Ed

SOUTHEASTERN LOUISIANA STATE UNIV. (LA) .... selu.edu   **1000/1500/21**
Communic, Comp Sci, Ed, English

SOUTHEASTERN OKLAHOMA STATE UNIV. (OK) ..... sosu.edu   **1000/1500/21**
Bot, Bus Admin, Zoo

SOUTHERN CALIFORNIA, UNIVERSITY OF (CA) .... usc.edu   **1320/1980/30**
Astro, Arch, Bus Admin, Communic, Drama, Ed, Engine, Math, Music, Pharm, Psych

SOUTHERN CONNECTICUT STATE UNIV. (CT) .... southernct.edu   **1000/1500/21**
Chem, Communic, Comp Sci, Econ, Ed, English, Geog, Physics, Poli Sci, Psych, Soc

SOUTHERN ILLINOIS UNIV. (CARBONDALE) (IL) .... siuc.edu   **1030/1545/22**
Bot, Bus Admin, Chem, Communic, Engine, Forestry, Geog, Hist, Music, Poli Sci, Psych, Zoo

SOUTHERN ILLINOIS UNIV. (EDWARDSVILLE) (IL) .... siue.edu   **1010/1515/21**
Ed, Engine, Nurs, Poli Sci

SOUTHERN MAINE, UNIVERSITY OF (ME) .... usm.maine.edu   **1050/1575/22**
Art, Bus Admin, Chem, Communic, Comp Sci, Drama, Engine, Music, Nurs

SOUTHERN METHODIST UNIVERSITY (TX) .... smu.edu   **1200/1800/26**
Anthro, Art, Art Hist, Bus Admin, Communic, Drama, Econ, Engine, Hist, Reli Stu

SOUTHERN MISSISSIPPI, UNIVERSITY OF (MS) .... usms.edu   **1010/1515/21**
Bus Admin, Drama Ed, Hist, Music, Nurs

SOUTHERN NAZARENE UNIVERSITY (OK) .... snu.edu   **1050/1575/22**
Ed, English, Nurs, Reli Stu

SOUTHERN OREGON UNIVERSITY (OR) .... sou.edu   **1040/1560/22**
Art, Bio, Bus Admin, Chem, Ed, For Lang, Soc

SOUTHERN POLYTECHNIC UNIVERSITY (GA) .... spsu.edu   **1080/1620/23**
Arch, Comp Sci, Engine, Math

SOUTHERN UTAH UNIVERSITY (UT) .... suu.edu   **1000/1500/21**
Communic, Drama, Econ, Ed, English

SOUTHWEST BAPTIST UNIVERSITY (MO) .... sbuniv.edu   **1060/1590/23**
Ed, Music, Reli Stu

SOUTHWEST MISSOURI STATE UNIVERSITY (MO) .. smsu.edu **1090/1635/24**
Classics, Drama, Ed, Math, Poli Sci, Pre-Law, Soc

SOUTHWEST TEXAS STATE UNIVERSITY (TX) ...... txstate.edu **1035/1550/22**
Ag, Anthro, Bio, Bus Admin, Comp Sci, Drama, Ed, Geog, Hist, Math

SOUTHWESTERN COLLEGE (KS) .... sckans.edu **1040/1560/22**
English, Music, Nurs

SOUTHWESTERN OKLAHOMA STATE UNIV. (OK) .. swosu.edu **1000/1500/21**
Bus Admin, Chem, Ed, Pharm

SOUTHWESTERN UNIVERSITY (TX) .... southwestern.edu **1245/1865/26**
*Art, Bio, Bus Admin, Chem, Communic, Drama, Econ, English, For Lang, Hist, Music,
Philo, Poli Sci, Pre-Law, Pre-Med/Pre-Dental, Psych, Reli Stu, Soc*

SPELMAN COLLEGE (GA) .... spelman.edu **1080/1630/24**
Bio, Chem, Comp Sci, Econ, English, Poli Sci, Pre-Law, Pre-Med/Pre-Dental, Soc

SPRING HILL COLLEGE (AL) .... shc.edu **1110/1665/24**
Bio, Bus Admin, Chem, Communic, English, Hist, Poli Sci, Pre-Law, Pre-Med/Pre-Dental

SPRINGFIELD COLLEGE (MA) .... spfldcol.edu **1010/1515/21**
Psych

STANFORD UNIVERSITY (CA) .... stanford.edu **1450/2175/32**
*Amer St, Anthro, Art, Art Hist, Bio, Chem, Classics, Communic, Comp Sci, Drama,
Econ, Ed, Engine, English, For Lang, Math, Music, Physics, Poli Sci, Pre-Law,
Pre-Med/Pre-Dental, Psych, Reli Stu, Soc*

STEPHEN F. AUSTIN STATE UNIVERSITY (TX) .... sfasu.edu **1000/1500/21**
Forest

STEPHENS (MO) .... stephens.edu **1080/1630/23**
Bus Admin, Communic, Drama, Ed, Pre-Law, Psych

STERLING COLLEGE (KS) .... sterling.edu **1040/1560/22**
Drama, Ed, Music

STETSON UNIVERSITY (FL) .... stetson.edu **1130/1700/25**
*Bus Admin, Chem, Comp Sci, Ed, English, Hist, Math, Music, Pre-Law,
Pre-Med/Pre-Dental, Psych, Reli Stu*

STEVENS INSTITUTE OF TECHNOLOGY (NJ) . stevens-tech.edu **1280/1920/29**
Comp Sci, Engine

STONEHILL COLLEGE (MA) .... stonehill.edu **1160/1740/25**
Bio, Bus Admin, Chem, Comp Sci, Poli Sci, Pre-Law, Psych

SUFFOLK UNIVERSITY (MA) .... suffolk.edu **1070/1600/23**
Bus Admin, Communic, Poli Sci, Soc

SUNY COLL. OF ENVIRONMENTAL SCIENCE & FORESTRY (NY) esf.edu **1160/1740/25**
Forest

SUSQUEHANNA UNIVERSITY (PA) .... susqu.edu **1160/1740/25**
*Bio, Biochem, Bus Admin, Chem, Communic, Drama, Econ, Ed, English,
Music, Poli Sci, Pre-Med/Pre-Dental, Psych*

SWARTHMORE COLLEGE (PA) ....swarthmore.edu **1420/2130/32**
Art Hist, Biochem, Bio, Classics, Econ, Ed, Engine, English, Hist,
Philo, Physics, Poli Sci, Pre-Law, Pre-Med/Pre-Dental, Psych

SWEET BRIAR COLLEGE (VA) .... sbc.edu **1170/1760/26**
Anthro, Art Hist, Chem, Drama, Engine, For Lang, Math, Poli Sci, Pre-Law, Psych

SYRACUSE UNIVERSITY (NY) .... syracuse.edu **1200/1800/26**
Anthro, Arch, Art, Art Hist, Bus Admin, Chem, Communic, Comp Sci, Drama,
Engine, Forest, Geog, Music, Physics, Poli Sci, Pre-Law, Psych, Reli Stu, Soc

TABOR COLLEGE (KS) .... tabor.edu **1060/1600/23**
Ed

TAMPA, UNIVERSITY OF (FL)............................utampa.edu **1095/1645/23**
Bus Admin, Communic, Music

TARLETON STATE UNIVERSITY (TX)......................tarleton.edu **1000/1500/21**
Ag, Drama, English, Hist, Music, Soc

TAYLOR UNIVERSITY (IN) .... taylor.edu **1090/1635/23**
Bus Admin, Comp Sci, Psych, Reli Stu

TEMPLE UNIVERSITY (PA) .... temple.edu **1100/1650/24**
Arch, Art, Biochem, Bio, Bus Admin, Chem, Communic, Comp Sci, Drama, English,
For Lang, Music, Pharm, Pre-Law, Pre-Med/Pre-Dental, Soc

TENNESSEE TECHNOLOGICAL UNIVERSITY (TN).. tntech.edu **1050/1575/22**
Ed, Engine

TENNESSEE, UNIVERSITY OF (TN) .... utk.edu **1110/1660/24**
Ag, Anthro, Arch, Art, Bot, Bus Admin, Chem, Classics, Ed, Engine, English, Forest, Hist,
Physics, Poli Sci, Pre-Law, Pre-Med/Pre-Dental, Reli Stu, Zoo

TEXAS, UNIVERSITY OF, AT
       ARLINGTON... uta.edu **1030/1550/22**
       Arch, Bio, Bus Admin, Communic, Comp Sci, Engine, Nurs, Poli Sci
       AUSTIN .... utexas.edu **1220/1830/26**
       Amer St, Arch, Astro, Bio, Bot, Bus Admin, Classics, Communic, Comp Sci,
       Drama, Ed, Engine, For Lang, Geog, Geol, Hist, Math, Music, Pharm, Philo,
       Physics, Poli Sci, Pre-Med/Pre-Dental, Psych, Zoo
       DALLAS ....utdallas.edu **1225/1830/26**
       Bus Admin, Comp Sci, Econ, Engine, Hist, Physics
       SAN ANTONIO .... utsa.edu **1000/1500/21**
       Arch, Art, Bio, Bus Admin, Engine, English, Hist, Music, Pre-Med/Pre-Dental, Psych
       SAN ANTONIO (HEALTH SCIENCE CENTER) .. uthscsa.edu **1100/1650/24**
       Nurs (No Frosh - Transfers Only)
       TYLER .... uttyl.edu **1067/1600/22**
       Bus Admin, Comp Sci, Engine, English, Math, Nurs, Psych

TEXAS A&M (TX) .... tamu.edu **1178/1770/26**
Ag, Anthro, Arch, Bus Admin, Chem, Communic, Econ, Ed, Engine, English, Forest,
Geol, Hist, Philo, Poli Sci, Pre-Med/Pre-Dental, Zoo

TEXAS A&M - CORPUS CHRISTI (TX)....................tamucc.edu **1000/1500/21**
Art, Bio, Bus Admin, Chem, Ed, English, Geog, Geol, Hist, Math, Nurs, Psych

TEXAS A&M - GALVESTON (TX) .... tamug.edu **1110/1665/24**
Bus Admin

TEXAS A&M - KINGSVILLE (TX) .... tamuk.edu **1000/1500/21**
Engine

TEXAS CHRISTIAN UNIVERSITY (TX) .... tcu.edu **1130/1700/25**
Bio, Bus Admin, Communic, Drama, Ed, Geol, Hist, Music, Nurs, Reli Stu

TEXAS LUTHERAN UNIVERSITY (TX) .... tlu.edu **1080/1620/23**
Bio, Bus Admin, Chem, Ed, Hist, Music, Reli Stu

TEXAS TECH UNIVERSITY (TX) .... ttu.edu **1110/1665/24**
Ag, Arch, Art, Bus Admin, Ed, Engine, English, Hist, Home Ec, Math

TEXAS WESLEYAN UNIVERSITY (TX) .... txwesleyan.edu **1010/1510/21**
Bus Admin, Communic, Ed, Psych

THOMAS MORE COLLEGE (KY) .... thomasmore.edu **1040/1560/22**
Bio, Bus Admin, Chem, Comp Sci, Ed, Nurs, Physics, Pre-Med/Pre-Dental

TOLEDO, UNIVERSITY OF (OH) .... utoledo.edu **1040/1560/22**
Bus Admin, Econ, Engine, Hist, Pharm

TOUGALOO COLLEGE (MS) .... tougaloo.edu **1000/1500/21**
Bio, Ed

TOWSON UNIVERSITY (MD) .... towson.edu **1095/1645/24**
Anthro, Art, Bus Admin, Chem, Communic, Drama, Ed, Music, Nurs, Psych, Soc

TRANSYLVANIA UNIVERSITY (KY) .... transy.edu **1200/1800/26**
Bio, Bus Admin, Chem, Comp Sci, Ed, Philo, Pre-Med/Pre-Dental, Psych

TRINITY COLLEGE (CT) .... trincoll.edu **1310/1965/29**
Amer St, Art Hist, Bio, Bus Admin, Chem, Econ, Engine, English, Hist, Math,
Philo, Pre-Law, Pre-Med/Pre-Dental, Reli Stu

TRINITY COLLEGE (DC) .... trinitydc.edu **1050/1575/22**
Bus Admin, For Lang, Math, Poli Sci, Pre-Law, Soc

TRINITY UNIVERSITY (TX) .... trinity.edu **1298/1948/29**
Art, Art Hist, Bio, Bus Admin, Chem, Classics, Communic, Econ, Ed, English,
For Lang, Hist, Philo, Physics, Poli Sci, Pre-Law, Pre-Med/Pre-Dental, Soc

TRI-STATE UNIVERSITY (IN) .... tristate.edu **1090/1640/24**
Engine

TROY STATE UNIVERSITY (AL) .... troy.edu **1000/1500/21**
Bus Admin. Ed, English, Nurs

TRUMAN STATE UNIVERSITY (MO) .... truman.edu **1220/1830/27**
Bio, Bus Admin, Chem, Econ, Ed, English, For Lang, Math, Nurs, Pre-Med/Pre-Dental

TUFTS UNIVERSITY (MA) .... tufts.edu **1340/2000/30**
Bio, Chem, Classics, Drama, Econ, Engine, English, Hist, Philo, Poli Sci,
Pre-Law, Pre-Med/Pre-Dental, Psych

TULANE UNIVERSITY (LA) .... tulane.edu **1270/1900/28**
Amer St, Anthro, Arch, Art, Bio, Biochem, Bus Admin, Drama, Engine, For Lang, Hist, Math, Philo, Poli Sci, Pre-Law, Pre-Med/Pre-Dental, Psych

TULSA, UNIVERSITY OF (OK) .... utulsa.edu **1230/1850/27**
Anthro, Art, Bio, Bus Admin, Communic, Comp Sci, Engine, English, Geol, Hist, Music, Physics, Psych

TUSKEGEE UNIVERSITY (AL) .... tuskegee.edu **1000/1500/21**
Ag, Arch, Engine, Nurs, Physics, Pre-Law, Pre-Med/Pre-Dental

UNION COLLEGE (NE) .... ucollege.edu **1050/1575/22**
Nurs, Reli Stu

UNION COLLEGE (NY) .... union.edu **1240/1860/28**
Bio, Chem, Engine, Hist, Math, Poli Sci, Pre-Law, Pre-Med/Pre-Dental, Psych

UNION UNIVERSITY (TN) .... uu.edu **1100/1650/24**
Art, Chem, Music, Nurs, Physics, Reli Stu

U. S. AIR FORCE ACADEMY (CO) .... usafa.edu **1280/1920/29**
Bus Admin, Comp Sci, Engine, Math, Physics, Poli Sci

U. S. COAST GUARD ACADEMY (CT) .... cga.edu **1260/1880/28**
Engine

U. S. MILITARY ACADEMY (NY) .... usma.edu **1270/1900/28**
Econ, Engine, Hist, Poli Sci

U. S. NAVAL ACADEMY (MD) .... usna.edu **1325/1980/30**
Chem, Engine, Poli Sci

URSINUS COLLEGE (PA) .... ursinus.edu **1200/1800/26**
Bio, Bus Admin, Chem, Econ, Ed, Physics, Poli Sci, Pre-Law, Pre-Med/Pre-Dental

UTAH, UNIVERSITY OF (UT) .... utah.edu **1100/1650/24**
Art, Art Hist, Bio, Bus Admin, Chem, Comp Sci, Drama, Engine, English, For Lang, Geol, Hist, Home Ec, Pharm, Philo, Poli Sci, Pre-Law, Pre-Med/Pre-Dental

UTAH STATE UNIVERSITY (UT) .... usu.edu **1090/1635/24**
Ag, Bio, Chem, Drama, Ed, Engine, English, Forest, Home Ec, Music, Poli Sci

UTICA COLLEGE (NY) .... ucsu.edu **1010/1510/22**
Bus Admin

VALPARAISO UNIVERSITY (IN) .... valpo.edu **1170/1755/26**
Bio, Bus Admin, Ed, Engine, For Lang, Math, Music, Nurs, Pre-Med/Pre-Dental, Psych, Reli Stu

VANDERBILT UNIVERSITY (TN) .... vanderbilt.edu **1350/2025/30**
Anthro, Art Hist, Bio, Classics, Econ, Ed, Engine, English, Geol, Hist, Music, Nurs, Philo, Physics, Poli Sci, Pre-Law, Pre-Med/Pre-Dental, Psych

VASSAR COLLEGE (NY) .... vassar.edu **1375/2065/30**
Art, Art Hist, Astro, Bio, Comp Sci, Drama, Econ, English, Hist, Math, Music, Philo, Pre-Law, Pre-Med/Pre-Dental, Psych

VERMONT, UNIVERSITY OF (VT) .... uvm.edu **1160/1740/25**
Ag, Bio, Bot, Bus Admin, Chem, Econ, For Lang, Geog, Geol, Hist, Nurs,
Physics, Poli Sci, Pre-Law, Pre-Med/Pre-Dental, Reli Stu, Psych, Zoo

VILLA JULIE COLLEGE (MD) .... vjc.edu **1050/1575/22**
Nurs

VILLANOVA UNIVERSITY (PA) .... villanova.edu **1260/1890/28**
Astro, Bio, Bus Admin, Communic, Econ, Engine, Math, Nurs, Philo,
Poli Sci, Pre-Law, Pre-Med/Pre-Dental

VIRGINIA, UNIVERSITY OF (VA) .... virginia.edu **1320/1980/30**
Amer St, Arch, Art, Astro, Bio, Biochem, Bus Admin, Chem, Classics, Econ, Engine, English,
For Lang, Hist, Music, Nurs, Poli Sci, Pre-Law, Pre-Med/Pre-Dental, Psych, Reli Stu, Soc

VIRGINIA COMMONWEALTH UNIVERSITY (VA) ....vcu.edu **1050/1575/22**
Art, Bus Admin, Drama, Engine, For Lang, Music, Nurs, Pharm, Pre-Med/Pre-Dental,
Pre-Law, Psych, Reli Stu

VIRGINIA MILITARY INSTITUTE (VA) .... vmi.edu **1120/1680/24**
Bus Admin, Chem, Econ, Engine, Hist, Pre-Law

VIRGINIA POLYTECHNIC INSTITUTE (VA) .... vt.edu **1200/1800/26**
Ag, Arch, Bio, Biochem, Bus Admin, Chem, Communic, Comp Sci, Engine, Forest, Hist, Psych

VIRGINIA WESLEYAN UNIVERSITY (VA) .... vwc.edu **1007/1510/20**
Bio, Bus Admin, Communic, Poli Sci, Pre-Law, Pre-Med/Pre-Dental, Psych, Reli Stu, Soc

VISUAL ARTS, SCHOOL OF (NY) .... schoolofvisualarts.edu **1064/1600/23**
Art, Bus Admin

VITERBO UNIVERSITY (WI) .... viterbo.edu **1055/1590/23**
Chem, Drama, Music, Nurs

WABASH COLLEGE (IN) .... wabash.edu **1185/1780/26**
Bio, Chem, Classics, Econ, English, Hist, Math, Philo, Poli Sci, Pre-Law, Pre-Med/Pre-Dental,
Psych, Reli Stu

WAGNER COLLEGE (NY) .... wagner.edu **1100/1650/24**
Amer St, Bus Admin, Drama, Ed, Soc

WAKE FOREST UNIVERSITY (NC) .... wfu.edu **1310/1965/29**
Bio, Bus Admin, Chem, Econ, English, For Lang, Hist, Math, Physics,
Poli Sci, Pre-Law, Pre-Med/Pre-Dental, Psych, Reli Stu

WALLA WALLA COLLEGE (WA) .... wwc.edu **1030/1550/22**
Communic, Engine, English, Nurs, Pre-Med/Pre-Dental

WALSH UNIVERSITY (OH) .... walsh.edu **1000/1500/21**
Ed, English, Nurs

WARREN WILSON COLLEGE (NC) .... warren-wilson.edu **1170/1765/26**
English, Hist, Pre-Law

WARTBURG COLLEGE (IA) .... wartburg.edu **1140/1700/25**
Bio, Bus Admin, Communic, Ed, English, Hist, Music, Pre-Med/Pre-Dental, Reli Stu

WASHBURN UNIVERSITY (KS) .... washburn.edu   **1140/1700/22**
Ed, Nurs, Physics

WASHINGTON COLLEGE (MD) .... washcoll.edu   **1155/1715/25**
Amer St, Bio, Bus Admin, Hist, Pre-Med/Pre-Dental, Psych

WASHINGTON & JEFFERSON COLLEGE (PA) ..... washjeff.edu   **1110/1665/24**
*Art, Bio, Bus Admin, Chem, Econ, Ed, English, Hist, Poli Sci, Pre-Law,
Pre-Med/Pre-Dental, Psych*

WASHINGTON & LEE UNIVERSITY (VA) .... wlu.edu   **1340/2010/30**
*Art, Bio, Bus Admin, Chem, Communic, Econ, English, For Lang, Geol, Hist, Math,
Physics, Poli Sci, Pre-Law, Pre-Med/Pre-Dental*

WASHINGTON UNIVERSITY IN ST. LOUIS (MO) .... wustl.edu   **1380/2070/31**
*Anthro, Arch, Art, Art Hist, Bio, Bus Admin, Chem, Comp Sci, Engine, English,
For Lang, Geol, Math, Philo, Physics, Pre-Law, Pre-Med/Pre-Dental, Psych*

WASHINGTON STATE UNIVERSITY (WA) .... wsu.edu   **1060/1590/23**
*Amer St, Ag, Anthro, Arch, Biochem, Bus Admin, Communic, Econ, Ed, Engine, English,
Hist, Home Ec, Pharm, Physics, Soc, Zoo*

WASHINGTON, UNIVERSITY OF (WA) .... washington.edu   **1160/1740/25**
*Anthro, Arch, Art, Art Hist, Astro, Biochem, Bot, Bus Admin, Chem, Classics, Comp Sci,
Drama, Econ, Ed, Engine, English, Forest, Geol, Hist, Math, Nurs, Philo, Physics, Pre-Law,
Pre-Med/Pre-Dental, Psych, Soc, Zoo*

WAYNE STATE COLLEGE (NE) .... wsc.edu   **1000/1500/21**
Chem, Ed, Psych

WAYNE STATE UNIVERSITY (MI) .... wayne.edu   **1000/1500921**
Engine, For Lang, Nurs, Pharm, Pre-Med/Pre-Dental

WAYNESBURG COLLEGE (PA) .... waynesburg.edu   **1000/1500/21**
Communic, Nurs

WEBER STATE UNIVERSITY (UT) .... weber.edu   **1020/1530/22**
Art, Bus Admin, Communic, Comp Sci, Drama, Econ, Ed, Math, Music, Nurs, Physics, Zoo

WEBSTER UNIVERSITY (MO) .... webster.edu   **1130/1700/25**
Comp Sci, Drama, Hist, Music, Nurs, Philo, Poli Sci, Psych

WELLESLEY COLLEGE (MA) .... wellesley.edu   **1360/2040/30**
*Art, Art Hist, Bio, Chem, Econ, Ed, English, For Lang, Hist, Math, Physics,
Poli Sci, Pre-Law, Pre-Med/Pre-Dental, Reli Stu*

WELLS COLLEGE (NY) .... wells. edu   **1130/1700/25**
*Amer St, Bio, Bus Admin, Chem, Drama, Ed, English, For Lang, Hist, Music,
Pre-Law, Pre-Med/Pre-Dental, Psych, Soc*

WESLEYAN COLLEGE (GA) .... wesleyan-college.edu   **1135/1700/25**
Amer St, Art, Bus Admin

WESLEYAN UNIVERSITY (CT) .... wesleyan.edu   **1380/2075/31**
*Amer St, Art, Astro, Bio, Chem, Drama, Econ, English, Hist, Math, Poli Sci,
Pre-Law, Pre-Med/Pre-Dental, Psych, Reli Stu*

WEST CHESTER UNIVERSITY (PA) .... wcupa.edu **1130/1700/25**
Art, Bio, Bus Admin, Chem, Communic, Comp Sci, English, For Lang, Music, Philo, Poli Sci, Pre-Law, Soc

WEST FLORIDA, UNIVERSITY OF (FL) .... uwf.edu **1120/1680/24**
Bus Admin, Chem, Comp Sci, Ed, Psych

WEST VIRGINIA UNIVERSITY (WV) .... wvu.edu **1060/1600/23**
Art, Bus Admin, Communic, Drama, Engine, Forest, Music

WEST VIRGINIA WESLEYAN COLLEGE (WV) .... wvwc.edu **1040/1560/22**
Art, Bio, Comp Sci, Drama, Ed, English, Hist, Physics

WESTERN CAROLINA UNIVERSITY (NC) .... wcu.edu **1030/1545/22**
Bus Admin, Chem, Comp Sci, Ed, English, Math, Music, Nurs

WESTERN CONNECTICUT STATE UNIV. (CT) .... wcsu.ctstateu.edu **1000/1500/21**
Amer St, Anthro, Art, Astro, Bus Admin, Ed, English, Music, Nurs, Soc

WESTERN ILLINOIS UNIVERSITY (IL) .... wiu.edu **1010/1515/21**
Ag, Chem, Communic, Ed, English, Geog, Music, Soc

WESTERN KENTUCKY UNIVERSITY (KY) .... wku.edu **1040/1560/22**
Ag, Bio, Comp Sci, Ed, Hist, Nurs, Physics, Psych, Soc

WESTERN MICHIGAN UNIVERSITY (MI) .... wmich.edu **1070/1600/23**
Art, Bus Admin, Communic, Comp Sci, Drama, Ed, English, Engine, For Lang, Hist, Home Ec, Music, Nurs, Physics, Psych

WESTERN NEW ENGLAND COLLEGE (MA) .... wnec.edu **1060/1590/23**
Bus Admin, Comp Sci, Ed, Engine, Psych

WESTERN STATE COLLEGE OF COLORADO .... western.edu **1000/1500/21**
Bio, Bus Admin, Drama, English, Hist, Geol, Music

WESTERN WASHINGTON UNIVERSITY (WA) .... wwu.edu **1120/1680/24**
Anthro, Art, Communic, Ed, English, Geog, Poli Sci, Pre-Law, Psych, Soc

WESTFIELD STATE COLLEGE (MA) .... wsc.mass.edu **1030/1550/22**
Ed, English, Music, Poli Sci, Psych

WESTMINSTER COLLEGE (MO) .... wcmo.edu **1120/1680/24**
Bio, Bus Admin, Econ, English, Hist, Poli Sci, Pre-Law, Pre-Med/Pre-Dental, Psych

WESTMINSTER COLLEGE (PA) .... westminster.edu **1090/1635/24**
Bio, Comp Sci, Pre-Med/Pre-Dental, Soc

WESTMINSTER COLLEGE (UT) .... westminstercollege.edu **1130/1700/25**
Art, Bio, Bus Admin, Chem, Communic, Comp Sci, Ed, Engine, English, Hist, Nurs, Philo, Physics, Poli Sci, Psych

WESTMONT COLLEGE (CA) .... westmont.edu **1220/1830/27**
Bio, Chem, Econ, Hist, Pre-Law, Pre-Med/Pre-Dental, Psych, Reli Stu

WHEATON COLLEGE (IL) .... wheaton.edu **1330/2000/29**
Art, Bio, Chem, Communic, Ed, English, Hist, Math, Music, Philo, Physics, Pre-Law, Pre-Med/Pre-Dental, Psych, Reli Stu, Soc

WHEATON COLLEGE (MA) ....wheatonma.edu **1230/1850/27**
Art, Art Hist, Astro, Bio, Drama, Econ, English, For Lang, Hist, Math,
Poli Sci, Pre-Law, Pre-Med/Pre-Dental, Psych, Soc

WHEELING JESUIT (WV) .... wju.edu **1045/1570/22**
Bio, Bus Admin, Chem, English, Hist, Math, Nurs, Philo, Psych, Reli Stu

WHEELOCK COLLEGE (MA) .... wheelock.edu **1020/1530/22**
Ed

WHITMAN COLLEGE (WA) .... whitman.edu **1340/2010/30**
Art, Astro, Bio, Chem, Classics, Drama, Econ, English, For Lang, Geol, Hist, Math, Music,
Philo, Physics, Poli Sci, Pre-Law, Pre-Med/Pre-Dental, Psych, Soc

WHITTIER COLLEGE (CA) .... whittier.edu **1090/1640/24**
Bus Admin, Chem, Econ, Ed, English, Poli Sci, Pre-Law

WHITWORTH COLLEGE (WA) ....whitworth.edu **1160/1740/26**
Art, Bus Admin, Chem, Communic, Ed, English, Hist, Music, Physics, Psych, Reli Stu

WICHITA STATE UNIVERSITY (KS) .... wichita.edu **1000/1500/21**
Bus Admin, Communic, English

WIDENER UNIVERSITY (PA) .... widener.edu **1030/1545/22**
Bus Admin, Ed, Engine, Nurs

WILBERFORCE UNIVERSITY (OH) .... wilberforce.edu **1000/1500/21**
Bus Admin, Poli Sci, Pre-Law

WILKES UNIVERSITY (PA) .... wilkes.edu **1080/1620/23**
Bio, Comp Sci, Engine, English, Hist, Math, Nurs, Pre-Med/Pre-Dental, Psych

WILLAMETTE UNIVERSITY (OR) .... willamette.edu **1230/1845/27**
Art Hist, Bio, Chem, Classics, Econ, English, Hist, Math, Music, Philo,
Poli Sci, Pre-Law, Pre-Med/Pre-Dental, Psych, Reli Stu, Soc

WILLIAM JEWELL COLLEGE (MO) .... jewell.edu **1170/1755/26**
Bio, Bus Admin, Chem, Comp Sci, Ed, English, Music, Nurs, Physics

WILLIAM & MARY, COLLEGE OF (VA) .... wm.edu **1350/2030/30**
Amer St, Bio, Bus Admin, Classics, Comp Sci, Drama, Econ, Ed, English,
For Lang, Geol, Hist, Philo, Physics, Poli Sci, Pre-Med/Pre-Dental, Reli Stu

WILLIAM PATERSON UNIVERSITY (NJ) .... wpunj.edu **1060/1590/23**
Anthro, Communic, Comp Sci, English, Hist, Music, Psych, Soc

WILLIAMS COLLEGE (MA) .... williams.edu **1400/2100/32**
Amer St, Art, Art Hist, Astro, Bio, Chem, Classics, Comp Sci, Econ, English, Hist,
Poli Sci, Pre-Law, Pre-Med/Pre-Dental, Psych

WILMINGTON COLLEGE (OH) .... wilmington.edu **1000/1500/21**
Ag, Ed, English, Hist

WILSON COLLEGE (PA) .... wilson.edu **1000/1500/21**
Econ, Pre-Law, Psych, Soc

WINGATE UNIVERSITY (NC) .... wingate.edu **1040/1560/22**
Art, Communic, Hist, Music

WINONA STATE UNIVERSITY (MN) .... winona.msus.edu **1090/1635/24**
Bio, Bus Admin, Chem, Communic, Comp Sci, Ed, English, Hist, Pre-Med/Pre-Dental, Soc

WINTHROP UNIVERSITY (SC) .... winthrop.edu **1055/1585/22**
Art, Bio, Bus Admin, Chem, Drama, Ed, English, Hist, Math, Poli Sci, Psych

WISCONSIN LUTHERAN COLLEGE (WI) ....wlc.edu **1100/1650/24**
Art, Chem, Communic, Ed, Math, Music, Reli Stu

WISCONSIN, UNIVERSITY OF, AT
    EAU CLAIRE ....uwec.edu **1099/1650/24**
    Bio, Bus Admin, Chem, English, Math, Nurs
    GREEN BAY .... uwgb.edu **1060/1590/23**
    Art, Bus Admin, Hist, Psych
    LA CROSSE .... uwlax.edu **1090/1635/24**
    Astro, Bus Admin, Chem, Communic, Comp Sci, Geog, Soc
    MADISON .... wisc.edu **1250/1875/27**
    Ag, Anthro, Art, Art Hist, Astro, Biochem, Bot, Bus Admin, Chem, Classics, Communic, Comp Sci, Drama, Ed, Engine, English, For Lang, Forest, Geog, Geol, Hist, Home Ec, Math, Music, Nurs, Pharm, Philo, Physics, Poli Sci, Pre-Law, Pre-Med/Pre-Dental, Psych, Soc, Zoo
    MILWAUKEE .... uwm.edu **1080/1620/23**
    Anthro, Arch, Bio, Bus Admin, Chem, Drama, Econ, Ed, English, For Lang, Hist, Nurs, Physics, Poli Sci, Pre-Law
    PLATTEVILLE .... uwplatt.edu **1050/1575/23**
    Ag, Bio, Chem, Ed, Engine, English
    STEVENS POINT .... uwsp.edu **1100/1650/24**
    Art, Bio, Bus Admin, Chem, Communic, Drama, Ed, Home Ec, Math, Music, Soc
    STOUT .... uwstout.edu **1000/1500/21**
    Bus Admin, Home Ec, Psych

WITTENBERG UNIVERSITY (OH) .... wittenberg.edu **1160/1720/26**
Art, Bio, Bus Admin, Chem, Ed, English, Geog, Hist, Music, Poli Sci, Pre-Law, Pre-Med/Pre-Dental, Psych, Reli Stu

WOFFORD COLLEGE (SC) .... wofford.edu **1200/1800/26**
Bio, Chem, Comp Sci, Econ, Ed, English, For Lang, Hist, Math, Philo, Pre-Law, Pre-Med/Pre-Dental, Psych, Soc

WOODBURY UNIVERSITY (CA) .... woodburyu.edu **1000/1500/21**
Arch, Bus Admin

WOOSTER, COLLEGE OF (OH) .... wooster.edu **1200/1800/26**
Art Hist, Bio, Chem, Classics, Drama, Econ, English, Geol, Hist, Math, Music, Poli Sci, Pre-Law, Pre-Med/Pre-Dental, Reli Stu, Soc

WORCESTER POLYTECHNIC INSTITUTE (MA) .... wpi.edu **1285/1925/29**
Bio, Biochem, Bus Admin, Comp Sci, Econ, Engine, Math, Physics, Pre-Law

WORCESTER STATE COLLEGE (MA) .... worcester.edu **1000/1500/21**
Bus Admin, Chem, Communic, Ed, Nurs, Philo, Psych

WRIGHT STATE UNIVERSITY (OH) .... wright.edu **1050/1575/22**
Econ, Engine, Geol, Nurs

WYOMING, UNIVERSITY OF (WY) .... uwyo.edu **1080/1620/24**
Ag, Amer St, Anthro, Astro, Bio, Bot, Bus Admin, Chem, Econ, Ed, Engine, English, Geog, Geol, Nurs, Pharm, Pre-Law, Pre-Med/Pre-Dental, Psych, Zoo

XAVIER UNIVERSITY (OH) .... xu.edu **1160/1740/25**
Bio, Bus Admin, Chem, Classics, Communic, Econ, Hist, Philo, Physics, Psych, Reli Stu

XAVIER UNIVERSITY OF LOUISIANA (LA) .... xula.edu **1080/1620/23**
Bio, Bus Admin, Chem, Ed, Music, Pharm, Pre-Med/Pre-Dental, Psych

YALE UNIVERSITY (CT) .... yale.edu **1475/2210/32**
Amer St, Anthro, Arch, Art, Art Hist, Bio, Biochem, Classics, Drama, Econ, English, For Lang, Hist, Math, Music, Philo, Poli Sci, Pre-Law, Pre-Med/Pre-Dental, Psych, Reli Stu, Soc

YESHIVA UNIVERSITY (NY) .... yu.edu **1200/1800/26**
Bio, Bus Admin, Comp Sci, Hist, Physics, Poli Sci, Pre-Med/Pre-Dental, Psych

YORK COLLEGE (NE) .... york.edu **1050/1575/22**
Ed, Psych, Reli Stu

YORK COLLEGE OF PENNSYLVANIA (PA) .... ycp.edu **1090/1635/24**
Bus Admin, Communic, Ed, Nurs

YOUNGSTOWN STATE UNIVERSITY (OH) .... ysu.edu **1000/1500/21**
Art, Bus Admin

SECTION FOUR

APPENDICES

APPENDIX A
The 1050 Colleges Used In This Study

A
Abilene Christian University
Abilene, Texas 79699

Adelphi University
Garden City, NY 11530

Adrian College
Adrian, Michigan 49221

◆ **Agnes Scott College**
Decatur, Georgia 30030

Akron, University of
Akron, Ohio 44325

◆ **Alabama, University of**
Tuscaloosa, Alabama 35487

Alaska Pacific University
Anchorage, Alaska 99508

Alaska, University of
Anchorage, Alaska 99508

Alaska, University of
Fairbanks, Alaska 99775

Albany College of Pharmacy
Albany, New York 12208

Albertson College of Idaho
Caldwell, Idaho 83605

◆ **Albion College**
Albion, Michigan 49224

Albright College
Reading, Pennsylvania 19612

Alderson-Broaddus College
Phillipi, West Virginia 26416

◆ **Alfred University**
Alfred, New York 14802

◆ **Allegheny College**
Meadville, Pennsylvania 16335

◆ **Alma College**
Alma, Michigan 48801

Alverno College
Milwaukee, Wisconsin 53234

American Academy of Dramatic Arts
New York, New York 10016

American International College
Springfield, Massachusetts 01109

◆ **American University**
Washington, DC 20016

◆ **Amherst College**
Amherst, Massachusetts 01002

Anderson University
Anderson, Indiana 46012

Andrews University
Berrien Springs, Michigan 49104

Anna Maria College
Paxton, Massachusetts 01612

Appalachian State University
Boone, North Carolina 28608

Aquinas College
Grand Rapids, Michigan 49506

Arcadia University
Glenside, Pennsylvania 19038

◆ **Arizona, University of**
Tucson, Arizona 85721

◆ **Arizona State University**
Tempe, Arizona 85287

◆ **Arkansas, University of**
Fayetteville, Arkansas 72701

Art Center College of Design
Pasadena, California 91103

Art Institute of Chicago, School of the
Chicago, Illinois 60603

Arts, University of the
Philadelphia, Pennsylvania 19102

Asbury College
Wilmore, Kentucky 40390

Ashland University
Ashland, Ohio 44805

Assumption College
Worcester, Massachusetts 01609

◆ **Auburn University**
Auburn University, Alabama 36849

Augsburg College
Minneapolis, Minnesota 55454

Augusta State University
Augusta, Georgia 30964

◆ **Augustana College**
Rock Island, Illinois 61201

Augustana College
Sioux Falls, South Dakota 57197

◆ **Austin College**
Sherman, Texas 75091

Averett University
Danville, Virginia 24541

Avila University
Kansas City, Missouri 64145

◆ Phi Beta Kappa Schools   ∎ Predominantly African-American Institutions

Azusa Pacific University
Azusa, California 91702

B **Babson College**
Wellesley, Massachusetts 02157

Baker University
Baldwin City, Kansas 66006

Baldwin-Wallace College
Berea, Ohio 44017

Ball State University
Muncie, Indiana 47306

Bard College,
Annandale-on-Hudson, New York 12504

Barry University
Miami Shores, Florida 33161

◆ **Bates College**
Lewiston, Maine 04240

Bay Path College
Longmeadow, MA 01106

◆ **Baylor University**
Waco, Texas 76798

Belhaven College
Jackson, Mississippi 39202

Bellarmine University
Louisville, Kentucky 40205

Belmont Abbey College
Belmont, North Carolina 28012

Belmont University
Nashville, Tennessee 37212

◆ **Beloit College**
Beloit, Wisconsin 53511

Bemidji State University
Bemidji, Minnesota 56601

Benedictine College
Atchison, Kansas 66002

Benedictine University
Lisle, Illinois 60532

▮ **Bennett College**
Greensboro, North Carolina 27401

Bennington College
Bennington, Vermont 05201

Bentley College
Waltham, Massachusetts 02154

Berea College
Berea, Kentucky 40404

Berklee College of Music
Boston, Massachusetts 02215

Berry College
Rome, Georgia 30149

Bethany College
Lindsborg, Kansas 67456

Bethany College
Bethany, West Virginia 26032

Bethany College
North Newton, Kansas 67117

Bethel College
St. Paul, Minnesota 55112

Biola University
La Mirada, California 90639

◆ **Birmingham-Southern College**
Birmingham, Alabama 35254

Blackburn College
Carlinville, Illinois 62626

Bloomsburg University
Bloomsburg, Pennsylvania 17815

Bluffton College
Bluffton, Ohio 45817

Boise State University
Boise, Idaho 83725

Boston Architectural Center
Boston, Massachusetts 02115

◆ **Boston College**
Chestnut Hill, Massachusetts 02167

Boston Conservatory
Boston, Massachusetts 02215

◆ **Boston University**
Boston, Massachusetts 02215

◆ **Bowdoin College**
Brunswick, Maine 04011

◆ **Bowling Green State University**
Bowling Green, Ohio 43403

Bradley University
Peoria, Illinois 61625

◆ **Brandeis University**
Waltham, Massachusetts 02254

Brescia University
Owensboro, Kentucky 42301

Briar Cliff University
Sioux City, Iowa 51104

Bridgewater College
Bridgewater, Virginia 22812

Bridgewater State College
Bridgewater, Massachusetts 02325

Brigham Young University
Provo, Utah 84602

◆ Phi Beta Kappa Schools ▮ Predominantly African-American Institutions

◆ **Brown University**
Providence, Rhode Island 02912

Bryan College
Dayton, Tennessee 37321

Bryant University
Smithfield, Rhode Island 02917

Bryn Athyn College of the New Church
Bryn Athyn, Pennsylvania 19009

Bryn Mawr College
Bryn Mawr, Pennsylvania 19010

◆ **Bucknell University**
Lewisburg, Pennsylvania 17837

Buena Vista University
Storm Lake, Iowa 50588

Butler University
Indianapolis, Indiana 46208

C

Caldwell College
Caldwell, New Jersey 07006

California College of Arts and Crafts
San Francisco, California 94107

California Institute of the Arts
Valencia, California 91355

California Institute of Technology
Pasadena, California 91125

California, University of, at
◆ **Berkeley,** California 94720
◆ **Davis,** California 95616
◆ **Irvine,** California 92717
◆ **Los Angeles,** California 90024
◆ **Merced,** California 95344
◆ **Riverside,** California 92521
◆ **San Diego,** California 92093
◆ **Santa Barbara,** California 93106
◆ **Santa Cruz,** California 95064

California Lutheran University
Thousand Oaks, California 91360

California Maritime Academy
Vallejo, California 94590

California Polytechnic State University
Pomona, California 91768

California Polytechnic State University
San Luis Obispo, California 93407

California, State University of, at
Bakersfield, California 93311
Camarillo, California 93012
◆ **Chico,** California 95929
Dominguez Hills, Carson, California 90747
East Bay, California 94542
Fresno, California 93740
Fullerton, California 92834
Long Beach, California 90840

California, State University of, at (*Cont.*)
Los Angeles, California 90032
Monterey Bay, California 93955
Northridge, California 91330
Sacramento, California 95819
San Bernardino, California 92407
San Jose, California 95192
San Marcos, California 92096
Stanislaus, California 95382

Calvin College
Grand Rapids, Michigan 49456

Campbell University
Buies Creek, North Carolina 27506

Capital University
Columbus, Ohio 43209

◆ **Carleton College**
Northfield, Minnesota 55057

◆ **Carnegie Mellon University**
Pittsburgh, Pennsylvania 15213

Carroll College
Helena, Montana 59625

Carroll College
Waukesha, Wisconsin 53186

Carson-Newman College
Jefferson City, Tennessee 37760

Carthage College
Kenosha, Wisconsin 53140

◆ **Case Western Reserve University**
Cleveland, Ohio 44106

Catawba College
Salisbury, North Carolina 28144

Catholic University of America
Washington, DC 20064

Cedar Crest College
Allentown, Pennsylvania 18104

Cedarville University
Cedarville, Ohio 45314

Centenary College of Louisiana
Shreveport, Louisiana 71104

Central Arkansas, University of
Conway, Arkansas 72035

Central College
Pella, Iowa 50219

Central Connecticut State University
New Britain, Connecticut 06050

Central Florida, University of
Orlando, Florida 32816

Central Michigan University
Mount Pleasant, Michigan 48859

Central Missouri State University
Warrensburg, Missouri 64093

Central Oklahoma, University of
Edmond, Oklahoma 73034

Centre College
Danville, Kentucky 40422

Chaminade University
Honolulu, Hawaii 96816

Champlain College
Burlington, Vermont 05402

Chapman College
Orange, California 92866

Coastal Carolina University
Conway, South Carolina 29528

College of Charleston
Charleston, South Carolina 29424

Charleston Southern University
Charleston, South Carolina 29423

Charleston, University of
Charleston, West Virginia 25304

◆ **Chatham College**
Pittsburgh, Pennsylvania 15232

Chestnut Hill College
Philadelphia, Pennsylvania 19118

Cheyney University of Pennsylvania
Cheyney, Pennsylvania 19319

◆ **Chicago, University of**
Chicago, Illinois 60637

Chowan College
Murfreesboro, North Carolina 27855

Christian Brothers University
Memphis, Tennessee 38104

Christopher Newport University
Newport News, Virginia 23606

Christendom College
Front Royal, Virginia 22630

◆ **Cincinnati, University of**
Cincinnati, Ohio 45221

Citadel, The
Charleston, South Carolina 29409

◆ **Claremont McKenna College**
Claremont, California 91711

▌**Clark Atlanta University**
Atlanta, Georgia 30314

◆ **Clark University**
Worcester, Massachusetts 01610

Clarke College
Dubuque, Iowa 52001

Clarkson University
Potsdam, New York 13676

Clemson University
Clemson, South Carolina 29634

Cleveland Institute of Art
Cleveland, Ohio 44106

Cleveland Institute of Music
Cleveland, Ohio 44106

◆ **Coe College**
Cedar Rapids, Iowa 52402

Cogswell Polytechnic College
Sunnyvale, California 94089

Coker College
Hartsdale, South Carolina 29550

◆ **Colby College**
Waterville, Maine 04901

Colby-Sawyer College
New London, New Hampshire 03257

◆ **Colgate University**
Hamilton, New York 13346

◆ **Colorado College**
Colorado Springs, Colorado 80903

◆ **Colorado, University of**
Boulder, Colorado 80309

Colorado, University of
Colorado Springs, Colorado 80933

Colorado, University of
Denver, Colorado 80217

Colorado School of Mines
Golden, Colorado 80401

◆ **Colorado State University**
Fort Collins, Colorado 80523

Columbia College
Chicago, Illinois 60605

Columbia College
Columbia, Missouri 65216

Columbia College
Columbia, South Carolina 29203

◆ **Columbia University**
New York, New York 10027
 ◆ **Barnard College,** New York, NY 10027

Concordia University
Irvine, California 92612

Concordia College
Moorhead, Minnesota 56560

◆ Phi Beta Kappa Schools ▌ Predominantly African-American Institutions

Concordia University
Seward, Nebraska 68434

♦ **Connecticut, University of**
Storrs, Connecticut 06269

♦ **Connecticut College**
New London, Connecticut 06320

Converse College
Spartanburg, South Carolina 29302

Cooper Union College, The
New York, New York 10003

♦ **Cornell College**
Mount Vernon, Iowa 52314

♦ **Cornell University**
Ithaca, New York 14853

Cornish College of the Arts
Seattle, Washington 98102

Covenant College
Lookout Mountain, Georgia 30750

Creighton University
Omaha, Nebraska 68178

Culver-Stockton College
Canton, Missouri 63435

Cumberland College
Williamsburg, Kentucky 40769

Curtis Institute of Music
Philadelphia, Pennsylvania 19103

D **Daemen College**
Amherst, New York 14226

♦ **Dallas, University of**
Irving, Texas 75062

Dana College
Blair, Nebraska 68008

♦ **Dartmouth College**
Hanover, New Hampshire 03755

♦ **Davidson College**
Davidson, North Carolina 28036

Dayton, University of
Dayton, Ohio 45469

Delaware State University
Dover, Delaware 19901

♦ **Delaware, University of**
Newark, Delaware 19716

Delaware Valley College of Pennsylvania
Doylestown, Pennsylvania 18901

♦ **Denison University**
Granville, Ohio 43023

♦ **Denver, University of**
Denver, Colorado 80208

DePaul University
Chicago, Illinois 60604

♦ **DePauw University**
Greencastle, Indiana 46135

DeSales University
Center Valley, Pennsylvania 18034

Detroit Mercy, University of
Detroit, Michigan 48221

♦ **Dickinson College**
Carlisle, Pennsylvania 17013

▮ **Dillard University**
New Orleans, Louisiana 70122

Doane College
Crete, Nebraska 68333

Dominican University
River Forest, Illinois 60305

Dominican University of California
San Rafael, California 94901

Dordt College
Sioux Center, Iowa 51250

♦ **Drake University**
Des Moines, Iowa 50311

♦ **Drew University**
Madison, New Jersey 07940

Drexel University
Philadelphia, Pennsylvania 19104

Drury University
Springfield, Missouri 65802

Dubuque, University of
Dubuque, Iowa 52001

♦ **Duke University**
Durham, North Carolina 27706

Duquesne University
Pittsburgh, Pennsylvania 15282

D'Youville College
Buffalo, New York 14201

E ♦ **Earlham College**
Richmond, Indiana 47374

East Carolina University
Greenville, North Carolina 27858

East Central State University
Ada, Oklahoma 74820

East Stroudsburg University
East Stroudsburg, Pennsylvania 18301

East Tennessee State University
Johnson City, Tennessee 37614

Eastern College
St. Davids, Pennsylvania 19087

Eastern Connecticut State University
Willimantic, Connecticut 06226

Eastern Kentucky University
Richmond, Kentucky 40475

Eastern Illinois University
Charleston, Illinois 61920

Eastern Mennonite University
Harrisonburg, Virginia 22802

Eastern Michigan University
Ypsilanti, Michigan 48197

Eastern Nazarene College
Quincy, Massachusetts 02170

Eastern Oregon University
La Grande, Oregon 97850

Eastern Washington University
Cheney, Washington 99034

♦ **Eckerd College**
St. Petersburg, Florida 33733

Edgewood College
Madison, Wisconsin 53711

Edinboro University of Pennsylvania
Edinboro, Pennsylvania 16444

Elizabethtown College
Elizabethtown, Pennsylvania 17022

Elon University
Elon University, North Carolina 27244

Elmhurst College
Elmhurst, Illinois 60126

♦ **Elmira College**
Elmira, New York 14901

Elms College
Chicopee, Massachusetts 01013

Embry-Riddle Aeronautical University
Daytona Beach, Florida 32114

Emerson College
Boston, Massachusetts 02116

Emmanuel College
Boston, Massachusetts 02115

Emory and Henry College
Emory, Virginia 24327

♦ **Emory University**
Atlanta, Georgia 30322

Endicott College
Beverly, MA 01915

Erskine College
Due West, South Carolina 29639

Eureka College
Eureka, Illinois 61530

Evansville, University of
Evansville, Indiana 47722

F ♦ **Fairfield University**
Fairfield, Connecticut 06430

Fairleigh Dickinson University
Teaneck, New Jersey 07666

Fairmont State University
Fairmont, West Virginia 26554

Faulkner University
Montgomery, Alabama 36109

Ferris State University
Big Rapids, Michigan 49307

♦■ **Fisk University**
Nashville, Tennessee 37208

Fitchburg State College
Fitchburg, Massachusetts 01420

Five Towns College
Dix Hills, New York 11746

Flagler College
St. Augustine, Florida 32085

♦ **Florida, University of**
Gainesville, Florida 32611

♦ **Florida A&M University**
Tallahassee, FL 32307

Florida Atlantic University
Boca Raton, Florida 33431

Florida Gulf Coast University
Fort Myers, Georgia 33965

Florida Institute of Technology
Melbourne, Florida 32901

♦ **Florida International University**
Miami, Florida 33199

Florida Southern College
Lakeland, Florida 33801

♦ **Florida State University**
Tallahassee, Florida 32306

Fontbonne University
St. Louis, Missouri 63105

♦ **Fordham University**
Bronx, New York 10458

Fort Hays State University
Hays, Kansas 67601

Fort Lewis College
Durango, Colorado 81301

♦ Phi Beta Kappa Schools   ■ Predominantly African-American Institutions

Framingham State College
Framingham, Massachusetts 01701

Franciscan University of Steubenville
Steubenville, Ohio 43952

Franklin College
Franklin, Indiana 46131

◆ **Franklin & Marshall College**
Lancaster, Pennsylvania 17604

Freed-Hardeman University
Henderson, Tennessee 38340

Friends University
Wichita, Kansas 67213

Frostburg State University
Frostburg, Maryland 21532

◆ **Furman University**
Greenville, South Carolina 29613

G

Gannon University
Erie, Pennsylvania 16541

Gardner-Webb University
Boiling Springs, North Carolina 28017

Geneva College
Beaver Falls, Pennsylvania 15010

Georgetown College
Georgetown, Kentucky 40324

◆ **Georgetown University**
Washington, DC 20057

George Fox University
Newberg, Oregon 97132

George Mason University
Fairfax, Virginia 22030

◆ **George Washington University**
Washington, DC 20052

◆ **Georgia, University of**
Athens, Georgia 30602

Georgia Institute of Technology
Atlanta, Georgia 30332

Georgia Southern University
Statesboro, Georgia 30460

Georgia Southwestern University
Americus, Georgia 31704

Georgia State University
Atlanta, Georgia 30303

◆ **Gettysburg College**
Gettysburg, Pennsylvania 17325

Gonzaga University
Spokane, Washington 99258

Gordon College
Wenham, Massachusetts 01984

Goshen College
Goshen, Indiana 46526

◆ **Goucher College**
Towson, Maryland 21204

Graceland University
Lamoni, Iowa 50140

Grambling State University
Grambling, Louisiana 71245

Grand Valley State University
Allendale, Michigan 49401

Great Falls, University of
Great Falls, Montana 59405

Greensboro College
Greensboro, North Carolina 27401

◆ **Grinnell College**
Grinnell, Iowa 50112

Grove City College
Grove City, Pennsylvania 16127

Guilford College
Greensboro, North Carolina 27410

◆ **Gustavus Adolphus College**
St. Peter, Minnesota 56082

Gwynedd-Mercy College
Gwnedd Valley, Pennsylvania 19437

H ◆ **Hamilton College**
Clinton, New York 13323

◆ **Hamline University**
St. Paul, Minnesota 55104

◆ **Hampden-Sydney College**
Hampden-Sydney, Virginia 23943

◆ **Hampton University**
Hampton, Virginia 23668

Hannibal-La Grange College
Hannibal, Missouri 63401

Hanover College
Hanover, Indiana 47243

Harding University
Searcy, Arkansas 72149

Hardin-Simmons University
Abilene, Texas 79698

Hartford, University of
Hartford, Connecticut 06117

Hartwick College
Oneonta, New York 13820

◆ **Harvard University**
Cambridge, Massachusetts 02138

◆ Phi Beta Kappa Schools ∎ Predominantly African-American Institutions

Harvey Mudd College
Claremont, California 91711

Hastings College
Hastings, Nebraska 68901

◆ **Haverford College**
Haverford, Pennsylvania 19041

Hawaii Pacific University
Honolulu, Hawaii 96813

◆ **Hawaii, University of**
Manoa, Honolulu, Hawaii 96822

Heidelberg College
Tiffin, Ohio 44883

Henderson State University
Arkadelphia, Arkansas 71999

◆ **Hendrix College**
Conway, Arkansas 72032

High Point University
High Point, North Carolina 27262

Hillsdale College
Hillsdale, Michigan 49242

◆ **Hiram College**
Hiram, Ohio 44234

◆ **Hobart & William Smith Colleges**
Geneva, New York 14456

◆ **Hofstra University**
Hempstead, New York 11550

◆ **Hollins University**
Roanoke, Virginia 24020

◆ **Holy Cross, College of the**
Worcester, Massachusetts 01610

Holy Names University
Oakland, California 94619

Hood College
Frederick, Maryland 21701

◆ **Hope College**
Holland, Michigan 49423

Houghton College
Houghton, New York 14744

Houston Baptist University
Houston, Texas 77074

Houston, University of
Houston, Texas 77004

◆▮ **Howard University**
Washington, DC 20059

Humboldt State University
Arcata, California 95521

Huntingdon College
Montgomery, Alabama 36106

Huntington College
Huntington, Indiana 46750

Husson College
Bangor, Maine 04401

I ◆ **Idaho, University of**
Moscow, Idaho 83844

Idaho State University
Pocatello, Idaho 83209

Illinois, University of, at
◆ **Urbana-Champaign,** Illinois 61801
◆ **Chicago,** Illinois 60680

◆ **Illinois College**
Jacksonville, Illinois 62650

Illinois Institute of Technology
Chicago, Illinois 60616

Illinois State University
Normal, Illinois 61761

◆ **Illinois Wesleyan University**
Bloomington, Illinois 61702

Immaculata University
Immaculata, Pennsylvania 19345

Indiana State University
Terre Haute, Indiana 47809

◆ **Indiana University**
Bloomington, Indiana 47405

Indiana University of Pennsylvania
Indiana, Pennsylvania 15705

I.U. - P.U. - Indianapolis University
Indianapolis, Indiana 46202

Indiana University of Technology
Fort Wayne, Indiana 46803

Iona College
New Rochelle, New York 10801

◆ **Iowa, University of**
Iowa City, Iowa 52242

◆ **Iowa State University of Science & Technology**
Ames, Iowa 50011

Ithaca College
Ithaca, New York 14850

J **Jacksonville State University**
Jacksonville, Alabama 36265

Jacksonville University
Jacksonville, Florida 32211

James Madison University
Harrisonburg, Virginia 22807

Jamestown College
Jamestown, North Dakota 58405

John Brown University
Siloam Springs, Arkansas 72761

John Carroll University
Cleveland, Ohio 44118

◆ **Johns Hopkins University**
Baltimore, Maryland 21218

Johnson State College
Johnson, Vermont 05656

Johnson C. Smith University
Charlotte, North Carolina 28216

Judson College
Marion, Alabama 36756

Juilliard School
New York, New York 10023

Juniata College
Huntingdon, Pennsylvania 16652

K ◆ **Kalamazoo College**
Kalamazoo, Michigan 49006

Kansas City Art Institute
Kansas City, Missouri 64111

◆ **Kansas, University of**
Lawrence, Kansas 66045

◆ **Kansas State University**
Manhattan, Kansas 66506

Kean University of New Jersey
Union, New Jersey 07083

Keene State College
Keene, New Hampshire 03435

Kennesaw State College
Marietta, Georgia 30144

◆ **Kent State University**
Kent, Ohio 44242

◆ **Kentucky, University of**
Lexington, Kentucky 40506

Kentucky Wesleyan College
Owensboro, Kentucky 42301

◆ **Kenyon College**
Gambier, Ohio 43022

Kettering University
Flint, Michigan 48504

King College
Bristol, Tennessee 37620

King's College
Wilkes-Barre, Pennsylvania 18711

◆ **Knox College**
Galesburg, Illinois 61401

Kutztown University
Kutztown, Pennsylvania 19530

L ◆ **Lafayette College**
Easton, Pennsylvania 18042

◆ **Lake Forest College**
Lake Forest, Illinois 60045

Lamar University
Beaumont, Texas 77710

Lambuth University
Jackson, Tennessee 38301

LaSalle University
Philadelphia, Pennsylvania 19141

Lasell College
Newton, Massachusetts 02466

La Verne, University of
La Verne, California 91750

◆ **Lawrence University**
Appleton, Wisconsin 54912

Lebanon Valley College
Annville, Pennsylvania 17003

◆ **Lehigh University**
Bethlehem, Pennsylvania 18015

LeMoyne College
Syracuse, New York 13214

Lenoir Rhyne College
Hickory, North Carolina 28603

Lesley University
Cambridge, Massachusetts 02138

Letourneau College
Longview, Texas 75607

◆ **Lewis & Clark College**
Portland, Oregon 97219

Lewis-Clark State College
Lewiston, Idaho 83501

Liberty University
Lynchburg, Virginia 24502

Lindenwood University
St. Charles, Missouri 63301

Linfield College
McMinnville, Oregon 97128

Lipscomb University
Nashville, Tennessee 37204

Lock Haven University of Pennsylvania
Lock Haven, Pennsylvania 17745

Long Island University-Brooklyn
Brooklyn, New York 11201

◆ Phi Beta Kappa Schools   ∎ Predominantly African-American Institutions

Long Island University-C.W. Post
Brookville, New York 11548

Longwood University
Farmville, Virginia 23909

Loras College
Dubuque, Iowa 52001

Louisiana College
Pineville, Louisiana 71360

Louisiana-Lafayette, University of
Lafayette, Louisiana 70504

◆ **Louisiana State University**
Baton Rouge, Louisiana 70803

Louisville, University of
Louisville, Kentucky 40292

Lowell, University of
Lowell, Massachusetts 01854

◆ **Loyola College**
Baltimore, Maryland 21210

◆ **Loyola Marymount University**
Los Angeles, California 90045

◆ **Loyola University of Chicago**
Chicago, Illinois 60611

Loyola University
New Orleans, Louisiana 70118

◆ **Luther College**
Decorah, Iowa 52101

Lycoming College
Williamsport, Pennsylvania 17701

Lynchburg College
Lynchburg, Virginia 24501

Lyndon State College
Lyndonville, Vermont 05851

Lyon College
Batesville, Arkansas 72503

M ◆ **Macalester College**
St. Paul, Minnesota 55105

MacMurray College
Jacksonville, Illinois 62650

Maine, University of
Farmington, Maine 04938

◆ **Maine, University of**
Orono, Maine 04469

Malone College
Canton, Ohio 44709

Manchester College
North Manchester, Indiana 46962

◆ **Manhattan College**
Riverdale, New York 10471

Manhattan School of Music
New York, New York 10027

Manhattanville College
Purchase, New York 10577

Mannes School of Music
New York, New York 10024

Mansfield University of Pennsylvania
Mansfield, Pennsylvania 16933

◆ **Marietta College**
Marietta, Ohio 45750

Marist College
Poughkeepsie, NY 12601

◆ **Marquette University**
Milwaukee, Wisconsin 53201

Marshall University
Huntington, West Virginia 25755

◆ **Mary Baldwin College**
Staunton, Virginia 24401

▌ **Marygrove College**
Detroit, Michigan 48221

Maryland Institute-College of Art
Baltimore, Maryland 21217

◆ **Maryland, University of Baltimore County**
Baltimore, Maryland 21250

◆ **Maryland, University of**
College Park, Maryland 20742

Marymount Manhattan College
New York, New York 10021

Marymount University
Arlington, Virginia 22207

Maryville College
Maryville, Tennessee 37804

Maryville University-Saint Louis
St. Louis, Missouri 63141

◆ **Mary Washington, University of**
Fredericksburg, Virginia 22401

Marywood University
Scranton, Pennsylvania 18509

Massachusetts College of Art
Boston Massachusetts 02215

Massachusetts College of Liberal Arts
North Adams, Massachusetts 01247

Massachusetts College of Pharmacy
Boston, Massachusetts 02115

◆ **Massachusetts, University of**
Amherst, Massachusetts 01003

Massachusetts, University of
Boston, Massachusetts 02125

Massachusetts, University of
Lowell, Massachusetts 01854

Massachusetts, University of
North Dartmouth, Massachusetts 02747

◆ **Massachusetts Institute of Technology**
Cambridge, Massachusetts 02139

Massachusetts Maritime Academy
Buzzards Bay, Massachusetts 02532

Master's College, The
Santa Clarita, California 91321

McDaniel College
Westminster, Maryland 21157

◆ **McKendree College**
LeBaron, Illinois 62254

McMurry University
Abilene, Texas 79697

McPherson College
McPherson, Kansas 67460

Memphis College of Art
Memphis, Tennessee 38112

Memphis, University of
Memphis, Tennessee 38152

Mercer University
Macon, Georgia 31207

Mercy College
Dobbs Ferry, New York 10522

Mercyhurst College
Erie, Pennsylvania 16546

Meredith College
Raleigh, North Carolina 27607

Merrimack College
No. Andover, Massachusetts 01845

Messiah College
Grantham, Pennsylvania 17027

◆ **Miami University**
Oxford, Ohio 45056

◆ **Miami, University of**
Coral Gables, Florida 33124

◆ **Michigan, University of**
Ann Arbor, Michigan 48109

Michigan, University of
Dearborn, Michigan 48128

◆ **Michigan State University**
East Lansing, Michigan 48824

Michigan Technological University
Houghton, Michigan 49931

◆ **Middlebury College**
Middlebury, Vermont 05753

Middle Tennessee State University
Murfreesboro, Tennessee 37132

Midwestern State University
Wichita Falls, Texas 76308

Millersville University of Pennsylvania
Millersville, Pennsylvania 17551

Milligan College
Milligan College, Tennessee 37682

Millikin University
Decatur, Illinois 62522

◆ **Mills College**
Oakland, California 94613

◆ **Millsaps College**
Jackson, Mississippi 39210

Milwaukee School of Engineering
Milwaukee, Wisconsin 53201

Minnesota State University - Mankato
Mankato, Minnesota 56001

Minnesota State University - Moorhead
Moorhead, Minnesota 56563

Minnesota, University of
Duluth, Minnesota 55812

◆ **Minnesota, University of**
Minneapolis, Minnesota 55455

Minnesota, University of
Morris, Minnesota 56267

Misericordia, College
Dallas, Pennsylvania 18612

Mississippi College
Clinton, Mississippi 39058

Mississippi State University
Mississippi State, Mississippi 39762

◆ **Mississippi, University of**
University, Mississippi 38677

Mississippi University for Women
Columbus, Mississippi 39701

Missouri Baptist College
St. Louis, Missouri 63141

Missouri Southern State University
Joplin, Missouri 64801

◆ **Missouri, University of**
Columbia, Missouri 65211

Missouri, University of
Kansas City, Missouri 64110

Missouri, University of
Rolla, Missouri 65401

Missouri, University of
St. Louis, Missouri 63121

Mobile, University of
Mobile, Alabama 36663

Molloy College
Rockville Centre, New York 11571

Monmouth College
Monmouth, Illinois 61462

Monmouth University
West Long Branch, New Jersey 07764

Montana Tech. of the U. of Montana
Butte, Montana 59701

Montana, University of
Missoula, Montana 59812

Montana State University
Billings, Montana 59101

Montana State University
Bozeman, Montana 59717

Montevallo, University of
Montevallo, Alabama 35115

Montclair State College
Upper Montclair, New Jersey 07043

Montreat College
Montreat, North Carolina 28757

Montserrat College of Art
Beverly, Massachusetts 01915

Moore College of Art
Philadelphia, Pennsylvania 19103

Moravian College
Bethlehem, Pennsylvania 18018

◆▎**Morehouse College**
Atlanta, Georgia 30314

▎**Morgan State University**
Baltimore, Maryland 21257

Morningside College
Sioux City, Iowa 51106

◆ **Mount Holyoke College**
South Hadley, Massachusetts 01075

Mount Mercy College
Cedar Rapids, Iowa 52402

Mount St. Joseph, College of
Cincinnati, Ohio 45233

Mount St. Mary's College
Emmitsburg, Maryland 21727

Mount St. Mary's College
Los Angeles, California 90049

Mount St. Mary College
Newburgh, New York, 12550

Mount Union College
Alliance, Ohio 44601

◆ **Muhlenberg College**
Allentown, Pennsylvania 18104

Murray State University
Murray, Kentucky 42071

Museum of Fine Arts, School of the
Boston, Massachusetts 02115

Muskingum College
New Concord, Ohio 43762

N **Nazareth College of Rochester**
Rochester, New York 14618

Nebraska, University of
Kearney, Nebraska 68849

◆ **Nebraska, University of**
Lincoln, Nebraska 68588

Nebraska, University of
Omaha, Nebraska 68182

Nebraska Wesleyan University
Lincoln, Nebraska 68504

Nevada, University of, at
Las Vegas, Nevada 89154
Reno, Nevada 89557

New College of Florida
Sarasota, Florida 34243

New England Conservatory of Music
Boston, Massachusetts 02115

◆ **New Hampshire, University of**
Durham, New Hampshire 03824

New Jersey, College of
Ewing, New Jersey 08628

New Jersey Institute of Technology
Newark, New Jersey 07102

Newman University
Wichita, Kansas 67213

New Mexico Institute of Mining and Technology
Socorro, New Mexico 87801

New Mexico State University
Las Cruces, New Mexico 88003

◆ **New Mexico, University of**
Albuquerque, New Mexico 87131

◆ Phi Beta Kappa Schools ▎Predominantly African-American Institutions

New Orleans, University of
New Orleans, Louisiana 70148

**New School University -
Eugene Lang College**
New York, New York 10011

New York, City University of, at
- ♦ **Baruch College,** New York, NY 10010
- ♦ **Brooklyn College,** Brooklyn, NY 11210
- ♦ **City College,** New York, New York 10031
- ♦ **Herbert H. Lehman Coll.,** Bronx, NY 10468
- ♦ **Hunter College,** New York, NY 10021
- **John Jay College,** New York, NY 10019
- ♦ **Queens College,** Flushing, NY 11367

New York Institute of Techology
Old Westbury, New York 11568

New York, State University of, at
- ♦ **Albany,** New York 12222
- ♦ **Binghamton,** New York 13902
- **Brockport,** New York 14420
- ♦ **Buffalo,** New York 14214
- **Fredonia,** New York 14063
- ♦ **Geneseo,** New York 14454
- **Maritime College (TNS),** New York 10465
- **New Paltz,** New York 12561
- **Oneonta,** New York 13820
- **Oswego,** New York 13126
- **Plattsburgh,** New York 12901
- **Potsdam,** New York 13676
- **Purchase,** New York 10577
- ♦ **Stony Brook,** New York 11794

♦ **New York University**
New York, New York 10011

Niagara University
Niagara Falls, New York, 14109

Nichols State University
Thibodaux, Louisiana 70310

North Carolina School of the Arts
Winston-Salem, North Carolina 27117

North Carolina, University of, at
- **Asheville,** North Carolina 28804
- ♦ **Chapel Hill,** North Carolina 27599
- **Charlotte,** North Carolina 28223
- ♦ **Greensboro,** North Carolina 27412
- **Pembroke,** North Carolina 28372
- **Wilmington,** North Carolina 28403

♦ **North Carolina State University**
Raleigh, North Carolina 27695

North Central College
Naperville, Illinois 60566

North Dakota State University
Fargo, North Dakota 58105

♦ **North Dakota, University of**
Grand Forks, North Dakota 58202

North Florida, University of
Jacksonville, Florida 32216

North Georgia College
Dahlonega, Georgia 30597

North Texas, University of
Denton, Texas 76203

Northeastern Illinois University
Chicago, Illinois 60625

Northeastern State University
Tahlequah, Oklahoma 74464

Northeastern University
Boston, Massachusetts 02115

Northern Arizona University
Flagstaff, Arizona 86011

Northern Colorado University
Greeley, Colorado 80639

Northern Illinois University
DeKalb, Illinois 60115

Northern Iowa, University of
Cedar Falls, Iowa 50614

Northern Kentucky University
Highland Heights, Kentucky 41099

Northern Michigan University
Marquette, Michigan 49855

Northwestern College
Orange City, Iowa 51041

Northwestern College
St. Paul, Minnesota 55113

♦ **Northwestern University**
Evanston, Illinois 60204

Northwestern University of Louisiana
Natchitoches, Louisiana 71497

Northwood University
Midland, Michigan 48640

Norwich University
Northfield, Vermont 05663

♦ **Notre Dame, University of**
Notre Dame, Indiana 46556

Nova Southeastern University
Ft. Lauderdale, Florida 33314

Nyack College
Nyack, New York 10960

O **Oakland City University**
Oakland City, Indiana 47660

Oakland University
Rochester, Michigan 48309

♦ Phi Beta Kappa Schools   ▌ Predominantly African-American Institutions

◆ **Oberlin College**
Oberlin, Ohio 44074

◆ **Occidental College**
Los Angeles, California 90041

Oglethorpe University
Atlanta, Georgia 30319

Ohio Northern University
Ada, Ohio 45810

◆ **Ohio State University**
Columbus, Ohio 43210

◆ **Ohio University**
Athens, Ohio 45701

◆ **Ohio Wesleyan University**
Delaware, Ohio 43015

Oklahoma Baptist University
Shawnee, Oklahoma 74801

Oklahoma Christian University
Olahoma, City, Oklahoma 73136

Oklahoma City University
Oklahoma City, Oklahoma 73106

◆ **Oklahoma, University of**
Norman, Oklahoma 73069

Oklahoma State University
Stillwater, Oklahoma 74078

Old Dominion University
Norfolk, Virginia 23529

Olivet Nazarene University
Bourbonnais, Illinois 60914

Olin College of Engineering
Needham, Massachusetts 02492

Oral Roberts University
Tulsa, Oklahoma 74171

Oregon Institute of Technology
Klamath Falls, Oregon 97601

◆ **Oregon, University of**
Eugene, Oregon 97403

Oregon State University
Corvallis, Oregon 97331

Otis College of Art and Design
Los Angeles, California 90057

Otterbein College
Westerville, Ohio 43081

Ouachita Baptist University
Arkadelphia, Arkansas 71998

Ozarks, College of the
Point Lookout, Missouri 65726

P **Pace University**
New York, New York 10038

Pacific Lutheran University
Tacoma, Washington 98447

Pacific Oaks College
Pasadena, California 91103

Pacific, U. of the
Stockton, California 95211

Pacific University
Forest Grove, Oregon 97116

Palm Beach Atlantic College
West Palm Beach, Florida 33416

Parsons School of Design
New York, New York 10011

Pennsylvania Academy of the Fine Arts
Philadelphia, Pennsylvania 19102

Pennsylvania State University at Erie
Erie, Pennsylvania 16563

◆ **Pennsylvania State University**
University Park, Pennsylvania 16802

◆ **Pennsylvania, University of**
Philadelphia, Pennsylvania 19104

Pepperdine University
Malibu, California 90263

Philadelphia Biblical University
Langhorne, Pennsylvania 19047

Philadelphia University
Philadelphia, Pennsylvania 19144

Pine Manor College
Chestnut Hill, Massachusetts 02167

Pittsburg State University
Pittsburg, Kansas 66762

Pittsburgh, University of
Bradford, Pennsylvania 16701

Pittsburgh, University of
Greensburg, Pennsylvania 15601

Pittsburgh, University of
Johnstown, Pennsylvania 15904

◆ **Pittsburgh, University of**
Pittsburgh, Pennsylvania 15260

Pitzer College
Claremont, California 91711

Plymouth State College
Plymouth, New Hampshire 03264

Point Loma Nazarene University
San Diego, California 92106

Point Park College
Pittsburgh, Pennsylvania 15222

Polytechnic Institute of New York
Brooklyn, New York 11201

◆ **Pomona College**
Claremont, California 91711

Portland State University
Portland, Oregon 97200

Portland, University of
Portland, Oregon 97203

Pratt Institute
Brooklyn, New York 11205

Presbyterian College
Clinton, South Carolina 29325

Presentation College
Aberdeen, South Dakota 57401

◆ **Princeton University**
Princeton, New Jersey 08544

Principia College
Elsah, Illinois 62028

Providence College
Providence, Rhode Island 02918

Puerto Rico, University of
Cayey, Puerto Rico 00736

Puerto Rico, University of
Mayaguez, Puerto Rico 00680

Puerto Rico, University of
Rio Piedras, Puerto Rico 00931

◆ **Puget Sound, University of**
Tacoma, Washington 98416

◆ **Purdue University**
W. Lafayette, Indiana 47907

Q **Queens College**
Charlotte, North Carolina 28274

Quincy University
Quincy, Illinois 62301

Quinnipiac University
Hamden, Connecticut 06518

R **Radford University**
Radford, Virginia 24142

Ramapo College
Mahwah, New Jersey 07430

◆ **Randolph-Macon College**
Ashland, Virginia 23005

◆ **Randolph-Macon Woman's College**
Lynchburg, Virginia 24503

◆ **Redlands, University of**
Redlands, California 92373

◆ **Reed College**
Portland, Oregon 97202

Regis College
Weston, Massachusetts 02193

Regis University
Denver, Colorado 80221

Reinhardt College
Waleska, Georgia 30183

Rensselaer Polytechnic Institute
Troy, New York 12180

Rhode Island College
Providence, Rhode Island 02908

Rhode Island School of Design
Providence, Rhode Island 02903

◆ **Rhode Island, University of**
Kingston, Rhode Island 02881

◆ **Rhodes College**
Memphis, Tennessee 38112

◆ **Rice University**
Houston, Texas 77251

Richard Stockton College of New Jersey
Pomona, New Jersey 08240

◆ **Richmond, University of**
Richmond, Virginia 23173

Rider University
Lawrenceville, New Jersey 08648

◆ **Ripon College**
Ripon, Wisconsin 54971

◆ **Roanoke College**
Salem, Virginia 24153

Robert Morris College
Moon Township, Pennsylvania 15108

◆ **Rochester, University of**
Rochester, New York 14627

Rochester Institute of Technology
Rochester, New York 14623

◆ **Rockford College**
Rockford, Illinois 61108

Rockhurst University
Kansas City, Missouri 64110

Rocky Mountain College
Billings, Montana 59102

Roger Williams University
Bristol, Rhode Island 02809

Rollins College
Winter Park, Florida 32789

◆ Phi Beta Kappa Schools   ▌ Predominantly African-American Institutions

Roosevelt University
Chicago, Illinois 60605

Rose-Hulman Institute of Technology
Terre Haute, Indiana 47803

Rosemont College
Rosemont, Pennsylvania 19010

Rowan University
Mahwah, New Jersey 08028

◆ **Rutgers University**
New Brunswick, New Jersey 08854

Rutgers University
Camden, New Jersey 08101

S   **Sacred Heart University**
Fairfield, Connecticut 06432

Sage Colleges
Troy, New York 12180

Saginaw Valley State University
University Center, Michigan 48710

St. Ambrose University
Davenport, Iowa 52803

St. Andrews Presbyterian College
Laurinburg, North Carolina 28352

St. Anselm College
Manchester, New Hampshire 03102

St. Bonaventure University
St. Bonaventure, New York 14778

◆ **St. Catherine, College of**
St. Paul, Minnesota 55105

St. Cloud University
St. Cloud, Minnesota 56301

St. Edward's University
Austin, Texas 78704

St. Francis College
Brooklyn, New York 11201

St. John Fisher College
Rochester, New, York 14618

St. John's University
Jamaica, New York 11439

Saint John's University/College of Saint Benedict
Collegeville, Minnesota 56321

Saint Joseph College
W. Hartford, Connecticut 06117

St. Joseph's College
Rensselaer, Indiana 47978

St. Joseph's College
Standish, Maine 04084

St. Joseph's College
Patchogue, New York 11772

◆ **Saint Joseph's University**
Philadelphia, Pennsylvania 19131

◆ **St. Lawrence University**
Canton, New York 13617

St. Louis College of Pharmacy
St. Louis, Missouri 63110

◆ **Saint Louis University**
St. Louis, Missouri 63103

Saint Martin's College
Lacey, Washington 98503

Saint Mary, College of
Omaha, Nebraska 68124

Saint Mary's College
Notre Dame, Indiana 46556

Saint Mary's College of California
Moraga, California 94575

Saint Mary, University of
Leavenworth, Kansas 66048

◆ **St. Mary's College of Maryland**
St. Mary's City, Maryland 20686

St. Mary's University of Minnesota
Winona, Minnesota 55987

St. Mary's University
San Antonio, Texas 78228

◆ **Saint Michael's College**
Colchester, Vermont 05439

St. Norbert College
DePere, Wisconsin 54115

◆ **St. Olaf College**
Northfield, Minnesota 55057

St. Peter's College
Jersey City, New Jersey 07306

Saint Rose, College of
Albany, New York 12203

St. Scholastica, College of
Duluth, Minnesota 55811

St. Thomas Aquinas College
Sparkhill, New York 10976

Saint Thomas, University of
St. Paul, Minnesota 55105

St. Thomas, University of
Houston, Texas 77006

St. Vincent College
Latrobe, Pennsylvania 15650

◆ Phi Beta Kappa Schools   ▮ Predominantly African-American Institutions

Salem College
Winston-Salem, North Carolina 27108

Salem State College
Salem, Massachusetts 01970

Salisbury University
Salisbury, Maryland 21801

Samford University
Birmingham, Alabama 35229

◆ **San Diego State University**
San Diego, California 92182

◆ **San Diego, University of**
San Diego, California 92110

San Francisco Art Institute
San Francisco, California 94133

San Francisco Conservatory of Music
San Francisco, California 94122

San Francisco, University of
San Francisco, California 94117

◆ **San Francisco State University**
San Francisco, California 94132

San Jose State University
San Jose, California 95192

◆ **Santa Clara University**
Santa Clara, California 95053

Santa Fe, College of
Santa Fe, New Mexico 87501

Sarah Lawrence College
Bronxville, New York 10708

School of the Art Institute of Chicago
Chicago, Illinois 60603

Schreiner University
Kerrville, Texas 78028

Sciences in Philadelphia, University of the
Philadelphia, Pennsylvania 19104

Scranton, University of
Scranton, Pennsylvania 18510

◆ **Scripps College**
Claremont, California 91711

Seattle Pacific University
Seattle, Washington 98119

Seattle University
Seattle, Washington 98122

Seton Hall University
South Orange, New Jersey 07079

Seton Hill College
Greensburg, Pennsylvania 15601

∎ **Shaw University**
Raleigh, North Carolina 27601

Shawnee State University
Portsmouth, Ohio 45662

Shenandoah University
Winchester, Virginia 22601

Shepherd College
Shepherdstown, West Virginia 25443

Shippensburg University
Shippensburg, Pennsylvania 17257

Shorter College
Rome, Georgia 30165

Siena College
Loudonville, New York 12211

Siena Heights University
Adrian, Michigan 49221

Silver Lake College
Mantiowoc, Wisconsin 54220

Simmons College
Boston, Massachusetts 02115

Simpson College
Indianola, Iowa 50125

◆ **Skidmore College**
Saratoga Springs, New York 12866

Slippery Rock University
Slippery Rock, Pennsylvania 16057

◆ **Smith College**
Northampton, Massachusetts 01063

◆ **South, University of the**
Sewanee, Tennessee 37383

South Alabama, University of
Mobile, Alabama 36688

◆ **South Carolina, University of**
Columbia, South Carolina 29208

◆ **South Dakota, University of**
Vermillion, South Dakota 57069

South Dakota School of Mines and Technology
Rapid City, South Dakota 57701

South Dakota State University
Brookings, South Dakota 57006

South Florida, University of
Tampa, Florida 33620

Southeast Missouri State University
Cape Girardeau, Missouri 63701

Southeastern Louisiana State
Hammond, Louisiana 70402

◆ Phi Beta Kappa Schools   ∎ Predominantly African-American Institutions

Southeastern Oklahoma State University
Durant, Oklahoma 74701

◆ **Southern California, University of**
Los Angeles, California 90089

Southern Connecticut State University
New Haven, Connecticut 06515

Southern Illinois University
Carbondale, Illinois 62901

Southern Illinois University
Edwardsville, Illinois 62026

Southern Maine, University of
Portland, Maine 04103

◆ **Southern Methodist University**
Dallas, Texas 75275

Southern Mississippi, University of
Hattiesburg, Mississippi 39406

Southern Nazarene University
Bethany, Oklahoma 73008

Southern Oregon University
Ashland, Oregon 97520

Southern Polytechnic University
Marietta, Georgia 30060

Southern Utah University
Cedar City, Utah 84720

Southwest Baptist University
Bolivar, Missouri 65613

Southwest Missouri State University
Springfield, Missouri 65804

Southwest Texas State University
San Marcos, Texas 78666

Southwestern College
Winfield, Kansas 67156

◆ **Southwestern University**
Georgetown, Texas 78627

◆∎ **Spelman College**
Atlanta, Georgia 30314

Spring Hill College
Mobile, Alabama 36608

◆ **Stanford University**
Stanford, California 94305

Stephen F. Austin State University
Nagogdoches, Texas 75962

Sterling College
Sterling, Kansas 67579

◆ **Stetson University**
Deland, Florida 32720

Stevens Institute of Technology
Hoboken, New Jersey 07030

Stonehill College
North Easton, Massachusetts 02357

Suffolk University
Boston, Massachusetts 02108

Susquehanna University
Selinsgrove, Pennsylvania 17870

◆ **Swarthmore College**
Swarthmore, Pennsylvania 19081

◆ **Sweet Briar College**
Sweet Briar, Virginia 24595

◆ **Syracuse University**
Syracuse, New York 13210

T **Tabor College**
Hillsboro, Kansas 67063

Tampa, University of
Tampa, Florida 33606

Tarleton State University
Stephenville, Texas 76402

Taylor University
Upland, Indiana 46989

◆ **Temple University**
Philadelphia, Pennsylvania 19122

Tennessee Tech University
Cookeville, Tennessee 38505

◆ **Tennessee, University of**
Knoxville, Tennessee 37996

Texas, University of, at
  Arlington, Texas 76019
◆ **Austin,** Texas 78712
  Dallas, Richardson, Texas 75083
  Health Science Center
    San Antonio, Texas 78284
  San Antonio, Texas 78249
  Tyler, Texas 75799

◆ **Texas A & M**
College Station, Texas 77843

Texas A & M - Corpus Christi
Corpus Christi, Texas 78412

Texas A & M - Galveston
Galveston, Texas 77553

Texas A & M - Kingsville
Kingsville, Texas 78363

◆ **Texas Christian University**
Fort Worth, Texas 76129

Texas Lutheran University
Seguin, Texas 78155

Texas Tech University
Lubbock, Texas 79409

Texas Wesleyan University
Fort Worth, Texas 76105

Thomas College
Waterville, Maine 04901

Thomas More College
Crestview Hills, Kentucky 41017

Toledo, University of
Toledo, Ohio 43606

▌ **Tougaloo College**
Tougaloo, Mississippi 39174

Towson University
Towson, Maryland 21204

Transylvania University
Lexington, Kentucky 40508

◆ **Trinity College**
Hartford, Connecticut 06106

◆ **Trinity College**
Washington, DC 20017

◆ **Trinity University**
San Antonio, Texas 78212

Tri-State University
Angola, Indiana 46703

◆ **Truman State University**
Kirksville, Missouri 63501

◆ **Tufts University**
Medford, Massachusetts 02155

◆ **Tulane University**
New Orleans, Louisiana 70118

◆ **Tulsa, University of**
Tulsa, Oklahoma 74104

▌ **Tuskegee University**
Tuskegee, Alabama 36088

U   **Union College**
Lincoln, Nebraska 68506

◆ **Union College**
Schenectady, New York 12308

Union University
Jackson, Tennessee 38305

U.S. Air Force Academy
Colorado Springs, Colorado 80840

U.S. Coast Guard Academy
New London, Connecticut 06320

U.S. Military Academy
West Point, New York 10996

U.S. Naval Academy
Annapolis, Maryland 21402

◆ **Ursinus College**
Collegeville, Pennsylvania 19426

◆ **Utah, University of**
Salt Lake City, Utah 84112

Utah State University
Logan, Utah 84322

Utica College
Utica, New York 13502

V ◆ **Valparaiso University**
Valparaiso, Indiana 46383

◆ **Vanderbilt University**
Nashville, Tennessee 37240

◆ **Vassar College**
Poughkeepsie, New York 12601

◆ **Vermont, University of**
Burlington, Vermont 05401

Villa Julie College
Stevenson, Maryland 21153

◆ **Villanova University**
Villanova, Pennsylvania 19085

◆ **Virginia, University of**
Charlottesville, Virginia 22904

Virginia Commonwealth University
Richmond, Virginia 23284

Virginia Military Institute
Lexington, Virginia 24450

◆ **Virginia Polytechnic Institute**
Blacksburg, Virginia 24061

Virginia Wesleyan College
Norfolk, Virginia 23502

Visual Arts, School of
New York, New York 10010

Viterbo University
La Crosse, Wisconsin 54601

W ◆ **Wabash College**
Crawfordsville, Indiana 47933

Wagner College
Staten Island, New York 10301

◆ **Wake Forest University**
Winston-Salem, North Carolina 27109

Walla Walla College
College Place, Washington 99324

Walsh University
North Canton, Ohio, 44720

Warren Wilson College
Asheville, North Carolina 28815

◆ Phi Beta Kappa Schools   ▌ Predominantly African-American Institutions

Wartburg College
Waverly, Iowa 50677

Washburn University
Topeka, Kansas 66621

Washington College
Chestertown, Maryland 21620

◆ **Washington & Jefferson College**
Washington, Pennsylvania 15301

◆ **Washington & Lee University**
Lexington, Virginia 24450

◆ **Washington University in St. Louis**
St. Louis, Missouri 63130

◆ **Washington, University of**
Seattle, Washington 98195

◆ **Washington State University**
Pullman, Washington 99164

◆ **Wayne State College**
Wayne, Nebraska 68787

Wayne State University
Detroit, Michigan 48202

Waynesburg College
Waynesburg, Pennsylvania 15370

Weber State University
Ogden, Utah 84408

Webster University
St. Louis, Missouri 63119

◆ **Wellesley College**
Wellesley, Massachusetts 02481

◆ **Wells College**
Aurora, New York 13026

Wesleyan College
Macon, Georgia 31210

◆ **Wesleyan University**
Middletown, Connecticut 06457

West Chester University
West Chester, Pennsylvania 19383

West Florida, University of
Pensacola, FL 32514

◆ **West Virginia University**
Morgantown, West Virginia 26506

West Virginia Wesleyan College
Buckhannon, West Virginia 26201

Western Carolina University
Cullowhee, North Carolina 28723

Western Connecticut State University
Danbury, Connecticut 06810

Western Illinois University
Marcomb, Illinois 61455

Western Kentucky University
Bowling Green, Kentucky 42101

◆ **Western Michigan University**
Kalamazoo, Michigan 49008

Western New England College
Springfield, Massachusetts 01119

Western State College of Colorado
Gunnison, Colorado 81231

Western Washington University
Bellingham, Washington 98225

Westfield State College
Westfield, Massachusetts 01086

Westminster College
Fulton, Missouri 65251

Westminster College
Wilmington, Pennsylvania 16172

Westminster College
Salt Lake City, Utah 84105

Westmont College
Santa Barbara, California 93108

Wheaton College
Wheaton, Illinois 60187

◆ **Wheaton College**
Norton, Massachusetts 02766

Wheeling Jesuit University
Wheeling, West Virginia 26003

Wheelock College
Boston, Massachusetts 02215

◆ **Whitman College**
Walla Walla, Washington 99362

Whittier College
Whittier, California 90608

Whitworth College
Spokane, Washington 99251

Wichita State University
Wichita, Kansas 67260

Widener University
Chester, Pennsylvania 19013

▮ **Wilberforce University**
Wilberforce, Ohio 45384

Wilkes University
Wilkes-Barre, Pennsylvania 18766

◆ **Willamette University**
Salem, Oregon 97301

William Jewell College
Liberty, Missouri 64068

◆ Phi Beta Kappa Schools   ▮ Predominantly African-American Institutions

◆ **William & Mary, College of**
Williamsburg, Virginia 23187

William Paterson University
Wayne, New Jersey 07470

◆ **Williams College**
Williamstown, Massachusetts 01267

Wilmington College
Wilmington, Ohio 45177

◆ **Wilson College**
Chambersburg, Pennsylvania 17201

Wingate University
Wingate, North Carolina 28174

Winona State University
Winona, Minnesota 55987

Winthrop University
Rock Hill, South Carolina 29733

Wisconsin Lutheran College
Milwaukee, Wisconsin 53226

◆ **Wisconsin, University of, at**
   Eau Claire, Wisconsin 54701
   Green Bay, Wisconsin 54311
   LaCrosse, Wisconsin 54601
 ◆ **Madison,** Wisconsin 53706
 ◆ **Milwaukee,** Wisconsin 53201
   Platteville, Wisconsin 53818
   Stevens Point, Wisconsin 54481
   Stout, Menomonie, Wisconsin 54751

◆ **Wittenberg University**
Springfield, Ohio 45501

◆ **Wofford College**
Spartanburg, South Carolina 29303

Woodbury University
Burbank, California 91510

◆ **Wooster, College of**
Wooster, Ohio 44691

Worcester Polytechnic Institute
Worcester, Massachusetts 01609

Worcester State College
Worcester, Massachusetts 01602

Wright State University
Dayton, Ohio 45435

◆ **Wyoming, University of**
Laramie, Wyoming 82071

X **Xavier University**
Cincinnati, Ohio 45207

▮ **Xavier University of Louisiana**
New Orleans, Louisiana 70125

Y ◆ **Yale University**
New Haven, Connecticut 06520

✡ **Yeshiva University**
New York, New York 10033

York College
York, Nebraska 68467

York College of Pennsylvania
York, Pennsylvania 17403

Youngstown State University
Youngstown, Ohio 44555

APPENDIX B
The Miscellaneous Majors Colleges Used In This Study

Aeronautics, College of
Flushing, NY 11369

Andrews University
Berrien Springs, MI 49104

Antioch College
Yellow Springs, OH 45387

Atlantic, College of the
Bar Harbor, ME 04609

Aurora University
Aurora, Il 60506

Bellevue University
Bellevue, NE 68005

Black Hills State University
Spearfish, SD 57799

Bradford College
Haverhill, MA 01835

Brooks Institute of Photography
Santa Barbara, CA 93108

Cabrini College
Radnor, PA 19087

Carlow College
Pittsburgh, PA 15213

Central Oklahoma University
Edmond, OK 73034

■ **Central State University**
Wilberforce, OH 45384

Centenary College
Hackettstown, NJ 07840

Chadron State University
Chadron, Nebraska 69337

Cincinnati College of Mortuary Science
Cincinnati, OH 45224

Clarion University of Pennsylvania
Clarion, PA 16214

Cleveland State University
Cleveland, OH 44115

Columbia College - Hollywood
Tarzana, CA 91356

Columbus College of Art & Design
Columbus, OH 43215

Cortland State College
Cortland, NY 13045

Curry College
Milton, MA 02186

Daniel Webster College
Nashua, NH 03063

David Lipscomb University
Nashville TN 37204

Davis & Elkins College
Elkins, WV 26241

Deep Springs College
Deep Springs Via Dyer, NV 89010

Defiance College, The
Defiance, OH 43512

Eastern Montana College
Billings, MT 59101

Eastern New Mexico University
Portales, NM 88130

**Eugene Lang College
(New School Social Research)**
New York, NY 11743

Fashion Institute of Technology
New York, NY 10001

Findlay, University of
Findlay, OH 45840

Hampshire College
Amherst, MA 01002

Holy Family College
Philadelphia, PA 19114

Kendall College of Art and Design
Grand Rapids, MI 49503

Lake Erie College
Painesville, OH 44077

Landmark College
Putney, VT 05346

Langston University
Langston, OK 73050

Lees-McRae College
Banner Elk, NC 28604

Loma Linda University
Loma Linda, CA 92350

Lourdes College
Sylvania, OH 43560

Madonna University
Livonia, MI 48150

Maine Maritime
Castine, Maine 04420

Maine, University of
Machias, Maine 04654

Marian College of Fond du Lac
Fond du Lac, WI 54935

APPENDIX B (Continued)

The Miscellaneous Majors Colleges Used In This Study

Mesa State College
Grand Junction, CO 81502

Metropolitan State College
Denver, CO 80204

Midwestern State University
Wichita Falls, TX 76308

Mitchell College
New London, CT 06320

Mount Ida College
Newton Centre, Massachusetts 02459

Mt. St. Claire
Clinton, IA 52732

Neumann College
Aston, PA 19014

University of New England
Biddeford, ME 04005

New Haven, University of
New Haven, CT 06516

New School for Social Research
New York, NY 11743

New York School of Interior Design
New York, NY 10021

North Carolina Wesleyan College
Rocky Mount, NC 27804

Northeastern Louisiana University
Monroe, LA 71209

Northwestern Oklahoma State University
Alva, OK 73717

Park University
Cahokia, IL 62206

Pfeiffer College
Misenheimer, NC 28109

Prescott College
Prescott, AZ 86301

Ringling School of Art & Design
Sarasota, FL 34234

St. Elizabeth, College of
Convent Station, NJ 07960

Saint John's College
Annapolis, MD 21404

Saint Leo College
Saint Leo, FL 33574

Saint Thomas University
Miami, FL 33054

Salem International University
Salem, WV 26426

Salve Regina-The Newport College
Newport, RI 02840

Sam Houston State University
Huntsville, TX 77341

Science and Arts of Oklahoma
Chickasha, Oklahoma 73018

Simon's Rock College of Bard
Great Barrington, MA 01230

Southern Illinois, U. of
Edwardsville, IL 62026

Southern New Hampshire, University of
Manchester, NH 03106

Spring Arbor College
Spring Arbor, MI 49283

SUNY-Farmingdale
Farmingdale, NY 11735

■ **Texas Southern University**
Houston, TX 77004

Texas Woman's University
Denton, TX 76204

Thomas Aquinas College
Santa Paula, CA 93060

Tusculum College
Greenville, TN 37743

United States Merchant Marine Academy
Kings Point, NY 11024

Unity College
Unity, ME 04988

Virginia Intermont College
Bristol, VA 24201

Webb Institute
Glen Cove, NY 11542

APPENDIX C

Single Sex Colleges Included In This Study

WOMEN'S COLLEGES

Agnes Scott College (GA)
Alverno (WI)
Bay Path College (MA)
Bennett College (NC)
Bryn Mawr College (PA)
Cedar Crest College (PA)
Chatham College (PA)
Converse College(SC)
Hollins College (VA)
Judson College (AL)
Mary Baldwin College (VA)
Meredith College (NC)
Mills College (CA)

Mount Holyoke College (MA)
Pine Manor College (MA)
Randolph-Macon Woman's Coll. (VA)
Regis (MA)
Rosemont College (PA)
St. Catherine, College of (MN)
Saint Joseph's (CT)
Saint Mary's College (IN)
Salem College (NC)
Scripps College (CA)
Seton Hill (PA)
Simmons College (MA)
Smith College (MA)

Spelman College (GA)
Sweet Briar College (VA)
Texas Woman's College
Trinity College (DC)
Wellesley College (MA)
Wesleyan College (GA)

MEN'S COLLEGES

Hampden-Sydney College (VA)
Morehouse College (GA)
Wabash College (IN)

APPENDIX D

Anyone who has been touched by the problem of alcohol or substance abuse, or who has worked with those struggling in recovery, knows that higher education will increasingly have to meet the needs of these persons. Several colleges are trying to address the needs of these students, and The Wellness Institute at Ball State has published a list of wellness dorms. Unfortunately, the grant for this no longer exists, but Ball State in Muncie, Indiana has done a fine job with young people in this area. You might call them at 765-285-8259.

Respectfully submitted,
Joseph W. Streit
Long-time Secondary School Counselor in New Jersey

APPENDIX E

A Simplified Timetable and Checklist for Seniors Planning on College*

SEPTEMBER - OCTOBER	Write for college catalogs, applications, financial aid information and pick up a financial aid booklet, continuing from your junior year.
SEPTEMBER-OCTOBER	Inquire at your high school Guidance Office about upcoming college nights.
SEPTEMBER-NOVEMBER	Continue campus visits as senior year academic commitments permit.
SEPTEMBER	Deadline for mailing in the late October or early November National College Exam Forms.
OCTOBER	Think about which two teachers you will ask to write college recommendations for you.
LATE OCTOBER	Deadline for mailing in the December National College Exam Forms.
NOVEMBER	Prepare a final list of colleges. Talk to your counselor about need-based funds. And look into merit-based money awarded by the colleges themselves.
	Talk to your counselor and/or a favorite teacher - show them your completed college essay, if your colleges require one.
NOVEMBER 1-15	Many early applications due.
NOVEMBER OR DECEMBER	Attend, with your parents, a local financial aid night given by an area high school.
NOVEMBER - DECEMBER	Apply to colleges. But always check deadlines. Some may be earlier.
DECEMBER 1	ROTC Scholarship applications to be in.
EARLY DECEMBER	Last call for mailing in the National College Exam Forms (SAT/ACT).
DECEMBER 15	Profile of Financial Aid Form (Step 1) due to College Scholarship Service (CSS).
JANUARY	Fill out the Financial Aid Form (FAF/FAFSA/PROFILE) or Family Financial Statement. Your counselor has it. This form will probably help you get a good deal of your total scholarships, jobs, and loans. It is the big one.
JANUARY - FEBRUARY	Send mid-year reports to colleges.
FEBRUARY 1	Profile application (Step 2) to College Scholarship Service (CSS).
MARCH	Local scholarship forms available in the guidance office.
EARLY APRIL	All colleges will notify you by this time if they will accept you or not. The more competitive colleges usually deliberate longer and many of these top schools wait until the first week of April to notify you.
MID-APRIL	If unhappy with the financial aid package at any of the colleges where you have been accepted, call that office and discuss it.
LATE APRIL	Send deposit to selected college.
MAY 1	Inform all colleges which accepted you whether or not you plan to attend.
MAY 1	Notify Guidance Office of your choice of college.
MAY - JUNE	Apply for summer jobs so that you can meet summer earnings expectations.
	Don't forget to graduate from high school!
SUMMER	Attend college orientation.
LATE SUMMER	Write Thank You notes to organizations that awarded you money.

*NOTE: Before your senior year, prepare preliminary list of colleges you're interested in and those you would like to visit. Spring visits in the junior year are advised.

APPENDIX F

The Get-Going Form

A simple, useful form to use with the college-bound to get them started applying to colleges.
The student and/or counselor and/or parent should fill in four colleges below,
complete with address and zip codes.

Dear Student:

Within the next two weeks, please write to the Director of Admissions at the schools listed below, requesting information. A sample letter is included at the bottom of the page.

1. _____
   _____
   _____

2. _____
   _____
   _____

3. _____
   _____
   _____

4. _____
   _____
   _____

SAMPLE LETTER

Date

Director of Admissions
Name of College
Address of College and Zip Code

Dear Director:

   I am a student of Easthampton High School in Easthampton, Massachusetts and expect to graduate in June, 2007.

   I am interested in your school and would appreciate your sending me an application for admission and information concerning your financial aid program, and your _____ program of studies. Thank you.

   Very truly yours,

Your signature
Your Name
Your Address and Zip Code

COUNSELOR'S NOTES

ABOUT THE AUTHOR

Fred Rugg

Raised by an older sister, FRED RUGG was one of a handful of "Huckleberry Finn" cases that the top universities accepted in the 1960's. He is a writer, speaker, workshop presenter, and author. Unlike virtually all other college guidebook people, Rugg is one of the true professionals, having directed secondary college counseling programs for 20 years in all types of communities. A 1967 Applied Math graduate from Brown, Rugg is the holder of advanced degrees in secondary school guidance and administration. Early in his career he was employed as a statistician for two New England companies and worked his way through Ivy League Brown - the only member of his class to enter public school teaching. Offering dozens of workshops yearly from coast to coast, Fred is an often animated, charismatic and humorous speaker, and is the only one giving monthly seminars who draws a crowd. In addition, he is a consultant to dozens of secondary schools and his evening speaking engagements for parents and students are popular and fun. He has lived and worked just about everywhere in America, has been married for over 38 years, and has two daughters. Beginning with his first volunteer assignment (Brown Youth Guidance), Rugg has been a perennial volunteer, and he's taught courses at four colleges. A native of New England, he has been based in Colorado and Florida, and now resides in California. As always, he is totally independent of the colleges.

PARENTS

Do you have a few questions on the colleges that you'd like to pose to Fred Rugg?
For $100.⁰⁰, you can talk to him for 30 minutes. Master and Visa Cards accepted.

FROM RUGG'S RECOMMENDATIONS...

INFORMATION THAT IS TO THE POINT, THAT YOU CAN USE IMMEDIATELY

Saving the college counselor enormous time with lists and answers found nowhere else - presented from the secondary school point of view!

FROM RUGG, YOU ALWAYS GET A NEW SLANT ON THE COLLEGES

---

1. THE NEW BOOK: *RUGG'S RECOMMENDATIONS ON THE COLLEGES 23rd Ed.*

Locating Quality Undergraduate Colleges For Counselors, Parents & Students.
ISBN #1-883062-63-2 • LC89-062896 • $24.95 • © 2006 by Frederick E. Rugg

★ Over 1000 Entry Changes in the New BLUE Book ★

Rugg's Recommendations on the Colleges recommends quality departments at quality colleges. It is the primary brainstorming source for secondary public school counselors in creating a student's initial college list. Two new majors have been added and there are wholesale changes on over 30 others. Rugg's 23rd edition is available listing 10,000 quality departments at 1060 quality colleges. The guidebook has been designated nationally as "a revered staple, the book parents and students must start with" in the search for a college to attend. The 23rd edition is the accumulation of 35 years of work in the undergraduate college admissions process, and as always, ***Rugg's*** is independent of the colleges. There are over 1000 entry changes since the 22nd edition, 110 majors, 150 recommended departments per major.

"A Revered Staple."
—West Coast Library Reviewer

"Thank you for delivering such an incredibly useful tool for our students."
—Mrs. Lynn Reed
Niagara-Wheatfield H.S. (NY)

"A gem."
—College Bound, Evanston, Illinois

"It took four other books to tell us what your book provided!"
—A parent

---

2. THE SPECIAL REPORT: *TWENTY MORE TIPS ON THE COLLEGES, Revised*

Twenty new behind the scenes tips. Ideal for counselors, parents, and students. 12th Edition.
ISBN #1-883062-64-0• $8.95 • © 2006

Brutally honest information about colleges and the application process. This Special Report, ***Twenty More Tips on the Colleges,*** offers insights into assessing a college or university from the first "hello." Author Rugg succinctly presents 20 key tips to assist counselors, parents and students in selecting the best college for a student. Rugg honestly assesses the value of several college rating and reference books. Tips include colleges with high success rates for medical school acceptance, and what to consider before deciding to attend a military school. Overlooked state institutions, as well as other important and helpful comments, are included. The college search and selection process is incomplete without reading the valuable information contained within this Special Report.

"I have known Fred Rugg for over thirty years, since we were on the staff together at Bristol (RI) High School. Fred has developed an uncanny insight and he is able to ask the right questions of both student and admission officer. Always up-to-date; never disappointing. Read his material; attend the seminars. They are great!"
—Robert Jeffrey, Independent Consultant
Orlando, FL

"I have used your information for years. It is a wonderful resource."
—Harriet Gershman, Academic
Counseling Services, Evanston, IL

---

3. FORTY TIPS ON THE COLLEGES: THE REVISED SPECIAL REPORT 12th edition

For all college bound students, parents, and their counselors. 20 pages. Over 32 college entry changes for 2006.
ISBN # 1-883062-65-9 • $9.95 (money back guarantee) • Revised 2006

Get the "insider's" advice on college admissions. In ***Forty Tips on the Colleges,*** author Rugg shares with the reader 40 key tips on the college admissions process. Rugg spent in excess of 3000 hours visiting with over 8000 secondary school counselors in 47 states, to compile the information contained in this transcript. These insightful suggestions provide the reader with some of the unwritten do's and don'ts in the college admissions process. Rugg presents his 40 tips, accompanied by his personal observations of the campuses, with honesty and a sense of humor. ***Forty Tips on the Colleges*** offers straight talk about selecting a college and gaining admission. The special report contains helpful advice for the student, parent and school counselor alike. Topics include previously unpublished tips on which colleges really care about their students; colleges with good learning disabilities programs; and how to choose a college where the student "fits in." The tips also contain helpful information concerning financial aid, college applications and SAT/ACT scores. Throughout this transcript, Rugg cites several helpful reference books. This **must read** is our most popular special report.

*"I give **Rugg's Recommendations** five stars. This reference book for college search is a good place to start. Each year Mr. Rugg updates information for the college clients and counselors themselves, not ivy-towered college presidents. He lists "Quality departments in quality colleges." He includes schools by major and highlights miscellaneous majors such as art therapy, criminal justice, atmospheric sciences, orthotics and prosthetics alternative colleges and mortuary science. This is by far the best starting place for students who know or don't know a preferred major or possible college "fit." The book is easy to use and full of current information on 1050 participating colleges. Take a look for yourself.*
—Jan Livingston, Independent Counselor
Northridge, CA

4. THE SPECIAL REPORT: *THIRTY QUESTIONS ON THE COLLEGES,*
Revised 12th Edition

For all college bound students, parents and their counselors. 21 pages.

ISBN # 1-883062-66-7• $9.95 • Revised 2006 • Over 42 college entry changes

Thirty frequently asked questions with some answers even Deans of Admissions can't give you. This Special Report includes: The state university all others should visit and copy • 150 recommended colleges where black youngsters will maximize their education • What makes individuals happy at college? • Community college graduates – how do top colleges really view them at transfer time? • The best of the best journalism schools • Understanding student body make-up • Engineering schools – how to choose them and the best bets around the USA. And 22 other topics based on over 300 counselor meetings across the country. Counselors and parents find this transcript form extremely useful (yes, it's O.K. to copy it with appropriate acknowledgement).

"When I attended the college admissions institute this past summer, all of the private H.S. counselors and Ivy School directors of admission said that Rugg's work was the best."

—Colorado Public Secondary School Counselor

5. THIRTY SEMINAR SHEETS $25

Our most popular lists are now available separately. Includes all of the rankings in #6 below, plus colleges where the following youngsters maximize their education: Jewish (140), Hispanic (140), Asian (120), and Black (160). *Call us for a sample—5 sheets for $5.*

"Rugg's Recommendations is not only a crucial starting point in the student's college search, but it is also an essential tool in teaching them how to make an important life decision. Keep up the important work."

—Michelle Koetke, Ind. College Counselor Newbury Park, CA

6. THE COLLEGE SEMINAR SUBSTITUTE

For Secondary School Counselors, public and private   • $55 (lists updated monthly)

Can't make it to a college seminar? Do the next best thing: Order this special package. *The College Seminar Substitute* provides you with 96% of the 60 items covered in our seminar agenda. In this package you receive Rugg's three Special Reports, *Twenty More Tips on the Colleges, Forty Tips on the Colleges, Thirty Questions and Answers,* plus 30 seminar handouts. These handouts contain over 1900 entries—a wealth of information. Topics covered include: a listing of safe campuses, college guidebook ratings, up-and-coming colleges; snob schools; prestigious school rankings; underrated schools, the top 200 schools for the learning disabled, the most generous schools, new information on financial aid; advice on school recommendations; a listing of intense (rigorous) schools; big colleges that play small; rated Catholic colleges; and four minority lists. This package gives the counselor a foundation in understanding and navigating the admission game. See why over 8000 secondary school counselors have attended Rugg's College Admission Seminars.

"It is the best single source of information that we have. It answers the questions most frequently asked by parents. Your college materials help both the beginning and experienced counselor. The various ratings and lists inspire both students and their parents to further research the college scene. When parents and students are clueless, your information provides direction and humor in beginning the college selection process."

—Ira Lipton, Counselor, E. Hampton (NY)

7. SPECIAL! SEND IT ALL! $70

Includes 1 book, 3 special reports, 30 seminar sheets—all our products.

"I love your book!."

—Carol Gill, Educational Consultant Dobbs Ferry, NY

➡ *ORDER FORM ON REVERSE*

Rugg's advice and comments have appeared in such diverse publications as USA TODAY, ROLLING STONE, COLLEGE BOUND, THE BOSTON GLOBE, THE CLEVELAND PLAIN DEALER, NEW JERSEY MONTHLY, ROCKY MOUNTAIN NEWS and YOUR MONEY.

THE 2006 RUGG COLLEGE ADMISSION SEMINAR SCHEDULE	San Francisco, CA January 18, 2006 La Jolla, CA February 24, 2006 Philadelphia, PA April 28, 2006	Boston, MA May 12, 2006 Denver, CO August 4, 2006	College Park, MD September 29, 2006 Parsippany, N.J. October 27, 2006

For more information: Call or write for a brochure; e-mail us at frugg@thegrid.net; or visit our Website at http://www.ruggsrecs.com

2006 PRODUCT ORDER FORM

ITEM #	TITLE OR DESCRIPTION	PRICE	QTY	AMOUNT
1	*Rugg's Recommendations on the Colleges:* The Book (23rd ed.)	$24.95		
2	*20 More Tips on the Colleges:* Revised Special Report (12th ed.)	$ 8.95		
3	*Forty Tips on the Colleges:* Revised Special Report (12th ed.)	$ 9.95		
4	*Thirty Questions & Answers:* Revised Special Report (12th ed.)	$ 9.95		
5	*Thirty Seminar Sheets: Colleges*	$25.00		
6	*College Seminar Substitute:* Includes 2 thru 5	$55.00		
7	**SEND IT ALL!!!** Send one of each (Items 1-5)	$70.00		

Order 5 or more books:	Only $22.00 each! Discount price available only on the book.	**SUBTOTAL**
Prepaid Orders over $89:	Subtract $4 from total.	Less $4 for prepaid orders over $89
International Orders:	Shipping and handling cost: Actual Cost.	Sales Tax (CA only) 7.75%
California Residents:	Please add 7.75% sales tax.	
SHIPPING CHARGES: (all orders mailed first class)	$ 0-15 Postage $2 $16-35 Postage $5 $36+ Postage $6	**Shipping** **TOTAL ENCLOSED**

Name _____

Address _____

City _____ State _____ Zip _____

Send to:

RUGG'S RECOMMENDATIONS
P.O. Box 417 • Fallbrook, CA 92088

For information on our 2006 COLLEGE ADMISSIONS SEMINARS,
call us at 760-728-4558 or Fax 760-728-4467 OR visit our Website at http://www.ruggsrecs.com